CHILDREN'S ISSUES, LA

MW01119671

VULNERABLE AND DISCONNECTED YOUTH: BACKGROUND AND POLICIES

CHILDREN'S ISSUES, LAWS AND PROGRAMS SERIES

Federal Programs for Troubled Youth
Killian Lucero
2009. ISBN: 978-1-60692-318-4

Federal Programs for Troubled Youth
Killian Lucero
2009. ISBN: 978-1-60876-701-4 (Online book)

Child Sexual Abuse: Pitfalls in the Substantiation Process
Anna Aprile, Cristina Ranzato, Melissa Rosa Rizzotto and Paola Facchin
2009. ISBN: 978-1-60741-427-8

Diet Quality of American Young Children
Calvin G. Parker (Editor)
2009. ISBN: 978-1-60692-771-7

Diet Quality of American School-Age Children
Kelly B. Volkarsky (Editor)
2009. ISBN: 978-1-60692-776-2

National School Lunch Program Assessment
Manuel P. Borges (Editor)
2009. ISBN: 978-1-60692-972-8

Reading First Impact Study
Beth C. Games , Howard S. Bloom, James J. Kemple, Robin Tepper Jacob, Beth Boulay, Laurie Bozzi, Linda Caswell, Megan Horst, W. Carter Smith, Robert G. St.Pierre, Fatih Unlu, Corinne Herlihy and Pei Zhu
2009. ISBN: 978-1-60741-529-9

Vulnerable and Disconnected Youth: Background and Policies
Dierk Neumann (Editor)
2010 ISBN: 978-1-60741-488-9

Foster Care and African-American Youth
Joanna Kaczmarek (Editor)
2010 ISBN: 978-1-60741-541-1

Preschool Children: Physical Activity, Behavioral Assessment and Developmental Challenges
Leone Colombo and Rachele Bianchi
2010 ISBN: 978-1-60876-026-8

Child Development and Child Poverty
Anselm Fiedler and Isidor Kuester
2010 ISBN: 978-1-60741-816-0

Child Protection, the Courts and Social Workers
Terrance R. Langely (Editor)
2010 ISBN: 978-1-60741-279-3

Child Labor in America
Ian C. Rivera and Natasha M. Howard (Editor)
2010 ISBN: 978-1-60876-769-4

Adam Walsh Child Protection and Safety Act: Analysis and Law
Terrell G. Sandoval (Editor)
2010 ISBN: 978-1-61668-808-0

Adam Walsh Child Protection and Safety Act: Analysis and Law
Terrell G. Sandoval (Editor)
2010 ISBN: 978-1-61668-808-0 (Online book)

Child Abduction Resources
Melanie H. Wilson (Editor)
2010 ISBN: 978-1-61668-247-7

Working with the Courts in Child Protection
Raymond T. Devon (Editor)
2010 ISBN: 978-1-61668-303-0

Working with the Courts in Child Protection
Raymond T. Devon (Editor)
2010 ISBN: 978-1-61668-303-0 (Online book)

CHILDREN'S ISSUES, LAWS AND PROGRAMS SERIES

VULNERABLE AND DISCONNECTED YOUTH: BACKGROUND AND POLICIES

DIERK NEUMANN
EDITOR

Nova Science Publishers, Inc.

New York

NOTICE TO THE READER

The Publisher has taken reasonable care in the preparation of this book, but makes no expressed or implied warranty of any kind and assumes no responsibility for any errors or omissions. No liability is assumed for incidental or consequential damages in connection with or arising out of information contained in this book. The Publisher shall not be liable for any special, consequential, or exemplary damages resulting, in whole or in part, from the readers' use of, or reliance upon, this material. Any parts of this book based on government reports are so indicated and copyright is claimed for those parts to the extent applicable to compilations of such works.

Independent verification should be sought for any data, advice or recommendations contained in this book. In addition, no responsibility is assumed by the publisher for any injury and/or damage to persons or property arising from any methods, products, instructions, ideas or otherwise contained in this publication.

This publication is designed to provide accurate and authoritative information with regard to the subject matter covered herein. It is sold with the clear understanding that the Publisher is not engaged in rendering legal or any other professional services. If legal or any other expert assistance is required, the services of a competent person should be sought. FROM A DECLARATION OF PARTICIPANTS JOINTLY ADOPTED BY A COMMITTEE OF THE AMERICAN BAR ASSOCIATION AND A COMMITTEE OF PUBLISHERS.

LIBRARY OF CONGRESS CATALOGING-IN-PUBLICATION DATA
Vulnerable and disconnected youth : background and policies / Dierk Neumann, editor.
    p. cm.
  Includes bibliographical references and index.
  ISBN 978-1-60741-488-9 (hbk. : alk. paper)
  1. Problem youth--United States. 2. Problem youth--Services for--United States. 3. Problem youth--Government policy--United States. I. Neumann, Dierk.
  HV1431.V85 2009
  362.7086'94--dc22
                          2009038427

Published by Nova Science Publishers, Inc. ✤ *New York*

CONTENTS

Preface   ix

Chapter 1   Disconnected & Disadvantaged Youth Hearing   1
             U.S. Government Printing Office

Chapter 2   Disconnected Youth: Federal Action Could Address Some of the
             Challenges Faced by Local Programs that Reconnect Youth to
             Education and Employment   113
             U.S. Government Accountability Office

Chapter 3   Vulnerable Youth: Background and Policies   161
             Adrienne L. Fernandes

Chapter 4   Vulnerable Youth: Federal Monitoring Programs and Issues   223
             Adrienne L. Fernandes

Chapter Sources   261

Index   263

PREFACE

This book provides an overview of the youth population and the increasing complexity of transitioning to adulthood for all adolescents. For vulnerable (or "at-risk") youth, the transition to adulthood is complicated by a number of challenges, including family conflict or abandonment and obstacles to securing employment that provides adequate wages and health insurance. These youth may be prone to outcomes that have negative consequences for their future development as responsible, self-sufficient adults. Risk outcomes include teenage parenthood, homelessness, drug abuse, delinquency, physical and sexual abuse, and school dropout. Detachment from the labor market and school or disconnectedness, may be the single strongest indicator that causes such an unsuccessful transition to adulthood. It also provides a separate discussion of the concept of "disconnectedness," as well as the protective factors youth can develop during childhood and adolescence that can mitigate poor outcomes. Further, the report describes the evolution of federal youth policy, focusing on three time periods, and provides a brief overview of current federal programs targeted at vulnerable youth.

Chapter 1 - This chapter is edited and excerpted testimonies before the SubCommittee on Income Security and Family Support of the Committee on Ways and Means, U.S. House of Representatives on June 19, 2009.

Chapter 2 - While most young people successfully transition to adulthood, a significant number of youth are disconnected from school and employment. These youth are more likely than others to engage in crime, become incarcerated, and rely on public systems of support. Several federal agencies oversee a number of programs and grants that assist local programs in serving this population at the local level. GAO reviewed the following: (1) characteristics of locally operated programs that serve disconnected youth, (2) the key elements of locally operated programs to which directors attribute their success in reconnecting youth to education and employment, and (3) challenges involved in operating these programs and how federal agencies are helping to address these challenges. GAO interviewed officials from four federal agencies, experts, and directors of 39 local programs identified by agencies and experts as helping youth meet educational and employment goals.

Chapter 3 - The majority of young people in the United States grow up healthy and safe in their communities. Most of those of school age live with parents who provide for their well-being, and they attend schools that prepare them for advanced education or vocational training and, ultimately, self-sufficiency. Many youth also receive assistance from their families during the transition to adulthood. During this period, young adults cycle between attending school, living independently, and staying with their families. On average, parents give their children an estimated $38,000, or about $2,200 a year, while they are between the ages of 18 and 34 to supplement wages, pay for college tuition, and assist with down payments on a house, among other types of financial help. Even with this assistance, the current move from adolescence to adulthood has become longer and increasingly complex.

For vulnerable (or "at-risk") youth populations, the transition to adulthood is further complicated by a number of challenges, including family conflict or abandonment and obstacles to securing employment that provides adequate wages and health insurance. These youth may be prone to outcomes that have negative consequences for their future development as responsible, self-sufficient adults. Risk outcomes include teenage parenthood; homelessness; drug abuse; delinquency; physical and sexual abuse; and school dropout. Detachment from the labor market and school — or disconnectedness — may be the single strongest indicator that the transition to adulthood has not been made successfully. Approximately 1.8 million noninstitutionalized civilian youth are not working or in school.

The federal government has not adopted a single overarching federal policy or legislative vehicle that addresses the challenges vulnerable youth experience in adolescence or while making the transition to adulthood. Rather, federal youth policy today has evolved from multiple programs established in the early 20th century and expanded in the years following the 1964 announcement of the War on Poverty. These programs are concentrated in six areas: workforce development, education, juvenile justice and delinquency prevention, social services, public health, and national and community service. They are intended to provide vulnerable youth with opportunities to develop skills to assist them in adulthood.

Despite the range of federal services and activities to assist disadvantaged youth, many of these programs have not developed into a coherent system of support. This is due in part to the administration of programs within several agencies and the lack of mechanisms to coordinate their activities. In response to concerns about the complex federal structure developed to assist vulnerable youth, Congress passed the Tom Osborne Federal Youth Coordination Act (P.L. 109-365) in 2006. This legislation, like predecessor legislation that was never fully implemented — the Claude Pepper Young Americans Act of 1990 (P.L. 101-501) — establishes a federal council to improve coordination of federal programs serving youth. Congress has also considered other legislation (the Younger Americans Act of 2000 and the Youth Community Development Block Grant of 1995) to improve the delivery of services to vulnerable youth and provide opportunities to these youth through policies with a "positive youth development" focus. This report will be updated periodically.

Chapter 4 - Youth mentoring refers to a relationship between youth — particularly those most at risk of experiencing negative outcomes in adolescence and adulthood — and the adults who support and guide them. The origin of the modern youth mentoring concept is credited to the efforts of charity groups that formed during the Progressive era of the early 1900s to provide practical assistance to poor and juvenile justice- involved youth, including help with finding employment.

Approximately 2.5 million youth today are involved in formal mentoring relationships through Big Brothers Big Sisters (BBBS) of America and similar organizations. Contemporary mentoring programs seek to improve outcomes and reduce risks among vulnerable youth by providing positive role models who regularly meet with the youth in community or school settings. Some programs have broad youth development goals while others focus more narrowly on a particular outcome. A 1995 evaluation of the BBBS program and studies of other mentoring programs demonstrate an association between mentoring and some positive youth outcomes, but the effects of mentoring on particular outcomes and the ability for mentored youth to sustain gains over time is less certain.

The current Administration has proposed new federal structured mentoring since FY2001 (though the Administration has also proposed phasing some of these services out beginning in FY2007). Two programs — the Mentoring Children of Prisoners (MCP) program and Safe and Drug Free Schools (SDFS) Mentoring program — provide the primary sources of dedicated federal funding for mentoring services. The Mentoring Children of Prisoners program was created in response to the growing number of children under age 18 with at least one parent who is incarcerated in a federal or state correctional facility. The program is intended, in part, to reduce the chance that mentored youth will use drugs and skip school. Similarly, the Mentoring program (proposed for elimination for FY2009 by the Administration) provides school-based mentoring to reduce school dropout and improve relationships for youth at risk of educational failure and with other risk factors. The Administration has also supported a pilot project, the Mentoring Initiative for System Involved Youth (MISIY), which seeks to identify and expand effective mentoring programs for youth in the juvenile justice or foster care systems (Congress appropriated funds for MISIY only in FY2006). Finally, other federal initiatives support mentoring efforts, including the Federal Mentoring Council and dedicated funding for mentoring organizations like BBBS.

Five bills have been introduced in the 110th Congress that primarily concern mentoring (S. 379, H.R. 2611/S. 1812, H.R. 5660, and H.R. 5810). Issues relevant to the federal role in mentoring include the limitations of research on outcomes for mentored youth, the potential need for additional mentors, grantees' challenges in sustaining funding, and the possible discontinuation of federal mentoring funding. This report will be updated as legislative activity warrants.

Since the mid-1990s, Congress has supported legislation to establish structured mentoring programs for the most vulnerable youth. The Department of Justice's Juvenile Mentoring Program (JUMP), the first structured federal mentoring program, was implemented in 1 994 to provide mentoring services for at-risk youth ages five to 20. The purpose of contemporary, structured mentoring programs is to reduce risks by supplementing (but not supplanting) a youth's relationship with his or her parents. Some of these programs have broad youth development goals while others focus more narrowly on a particular outcome such as reducing gang activity or substance abuse, or improving grades. Research has shown that mentoring programs have been associated with some positive youth outcomes, but that the long-term effects of mentoring on particular outcomes and the ability for mentored youth to sustain gains over time are less certain.

While there is no single overarching policy today on mentoring, the federal government supports multiple mentoring efforts for vulnerable youth. Since FY2001, Congress has passed legislation to provide mentoring services for three groups of these youth: children of prisoners through the Mentoring Children of Prisoners (MCP) program; children at risk of educational failure, dropping out of school, or involvement in delinquent activities through the Safe and Drug Free Schools (SDFS) Mentoring program; and youth in the foster care and juvenile justice systems through the Mentoring Initiative for System Involved Youth (MISIY). The purpose of the three programs is to improve the outcomes of vulnerable youth across a number of areas, including education, criminal activity, health and safety, and social and emotional development.

The federal government also supports other mentoring efforts. Programs under the Corporation for National and Community Service (CNCS) provide mentoring services, among other supportive activities for youth. In partnership with the U.S. Department of Health and Human Services (HHS), CNCS also leads the Federal Youth Mentoring Council, convened in 2006 to address the ways federal agencies can combine resources and training and technical assistance to federally administered mentoring programs. Further, the Office of Juvenile Justice and Delinquency Prevention in the U.S Department of Justice (DOJ) provides funding for Big Brothers and Big Sisters of America and other mentoring organizations.

This report begins with an overview of the purpose of mentoring, including a brief discussion on research of structured mentoring programs. The report then describes the evolution of federal policies on mentoring since the early 1 990s. The report provides an overview of the components and funding for each of the three major federal mentoring programs, as well as a discussion of other federal mentoring initiatives that are currently funded. Note that additional federal programs and policies authorize funding for mentoring activities, among multiple other activities and services.[1] These programs are not discussed in this report. The report concludes with an overview of issues that may be relevant to mentoring legislation in the 110th Congress and any discussions concerning the federal role in mentoring. These issues include the limitations of research on outcomes for mentored youth, the potential need for additional mentors, grantees' challenges in sustaining funding, and the possible discontinuation of federal mentoring funding.

In: Vulnerable and Disconnected Youth: Background...   ISBN: 978-1-60741-488-9
Editor: Dierk Neumann   © 2010 Nova Science Publishers, Inc.

Chapter 1

DISCONNECTED & DISADVANTAGED YOUTH HEARING

U.S. Government Printing Office

The Subcommittee met, pursuant to notice, at 10:03 a.m., in room B–318, Rayburn House Office Building, Hon. Jim McDermott (Chairman of the Subcommittee), presiding.

[The advisory announcing the hearing follows:]

MCDERMOTT ANNOUNCES HEARING ON DISCONNECTED AND DISADVANTAGED YOUTH

Congressman Jim McDermott (D–WA), Chairman of the Subcommittee on Income Security and Family Support of the Committee on Ways and Means, today announced that the Subcommittee will hold a hearing on disconnected and disadvantaged youth. **The hearing will take place on Tuesday, June 19, 2007, at 1:00 p.m. in room B–318, Rayburn House Office Building.**

In view of the limited time available to hear witnesses, oral testimony at this hearing will be from invited witnesses only. However, any individual or organization not scheduled for an oral appearance may submit a written statement for consideration by the Committee and for inclusion in the printed record of the hearing.

BACKGROUND

Approximately 2.3 million noninstitutionalized youth between the ages of 16 and 24 have neither attended school, nor worked at anytime over the last year according to the most recent data compiled by the Congressional Research Service. Additionally, past studies suggest that at least 1 million children between the ages of 12 to 17 experience some period of homelessness every year.

A myriad of issues may lead to youth becoming detached from school and work and/or becoming homeless, including poverty, inferior schools, the lack of economic opportunity, racial discrimination, substance abuse, teenage parenthood, interaction with the criminal justice system, family instability and violence, and a difficult transition from foster care. There are a number of programs that either specifically or indirectly focus on disadvantaged and vulnerable youth, but some experts have suggested the overall response is fragmented and serves only a fraction of those in need.

While the issue of disconnected youth is not new, the problem has increased in recent years for certain groups. For example, the percentage of African American men between the age of 20 and 24 who are both out of work and out of school rose from 9.5 percent in 1998 to 14.1 percent in 2005. This rate would climb significantly if it included young men who were incarcerated.

In announcing the hearing, Chairman McDermott stated, **"We cannot afford to lose the productive talents of millions of our youngest citizens who cannot find a place in the world of school and work. Nor can we stand by as some of them go without the bare essentials of life, starting with a place to call home. We need to search for a better way to reconnect these youth to what so many of us take for granted."**

FOCUS OF THE HEARING

The hearing will focus on disconnected, disadvantaged and homeless youth.

DETAILS FOR SUBMISSION OF WRITTEN COMMENTS

Please Note: Any person(s) and/or organization(s) wishing to submit for the hearing record must follow the appropriate link on the hearing page of the Committee website and complete the informational forms. From the Committee homepage, *http://waysandmeans.house.gov*, select *"110th Congress"* from the menu entitled, *"Hearing Archives"* (*http://waysandmeans.house.gov/Hearings.asp?congress=18*). Select the hearing for which you would like to submit, and click on the link entitled, *"Click here to provide a submission for the record."* Once you have followed the on-line instructions, completing all informational forms and clicking "submit" on the final page, an email will be sent to the address which you supply confirming your interest in providing a submission for the record. You *MUST REPLY* to the email and *ATTACH* your submission as a Word or WordPerfect document, in compliance with the formatting requirements listed below, by close of business **July 3, 2007.** Finally, please note that due to the change in House mail policy, the U.S. Capitol Police will refuse sealed-package deliveries to all House Office Buildings. For questions, or if you encounter technical problems, please call (202) 225–1721.

FORMATTING REQUIREMENTS

The Committee relies on electronic submissions for printing the official hearing record. As always, submissions will be included in the record according to the discretion of the Committee. The Committee will not alter the content of your submission, but we reserve the right to format it according to our guidelines. Any submission provided to the Committee by a witness, any supplementary materials submitted for the printed record, and any written comments in response to a request for written comments must conform to the guidelines listed below. Any submission or supplementary item not in compliance with these guidelines will not be printed, but will be maintained in the Committee files for review and use by the Committee.

1. All submissions and supplementary materials must be provided in Word or WordPerfect format and MUST NOT exceed a total of 10 pages, including attachments. Witnesses and submitters are advised that the Committee relies on electronic submissions for printing the official hearing record.
2. Copies of whole documents submitted as exhibit material will not be accepted for printing. Instead, exhibit material should be referenced and quoted or paraphrased. All exhibit material not meeting these specifications will be maintained in the Committee files for review and use by the Committee.
3. All submissions must include a list of all clients, persons, and/or organizations on whose behalf the witness appears. A supplemental sheet must accompany each submission listing the name, company, address, telephone and fax numbers of each witness.

Note: All Committee advisories and news releases are available on the World Wide Web at *http://waysandmeans.house.gov.*

The Committee seeks to make its facilities accessible to persons with disabilities. If you are in need of special accommodations, please call 202–225–1721 or 202–226– 3411 TTD/TTY in advance of the event (four business days notice is requested). Questions with regard to special accommodation needs in general (including availability of Committee materials in alternative formats) may be directed to the Committee as noted above.

Chairman McDermott. The Committee will come to order.

Today we're going to talk about homelessness. There are too many Americans out of school and out of work and out of their homes and really out of luck, and it's time for America to pay more attention, because we can make a difference and I believe we really must make a difference.

In 2005 there were 2.3 million youths between the ages of 16 and 24 who did not work or attend school at any time. That's a lot of kids. Estimates for the number of homeless youth are more dated and more varied, but there are likely more than 1 million in any given year.

The purpose of today's hearing is to discuss the pathways that lead to young people becoming detached from school, work and housing. We also hope to learn about both existing and potential programs designed to help prevent and respond to homelessness and separation from school and work.

Both our hearts and our heads should propel us toward improving our outreach to these young Americans. The thought of a teenage person confronting homelessness or pondering life without hope should stir the emotions in all of us.

The reality that reconnecting youth will improve so many other concerns confronting our nation illustrates the wisdom of moving forward. Issues like long-term economic development, crime, and poverty are all intertwined with the lives of these young people.

None of this is meant to suggest that there's a simple answer that will respond to all the needs of disadvantaged kids. There are a variety of circumstances that might lead to a young person becoming homeless or dropped out of the worlds of school or work. Poverty plays a lead role but family instability, teenage parenthood and many other factors also contribute to the problem.

While the issue of disconnected youth is certainly not new, data suggest the problem may be growing for certain groups, especially young black men. Additionally the long-term costs of dropping out of school may be higher than ever given the premium the global economy places on education and skills.

There are some very helpful programs that reach out to disadvantaged youth, one of which we'll hear about today. However questions still linger about whether there are enough of these programs, whether they address the myriad of new challenges kids face today from higher housing costs to declining manufacturing jobs and whether there is a way to tie them together in a more systematic way.

Furthermore, there are certain broader policies related to education and housing and making work pay that would likely provide significant dividends for disadvantaged youth. Finally, this Sub-committee takes special notice of the fact that youth coming out of the foster care system, they've been in the foster care system up to age 18, are suddenly dropped on the street cold, and they are at a particular risk of being both homeless and jobless. Our burden to help these kids is especially high since the government has acted as their legal parent. Your parents don't ordinarily shove you out of the house at 18 with nothing, but that's basically what we do to young people in the foster care system.

The Subcommittee will hold future hearings to look specifically at that particular part of the issue. I would like to now yield to the Subcommittee's ranking member, Mr. Weller. Jerry.

Mr. Weller. Thank you, Mr. Chairman, and thank you for conducting this important hearing today. Today's hearing is on disconnected youth. As we will hear, disconnected youth include those who drop out of school, do not work and often end up in the streets.

The very title "disconnected youth" begs the question how are kids connected. The answer is two ways, through their family and through their school. Kids are connected through their family starting with the love and support of their parents, and that goes beyond financial support to the deep sense of belonging associated with being a son or daughter who is loved, protected, and encouraged on the road of life.

As one of our witnesses puts it, we should all remain mindful that strengthening families is the best way to prevent the suffering and social disconnection among our young people. I totally agree.

The second way kids are connected, especially as they get older, is through their school. That really means through the circle of friends, teachers, coaches and other mentors they rely on as they become more independent and develop the habits and skills needed for life on their own.

Think about kids who don't have both or even one of those connections. Kids in foster care have been removed from their own parents due to abuse and neglect. That's traumatic enough, but now add in the fact that many foster children are bounced not only from home to home but also from school to school.

A 2004 study of young adults in the Midwest found that over a third of those who aged out of foster care reported having had five or more school changes. Five or more school changes for a group already separated from their parents, that's the definition of disconnection.

Studies show high school students who change schools even once are less than half as likely to graduate as those who don't change schools. No wonder there is a 20 percentage point difference between the high school graduation rates of foster youth and their peers according to the group Kids Count, all of which contributes to the often grim prospects for children of foster care, especially those who spend the most time in care and bounce from school to school and thus are the most likely to drop out.

According to the Nonpartisan American Youth Policy Forum, high school dropouts are substantially more likely to be unemployed and on welfare. Youth who drop out are three-and-a-half times more likely to be incarcerated during their lifetimes. Those who work earn 50 percent less than those with high school diplomas. Even the death rate for youth who drop out of school is higher.

So, it seems to me we should be doing everything we can to increase high school completion rates in general. For kids in foster care who are already disconnected from their parents it is especially important for them to stay connected to their school including the friends, teachers and mentors they trust and who know them.

I welcome the broader testimony we will hear today about home-lessness and the various funding sources beyond the scope of this Subcommittee addressing that. I am very eager, especially eager, to focus on what we can do within the foster care system to increase the chances these already vulnerable children at the very least get their high school diplomas.

Fortunately, as we will hear, there are good options some states are already putting into effect. We should spread the word and consider enacting Federal legislation that provides more foster youth the opportunity to stay better connected to their schools, to graduate and to create the foundation for productive and happy lives.

I look forward to hearing all of today's testimony. Thank you, Mr. Chairman.

Chairman McDermott. Thank you. Other members are welcome to make entries into the record, and without objection we will accept them.

We're going to begin today by having a couple of Members of Congress. It's very seldom that Members of Congress come and ask to testify at something, so I want you to realize that this is a unique event. Today John Yarmuth from the third congressional district in Kentucky will begin, and he'll be followed by Michele Bachmann from the sixth district of Minnesota. John.

STATEMENT OF HON. JOHN YARMUTH, A REPRESENTATIVE IN CONGRESS FROM THE STATE OF KENTUCKY

Mr. Yarmuth. Thank you, Mr. Chairman.

Chairman McDermott, Ranking Member Weller and colleagues, I appreciate the opportunity to testify today at this hearing on disconnected and disadvantaged youth.

As a member of the Education and Labor Committee, I, like you, have a high level of interest in youth who are detached from family, school, work and any sort of permanency. Our missions are similar, and I look forward to finding common ground where our Committees can work together to address the life challenges of our nation's disconnected youth.

Before coming to Washington I volunteered a considerable amount of time at organizations that work with disconnected youth. We are fortunate in my hometown of Louisville to house some of the finest services for disconnected youth in the nation with the headquarters of the National Safe Place and Boys' Haven.

There I saw firsthand the hardships and devastation resulting from homelessness. My experiences with these agencies and Kentucky's disconnected youth have served as a reminder that home-lessness is more than a collection of sociological and economic data, as it sometimes ends up being viewed here in the halls of Congress, but a myriad of human stories.

I am thankful that Jewel and DeCario Whitfield are here today to share some of those stories with us, to help us understand that of the 3 million children who run away or experience homelessness each year, each one has a story of abuse, physical, psychological or emotional, and each child is in need of structure, stability and permanency.

Unfortunately, despite the superb work of organizations across the country we are failing these children at every turn. The funds and personnel to accommodate the bare necessities of so many Americans in need have simply not been made available. We must explore and implement measures to incentivize careers that provide these badly needed services to our communities.

Last week in the Education and Labor Committee we adopted an amendment to the College Cost Reduction Act that will incentivize such work with $1,000 in loan forgiveness each year for five years. I believe this measure is a good start, but there is far more to do to build an infrastructure capable of responding to the pandemic problem of disconnected youth.

As I have found working with Congresswoman McCarthy on the reauthorization of the Runaway Homeless Youth Act, the story gets much worse once one realizes that the failings are not limited to just funding and personnel. The necessary infrastructure is simply not in place.

The upside is that we are in a position to change that if we focus our energy in the right areas. Luckily for us, the deficiencies are glaring and practically begging us to step in. For example, we have little to no ability to monitor success of programs serving disconnected youth.

Homeless youth enter these systems temporarily and then leave. There is currently no comprehensive system linking juvenile courts, foster care, homeless shelters, schools, hospitals and social service providers. So, we don't know where they go and we don't offer services once they have gone. They are simply out of the system, disconnected once more.

We must do more than just contain these little children while we have them. They have come into the system lost, reaching out, and we must set them on a path to adulthood prepared for the work-place and ready for the world without dragging the dead weight of a history of neglect.

They also face a hurdle that won't surprise anyone here because it is consistent with one out of six Americans: no access to health care. With our nation's disconnected youth, we are talking about children often living in unsanitary conditions, many the victims of abuse and all of whom are in need of care.

At a minimum, we have an obligation to tend to the health of these children through Medicaid or other means. Providing health care to these 3 million American children cannot be treated as an option any longer.

In my three-minute assessment of the failings in the area of disconnected youth, the hurdles may seem insurmountable, but we cannot let ourselves get so caught up in the distance we have to go that we become too intimidated to take the next step forward.

Ultimately, we need to consolidate our resources and services for the disconnected so that they no longer get lost in the system while seeking services. A homeless shelter can be more than a place to stay and eat a meal. It can be a place to access comprehensive services like health care, education, economic assistance and job training. When these scattered services can be found under one roof, we will truly be offering a path to housing, employment and independence.

In our reauthorization of the Runaway Homeless Youth Act we've taken steps to help children prepare for adulthood with the transitional living program that teaches homeless 15 to 18 year olds life's basics: cooking, laundry, financial literacy and the basics of finding a job.

The legislation also tackles the absolute basics with a national switchboard to provide help by phone or e-mail to those who need it, the Basic Center Program, that gives young people a place to stay while they reintegrate with their families and the Street Out-reach Program that will very simply make connections with kids on the streets.

It is my hope that our Committees can work together to make a much stronger and broader impact by exploring the possibilities of expanding temporary assistance for needy families to include disconnected youth who have children, fully utilizing the Social Service Block Grants to fund organizations that help foster children and runaways and ensuring that children are tapping into Federal welfare services that will help these young Americans pre-pare to face the world.

As we move forward together on issues facing disconnected youth, I hope we all feel not only the urgency to act but that we also share a sense of optimism for what we can accomplish together on behalf of youth in every corner of America. I look forward to the reauthorization of the Runaway Homeless Youth Act, the findings of this hearing and future progress we make in this institution. Thank you.

[The prepared statement of Mr. Yarmuth follows:]

Prepared Statement of the Honorable John Yarmuth, a Representative in Congress from the State of Kentucky

Thank you for the opportunity to testify today at this hearing on Disconnected and Disadvantaged Youth. As a member of the Education and Labor Committee, I, like you, have a high level of interest in youth who are detached from family, school, work, and any sort of permanency. Our missions are similar, and I look forward to finding common ground where our committees can work together to address the life challenges of our nation's disconnected youth.

Before coming to Washington, I volunteered a considerable amount of time at organizations that work with disconnected youth. We are fortunate in my hometown of Louisville to house some of the finest services for disconnected youth in the nation with the headquarters for National Safe Place and Boys' Haven. There, I saw first hand the hardships and devastation that comes as a result of homelessness.

My experiences with these agencies and Kentucky's disconnected youth have served as a reminder that homelessness is more than a collection of sociological and economic data—as it can sometimes seem here in the halls of Congress—but a myriad of human stories. I am thankful that Jewel and DeCario Whitfield are here today to share some of those stories with us, to help us understand that of the three million children who runaway or experience homelessness each year, each one has a story of story of abuse: physical, psychological, or emotional. And each child is in need of structure, stability, and permanency in their lives.

Unfortunately, despite the superb work of the organizations I named and others such as the National Network for Youth and Alliance to End Homelessness—the system is failing these children at every turn. The funds and personnel to accommodate the bare necessities of so many Americans in need are simply not available. We must explore and implement measures that incentivize careers that provide these badly needed services to our communities. Last week, I introduced an amendment to the College Cost Reduction Act that will incentivize work in such areas with $1,000 in loan forgiveness each year for five years. I believe that this measure is a good start, but there is far more to do to build an infrastructure capable of dealing with a problem of this magnitude.

As I found in my work with Congresswoman McCarthy and our work on the reauthorization for the Runaway Homeless Youth Act, the story gets much worse once one realizes that the failings are not limited to just funding and personnel; the necessary services are simply not in place. The upside is that we are in a position to change that if we focus our energy in the right areas. Luckily for us, the deficiencies are glaring and practically begging us to step in.

For example: We have little to no ability to monitor success. Homeless youth enter these systems temporarily and then leave. We don't know where they go, we don't offer services once they have gone, they are simply out of the system—disconnected once more. We cannot be content to simply contain these children while we have them. They have come into the system lost, reaching out, and we must set them on a path to adulthood prepared for the workplace and ready for the world, without dragging the dead weight of a history of neglect.

They also face a hurdle that won't surprise anyone here because it is consistent with one out of six Americans: No access to healthcare. With our nation's disconnected youth we are talking about children living in unsanitary conditions without guidance, many the victims of abuse, and all of whom are in need of care. We have an obligation to, at a bare minimum; tend to the health of these children, whether through Medicaid or other means. Providing healthcare to these three million American children cannot be treated as an option any longer.

In my three minute assessment of the failings in the area of disconnected youth, the hurdles seem insurmountable . . . even to me. But we cannot let ourselves get so caught up in the distance we have to go that we become too intimidated to take the next step forward.

In our reauthorization, we've taken steps to help children prepare for adulthood with a Transitional Living Program that teaches homeless 15 to 18 year-old to do the basics: cooking, laundry, learn financial literacy and the basics of finding a job. It tackles the absolute basics, with the National Switchboard to provide help by phone or email to those who need it, the Basic Center Program that gives young people a place to stay while they reintegrate with their families, and the Street Out-reach Program that will very simply make connections with kids on the streets.

Likewise, our committees can work together on the next relatively small but crucial steps: expanding Temporary Assistance for Needy Families to include disconnected youth who have children, utilizing the Social Service Block Grants to fund organizations that help foster children and runaways, and ensuring that children are tapping into federal welfare services that can ensure that when young Americans move on from these services, they are truly ready to face the world.

As we move forward together on issues facing disconnected youth, I hope that you are—like me—feeling the urgency to act, but also optimistic for what we can accomplish together on behalf of youth in every corner of America. I look forward to the reauthorization of the Runaway Homeless Youth Act, the findings of this hearing, and future progress we take in this institution. Thank you.

Chairman McDermott. Thank you.

Ms. Bachmann.

STATEMENT OF MICHELE BACHMANN, A REPRESENTATIVE IN CONGRESS FROM THE STATE OF MINNESOTA

Ms. Bachmann. Thank you, Chairman McDermott, Congressman Weller and members of the Subcommittee. I want to thank you for inviting me to discuss the educational challenges that are faced by disconnected and disadvantaged youth, specifically foster children.

My name is Michele Bachmann. I'm a first term Member of Congress, serving Minnesota's sixth district, and I have a very special interest in the quality of education received by foster children because, over the course of six years, my husband, who is present here today, Marcus Bachmann, and my family cared for 23 treatment-level foster children in our home.

We are the lucky parents of five biological children, but we feel that we were even more blessed by having 23 foster children come into our home. When the children came to us, they were not babies, Mr. Chairman, they were teenagers. They had come through a number of horrendous experiences. Many of them had been abused in many different ways.

They weren't your typical foster children. They were in need of greater depth of services. Many of them had lived in numerous homes throughout their lives and again had experienced various levels of abuse. We were honored to be able to bring these children into our home, Mr. Chair. What we saw is that what these children needed more than anything was love, acceptance and stability. While we were by no means a perfect family one thing that we could offer to these children was just a little bit of a picture of what the word normal looks like.

Here's a mom and a dad who love each other. Here is a fairly regular schedule. Here's a mom who cooks a meal, a dad who goes to work. This is what normal, a snapshot of normal might look like for the life of a child.

We immediately enrolled our children in our local public school system. We live in a nice suburban area of Minneapolis-St. Paul, and we were glad to be able to have our children in our local public schools system. Our biological children were enrolled in a local private school with fairly low class sizes and fairly low overall population in that school system.

Over the course of the years, our foster children often would ask me if I would be willing to home school them. Occasionally they asked if they could attend our children's private school and we had to tell them, no, we were unable to do that, that they needed to attend our local public school.

Again, our local public schools were good, but it was a new experience and they often had 700 children in the graduating class. Oftentimes, without exception our foster children all had an IEP, an individualized education plan. Without exception, they had a social worker assigned to them, a counselor assigned to them. They did have support systems but oftentimes they were in a situation where they were seen as transient and temporary.

One thing that we wanted to give our foster children, Mr. Chair and Members of the Committee was a sense of permanence and a sense of stability so they could feel that, as they went through their life there's something that they could count on, that they could always come back to. We wanted to make sure that they had that. Part of that—we know at the Federal level there's the Chafee Program for foster students that goes to the college level where students can attend a school of their choice in this transitional period.

One thing that we would like to ask the Committee to look at is the idea that there could also be a program available specifically for foster children of all ages that would allow for this possibility of choice for them as well so that they could have this idea of stability. If their parents, their biological parents would agree, if the social workers would agree, if there might be an option, whether it's a public school, a charter school, of which—my husband and I began a charter school in our city; it's the oldest charter school in the United States for K–12 at risk youth—or if they would choose a private school so that they could—if they changed homes they could still stay in the same school, so that they could have that sense of stability.

We still stay in communication with our foster children. We are grateful to say that all of our foster children, all 23 are doing well. They've graduated from high school. One of our foster daughters today is in college and plans to get her PhD.

This is the same foster child who said to me when she was enrolled in our public school, "you know, Mom, I was put into stupid people math." One thing that she felt is that, because she was seen as a temporary student she was put in lower level classes that weren't up to her ability. This is a student today who's planning to go for her PhD.

We believed in her. My husband and I loved her, as I'm sure many foster parents have done for their foster children, but what we want to do is to make sure that the potential in every child is fully realized, and I know that the Committee shares that same goal. We want to be able to do that, bringing and creating a life of stability and choice for every foster child just as our five biological children had that same opportunity. We want to make sure that's available for our foster children as well.

I want to thank you, Mr. Chair. It's obvious that you have a heart of gold and that the members of this Committee do as well— that we can work together and try to do something really good for America's foster children. I thank you. I thank the members of this Committee.

[The prepared statement of Ms. Bachmann follows:]

Prepared Statement of the Honorable Michele Bachmann, a Representative in Congress from the State of Minnesota

Mr. Chairman, Congressman Weller, and members of the Subcommittee, thank you for inviting me to discuss the educational challenges faced by disconnected and disadvantaged youth; specifically foster children.

I am Michele Bachmann, a first-term Member of Congress serving Minnesota's Sixth District. I have a special interest in the quality of education received by foster children because over the course of six years, my family cared for twenty-three high-need teenagers through the Lutheran Social Services' Treatment Foster Care program.

I believe every child deserves the chance to gain a high-quality education. Growing up, I attended public schools where I was taught using a rigorous curriculum despite the fact that my community was not particularly affluent. While I was in school, my parents divorced and almost overnight my stable, middle-class family was changed forever. Although times were extremely tough, whenever my three brothers and I would become frustrated my mother would tell us to concentrate on our schoolwork, because no matter what happened, no one could ever take our education away from us. She was right—I left my public high school with a quality education and went on to graduate from college, then law school, and finally to earn an L.L.M. in tax law.

Years later, when my family began to take in foster children, I felt that although our circumstances were very different, I could identify with their pain and frustration. All of them had challenges considered serious enough that they were unable to be placed through the traditional county foster care systems, and our family's role was to provide them with a safe home and see them through to their high school graduations.

We quickly learned that our foster children had very different needs than most children. Almost all of them had been given Individualized Education Plans—individual plans designed for students with special educational needs. Many of the kids had been under the care of counselors, many suffered from eating disorders, and others had difficult behavioral or learning issues. All of them had switched schools at least once, and as a result of their tumultuous home lives, none of them had very strong educational backgrounds.

While through the years some of our foster children performed better in school than others, my husband and I noticed some common problems. Many times, we got the impression that the kids were seen by both their peers and their teachers as if they were only going to be there short term. Although their teachers were welcoming, little special attention was provided to ensure that they caught up to their classmates, and their other needs were often not considered because there were so many other students to attend to. They became small fish swimming in a very large pond.

We also began to notice that not all of our foster children were presented with the quality of coursework we had thought they would receive. Many of them were placed in lower-level classes, as if they were not expected to succeed. One of the kids remarked to me once that she was in "stupid people math." Another brought home an 11th grade math assignment that involved coloring a poster. Yet another told me she had spent an entire week of classes watching movies, and others were being selected for the "School to Work" program, in which high school students attended classes for half of the day and were then sent to work minimum-wage jobs at local businesses. Although it had been evident to us from the beginning that because of their backgrounds, our foster children were going to struggle in school, it was frustrating to see that rather than being given the leg up they needed, so many of themfelt that they were being left behind. Unfortunately, national studies indicate that this is an extremely common experience for foster children.

What made this experience so heartbreaking is we could clearly see that despite our wishes, our foster children did not get the same opportunities or attention that our biological children received in their school. Our biological children's classes were smaller and more rigorous, the teachers knew all of the students, the students kneweach other, and parents were able to be much more involved in their children's educations—all goals which are not always attainable in a large school, but which could have done wonders for our foster children.

As a result of these experiences, I believe it is imperative that Congress examine creating a federal school choice program for foster children, through which foster parents are given the option to place children in their care in either a public or private school long-term, depending on their specific needs. Such a plan would allow foster children requiring more individual attention to attend a school better equipped to help them. Just as important, for the first time in their lives, these children who have become so used to being uprooted would have the chance to be placed in an environment where they could have their special educational needs met and feel as if they belong, where they could remain enrolled even if their homeschanged.

Currently, the federal government operates a program for older foster children—the Chafee Foster Care Independence Program—which assists them in transitioning from foster care to life on their own. Among other things, the Chafee Program provides vouchers of up to $5,000 to foster children ages 16 through 18 for education and training. Congress should consider extending this voucher program to fosterchildren of all ages, so foster parents are able to best meet the educational needs of the children in their care by either allowing them to choose a private school or providing them with the funds necessary to transport their children to their original school even if it is outside of their immediate area.

Additionally, Congress should consider extending the extremely successful D.C. school choice program aimed at low-income students, which has drawn more thanthree times the number of applications as there are available spots. Creating a similar program to serve D.C. foster children as well as those who come from low-income families would be an important step in the direction of giving the option of school choice to all foster children.

In closing, even if placed in the best families, foster children often face the possibility that they will have to change homes, and as a result they must find a safeplace of their own where they can become accepted and gain a sense of stability. Although for many foster children school can be such a place, the cases of many others show that under the current system, this is not always possible. I hope my family's experiences highlight the special challenges facing foster children as well as the need for an examination of whether limiting their educational options is truly in their best interests. I thank the Subcommittee for holding this hearing, and I thank you, Mr. Chairman, Congressman Weller, and Subcommittee Members for the opportunity to share our story today.

Chairman McDermott. Thank you. Mr. Weller will inquire.

Mr. Weller. Thank you, Mr. Chairman.

Ms. Bachmann, you elaborated in your testimony regarding some of your observations regarding education for children. First, let me just say, God bless you; that's a houseful over a lifetime, and we really, really want to thank you for the leadership you have shown on issues affecting foster children and also that you've demonstrated so much love and so much compassion, offering children an opportunity for a better life. I commend you for that.

I had mentioned in my opening statement that there was a study in the Midwest—and you represent Minnesota, I represent Illinois, we're Midwestern states—that over a third of those who aged out of foster care reported having five or more school changes. What has been your experience with children that you've provided a home for and the number of schools that they may have attended before they became part of your family and some of the transitions and challenges they had, leaving friends, leaving their peers and starting over again?

Ms. Bachmann. Mr. Chairman, Congressman Weller, you're exactly right, those are tremendous challenges. Since we were a treatment foster care home, which means we took in children who were considered more difficult than foster children out of a regular county system, we had children placed in our home from all across the State of Minnesota. In fact, I think we may have had one or two come to us from the State of Wisconsin, if I remember, that were placed in our home. They had been through numerous homes.

We had some identifying features. Almost none of our children had a father in their life. That was one thing that we could offer, but they had many, many school experiences. So, not to berate the public schools in any way, many foster children's experience is that they do tend to be at the lower achieving end because they've transitioned from school to school to school, and what one school may be studying at one time of the year may have nothing to do with what another school may be studying that a child has transferred into. So, there's not this level of continuity.

We also saw, from a number of the biological mothers whose foster children we were privileged to care for, they were also concerned about different aspects of the child's background, that they be able to have their values honored or upheld. So, we did have different foster mothers ask us if their children could attend our children's private school for instance, and we were unable to do that. We were prohibited from doing that. Even if we felt that we could afford the cost ourselves financially, that was not an option to allow foster children to be placed into the private schools.

Mr. Weller. So, the program prevented you from——

Ms. Bachmann. The program prevented us from placing the children either in a home school situation or in a private school situation.

We had children who graduated from high school and who remained with us because they just simply were not ready. I know the Chairman had made some remarks about some children, and yourself I believe made remarks that at age 18 they aren't necessarily ready and able to stand on their feet.

So, we did have—not all of the children but we had several children that we kept in our home and worked with over a period of time to help them gain the skills necessary so they could truly be independent. We've continued to this day to maintain contact with some of our foster children so that we can continue to offer that level of support.

Mr. Weller. As a follow up, many of these children, do they participate in special education programs? Are they in other programs in the school?

Ms. Bachmann. Yes, Mr. Chairman, Congressman Weller, our foster children were in special education programs. They were also in regular classrooms as well, but again, one of our foster daughters who had made the comment to me, "Mom, I've been put in stupid people math," also came home and told me that in her math class, for instance, in eleventh grade, she was coloring posters, she wasn't learning math.

In some classes she was watching feature length films all week. She wasn't doing academics. I was very concerned. Personally I had come out of a middle class home, and my parents were divorced when I was in junior high. Over night, financially we were below the poverty level, and I think that's why my heart was pricked to take in foster children. I knew what it had been like to be middle class. I knew what it had been like to be in a poverty situation, and I was very concerned that my foster children would have great academic opportunities in order to make something out of themselves.

Coming from a below poverty background, because we had a decent public school system I was able to work my way through college, work my way through law school, work my way through a post-doctorate in tax law and be able to support myself. If anyone needs a leg up in life, it is foster children. I can tell you that from personal experience.

That's why I want to make sure that we offer every parameter of opportunity to these great kids. They are really great kids. They just want to know someone loves them, someone cares for them, someone will be there to hold their back. Any amount of stability that we can offer these kids will go miles down the road for their future lives.

Mr. Weller. We've run out of time here but I also add, it's clear that these children also suffer from the disadvantage of low expectations.

Ms. Bachmann. Yes.

Mr. Weller. When they're placed in schools because of their circumstances people expect them to be able to perform less well as other kids, that's a disadvantage they also have to overcome. So, again, thank you for your commitment and taking care of so many kids and helping give other children opportunities.

Ms. Bachmann. Thank you. Thank you, Mr. Chairman.

Chairman McDermott. Thank you both for coming. We will see you again.

Our next panel will come up to the table. A group of people here, some who are working in homes for the homeless and some are people who have experienced the whole nine yards. We will begin with a young woman who has had the experience personally and we'll let her tell her own story. Jewel.

You want to push the button and put yourself in live.

STATEMENT OF JEWEL KILCHER, RECORDING ARTIST

Ms. Kilcher. How's that? You'd think I could work a microphone.

Chairman McDermott, Ranking Member Weller and members of the Subcommittee, thank you for allowing me to appear before you today on behalf of those who otherwise have no voice, America's homeless, disconnected and disadvantaged youth.

The issue of homeless youth is complicated by misperceptions about why kids become homeless. Many of us here today have probably seen youth homelessness but really didn't realize that it was staring us in the face. Maybe you walked by a kid who was sitting on a bench and rather than thinking he was homeless or someone who was forced into prostitution in order to make enough money to eat every day, you thought he looked like maybe just a punk kid who ditched school and was waiting for his friends.

You really have to consider what being homeless is like for a few confused, long and lonely days. The experience doesn't just last for a few days for most people. Consider spending years on the streets after being kicked out of your house by an abusive alcoholic mother. Consider being in foster care where your new foster parents don't seem to care whether you're there or not and never asked you what you need.

What if the home you've been placed in is abusive and dysfunctional? You may either run away because no one seems to care or you are told at age 18 you have to leave because you are too old for foster care. There are no resources available to you and you are now homeless.

Think about your children or grandchildren. Think for a second about a 12-year-old girl. What if her first sexual experience didn't come at a time of her choosing but after an uncle touched her and made her keep it a secret? Then the secret is exposed, the truth spirals out of control, forcing a needlessly ashamed and frightened girl onto the streets.

These girls and boys do not choose to live on the streets or be homeless. It is the sad truth that they feel safer there.

What is equally troubling is that many Americans look at someone's being homeless as the result of a choice he or she made, that they are lazy or that it is just a correctable condition because the United States is the land of so much opportunity.

These are just a few of the reasons why I do not believe America's homeless youth population is made up of kids who leave home because they want to. Most homeless kids are on the streets because they have been forced by circumstances to think that they are safer there than in any home they once knew. Others may have reached the end of their economic resources or those of their family and are left trying to get out of poverty from the disadvantageous position of America's streets.

I experienced homelessness firsthand. I moved out when I was 15 years old. I worked several jobs. I wasn't a lazy kid. It was just I thought I could do a better job than my parents.

I was able to get a scholarship to a performance arts high school and was able, while being homeless, to still go to a good school. Spring breaks were hard vacations. I would end up just hitchhiking around the country and street-singing for money because they wouldn't let you stay on campus during the breaks.

After many twists and turns I ended up in San Diego when I was 18, and I had a series of deadend jobs and finally one boss fired me because I wouldn't have sex with him and he wouldn't give me my paycheck that day. My rent was due and my landlord kicked me out.

I thought, I'll just stay—I had a little $200 car that a friend let me use—and I just slept in my car for the day, and it ended up lasting about a year. I was really sick at the time. I had sick kidneys and was turned away from every emergency room that there was to the point where you'd get blood poisoning because your kidneys weren't working, and I'd be throwing up in my car and nobody would help.

This lasted for about a year and I was able to finally get out. I'll never forget. Record labels started coming to see me. I was singing in a coffee shop. I wrote music just to help myself feel better, and it seemed to make other people feel better, and they started coming to my shows.

Atlantic Records was going to come see me, and I was so excited. I went to Denny's where I always washed my hair in a little shallow sink. I had to fit my head in sideways and use the hand soap to wash my hair and I was using paper towels to dry it off. I was humming to myself because I was so excited that a record label was coming to see me.

I looked up in the mirror and there were two women backed up against the wall and they were horrified. They looked at me just like I was a leper. I suddenly got really embarrassed because I realized what I was and what I looked like to them. As they walked out, the one woman said to the other, "well, she looked pretty enough; I wonder how she ended up like that."

I wanted to tell them so bad, "you're wrong about me. I'm an okay kid and a label is coming to see me." It ended up working out for me.

Some research estimates that about 1 million to 1.6 million youth experience homelessness each year. I personally would guess the number is higher. The number of kids turned away from shelters every day as well as the number of phone calls made to the National Runaway Hotline indicates some that it may be even higher.

Unfortunately, homeless kids are running from something, and that makes them difficult to find or to count as part of any single community. What is clear is that life in a shelter or on the streets puts homeless kids and youth at a higher risk for physical and sexual assault, abuse, and physical illness, including HIV/AIDS.

As I heard in testimony earlier, with education—I was never taught grammar, which is odd because I'm a writer and I now make my living as a writer. Every time they were teaching grammar at a school I just either showed up just after they finished the classes or just before they were starting and then I was gone again. I went to probably ten different schools between the ages of eight and sixteen, so it really is true.

Estimates suggest that 5,000 unaccompanied youths die each year as a result of assault, illness or suicide. That is an average of 13 kids dying every day on America's streets.

I was talking with—earlier who has an amazing story and amazing accomplishment. People prey on you. They know. I've never been solicited more and approached more than when I was homeless. I grew up bar singing, so you'd think it would be hard to top, but when I was homeless you're constantly being solicited, and I knew a lot of girls who were stripping and prostituting because it was really the best solution they had for making money.

Anxiety disorders, as you can imagine, depression, Post-Traumatic Stress Disorder and suicide are all more common among homeless children. Previous studies of the homeless youth population have shown high rates of parental alcohol and drug abuse. Substance abuse however is not characteristic; it doesn't define most youth who experience homelessness.

Despite all of the setbacks faced by homeless kids there is room to be optimistic. Most homeless children tend to try and make it to school. Most do make it to school at least for a period of time. If safe shelters, counseling and adequate support were available for these kids and if our schools and our job training programs were stronger, these children would be given opportunities to graduate high school and build the skills they need to go on to live healthy and productive lives.

It's funny, my boyfriend of nine years laughed when he met me because he always said I could end up in Wisconsin if I needed to on a shoestring with a stick of gum, but I didn't know how to do laundry when he met me. You know, I didn't know how to do really simple functional things.

You need to be taught that. You just aren't taught those things. You don't realize that that's what your parents are supposed to be teaching you.

As I prepared to be here today I learned Congress is taking steps in the right direction this year by increasing the level of Federal support for homeless youth-related programs. I understand the House of Representatives is poised to pass a $10 million increase for Runaway and Homeless Youth Act programs, and a $5 million increase for education of homeless children and youth programs.

This anticipated funding increase is crucial. I cannot tell you enough, support for shelters and transitional living and housing programs is necessary if we are going to change the landscape for homeless boys and girls in America.

Regrettably, I do also understand funding for street outreach programs may not receive an increase in funding this year. What I know about street outreach is that it is essential to dealing with the issue of youth homelessness.

We need people who work hard to find these kids and point them toward help because we know that they will not be looking for adults; adults most likely contributed to their situation in the first place. When they do seek help from adults, the system, police, they're just opening themselves up to be harmed and exploited or arrested again.

I am passionate about the work in this area by Virgin Mobile USA and its RE*Generation movement in supporting the homeless youth street outreach programs of StandUp For Kids and awareness building efforts by Youth Noise. The RE*Generation is also supported by Virgin Unite, the Virgin Group's charitable arm, created by Sir Richard Branson.

The fact is that businesses and organizations working together are crucial to the success of Federal programs, and broader support in this area is desperately needed.

I would like to thank Congress for its help in raising awareness of issues surrounding homeless youth by introducing resolutions that designate November as National Homeless Youth Awareness Month. I look forward to their passage so we can all make November a success by demonstrating to these forgotten youth that Congress is listening, people do want to help and that people care about their futures.

Today is an opportunity to discuss important problems facing families and children across the country. As you begin examining ways to prevent youth homelessness, improve community-based intervention programs that support families and older adolescents and assist youth aging out of foster care, it is my hope that your job becomes easier once the problem is absorbed into the consciousness of the American people.

This country has to stop looking in the other direction on these most heart-wrenching and complex issues facing America's youth. Through greater awareness people will view this as a problem with solutions. We must all work together to end youth homelessness in America.

I am pleased to be here today, and I will do my best to answer any questions you may have.

[The prepared statement of Ms. Kilcher follows:]

Prepared Statement of Jewel, Recording Artist

Chairman McDermott, Ranking Member Weller, and members of this Sub-committee, thank you for allowing me to appear before you today on behalf of those who otherwise have no voice—America's homeless, disconnected and disadvantaged youth.

The issue of homeless youth is complicated by misperceptions about why kids become homeless. Many of us here today have probably seen youth homelessness but didn't realize it was staring us in the face.

Maybe you walked by a kid who was sitting on a bench, and rather than thinking he was homeless, or someone who was forced into prostitution in order to make enough money to eat everyday, you thought he looked like a punk kid who ditched school and was waiting for his friends.

Consider being homeless for a few confused, long and lonely days. Consider spending years on the streets after being kicked out of home by an abusive, alcoholic mother. Consider being in foster care where your new foster parents don't seem to care whether you're there or not and never ask you what you need. What if the home you have been placed in is abusive and dysfunctional? You may either run away because no one seems to care, or you are told at age 18 you have to leave because you are too old for foster care. There are no resources available to you and you are now homeless.

Think about your children or grandchildren. Think for a second about a 12-year-old girl. What if her first sexual experience didn't come at a time of her choosing, but after an uncle touched her and made her keep it a secret. Then, the secret is exposed and the truth spirals out of control, forcing a needlessly ashamed and frightened girl onto the streets.

These girls and boys don't choose to live on the streets or to be homeless. It is the sad truth that they feel safer there. What is equally troubling is that many Americans look at someone's being homeless as the result of a choice he or she made, or that it is a correctable condition because the United States is the land of so much opportunity.

There are numerous causes and effects of youth homelessness. Thirty percent of shelter youth and 70% of street youth are victims of commercial sexual exploitation at a time in their lives when these boys and girls should be going to elementary school.

These are just a few of the reasons why I do not believe America's homeless youth population is made up of kids who leave home because they want to. Most homeless kids are on the streets because they have been forced by circumstances to think that they are safer there than in the home they once knew. Others may have reached the end of their economic resources, or those of their family's, and are left trying to get out of poverty from the disadvantageous position of America's streets.

I experienced homelessness first-hand. When I was 15 years old, I received a vocal scholarship to attend Interlochen in Michigan. I always enjoyed performing solo, and one Spring Break I took a train and hitchhiked in Mexico, earning money singing on street corners. Many twists and turns later, I moved to San Diego and because of a series of unfortunate events, I ended up living in a car. My car was then stolen so I had to borrow $1,000 from a friend to buy a van which ended up becoming my home. Living in a van was not romantic. I washed my hair in public bathroom sinks. People would often gawk and make comments about me. They would say how sad it was that I was homeless, but many more tried to pretend that I wasn't there. I was mortified and embarrassed of my condition, and the stigma that was being attached to me. I can assure you that kids do not want to be on the streets or without people who care about them.

Some researchers estimate that about 1 to 1.6 million youth experience homelessness each year. The number of kids turned away from shelters every day as well as the number of phone calls made to the National Runaway Hotline indicate some estimates that may be even higher. Unfortunately, homeless kids are running from something and that makes them difficult to find or to count as part of any single community.

What is clear is that life in a shelter or on the streets puts homeless youth at a higher risk for physical and sexual assault, abuse, and physical illness, including HIV/AIDS. Estimates suggest that 5,000 unaccompanied youths die each year as a result of assault, illness, or suicide; that's an average of 13 kids dying every day on America's streets.

Anxiety disorders, depression, Post Traumatic Stress Disorder, and suicide are all more common among homeless children. Previous studies of the homeless youth population have shown high rates of parental alcohol or drug abuse. Substance abuse, however, is not a characteristic that defines most youth who experience homelessness.

Despite all of the setbacks faced by homeless kids, there is room to be optimistic. Most homeless children tend to make it to school, at least for a period of time. If safe shelters, counseling, and adequate support were available for these kids, and if our schools and our job training programs were stronger, these children would be given opportunities to graduate high school and build the skills they need to go on to live healthy and productive lives.

As I prepared to be here with you today, I learned Congress is taking steps in the right direction this year by increasing the level of federal support for homeless youth-related programs. I understand the House of Representatives is poised to pass a $10 million increase for Runaway and Homeless Youth Act programs and a $5 million increase for Education of Homeless Children and Youth programs. This anticipated funding increase is crucial. Support for shelters and transitional living and housing programs is necessary if we are going to change the landscape for homeless boys and girls in America.

Regrettably, I also understand funding for street outreach programs may not receive an increase in funding this year. What I know about street outreach is that it is essential to dealing with the issue of youth homelessness. We need people who work hard to find these kids and point them toward help, because we know they won't be looking for adults. Adults most likely contributed to their situation in the first place. When they do seek help from adults, the system, or a police officer, they are opening themselves up to being harmed, exploited, or arrested—again.

I am passionate about the work in this area by Virgin Mobile USA and its RE*Generation movement in supporting the homeless youth street outreach programs of StandUp For Kids and awareness building efforts by YouthNoise. The RE*Generation is also supported by Virgin Unite, the Virgin Group's charitable arm created by Sir Richard Branson. The fact is that businesses and organizations working together are crucial to the success of federal programs, and broader support in this area is desperately needed.

I would like to thank Congress for its help in raising awareness of issues surrounding homeless youth by introducing resolutions that designate November as ''National Homeless Youth Awareness Month''. I look forward to their passage so we can all make November a success by demonstrating to these forgotten youth that Congress is listening, people do want to help, and that people care about their futures.

Today is an opportunity to discuss important problems facing families and children across the country. As you begin examining ways to prevent youth homelessness, improve community-based intervention programs that support families and older adolescents, and assist youth aging out of foster care, it is my hope that your job becomes easier once the problem is absorbed into the consciousness of the American people. This country has to stop looking in the other direction on these most heart-wrenching and complex issues facing America's youth. Through greater awareness, people will view this as a problem with solutions. We all must work together to end youth homelessness in America.

I am pleased to be here today and I will do my best to answer any questions you may have. Thank you.

Chairman McDermott. Thank you very much.

Ms. Shore is the executive director of Sasha Bruce Youthwork here in Washington, D.C. I did not say earlier, the full text of your remarks will be put in the record. We would like you to try and keep it to 5 minutes so we have some time to ask questions.

STATEMENT OF DEBORAH SHORE, EXECUTIVE DIRECTOR, SASHA BRUCE YOUTHWORK, INC.

Ms. Shore. I have tried to do that, thank you. Thank you, Chairman McDermott and all members of the Subcommittee. This is a wonderful opportunity today. My name is Deborah Shore and I am the founder and executive director of Sasha Bruce here in Washington, D.C. I am honored to offer the perspective of our agency's dedicated counselors who work incredibly hard on behalf of our city's disconnected youth population. I have submitted written testimony which will provide greater detail to my brief remarks today.

Please allow me to start by describing the work of our agency. The mission of Sasha Bruce is to improve the lives of runaway, homeless, neglected and at-risk youth and their families in the Washington, D.C. metropolitan area. This year, more than 1,500 of Washington, D.C.'s most troubled children, teenagers and young adults will receive our assistance.

We began as a street outreach program in 1975, specifically for homeless and runaway youth, but we have grown considerably since then in response to service gaps not just for homeless teenagers but to address the wide range of issues facing disconnected young people, including those who have dropped out or have been removed from school and older youth without employment or secure housing. Today, our 14 programs are financed through a mix of Federal and D.C. government dollars, as well as considerable private sector support. We operate the only youth-specific shelter in Washington, D.C., The Sasha Bruce House. I am very honored to be accompanied today by Mr. DeCario Whitfield, a current member and client of our Youth Build Program.

I want to underscore how pleased I am that the leadership of this Committee made the decision to call a hearing on the issues and needs of the broad category of disconnected young people. I believe you have correctly recognized that this is a group of young people who defy our current structures, and for whom solutions lay in creative, coordinated, new and targeted initiatives. It is plain to us, working on the ground, that coordinated efforts between social services, schools, health care, employment and training, juvenile justice and child welfare services are needed if we are to re-attach these youth to school, training, the job market, families and community.

Our organization has been working with this broad category of youth for a long time, and therefore we believe that we bring a perspective useful to this Committee and to the Subcommittee.

A variety of circumstances typically contribute to young people becoming disconnected: difficulty with school, family stresses and disruptions and the lack of intermediate institutions, such as churches or nonprofit, community-based agencies in young people's lives. Our experience is that the number of disconnected youth is increasing. We are seeing it everyday. Disconnected youth are those currently being served as part of the important Runaway and Homeless Youth Act funded programs but also are those youths who are entering the juvenile justice system, coming back out of the juvenile justice system, aging out of foster care, and quietly dropping out of school with no connection to training or a means to enter the workforce.

The current system of service funded through the Runaway and Homeless Youth Act is the most responsive to this broad population as it has both outreach, emergency shelter and assistance with independent and community group living programs. Some of these services, however, are limited to under 18 years so more responsive front-end services must be available to youth who are both under and over 18 and who are still struggling to be connected to a positive path toward independence. Family services, individual strength-based counseling and capacity to link youth to services is an important first entry point and should be further strengthened. These systems need to be strengthened and expanded to include additional youth and to create greater capacity.

Also, the disconnection for many from school is a point where intervention is paramount. Certainly, we know that for many youth school and family issues are the two most common reasons why they become homeless, get involved with the courts, become pregnant, do drugs, which leads to much of the negativity which is so much harder to sort out later. There is a need for there to be greater connection between the social service system and youth who are dropping out or at risk of dropping out. The school systems must be urged to put a greater priority on holding on to these youth in alternative school settings and/or establishing vocational schools and providing supplementary school services, including after school services.

Entering the workforce in this day and time, even with a high school diploma, is daunting for many of our young people and a great deal more needs to be done to construct workforce development programs, which provide help to youth, including those needing remedial assistance. It was clear that as part of the recent report done by The Brookings Institution that disconnected youth need to have targeted services available to both proceed with their basic education and get job skills, training and employment if they are to move into the middle class and not simply into poverty. Youth Build in this report was held up as a solid model of a program which should be expanded as it has all the features of what is needed and has proven to work.

As many people have mentioned already, youth who age out of foster care and who re-enter the community from the juvenile justice system are at high risk of becoming homeless and disconnected. Some estimates are as high as 50 percent of all former foster care youth become homeless at some point. These populations in my view should be specially targeted as they are at such high risk for continuing to be part of our institutional service system.

In my written testimony, I gave the Committee benefit of the alarming statistics about young people in D.C. and the grim outcomes for them, which argue loudly for more leadership to be taken toward reconnecting them to positive support systems. D.C. has dramatic statistics but is by no means alone in having so many disconnected youth in our country.

For this testimony, I would like to mention a few additional risk factors, which need to be considered——

Chairman McDermott. May I ask you to sum up?

Ms. Shore [continuing]. When constructing a program response.

Chairman McDermott. Okay?

Ms. Shore. Health care issues, sexually transmitted disease, teen pregnancy, health care in general, drug involvement, I absolutely agree with Jewel that we are not looking at young people who typically are involved in drugs themselves but who are at risk of it and many of their parents are drug involved. Violence is a major issue for the young people that we see. The effort to combat gang violence is a very important initiative that I think needs to be tied together. Then, of course, the issue of housing and the issue of being able to provide support to the entire family is of critical importance.

I would just say that I agree that the increase in the investment in the Runaway and Homeless Youth Act is critical. I also would urge there to be a look that these programs can go up to age 24 because under-18 year olds, there is no magic number to the 18 age anymore. I would urge the increase in resources to the Education of Homeless Youth, Children In Youth Act, the Chafee Independence Living Program Act, and we wholeheartedly support the National Network's Place to Call Home Campaign, which is taking off shortly.

Thank you for this opportunity. I really appreciate and hope to see some real change and development as a result of this activity.

[The prepared statement of Ms. Shore follows:]

Prepared Statement of Deborah Shore, Executive Director, Sasha Bruce Youthwork

The mission of *Sasha Bruce Youthwork* is to improve the lives of runaway, homeless, neglected and at-risk youth and their families in the Washington metropolitan area. This year more than 1,500 of Washington D.C.'s most troubled children, teenagers and young adults will receive our assistance. Sasha Bruce Youthwork was one of the original grantees of the landmark Runaway and Homeless Youth Act three decades ago. Our Sasha Bruce House remains the only emergency shelter for young people in the nation's capital.

We began as a street outreach project in 1974 specifically for homeless and run-away youth. But we have grown considerably since then in response to service gaps not just for homeless teenagers, but to address the wide range of issues facing *disconnected* young people, including those who have dropped-out or been removed from school and older youth without employment or secure housing. Today our fourteen programs are financed through a mix of federal and DC government dollars, as well as considerable private sector support. These include emergency shelter for runaway and homeless children; counseling within homes and on the street; counseling in pregnancy prevention; AIDS and substance abuse education; independent living programs for sixteen to twenty one year olds; after-school programming and positive youth development activities; an independent living and parenting program for young mothers and their babies; two group homes for children in the welfare system, one specifically for teen mothers; a service enriched residence as an alternative to detention for teenage boys; practical support for families leaving shelter or transitional housing; community capacity building to prevent diseases among youth exiting the juvenile justice system; and our *Youthbuild Program,* which involves classroom-based GED preparation and building trade apprenticeships in partnership with Habitat for Humanity specifically for high school dropouts.

SBY is the principal provider of services to runaway and homeless youth, as well as this broader category of "disconnected youth" in DC. Most youth-serving residential CBOs here limit access to those young people referred for services by the juvenile justice and child welfare systems. Thus, our shelter, transitional living and a host of non-residential counseling projects represent primary avenues for the *non-system-involved*, disconnected youth to receive barrier-free access to supportive services. It is by virtue of this unique mix of residential and non-residential "safety net" services for both homeless youth, disconnected youth and system-involved youth that I believe the perspective of our organization will be useful to Ways and Means and to this Subcommittee, specifically.

I want to underscore how pleased I am that the leadership of this Committeemade the decision to call a hearing on the issues for and needs of this broad category of "disconnected young people." This group of young people has needs which touch various existing systems and which fall through the gaps in the educational, vocational and service system. It is plain to those of us working on the ground that a new, coordinated effort needs to be made to help re-attach these youth to expanded and targeted systems of support if we are to reverse this worrying trend.One of the important points to make here is that where many systems which exist for youth have a cut off of age 18, the group which we identify as disconnected youth must go up to age 24 as this describes the group who are still in need of help entering the adult world and who are clearly at risk without such assistance.

A variety of circumstances typically contribute to young people becoming disconnected—whether it be from schools, or family support systems, or intermediate institutions such as churches or nonprofit community based agencies. All must be addressed if our adolescents are to develop fully. However, several primary service areas stand out and are most relevant to the work of responding to these young people.

Family supports and social services help cannot be understated. The importance of programs which provide outreach and emergency shelter like those funded under the Runaway and Homeless Youth Act and other prevention programs which help to identify youth before complete disconnection from school, family and community are paramount. These services need to be working closely with the school systems and with the courts to identify youth before they have dropped out or gotten into trouble with the law. According to the Ann E. Casey Foundation, in 2005 roughly 8% of DC youth between ages 16 to 19 were neither attending school nor working. This is about 1000 disconnected teenagers. Perhaps more troubling, 16%, or approximately 5,000 young people 18 to 24 years old were neither attending school nor working. Clearly, employment and educational gaps are large and much more needs to be in place to respond to the needs which exist.

Assistance with schooling is also key, both to stay in school if possible or to get an alternative education. Many of the youth who have populated both the runaway and homeless youth system and the juvenile justice system have as an underlying problem serious educational issues. Whether because of the disruptions in their lives due to family instability or undetected learning problems, missing out on a basic education in this modern world is tantamount to being relegated to deep poverty. At least in DC, there are few vocational education opportunities and adult education programs needs to be seriously expanded.

A workforce development plan and program targeted to disconnected youth is essential if youth are to become reconnected. The Brookings Institute did an analysis recently about how to reduce poverty locally and recognized "disconnected youth" as a category which needs targeted training along with social services and housing assistance as the recipe for creating ways for people out of poverty. Social services, health services, education, workforce development and housing are the true building blocks of a solution to the constellation of problems which lead to disconnection for youth.

In developing my thoughts for this testimony, it seemed important to point out the primary risk factors which stand out and are most relevant to solving the problem at hand. I have included the information I have about the District which I think represents dramatically some of the most intractable problems in our country and so perhaps can lead the way to creative problem solving.

Poverty, Family Instability and Child Neglect

In 2004, the District had one of the highest percentages of children in the United States under age 18 living below poverty (34% compared to 18% of children in the US). Family dissolution in DC is most evident among low-income people living in East-side Wards 7 and 8, where SBY operates several of its programs. These Wards are almost exclusively African-American, have the lowest per-capita income and are historically underserved. According to the *Kids Count 2006*, Wards 7 and 8 also have the highest crime rates and highest number of deaths among children and youth, death to teens and teen murders. And these wards have the highest rates for unemployment and for children receiving TANF, food stamps and Medicaid. According to the Urban Institute, more than 9,000 children receive TANF in Ward 8 alone—four times the rate for other sectors of the city, and more than half of DC's poor children live east of the Anacostia River.

These socio-economic indicators are primary risk factors for child neglect and family dissolution in DC, and in other major cities in this country. Other risk factors include a series of family-related factors such as family management problems, poor parental discipline practices, family conflict and social isolation. Other negative influences on family stability include lack of services, adolescent problem behaviors and academic failure. We need the full spectrum of federal government agencies to acknowledge and address these inter-connected socio-economic conditions as they develop public policy initiatives if we are to decrease the number of young people who are homeless and disconnected in our cities.

Housing

Voluminous research evidences the severe lack of affordable housing in DC relative to the number of families of modest or low incomes. Several credible projections of affordable housing availability indicate that DC's east side neighborhoods will continue to gentrify in the coming years, regardless of recent stabilization of home prices nationally.

While housing which is affordable for low-income families becomes scarcer in DC, the demand for emergency shelter for homeless youth continues to outstrip available capacity. It is difficult to determine the number of runaway and homeless youth in the District of Columbia, but knowledgeable estimates indicate that the problem is substantial. The Homeless Services Planning and Coordinating Committee of the Metropolitan Washington Council of Governments takes an annual "snapshot" of homeless persons in order to quantify the problem. In January 2006, the *point-in-time* count was 9,369, an increase of 4 percent from January, 2005. *The DC Kids Count Collaborative, 13th Annual Fact Book 2006*, notes that homelessness in the District has increased for the fifth consecutive year. Of the families applying for shelter for the first time in 2005, an estimated 6,100 were children.

While the National Runaway Switchboard handled 1,327 calls from DC youth in 2006, SBY's 24-hour emergency hotline during the past three months fielded 234 crisis calls from youth, families, schools, service agencies and police seeking our shelter services.

Education

The administrative problems with DC public and charter schools are well established, and correlate to low levels of academic achievement compared to similar-sized cities. Poor educational outcomes represent profound barriers to employment success, family stability and self-sufficiency among our agency's current and future clientele.

While it is essential to improve the DC school system and to provide under-performing youth with counseling and support services, the realities of DC's education system and workforce are such that there is a serious need for supplemental education services. In fact, supplemental academic instruction coupled with positive youth development activities, vocational training and civic engagement opportunities need to be offered during after-school time in our young peoples' neighborhoods if we are to have success in improving educational outcomes throughout this country.

Some other important ancillary problems need to be addressed if there is to be a full system of service in place.

Sexually Transmitted Diseases and Teen Pregnancy

Our counselors estimate that nearly 75% of our youth are sexually active and approximately half report having been sexually assaulted. Many lack the experience of healthy intimate relationships, infrequently attend school and the realities of dysfunctional situations in many of their homes often prevent appreciation of healthy dating behaviors. The belief that social acceptance can be realized through sex (especially between young females and older males) is widespread. Runaway, homeless and other street youth may take more risks to survive, can be exploited sexually and are more prone to drug experimentation because it often forms a significant part of the fabric of street life. These risks are exacerbated by difficult political circumstances facing homeless youth of color. Many are dealing with emotional trauma from years of neglect. Few have the experience to make the right choices in difficult circumstances. It is well established that DC has the highest rates of HIV of any major US city. Our programs focus primarily on DC Wards 6, 7, and 8, the city's poorest, east-side neighborhoods, which have a high density of sexually active youth with high rates of multiple sexual partners and low condom use. This risky sexual activity is the most significant behavior that places our clients at risk for HIV infection and other communicable diseases. It should not be surprising that young people faced with these significant health issues will have trouble prioritizing among life's many challenges and will be more likely to fail at school or become homeless.

This risky sexual activity also plays a large role in unwanted teenage pregnancies. Despite some well documented improvements in the past 2 years to onceastounding teen pregnancy rates, there continues to be an urgent need for pregnancy prevention education among young people in the District. The negative effects of adolescent childbearing are well documented and compelling, for mothers, fathers and theirchildren. For example, 59% of women who have children before they reach twenty do not have a high school diploma by the age of 30,[1] and almost half will begin receiving welfare within five years of having their first child.[2] Studies show that children of teenage mothers have lower birth weights and are more likely to perform poorly in school.[3] Children born to mothers aged 15 or less are twice as likely to be abused or neglected in their first five years than children born to mothers aged20–21.[4] Also, the Annie E. Casey Foundation report, *When Teens Have Sex: Issues and Trends*, found that fathers of children born to teen mothers earned on average $3,400 less annually than fathers of children born to 20- or 21-year-old women.[5]

Drug Use

It is a common and incorrect stereotype that homeless youth are addicted to drugs. Our experience is that many homeless and disconnected youth, like other youth, do use drugs, but the majority are doing so in an ill-advised effort to survive day-by-day. In fact, at Sasha Bruce Youthwork, it is far more typical for our young clients' parents to be addicted. This is one reason, among many which I will touch on later, that a holistic approach to engaging the entire family in services is the most effective way to help children and youth.

This is not to say that drug prevention education and treatment for young people and their families is not needed. In fact, nonjudgmental education about psycho-active substances and their effects is the best way to prevent their abuse among youth, and this is particularly the case among those who have become involved— or are at greatest risk for becoming involved—in the juvenile justice and child welfare systems. According to DC's Pre-Trial services, in February of 2006, 51% of juvenile arrestees tested positive for drugs. And approximately 85% of foster care placements in the District are reportedly due to substance use, whether by the parent, guardian or child.

Violence

According to the Casey Foundation's *Kids Count 2006*, the rate for teen deaths in DC has skyrocketed by 40% in recent years. The majority of these deaths may be reasonably attributed to violence perpetrated by teens on other teens, almost exclusively African American teens. Further, this youth-on-youth violence has been— and likely will continue to be—concentrated in DC's poorest, East-side neighborhoods.

Violence among youth negatively impacts school attendance. In the District in 2005, 16% of students were in a physical fight on school property one or more times during the past 12 months (compared to 15% in 2004). 9% of students did not go to school because they felt unsafe at school or on their way to school on one or more of the past 30 days. 12% of students were threaten or injured with a weapon such as a gun, knife, club on school property, one or more times during the past 12 months.

There is general acceptance that youth violence in DC can be correlated with gang membership. The reasons for joining a gang include the need for marginalized youth to feel accepted, the need for money, or protection from other youth. Therefore, to address the rising tide of violence in our communities, we will need to change these attitudes and beliefs concurrent to engaging young people at highest risk for violence and gang activity into positive alternative activities.

In addition to the core set of risk factors and problematic social conditions described above, I would like to turn now to **emerging issues and service gaps** here in DC, and which I believe are common elsewhere in this country. Relevant to the Ways and Means Committee's purview, three trends, or emerging issues, stand out and also should be considered as we seek to prevent social disconnection and home-lessness among youth.

First of all, here in DC, and across the country, we must put greater resources to address the growing problem of young people "aging out" of the child welfare system. According to the District's Child and Family Services Agency, as of October 2006, 2,313 children were in foster care and 1,681 children were enrolled in "the system" and living in their natural homes. These figures combined equal 2% of all children and youth in DC, which is significantly higher than any other jurisdiction. Importantly, youth age 12 and up make up about 61% of the total foster care population—a number which many authorities believe to be rising and which is extremely high compared to other jurisdictions. These figures are causing many public policy officials to call for alternatives to foster care placement (such as emergency respite and ongoing family counseling prior to entry into the child welfare system for young people who experience conflict at home) and for a larger number of housing and options for young adults "aging out" of the system, to name just two.

Second, the lack of affordable housing in DC and other major US cities must be addressed if we are to improve the lives of disconnected, urban youth. SBY oversees several transitional living contracts with DC and federal government specifically for young people who would be homeless otherwise. While it should remain the highest of priorities to secure permanent housing for our clients upon exit from these temporary residential programs, this is a particularly difficult challenge in DC (and several other major cities), especially among teenage and young adult populations, due to gentrification of neighborhoods and high housing costs. And while DC and federal government have been more apt in recent years to embrace new initiatives for permanent housing, we must not lose sight of the urgent and on-going need for emergency shelter and transitional living programs for young people with no where else to turn.

The promotion of affordable housing must be tied to workforce development targeted for DC's poorest communities if we are to have real success in promoting educational and employment opportunities for this city's disconnected youth. Martha Ross and Brooke DeRenzis of The Brooking's Institute's Greater Washington Research Program recently released a report *Reducing Poverty in Washington DC and Rebuilding the Middle Class from Within*. It concludes with several recommendations on how to help the city's low-income residents move into the middle class. Specifically, we need to improve the city's workforce development system and expand our education and training capacity, and the authors argue convincingly for the expansion of sector-specific programs, notably construction training, which would offer a greater number of low-income residents access to good-paying employment. This recommendation mirrors the objectives of our YouthBuild Program, which links GED attainment to building trades apprenticeships. Ross and DeRenzis also demonstrate the wisdom of enhanced programs for residents with low reading and math skills concurrent to employment preparation, as well as supported work for ex-of-fenders and out-of-school youth.

Third, I am happy to report that recent years in DC have seen an increased commitment to funding community based alternatives to incarceration for juvenile offenders. In DC in 2003, juveniles were committed and detained at a rate of 625 per 100,000. This rate far exceeds any other state in the nation and 90% of these youth were male, and 81% were African American. In 2004, the DC Inspector General released a report highlighting a number of deficiencies with the Youth Service Administration, the agency responsible for juvenile detention and rehabilitation, and recommended that the agency become a Mayoral cabinet level position. Since that time a new Director, Vincent Schiraldi, was appointed to the agency, which was renamed the Department of Youth Rehabilitative Services (DYRS). Since Mr. Schiraldi's appointment there has been a philosophical shift at DYRS, including a commitment to decrease the number of youth incarcerated at the District juvenile facility, Oak Hill, and a greater interest in placing detained and committed youth in community residential and non residential facilities.

In 2005, 1,228 youth were released from secure detention to relatives and non-residential community programs. Given the entrenched staffing and change-resistant bureaucracy of the juvenile justice system in DC historically, this number of releases represents a significant policy and operational shift (there were 1,006 releases in 2003 and 1,135 in 2004, respectively). The increasing number of young people returning post-incarceration to DC communities is consistent with DYRS's new direction and commitment to community placement. In fact, DYRS has developed several new initiatives including a program called REFAM (Return to Families), which is charged with providing youth with less serious offenses with community-based individualized plans.

Mr. Schiraldi believes that approximately 70% of youth at Oak Hill are confined with nonviolent offences and should be targeted for REFAM. DYRS has also recently begun funding community-based programs to provide Evening Reporting Center and Intensive Third Party Monitoring slots. This nascent movement to fund community alternatives to youth incarceration in DC is a positive one for disconnected youth,their families and our communities. Other cities would be well served to implement similar initiatives for arguably the most disconnected of youth—the so-called ''re-entry'' population.

There are two additional areas which I believe are urgent. Specifically, we need to do more to prevent dating violence among youth and to urge more positive sexual and social relationships and to provide programs in all major cities which give youthwho are drawn into commercial sex work a way out.

There are several federal programs which support homeless and disconnected youth. Yet these programs are small relative to the problems I've described above and they need greater congressional attention. I now would like to make several very specific suggestions for federal policy.

- Increase investment in the Runaway and Homeless Youth Act to expand housing and supportive services and to intervene and support homeless youth.
- Increase resources to schools through the Education of Homeless Children and Youth Act so that admission, transportation and school supports are provided to homeless youth and children.
- Expand resources for youth aging out of the foster care system through the Chafee Independence Living Act Programs—these programs help find housing resources for foster youth who don't have family ties and often end up home-less after emancipation at 21 from foster care systems.
- Promote cost-saving programs which emphasize alternatives to juvenile incarceration. The Juvenile Justice Delinquency & Prevention Act requires states to have early intervention, prevention programs to divert youth from crime and

incarceration, yet there is inadequate funding to establish these programs in many states.

- Pass the Place to Call Home Act, a legislative proposal of the national Network for Youth that is expected to be introduced in Congress in July. The Place to Call Home Act is a comprehensive legislative proposal to prevent, respond to, and end runaway and homeless situations among youth through age 24. Enactment of the bill's provisions will have a decisive positive impact for all disconnected youth, not solely youth experiencing homelessness.
- Increase investment in the Promoting Safe and Stable Families Program. This is a vital account that states use to establish prevention and early intervention supports for families at risk of child removal from the home, and support to homeless families.
- Increase funding and supports for the Youthbuild program so that serious expansion can occur for a model which has proven effective and could do somuch more.

Conclusion

The lives of thousands of Washington children and those across the country are impaired by severe poverty, disrupted families, teenage pregnancy, inadequate schools, poor health care and violence. For many children, the consequences of disintegrating families include parental neglect or abuse. Instead of security, they faceunsafe conditions in their homes, schools and neighborhoods. Some are abandoned or have little or no adult supervision. Too few of the young people at highest risk for homelessness and family dissolution are offered positive youth development activities which challenge them to achieve their highest potential and to become engaged positively in their communities.

I prepared this testimony this past weekend, during Father's Day. So it was bittersweet to consider this time of national familial celebration while organizing my thoughts on all of the many ways that young people become disconnected and disillusioned. Though it is with sadness and regret, we all must acknowledge the lack of strong and supportive families in our nation's poorest communities as a primary symptom of malaise among the vast majority of our very troubled youth. Whether the manifestations are dropping out of school or homelessness or unemployment, we all should remain mindful that strengthening families is the best way to prevent suffering and social disconnection among our young people.

Engaging entire families—rather than individual youth—in all services and supports whenever possible has been the operational philosophy of Sasha Bruce Youthwork for three decades. This cannot be over-stated. Through this testimony, I have endeavored to briefly outline the many issues facing troubled youth today, and to offer some recommendations, but I must emphasize the importance of approaching this multi-faceted and complicated problem with a steady eye to engaging entire families in trusting relationships that help them to identify and to build on their competencies. Indeed, we see this strength-based, family-focused approach as key to our success and it should be a fundamental part of any neighborhood-based, local, state-wide or national strategy to helping young people grow into healthy, loving and responsible adults.

Chairman McDermott. Thank you very much.

Mr. Whitfield?

STATEMENT OF DECARIO WHITFIELD

Mr. Whitfield. Good afternoon, ladies and gentlemen. My name is DeCario Whitfield. I am 19 years old and I am a student enrolled in the Sasha Bruce Youth Build Program. I came to the Youth Build Program after coming home from jail. I was locked up at the age of 16 for armed robbery. There were a lot of circumstances that led to this terrible time.

I was in high school. I was not getting the attention and assistance that I needed from my teachers. I did not understand any of the lessons, and I was constantly behind in my assignments just because I could not understand. I was scared to go to class because I knew I did not know the stuff. The classes were out of order, the students were running the halls, disrespectful to the teachers and each other. I was roaming the halls, smoking weed to escape the misery of feeling stupid and left behind. I could not wait for the 3:15 bell to ring.

Even though I lived with my grandmother, I did not have guidance at home. Although I was not starving and had a roof over my head, I was not getting attention from my family. My father was doing a 10-year sentence in jail, and my mother was running the streets too often to pay me attention. Her habit kept her busy. I had nowhere to run or turn to for structure. I led myself wherever I wanted to go. I was in charge of my life even though I was not wise enough to make decisions for myself. I lived in the ghetto where I saw people get shot, stabbed, using drugs and getting robbed everyday. It was easy to follow the crew and do the same thing.

After I was released, I was ashamed of the fact that I hurt others. I was sentenced to three years in jail. I was sentenced to a Title XVI sentence, when a 16 year old is being tried as an adult. I was in D.C. Jail, Shelby Training Center in Memphis, Tennessee, and the U.S. Penitentiary in Pennsylvania. I was not going to get an education, a job or any kind of direction and development in these places.

Then one day after serving 2.5 years of my sentence, I came home. I was released to my family, the same family that did not give the guidance that I needed in the first place. I was still on my own again. I knew I needed to make a change. I found out about the Sasha Bruce Youth Build Program while I was in jail. I wanted to get my GED because I did not graduate from high school. I wanted to be able to get a job so that I did not have to hustle. I knew I needed some kind of skill and training.

I came home on a Friday. Ms. Tara from the Free Minds Reading Book Club called Ms. Kym from the Sasha Bruce Youth Build Program and asked her if I could attend the orientation on the following Monday. I was in. She allowed me to come to the orientation even though I had not tested or interviewed. She took a chance on me, and I am glad.

Now that I am in the program, I feel that I am back on track. Some people feel that they are too old to go back to school to get an education. Youth Build made it possible for me to get a way to get my GED. I also get a chance to go to school and get money at the same time. I do not have to worry about getting to work after being in school all day. I get both in the same place. The environment stays the same. I am allowed the chance to have a regular stable environment.

In my classes, there are smaller amounts of people. I am able to get attention that I never got before. The teachers are respectful and they care about me. I have two teachers who care, instead of one who's all crazy and stressed out.

The counselors are there for me. I am able to get guidance whenever I need it. I can discuss trouble when it comes. Before, I would deal with it in any way I could without any outside help from a responsible adult. I am even able to talk about man stuff. I am able to hear from an adult and not feel like something is wrong with me. This program gave me a way to get back to what is supposed to be normal. I never knew normal. It feels almost strange.

When I am all done with this program, I will have training in a trade that I can use to get a job. I have other skills but they are illegal skills. I can only use them for other types of stuff. I was told that the construction piece could be seen as a means to an end. I have a career counselor to help me with any field I choose to enter. I have not made up my mind yet. I got some help with all that too. My counselor told me to redirect my other skills in a legal profession. Instead of breaking an entering, I could be a locksmith.

Programs for young people like Youth Build need to be everywhere. Not everybody is able to get the right people to help them get back straight. Not everybody who falls off the track is in a place where they get word of the chance to do better, fix the wrong stuff, and make something of themselves.

Without the program, I would be selling clothes at a stand in a mall with no GED or any type of good money. I would be stressed out and feeling stupid still. It would take me a long time to get my GED on my own. It would be a minute before I would be able to figure out that nothing was wrong with me. It would also take awhile to figure out the right things to do. Right now, I have supervision even though I am not on probation. People actually want to know where I am when I do not show up for class. I am responsible for learning instead of ducking the teachers and smoking weed. I even have some pocket change, enough to satisfy immediate needs for a little while. I am doing well and nothing is wrong with me. I am not a crazy kid running the streets.

Thank you.

[The prepared statement of Mr. Whitfield follows:]

Prepared Statement of DeCario Whitfield

Good afternoon ladies and gentlemen. My name is DeCario Whitfield. I am 19 years old and I am a student enrolled in the Sasha Bruce YouthBuild program. I came to the YouthBuild program after coming home from jail. I was locked up at the age of 16 for armed robbery. There were a lot of circumstances that led to thatterrible time.

I was in high school. I was not getting the attention and assistance that I needed from my teachers. I did not understand any of the lessons and I was constantly behind in my assignments just because I didn't understand. I was scared to go to class because I knew I didn't know the stuff. The classes were out of order. The students were running the halls, disrespectful to the teachers and each other. I was roaming the halls and smoking weed to escape the misery of feeling stupid and left behind. I couldn't wait for the 3:15 bell to ring.

Even though I lived with my grandmother, I did not have guidance at home. Although I was not starving and had a roof over my head, I was not getting attention from my family. My father was doing a ten-year sentence in jail and my mother was running the streets too often to pay me some mind. Her habit kept her busy getting her fix. I had nowhere to turn for structure. I led myself wherever I wanted to go. I was in charge of my life, even though I was not wise enough to make decisions for myself. I lived in the ghetto. I saw people getting shot, stabbed; using drugs, and getting robbed everyday. It was easy to follow the crew and do the same thing.

After I was arrested, I felt ashamed of the fact that I hurt others. I was sentenced to three years in jail. I was sentenced to a Title-16 sentence. It's when a 16 year old is charged and sentenced as an adult. I went to DC Detention Center, Shelby Training Center in Memphis TN, and United States Penitentiary in Pennsylvania. I was not going to get an education, a job, or any kind of direction and development in those places.

Then one day after serving $2\frac{1}{2}$ years of my sentence, I came home. I was released to my family; the same family that did not give the guidance that I needed in the first place. I was still on my own, again. I knew I needed to make a change. I found out about the Sasha Bruce YouthBuild while I was in jail. I wanted to get my GED because I didn't graduate from high school. I wanted to be able to get a job so I didn't ever have to hustle. I knew I needed some kind of skills and training.

I came home on a Friday. Ms. Tara from Free Minds Reading Club called Ms. Kym from Sasha Bruce YouthBuild and asked her if I could attend the orientation on the following Monday. I was in. She allowed me to come to the orientation even though I had not tested or interviewed. She took a chance on me. I'm glad.

Now that I'm in the program, I feel that I'm back on track. Some people feel that they are too old to go back to school to get an education. YouthBuild made it possible for me to get a way to get my GED. I also get a chance to go to school and get some money at the same time. I don't have to worry about getting to work after I have been to school all day. I get both in the same place. The environment stays the same. I am allowed the chance to have a regular stable environment.

In my classes, there is a smaller amount of people. I am able to get the attention that I never got before now. The teachers are respectful and they care about me. I have two teachers who care, instead of one all crazy and stressed out.

The counselors are there for me. I am able to get guidance when I need it. I can discuss trouble when it comes. Before, I would deal with it in any way I could without any outside help from a responsible adult. I'm even able to talk about man stuff. I'm able to hear from an adult and not feel like something is wrong with me. This program gave me a way to get back to what's supposed to be normal. I never knew normal. It feels almost strange.

When I'm all done with this program, I will have training in a trade to use to get a job. I have other skills, but they're all illegal skills. I can only use them for other type stuff. I was told that the construction piece could be seen as a means to an end. I have a career counselor to help me with any field I choose to enter. I have not made up my mind yet. I got some help with all that too. My counselor told me to redirect my other skills to use in legitimate professions. Instead of breaking and entering, I could be a locksmith.

Programs for young people, like YouthBuild, need to be everywhere. Not everybody is able to get to the right people to help them get back straight. Not everybody that fell off the track is in a place where they get word of the chance to do better, fix the wrong stuff, and make something of themselves.

Without the program I would be selling clothes at a stand in the mall with no GED or any type of good money. I would be stressed out and feeling stupid, still. It would take me a long time to get my GED on my own. It would be a minute before I would be able to figure out that nothing is wrong with me. It would also take awhile to figure out the right things to do.

Right now, I have supervision, eventhough I'm not on probation. People actually want to know where I've been when I don't show up for class. I am responsible for learning, instead of ducking the teachers and smoking weed. I even have some pocket change, enough to satisfy immediate needs for a little while. I'm doing good, and nothing is wrong with me. I'm not a crazy kid running the streets.

Chairman McDermott. Thank you very much for that testimony.

Dr. Mincy is a professor of social policy and social work at Columbia University's School of Social Work.

Dr. Mincy?

STATEMENT OF RONALD B. MINCY, MAURICE V. RUSSELL PROFESSOR OF SOCIAL POLICY AND SOCIAL WORK PRACTICE, COLUMBIA UNIVERSITY

Dr. Mincy. Good afternoon, Mr. Chairman. Since many young people between 16 and 24 years old are out of school and out of work, they are not acquiring the knowledge and skills needed to replace today's skilled, educated and experienced adult workers. These young people are called "disconnected youth." To remain competitive in a global economy, it is imperative that Congress act in order to reconnect these young people to school and work. Doing so would also provide an important progress on an important American ideal, namely, inter-generational social mobility. Finally, reconnecting these young people to school and work would save billions of dollars in future welfare, child welfare, unemployment and criminal justice expenditures. For these reasons, I applaud this Committee for holding these hearings, and I am grateful for the opportunity to testify.

I would like to set a big picture here. Between 1980 and 2000, the United States enjoyed two of the longest periods of economic growth this nation has ever seen. That growth was fueled by a steady increase in the size, skills, experience and education of the prime-age labor force. However, over the next 10 years, the prime-age labor force is expected to grow at less than half the pace it did during these prosperous years. Moreover, white workers, who generally have more education and occupational status than black, Latino and foreign-born workers, represented the majority of new workers during this prosperous time, but they will represent just 15 percent of net new workers over the next two decades.

Increases in the fraction of workers with college degrees help to fuel the economic growth of the 1980s to 2000s. However, we are expected to have very slow growth in the number of college-educated workers in the next 10 years.

For these reasons, maintaining our competitiveness demands that we get as much as we can out of every potential worker. However, youth between 16 and 24 years old, who are not in school and not in work, are not obtaining the skills they need to fill the void.

Disconnected youth represent about 5 to 29 percent of all young people between 16 and 24 years old. Estimates vary about how large this population is according to the age at which we are trying to begin these estimates or whether or not the estimates are narrow or broad. Some estimates include younger adolescence down to age 14. Some include, in addition to being out of school and out of work, women who are not married to students or workers or unmarried mothers. Some estimates rely not just on being out of school and out of work but whether or not someone is a high school dropout in the foster care system or in the juvenile justice system or whether or not someone suffers from long-term unemployment or incarceration.

Due to these variations, most studies estimate the population as being somewhere between 2 million and 10 million youth. Therefore, this population is by no means a drop in the bucket and it really represents an important potential labor force to replace retiring workers that if we do not act, we will lose.

Our tolerance for social and economic mobility is based on the idea that equal opportunity will mean that disadvantaged adults will not have disadvantaged children. However, the characteristics of most disconnected youth belie that. Blacks and Hispanics, particularly those of Puerto Rican descent, are over-represented among disadvantaged youth. The children of high school dropouts are also over-represented as are the children of public assistance recipients.

Not only are the children of the disadvantaged more likely to become disconnected in the first place, but they are also likely to experience recurring spells of disconnection and longer spells. For example, black men who are in this age group, one third of them have disconnection spells of up to two years and 12 percent of them have disconnection spells of up to three years. Someone who has three years of being out of school and out of work is unlikely to be hired by the private sector in the United States. This suggests that the idea of inter-generational mobility is being undermined by this notion of disconnected youth and it is for this reason that it is important for this Committee to act.

I want to then honor my time and the time of the other presenters by pointing out that we have heard of a number of effective programs for disadvantaged youth. Youth Build has been touted a number of times. There is also a CUNY Prep Program, which I discuss in my written testimony, that moves young people from being out of school and out of work to actually enrolling in college.

So, I want to again applaud this Committee for holding these hearings and I look forward to working with this Committee in the future to see that we can address these to a number of different Committees, a number of Federal programs and thank you very much.

[The prepared statement of Dr. Mincy follows:]

Prepared Statement of Ronald B. Mincy, Ph.D., Maurice V. Russell Professor of Social Policy and Social Work Practice, Columbia University School of Social Work

Because many young people between 16 and 24 years old are out-of-school and out-of work, they are not acquiring the knowledge and skills needed to replace today's skilled, educated, and experienced adult workers. These young people are called disconnected youth. To remain competitive in a global economy, it is imperative that Congress act in order to re-connect these young people to school and work. Doing so would also promote an important American ideal, namely inter-generational social mobility. Finally, reconnecting these young people to school and work would save billions of dollars in future welfare, unemployment, and criminal justice expenditures. For these reasons, I applaud this committee for holding these hearings, and I am grateful for the opportunity to testify.

As compared with the previous two decades, the U.S. labor force is expected to grow much more slowly and we can anticipate substantial shortages of skilled, educated, and experienced workers. The labor force (persons between 25 and 54 years old) grew by almost 50 percent between 1980 and 2000, but over the following 20 years, it is projected to grow by less than 16 percent. Only 15 percent of net new U.S. workers will be native-born whites, who represented over 54 percent of net new workers between 1980 and 2000. Black, Hispanic, and foreign-born workers will replace native born white workers between the ages of 25 and 54 years old, because the number of these prime age white workers will decline by 10 percent 2000 and 2020 (Ellwood, 2001). Since minority and foreign-born workers generally have lower levels of educational attainment and occupational status than white workers, this demographic transition implies declines in the skills and education of the American workforce. There is also direct evidence of such a decline. The fraction of workers with college degrees will increase by about 5 percentage points between 2000 and 2020; during the two decades before 2000 it increased by 11 percentage points (Ellwood, 2001).

Youth who are out of school and out of work are not acquiring the knowledge and skills needed to replace the skilled, educated, and experienced adult workers who will retiring in the coming decade. In the 1990s, observers began efforts to estimate the size and characteristics of these disconnected youth (Besharov 1999 and Donahoe and Tienda 2000). Though we know much more about them, we still lack a coherent national strategy to provide these young people with the supports they need to return to school and work, so that we remain competitive in a global economy.

Definitions of disconnected youth vary by age and other criteria. The most strict definition is a person between the 16 and 24 years old, who is neither working (in the private sector or the military), nor in school. When studying disconnection, some studies consider youth as young as 14 years old because it is clear that the process of disconnection begins before age 16. To take account of gender differences in the transition from youth to adulthood, early studies added teenaged mothers or women who were not married to a student or worker to the definition of disconnected youth (Brown and Emig, 1999). More recent studies also use factors that are highly associated with disconnection by the most strict definition (out-of-school and out of work) as criteria defining disconnection youth. For example, according to Wald and Martinez, (2006) any 14 to 17 year old who drops out of high school, or is involved with the juvenile justice system, or is an unmarried mother, or is in foster care is at risk of disconnection. Moreover, any 18-to-24 year old who experiences long-term unemployment or incarceration is disconnected. Because of these variations in criteria, estimates of the size of the disconnected-youth population vary widely. By the strictest definition, disconnected youth represent about 5 percent of all youth between 16 and 24 years old. By broader definitions, they represent as much as 29 percent of all youth in a given age range. Depending upon criteria, disconnected youth were reconnected to school and work, they could replace a small or more substantial fraction of the skilled, educated, and experienced workers who will retire over the next decade.

Besides replacing skilled, experienced, and educated workers, disconnected youth are evidence that a fundamental American ideal is failing. That ideal is intergenerational social-economic mobility. Our tolerance for social and economic inequality is based on the belief that equal opportunity will make it possible for the children of the disadvantaged to advance beyond their parents' station in life. However, a common finding of studies of disconnection is that blacks and native-born Hispanics, especially those of Puerto Rican descent, are more likely to become disconnected than other adolescents (Brown and Emig 1999, Donahoe and Tienda 2000, and MaCurdy, Keating, et al. 2006). For example, black males are twice as likely to be disconnected as white males, because of their high dropout, unemployment and incarceration rates. In addition to high dropout and unemployment rates, black females are more likely to be disconnected than white females because of their high rates of unmarried births.

Studies also show that race and ethnicity are not the only evidence, related to disconnection, that the American class structure is hardening. Instead, the probability of disconnection is inversely related to parental education and parental receipt of public assistance. So, for example, by age 22 the probability of disconnection for the adolescent children of high school dropouts is more than twice as high as the corresponding probability for the adolescent children of college graduates. What's more the probability of disconnection was 34 percent for the white adolescent children of high school dropouts, but 47 percent for the white adolescent children of high school dropouts, who also received public benefits (MaCurdy, Keating, et al. 2006).

Longitudinal studies, which examine outcomes over time, show that race and parental education are also strong predictors of recurring and longer spells of disconnection. For example, once an initial spell of disconnection is interrupted by a return to work or school, 13 percent of the adolescent children of high school dropouts experience a second spell of disconnection. By contrast, a second spell of disconnection occurs for only 7 percent of the adolescent children of high school graduates and only 4 the adolescent children of college graduates. Only 24 percent of white males had a first spell of disconnection lasting at least two years; while 33 percent of black males did so. Indeed, 12.3 percent of black males had first disconnections spells that lasted three years; only 8.3 percent of black females, 6.5 percent of white males and 4.9 percent of white females had a first disconnection spell of such long duration.

That the incidence, recurrence, and duration of disconnection spells is higher forblacks than whites, does not mean that white youth are immune to disconnection. The majority (58 percent) of disconnected youth are white.

Longitudinal studies of disconnection also providing information that may help policy makers target resources to disconnected youth. As stated above, the adolescent children of public assistance recipients are more likely to become disconnected as are youth in the foster care system and juvenile justice systems. Moreover, theprobability of the first spell of disconnection rises steadily with age, but peaks at 18 years old, when most youth should be graduating from high school. Finally, the probability of a second spell of disconnection is higher for youth who began their first spell of disconnection after dropping out of school or being convicted of a crime. These findings suggest strategic points during the life cycle when interventions should be targeting disconnected youth or youth at risk of becoming disconnected.An obvious intervention point is just before youth leave school. Another is while youth (or their parents) are receiving public benefits. Other points of intervention include the period just before youth age out of foster care or after youth have been convicted of a crime, perhaps in programs that divert non-violent offenders from incarceration. Welfare programs and programs serving teen mothers are obvious points of contact for serving disconnected young women. But because disconnectedyoung men are rarely served by publicly-funded programs, unless they are reached in school, foster care, or in the juvenile justice system, it may be difficult to reach them at all.

RECONNECTING DISCONNECTED YOUTH

Promising or effective interventions for disconnected youth are simple to conceptualize, but often difficult to design and implement. They tend to connect youth, to school or work, but they must also create comprehensive systems of support to address barriers to school attendance and employment. The basic model for connectingdisconnected youth to school is the alternative high school. Studies show that the most successful such high schools emphasize easy access. They tend to be free of charge and offer schedules that allow young people to handle their personal responsibilities and complete their coursework. The most promising approaches go beyond GED attainment, because studies show that the return to obtaining a GED is substantially lower than the returns to a high school diploma (Campbell and College, 2003). Moreover, these programs have small class sizes, a family atmosphere, a combination informality and structure and individualized strategies are all common in successful transitional schools. Student autonomy and accountability are also stressed in these programs (Dugger and Dugger 1998 and Reimer and Cash 2003). Other features of effective alternative schools include attention to students' psychological needs and efforts to build on student's social as well as their academic skills (Mitchell and Waiwaiole 2003).

CUNY Prep, collaboration between the Department of Youth and Community Development (DYCD), New York City Department of Education (DOE) and City University of New York (CUNY), is a good example of a alternative high school. The purpose of CUNY Prep is to prepare out-of-school students, between the ages of 16–18 years old, to reenter high school or to acquire their GED so they may attend college. With this goal in mind, CUNY Prep works to improve the confidence of the youth as students in a small school setting, where they are held to high expectations. Teachers and administrators work diligently with students to overcome current barriers, such as acquiring daycare for young mothers and housing or other barriers to reentry for ex-offenders. Besides high expectations and supports, CUNY Prep students are also held accountable for their actions. Failure to adhere to rules for student conduct often results in dismissal, although students are allowed to return the following semester with no retributions.

Connecting older youth or young adults to work is a more formidable task for several reasons. Young people between the ages of 18 and 24, usually face more obstacles to work than younger cohorts, attempting to return to school. Many 18-to-24 year-old disconnected youth are high school dropouts. Others graduated from high school despite having limited math and reading skills. Finally, few employers are willing to hire young people with no work experience. Despite these difficulties, there are programs that are successful in introducing or re-introducing these young adults to work.

Many of the characteristic of successful alternative education programs hold true for workforce development programs. However, diversity within the disconnected-young adult population requires multiple pathways to success (National League of Cities, 2000). Such designs often result when efforts are undertaken to include disconnected young adults in program design and implementation decisions.

YouthBuild USA is a nationally recognized program that works with disconnected young people, by creating meaningful employment opportunities in the construction industry. The Department of Housing and Urban Development has partnered with local nonprofit, faith-based and public agencies to replicate Youthbuild in several communities around the country.

Constructions jobs not only help the young adults, but also enable these young adults to contribute to their communities by building low-income housing. While learning job skills that will lead to sustainable employment, young adults are also encouraged to complete their high school diploma or obtain their GED at YouthBuild's own alternative school. Consistent with the comprehensive approach needed to work with disconnected youth, Youthbuild also provides social support and follow up services to participants.

More recently, Youthbuild has added several new features to its programming, which should increase success. Through a partnership with AmeriCorps young adults receive monetary compensation while learning new skills, which should increases retention. Additionally, AmeriCorps offers a stipend or a larger educational reward upon completion of the program, which should increase the number of young adults who successfully complete the program. Fifty-eight percent of the youth that enter the program complete it, of those 33 percent obtain their GED or high school diploma and 78 percent go onto to gainful employment or further education.

Financial literacy and leadership development are other new components of Youthbuild's programming. Upon graduation from the program, YouthBuild introduces its graduates to asset development through Individual Development Accounts (IDAs) and YouthBuild Asset Trust. After graduation from Youthbuild, participants have the opportunity to engage youth leadership activities. There are a variety of alumni youth leadership organizations for graduates of YouthBuild.

A final example of a promising program for disconnected youth is especially focused on homeless youth and youth in foster care system. The Metropolitan Atlanta Youth Opportunity Initiative (MAYOI) is a is a two year transitional program, sponsored by The Annie E. Casey Foundation and Casey Family Programs, targeting foster care youth or youth who have been previously homeless. MAYOI collaborates with local providers ensure these youth receive priority for housing and other social services, including education, health care, employment-training. The goal for participants is to become economically self-sufficient in two years and have their own home within three years.

These are just a few of the promising initiatives that have been developed by governments and non-profit agencies to respond to the needs of disconnected youth. A much more concerted effort is needed in the coming years to build effective systems to support these youth. One of the obstacles to such a system is the multiple jurisdictions involved. Disconnected youth (or those at risk) come from families receiving welfare, the foster care system, and the criminal justice system. We want to ensure that these youth return to school and to work. Though support from the federal government is desperately needed, no single federal departments and Congressional committees can do the job on its own. Nevertheless, I urge Members of Congress to begin with these hearings to work through the obstacles. Our position in the world economy and our commitment to a fundamental American ideal depend on our ability to act decisively, over the 10 years.

References

Besharov, D. (Ed.) (1999). *America's Disconnected Youth*. Washington, D.C.: American Enterprise Institute. Brown, B.V., & Emig, C. (1999). Prevalence, Patterns, and

Outcomes. In D. Besharov (Ed.), *America's Disconnected Youth*. Washington, D.C.: American Enterprise Institute.

Campbell, L. and College, N. (2003). As strong as the strongest link: Urban high school dropout. *The High School Journal, 87,* 2, 16–24.

Dugger, J.M. & Dugger, C.W. (1998). An evaluation of a successful alternative high school. *The High School Journal. 81(4),* 218–228.

Donahoe & Debra and Marta Tienda. (2000). "The Transition from School to Work: Is There a Crisis? What Can Be Done?" In Danziger, Sheldon, and Jane Waldfogel (Eds.) *Securing the Future: Investing in Children from Birth to College.* Russell Sage Foundation, New York, NY.

Ellwood, D.T. (2001). The Sputtering Labor Force of the 21st Century: Can Social Policy Help?: National Bureau of Economic Research.

MaCurdy, T., Keating, B. & Nagavarapu, S.S. (2006). *Profiling the plight of disconnected youth in America.* William and Flora Hewitt Foundation.

Metropolitan Atlanta Youth Opportunities Initiative. (2007). *Making My Way Home program overview.* Retrieved on June 17, 2007 from the World Wide Web: http://www.atlcf.org/www/documents/mywayinfo06b.pdf.

Metropolitan Atlanta Youth Opportunities Initiative. *Metropolitan Atlanta Youth Opportunities Initiative fact sheet.* Retrieved on June 17, 2007 from the World Wide Web: http://www.jimcaseyyouth.org/docs/mayoifactsheet.pdf.

Mitchell, S. & Waiaiola, G. (2003). Interim Evaluation of In-District Alternative Education High School Programs. Portland, OR: Author.

National League of Cities. (2006). *Reengaging disconnected youth.* Washington, DC: Author.

Reimer, M. & Cash, T. (2003). *Alternative schools: Best practices for development and evaluation.* Clemson, South Carolina: National Dropout Prevention Center.

The Jim Casey Youth Opportunity Initative. (2006). *Cross-Site Report: Progress on Performance Measures.* Retrieved on June 17, 2007 from the World Wide Web: http://www.atlcf.org/www/documents/perfreport06.pdf.

Wald, M. & Martinez, T. (2003). *Connected by 25: Improving the life chances of the countries most vulnerable 14–24 year olds.* William and Flora Hewitt Foundation Working Paper.

Chairman McDermott. Thank you very much for your testimony.

Ms. Burt is a research associate for the Center for Labor, Human Services and Population at The Urban Institute.

STATEMENT OF MARTHA R. BURT, RESEARCH ASSOCIATE, CENTER ON LABOR, HUMAN SERVICES AND POPULATION, THE URBAN INSTITUTE

Dr. Burt. Thank you, Chairman McDermott, Congressman Weller and other Members of the——

Chairman McDermott. I guess I should have addressed you as "Doctor," I am sorry.

Dr. Burt. Thank you. He is a doctor and I am a doctor. Thanks for inviting me to share my views related to homeless youth, and especially their involvement in public systems. I have been involved in policy-oriented research related to homeless populations since 1983 with the First Emergency Food and Shelter Act, and I have also, in addition to working on homeless issues, worked a lot on high-risk youth from a number of different directions, including teenage pregnancy, mental illness and community programs to assist multi-problem youth. So, I take a multi-system perspective, and I take a fairly long—who is getting into the potential place to become homeless among many youth who are at high risk and experience a lot of difficulties.

About a quarter of youth could be put in that category of those who have an elevated risk of homelessness. They are in fact showing up on the streets and the more vulnerabilities they have in the direction of many of the issues that people have said the higher likelihood that they are—that they will experience homelessness.

I have been asked to talk about how big the problem is, that is how many homeless youth are there, who they are and what might be promising types of intervention. I am not going to talk about who they are because I think you have heard that from everybody else. I have provided a number of statistics about the proportions that we know from research are in— have particular issues, but I will skip that.

I do want to talk about the issue of understanding how big the problem is and why it is so difficult for anybody to tell you the answer to that. The Committee is, at this point, interested in youth 16 to 24. That means you are interested in minors and adults. The same national surveys do not cover both minors and adults, and so we are always in a position of trying to piece together information from surveys that look at youth, like the Youth Risk Behavior Survey, and surveys that look at adults. In addition, the same systems do not serve both youth and adults. So, for instance, the homeless service system, for which we do have some national data and national estimates that I have included in my testimony, does not take anybody under 18. The Runaway and Homeless Youth system has its own data system and trying to put those together is rather difficult. The foster care system has yet another data system. Trying to figure out where the overlaps are makes it very difficult for us to give you estimates.

It also very much depends on what you mean by "homeless." When you look at estimates of 1.5 million, 1.6, 1.7 million, in the course of a year, is everything from youth who have left without parental permission for one night, so the definition in these telephone surveys is one night on the street without consent and not on vacation, of course, all the way to up kids who have basically been kicked out at the age of 12 because somebody found out or figured out that they were a sexual minority and they have no place to go except on the street from thereon. So, if you are looking at the very hardcore group of kids who have very long histories of homelessness, that is a smaller proportion of kids who have a lot more complex needs and a level of intervention that will be necessary to help them back is a lot higher.

Youth who use youth homeless shelters are most often homeless for the first time and have not been homeless very long. Mostly what we know about them we know because they are connected to the programs run by the Family and Youth Services Bureau and we have a data system on them. Street use is exactly the opposite. They are unattached to shelters, they are on their own without adult supervision for periods that can last for several years. In the National Survey of Homeless Assistance Providers and Clients, which I analyzed and published a lot about, we looked at the 18 and 19 year olds because this went only to adult shelters so we have analyzed the 18 and 19 year olds and the 20 to 24 year olds to look at the differences between those age groups and the homeless people over 25, and what you find is that up to 61 percent of the 18 and 19 year olds who are in adult shelters have been in foster care and have aged out of foster care, many have been in correctional institutions and that is where you get your really serious cases who have very long histories of homelessness, they are already chronically homeless.

In the 20 to 24 year old group, you have a lot of young mothers, who were teenage moms, have all the issues related to being a mother at a very young age, often not voluntarily, and are now turning up as the homeless families, and they are being talked about as if they were not teenage moms, they are just a normal family that was just one paycheck away from homelessness but that is not actually who they are.

I want to actually emphasize very much that the intervention point, there is a general rule of thumb, when you are looking at populations sort of as broad brush as homeless youth and that is to go for the hardest core you can find. If you are going to put significant money into people, people who are in trouble, the ones you really want to touch and touch deeply, intensively, and across the board, are those who have absolutely no chance of getting out of this on their own. Most of the children who go to runaway and homeless youth centers end up in fact reconnected to their families, thanks to the help they get at those places, with not no trouble but not huge amounts of trouble and huge investment in them.

The really hardcore kids, the kids who age out of foster care, the kids who run away from foster care, which is at least as many, the kids who get exited out of foster care before they are 18 because they are now in other institutions, like jails and correctional facilities, these populations are at least as big those that age out. The 200,000 a year who leave correctional institutions between the ages of 16 and 24 also are at very, very high risk for long-term less than productive lives. The most expensive interventions are also the interventions that will rescue the people who are least likely to rescue themselves.

Thank you very much.

[The prepared statement of Dr. Burt follows:]

Prepared Statement of Martha R. Burt, Ph.D., Research Associate, Center on Labor, Human Services and Population, the Urban Institute

Chairman McDermott and Members of the Committee:

Thank you for inviting me to share my views relating to homeless youth, and especially to their involvement in public systems under the supervision of this committee. I have been involved in policy-oriented research on homeless populations and homeless service systems since 1983, when the first Emergency Food and Shelter Program legislation was passed, and have also spent considerable time trying to understand strategies that are able to reach multiproblem youth and help them move toward a productive and responsible adulthood. So it is a pleasure for me to be asked to give testimony on a matter that has not received either the research or policy attention it deserves.[6]

I have been asked to address three issues: (1) How big is the problem—how many homeless youth are there? (2) Who are homeless youth—what are their characteristics, and what factors predispose youth to become homeless? and (3) What might be the most promising points and types of intervention? [7]

How Big Is the Problem?

There are no reliable statistics on the number of homeless youth, in part because this is a notoriously difficult population to find and count, and in part because everyone defines the population differently. This Subcommittee has stated that its interest is in the population of youth and young adults age 16 to 24. This age range includes both minors and adults, which usually means that data must be drawn from different ongoing national surveys just as different systems of public and private support and intervention serve minors and adults. There are also issues of what one means by ''homeless''—does one night away from home without permission count, or two nights, or do we want to focus on the youth who truly have no place to go back to and spend years on the streets? Estimates have to be cobbled together from different sources, or special surveys have to be conducted, each of which has its limitations. I am happy to say more about definitional and methodological issuesif asked, but assuming the Subcommittee is interested in our best guesses, they are the following:

- For youth age 12–17, two estimates from quite different sources fall in the range of 1.6 to 1.7 million a year (between 7 and 8 percent of all youth in those age ranges). This estimate is at the high end because it is very inclusive, counting short unauthorized absences from home or ''throwaway'' experiences of getting kicked out for a period of time as well as long-term separation from family or having nowhere to return (Ringwalt et al. 1998; Hammer,Finkelhor, and Sedlak 2002). A higher proportion of episodes occur among older than among younger youth. Further, most of these episodes are very short, with the result that about 300,000 to 400,000 youth might be expected to be homeless on any given day.

- Youth using homeless youth shelters are usually homeless for the first time and have not been homeless long. Information about youth in these shelters,which are usually funded by the Family and Youth Services Bureau of the Department of Health and Human Services (DHHS), can be obtained through RHYMIS, that system's management information database. Street youth are the opposite—unattached to shelters and on their own without adult supervision for periods that can exceed several years. Information about this part of the homeless youth population is only available through special studies.

- Homelessness among young adults, age 18 to 24, may be studied within the homeless assistance system that serves adults. Still the best source of that information, although now dated, is the National Survey of Homeless Assistance Providers and Clients (NSHAPC), which was conducted in 1996. Urban Institute researchers developed estimates of the homeless population from NSHAPC, from which we can estimate the numbers of 18- to 19-year-olds and20- to 24-year-olds among the adult homeless population (Burt, Aron, and Lee 2001).
  - 18- to 19-year-olds are 5 percent, or 22,000 to 44,000, of the homeless population on a single day, or about 80,000 to 170,000 over the course of a year.
  - 20- to 24-year-olds are 7 percent, or 31,000 to 59,000, of the homeless population on a single day, or about 124,000 to 236,000 over the course of a year.

Who Are Homeless Youth?

- **Gender**—In shelter samples, whether in youth or adult shelters, the proportions of males and females tend to be about equal. The older and the more "street" the sample, the more males.

- **Race/ethnicity**—As with samples of homeless adults, race/ethnicity distributions depend heavily on the race/ethnicity distribution of the entire community.

- **Sexual minorities**—Research findings on the proportion of homeless youth who are gay, lesbian, or bisexual vary, from a low of about 6 percent from youth-services-center samples to as high as 11 to 35 percent in street samples. Sexual minority status is a powerful risk factor for youth homelessness, as disclosure to a parent or a parent's discovery of that status may lead to being thrown out or running away.

- **Pregnancy**—Homeless youth are three times as likely as national samples of youth to be pregnant, to have impregnated someone, or to already be a parent. Pregnancy may be the result of having no way to obtain money other than through prostitution (survival sex) when already homeless or ejection from home because of the pregnancy. This trend continues for homeless young adults age 18 to 24 (see appendix, table 1).

- **Length of time homeless**—As noted, youth using runaway and homelessyouth shelters tend to have been homeless only once and for a short period of time. NSHAPC data on young adults shows that more than half had been homeless for 2 to 9 years. Two-thirds of those age 18 to 19 had first become homeless before they were 18; the same was true for a third of those age 20 to 24 (see appendix, table 1).

Risk Factors for Homelessness Among Youth

In addition to pregnancy and sexual minority status, a number of factors may contribute to a youth becoming homeless and to the separate issue of a youth remaining homeless.

- **School difficulties**—About half of homeless youth have not finished high school, with the proportion going up the younger the youth. Between one-fourth and two-fifths of homeless youth have had to repeat at least one grade inschool. Among young adult homeless people, the majority have been suspended and/or expelled from school (see appendix, table 2).

- **Substance abuse**—Thirty to 40 percent of homeless youth report alcohol problems in their lifetime, and 40 to 50 percent report drug problems. These percentages are smaller than for older homeless people, but homeless youth tend to have started younger, often before age 15. This early use and abuse is predictive of serious adult addiction problems and long-term homelessness (of 18-to 19-year-olds in NSHAPC, 23 percent began drinking to get drunk before age 15, and 20 percent began using drugs regularly at that early age) (see appendix, table 2).

- **Mental health problems**—Forty-five percent of homeless youth reported mental health problems in the past year, 50 to 56 percent did so over their lifetime. These rates are not different than for older homeless adults, but they are predictive of becoming homeless and remaining homeless (see appendix, table 2).

- **Family conflict and child maltreatment**—Very high proportions of homeless youth report family conflict as a reason for being homeless. Almost twice as many young adult homeless people report abuse and neglect experiences as do older homeless people (see appendix, table 3).

- **Out-of-home placement and foster care**—Abuse and neglect experiences increase the likelihood of child welfare involvement and out-of-home placement, and life on the street increases the likelihood of criminal involvement.
  - 61 percent of 18- to 19-year-old NSHAPC young adults had been in out-of-home placements—a rate more than two and a half times that reported by homeless adults 25 and older. The 20- to 24-year-old NSHAPC population was in the middle. Further, the younger group was more likely to have been removed from their home before age 13 and to have spent more time in out-of-home placement. Half had been forced to leave home when they were a minor (see appendix, table 3). About a quarter of NSHAPC young adults had been in juvenile detention, compared with 15 percent of older homeless people.
  - The association between child welfare involvement and shelter use as an adult works both ways. Studies in New York City indicate that 29 percent of emergency shelter users had been involved with child welfare services, of whom three-quarters had been placed outside the home (Park, Metraux, and Culhane 2005). Thus, out-of-home placement is a decided risk for homelessness (in the general population, only about 3 percent of adults have been so placed). Looked at from the child welfare perspective, 19 percent of former child welfare service users entered public shelters within 10 years of leaving child welfare. Those placed outside the home were twice as likely as those that just received preventive services to enter a shelter (22 versus 11 percent), while absconders from foster care had the highest rate of subsequent homelessness (Park et al. 2004a).
  - Finally, having been homeless as a child, with one's parent(s), is associated with subsequent child welfare involvement. Eighteen percent of such children became involved with child welfare within 5 years of their first shelter admission, with recurrent use of shelters (i.e., repeated homeless episodes) being a strong predictor of child welfare involvement (Park et al. 2004b).

- **Juvenile justice involvement**—Every year about 200,000 youth age 10 to 24 leave detention and correctional facilities. Most do not have a high school diploma, nor have they ever held a job. They frequently have physical health, mental health, and/or substance abuse problems. And they most commonly go back to neighborhoods that will expose them to the same risk factors for getting into trouble that put them into the justice system in the first place. Severalstudies, summarized by

Toro et al. (2007), indicate that these youth have high probabilities of ending up homeless.

All the statistics we can assemble suggest that many kinds of trouble may lead to youth homelessness. The very large majority of youth who experience a runaway, throwaway, or homeless episode manage to leave homelessness and not return. But the longer a youth has been homeless, the more likely he or she is to be in many kinds of trouble and to have been for a long time (Toro, Dworsky, and Fowler 2007). Further, the longer the period of youth homelessness is and the more barriers ayouth faces, the higher the risk that the youth will end up as a chronically homeless adult. Indeed, many homeless street youth today would meet HUD criteria for chronic homelessness if they were adults.

Intervention Options

A general rule of thumb for selecting among intervention points and intervention types is ''go for the hardest-core you can find.'' Thus, with homeless youth, the largest waste of human potential, along with the biggest costs to society, lies with multiproblem youth, who are quite often involved with two or more public systems and who have the highest risk of becoming and remaining homeless. This may seem counterintuitive, and it is often not politically popular. But a good deal of researchindicates that while interventions with the ''hardest-core'' parts of a population are the most expensive, they also yield the most impact for the investment. This is because these are the people who are pretty much guaranteed *not* to solve their own problems if left to their own devices.

The runaway and homeless youth shelter network, supported and overseen by the Family and Youth Services Bureau of the DHHS, already focuses on the large component of the runaway youth population that potentially has a home to go back to. Follow-up studies indicate that the very large majority of these youth (up to 90+ percent) reunite with their parents, progress to living on their own, or live with friends, but do not continue in or return to homelessness. While expanding the numbers and locations of these programs would always be desirable, such an expansion would not make much difference for the street youth population because very fewof the latter population use these programs.

The intervention points that are likely to yield maximum payoff are the periods surrounding institutional release—the 24,000+ youth who turn 18 while in foster care and the 200,000+ youth who leave juvenile or corrections facilities every year are those among the general youth population who have the highest risk of becoming homeless and of staying homeless or reentering institutions if nothing is done to intervene.[8] The period surrounding the end of substance abuse treatment or psychiatric hospitalization is another potentially fruitful intervention point.

Some research on the Chafee Foster Care Independence Program (FCIA) indicates that this strategy has promise. The FCIA doubled allocations to states to ease transition from foster care and allows states to use 30 percent of funds to pay for housing for youth older than 18 but not yet 21. Research summarized by Toro et al. (2007, 14–17) indicates that the youth who receive this type of support are less likely to become homeless during the transition period, and are also more likely to be in college, have access to health care, and not be involved in the criminal justice system. Further follow-up interview waves will shed light on whether these differences persist once youth reach age 21.

In Denver, Urban Peak runs two housing programs that address, respectively, the needs of youth aging out of foster care and long-term street youth. The first is a partnership between Urban Peak and the state child welfare department to provide permanent supportive housing for children in or about to leave state custody who are or have been homeless. The second uses HUD funding and local service dollars to create permanent supportive housing for street youth with disabilities, to allow them to stabilize and get their lives together (Burt, Pearson, and Montgomery 2005).

Throughout the country, adult corrections departments are realizing that it is in their interest to partner with homeless assistance networks as well as employment, mental health and substance abuse agencies to ease the transition from incarceration to community. This movement is driven by the bottom line for corrections departments—two-thirds of releasees will be back within three years if they do not receive transitional assistance. The return of such a large proportion of releasees is extremely expensive for corrections departments, and they are finally realizing that it is in their interest to do something about it. The same could be happening with juvenile justice institutions and the young adult facilities run by adult corrections departments.

Conclusions

A surprisingly large proportion of youth age 16 to 24 will experience at least one night of homelessness. A much smaller proportion will spend a lot of time homeless, as youth and later as adults. The factors that propel youth toward homelessness are often the same ones that keep them there or that create the conditions for repeat episodes. We do not have much research evidence capable of guiding us toward the most effective interventions to prevent or end youth homelessness. What we do have suggests that we should pick points of maximum leverage, such as when youth are leaving institutional care, and provide "whatever it takes" to ensure that they can avoid homelessness and ultimately transition to lives of self-sufficiency.

References

Burt, Martha R., Laudan Aron & Edgar Lee. (2001). *Helping America's Homeless: Emergency Shelter or Affordable Housing?* Washington, DC: Urban Institute Press. Burt, Martha R., Carol Pearson, and Ann Elizabeth Montgomery. (2005). *Strategies for Preventing Homelessness.* Washington, DC: Department of Housing and Urban Development.

Hammer, H. David Finkelhor & Andrea Sedlak. (2002). *Runaway/Thrownaway Children: National Estimates and Characteristics.* National Incidence Studies of Missing, Abducted, Runaway, and Thrownaway Children (NISMART), October 2002. Washington, DC: Office of Juvenile Justice and Delinquency Prevention, Department of Justice.

Orlebeke, Britany. (2007). "*Making the Child Welfare System Work for Older Youth.*" Presentation at Thursday's Child, Urban Institute, Washington, DC, June 14, 2007.

Park, Jung M., Stephen Metraux & Dennis P. Culhane. 2005. ''Childhood Out-of-Home Placement and Dynamics of Public Shelter Utilization among Young Homeless Adults.'' *Children and Youth Services Review 17(5):* 533–46.

Park, Jung M., Stephen Metraux, Gabriel Brodbar & Dennis P. Culhane. (2004a). ''Public Shelter Admission among Young Adults with Child Welfare Histories by Type of Service and Type of Exit.'' *Social Services Review 78:* 284–303.

————. 2004b. ''Child Welfare Involvement among Children in Homeless Families.'' *Child Welfare 83(5):* 423–36.

Ringwalt, Chris, James M. Greene, Marjorie Robertson & M. McPheeters. (1998). ''The Prevalence of Homelessness Among Adolescents in the United States.'' *American Journal of Public Health 88(9):* 1325–29.

Toro, Paul, Amy Dworsky & Peter Fowler. (2007). ''*Homeless Youth in the United States: Recent Research Findings and Intervention Approaches.*'' Paper presented at the Second National Homelessness Research Symposium, March 1–2, Washington, D.C.

APPENDIX

Table 1 Basic Demographic Characteristics of Young Homeless Clients (weighted percentages)			
	Clients Under 20 Years Old (UN=125)	Clients Aged 20 to 24 (UN=217)	Clients Age 25 and Older (UN=2,578)
Percent of All Homeless Clients	5	7	88
Gender			
Male	44	42	72
Female	56	58	28
Race/Ethnicity			
White non-Hispanic	42	45	41
Black non-Hispanic	42	36	40
Hispanic	14	19	10
American Indian	1	1	9
Other	1	*	1
High school graduate or more	49	49	64
In homeless family or pregnant			
Not in a homeless family (not living with own child[ren])	86	59	88
Not pregnant	85	57	87
Pregnant	1	2	1
In a homeless family (living with own child[ren])	14	41	12
Not pregnant	14	34	11
Pregnant	*	7	1
Urban-Rural Status			
Central city	88	66	70
Suburban/balance MSA	7	29	21
Rural	5	5	9
Age first homeless			
Under 12	1	*	1
12 to 17 years	65	35	17
18 to 19 years	35	23	5
20 to 24 years	0	42	13
25 or older	N.A.	N.A.	64
Years since first homeless			
1 year or less	42	40	21
2 to 9 years	58	52	37
10 years or more	0	9	42
Spent time with family/friends[a]	52	66	51
Received money from family/friends[b]	49	34	18

Source: Burt, Aron, and Lee, 2001, *Helping America's Homeless*, , Chapter 5, Table 5.4. Urban Institute analysis of weighted 1996 NSHAPC client data; Ns given at top of table are unweighted (designated "UN"). [a] Within the past 30 days.

Table 2 History of Alcohol, Drug, and Mental Health Problems Among Young Homeless Clients (weighted percentages)	Clients Under 20 Years Old (UN=125)	Clients Aged 20 to 24 (UN=217)	Clients Age 25 and Older (UN=2,578)
Adverse Experience Occurred Before Age 18			
First Started Drinking			
Before age 15	32	15	26
Between age 15 and 17	9	17	22
First Started Drinking to Get Drunk			
Before age 15	23	11	13
Between age 15 and 17	12	14	15
First Started Using Drugs			
Before age 15	31	12	19
Between age 15 and 17	17	15	20
First Started Using Drugs Regularly			
Before age 15	20	9	11
Between age 15 and 17	23	13	15
Problems in Past Year			
Alcohol Problems	26	27	49
Drug Problems	43	29	38
Mental Health Problems	46	46	45
Problems in Lifetime			
Alcohol Problems	37	40	66
Drug Problems	48	38	60
Mental Health Problems	50	56	57
Less than High School Degree	51	51	37
Ever Repeated a Grade			
One grade	33	33	24
More than one grade	10	7	6
Ever Dropped Out of School			
Elementary school	1	1	2
Junior high/middle school	8	16	7
Senior high school	46	51	42
Ever Suspended From School	72	41	43
Ever Expelled From School	32	17	18
Juvenile Detention Before Age 18	23	23	15

Source: Burt, Aron, and Lee, 2001, *Helping America's Homeless*, Chapter 5, Table 5.6. Urban Institute analysis of weighted 1996 NSHAPC client data. Ns given at top of table are unweighted (designated "UN").

Table 3
Childhood Neglect, Abuse, and Out-of-Home Experiences of Young Homeless Clients
(weighted percentages)

	Clients Under 20 Years Old (UN=125)	Clients Aged 20 to 24 (UN=217)	Clients Age 25 and Older (UN=2,578)
Before Age 18 Someone You Lived With			
Left you without adequate food or shelter	22	14	12
Physically abused you, to cause physical harm	33	33	21
Forced you or pressured you to do sexual acts that you did not want to do	16	21	12
Abuse/ Neglect Combinations Before Age 18			
Physical and/or sexual abuse but not neglect	42	40	23
One or more abuse/neglect experiences	51	41	27
Before Age 18, Ever Placed In:			
Foster care, Group Home, or Institution	61	34	23
Foster care	40	18	9
Group home	41	21	7
Institution	27	13	15
Before Age 13, Ever Placed In:			
Foster Care, Group Home, or Institution	35	21	13
Foster care	20	18	8
Group home	23	13	5
Institution	16	6	6
Between Ages 13 and 17, Ever Placed In:			
Foster Care, Group Home, or Institution	54	28	18
Foster care	36	10	6
Group home	39	18	5
Institution	24	12	12
Length of Time in Out-of-Home Placement Before Age 18ª			
Less than one week	6	1	2
1 to 4 weeks	3	21	5
1 to 6 months	6	12	16
7 to 12 months	9	6	13
13 to 24 months	19	9	12
More than 2 years	56	51	51
Ever Run Away From Home for More Than 24 Hours Before Age 18	51	38	32
Ever Forced to Leave Home for More Than 24 Hours Before Age 18	60	36	20
First Time Became Homeless Occurred Before Age 18	64	35	18

Source: Burt, Aron, and Lee, 2001, Helping America's Homeless, Chapter 5, Table 5.5. Urban Institute analysis of weighted 1996 NSHAPC client data; Ns given at top of table are unweighted (designated "UN"). Note: Percentages do not sum to 100% due to rounding. ª Among homeless clients who spent time in foster care, a group home, or an institution before they were 18 years old.

Chairman McDermott. Thank you very much for your testimony.

Dan Lips is an educational analyst for the Heritage Institute— the Heritage Foundation, excuse me.

Dan?

STATEMENT OF DANIEL LIPS, EDUCATION ANALYST, THE HERITAGE FOUNDATION

Mr. Lips. Mr. Chairman, Congressman Weller, members of the Subcommittee, thank you for having me here to testify today. My name is Dan Lips and I am an education analyst at The Heritage Foundation. The views that I express today are my own and should not be construed as representing any official position of The Heritage Foundation.

I am here today to testify about the need to improve educational opportunities for children in foster care, and specifically why Federal and State policy-makers should give foster children and their guardians more control over where they go to school. As this Committee knows, the more than 500,000 American children currently in foster care are among the most at-risk in our society. Research shows that adults who were formerly in foster care are more likely than the general population to be homeless, dependent on State services and to be convicted of crimes and incarcerated.

Early warning signs of these problems are evident in the classroom where foster children often struggle. Compared to the general population, foster children have lower scores on standardized tests and higher dropout rates. This is not surprising when one considers the problems that foster children often face in the classroom, such as instability and frequent school transfers, the kinds of things we have heard about today.

Here in Washington, D.C., 40 percent of the children in foster care have experienced four or more placements. Research has shown that across the country home transfers often lead to school transfers since one's school is often determined by one's address. This instability has a damaging effect on a child's academic progress and it also has harmful social effects since a school transfer can mean the end of friendships, social networks and relationships with adults, all of which can be very important for kids in foster care who have unstable family lives.

One way to address this and other problems and to provide better educational opportunities would be to give foster children more control and more options over where they attend school. Offering tuition scholarships, or school vouchers, to children in foster care could yield important benefits. First, a scholarship could provide foster children with stability. A scholarship or choice option could often allow a child to remain in the same school even when he or she changes homes. Second, for other children, a scholarship could provide an option to transfer into a school that offers a better educational experience. Third, a tuition scholarship program could allow students to attend schools that offer specialized services that cater to a foster child's specific needs.

So, what can Congress do to advance this important policy goal? Providing social services and education is primarily the responsibility of State and local governments, not the Federal Government. However, the Congress can take a number of steps to advance this reform initiative and improve educational opportunities for children in foster care. First, Congress should request that GAO compile research on the frequency of foster children's school transfers and the need to improve educational opportunities for children in foster care. Second, Congress should reform the Chafee Foster Care Independence Program to allow states to improve educational opportunities for younger children.

Through the Chafee program, states currently can provide education and job training vouchers to foster children who are sixteen years old or older. For many foster children, this assistance can come too late. Congress should give states the flexibility to use funds allocated through the Chafee program to provide K–12 scholarships if State leaders believe this is the best use of funds.

Finally, since the Federal Government has oversight over the District of Columbia, Congress should provide opportunity scholarships to foster children in Washington, D.C. In 2004, Congress created a school voucher program for low-income students in the District. This program has proven very popular with parents and participating families. Congress should expand this program or create a new program to give scholarships to foster children living in the District.

I have expanded on these ideas in my written testimony, but I will honor my time and close by saying: Giving foster children the ability to attend the school of their choice will not address all the problems they face in life or in the classroom but it can give some of our most at-risk kids a chance for a better life. Since they are charges of the State, foster children are, in a sense, ''all of our children.'' We should not be satisfied until every child in foster care has a stable and high-quality education, the foundation for a successful life. Giving foster children school choice would be a promising step toward accomplishing this important goal.

Thank you again, Mr. Chairman, for the opportunity to be here today, and I look forward to your questions.

[The prepared statement of Mr. Lips follows:]

Prepared Statement of Dan Lips, Education Analyst, The Heritage Foundation

Mr. Chairman and Members of the Committee, thank you for this opportunity totestify today. My name is Dan Lips. I am an Education Analyst at The Heritage Foundation. The views I express in this testimony are my own, and should not be construed as representing any official position of The Heritage Foundation.

I am here today to testify about the need to improve educational opportunities for children in foster care. Specifically, I will discuss why Federal and State policy-makers should reform education policies to provide greater school choice options forfoster children.

Introduction

The more than 500,000 children currently in foster care are among the most at-risk children in American society. Research shows that adults who were formerly in foster care are more likely than the general population to succumb to poor life outcomes.

They are more likely to be homeless, unprepared for employment and limited to low-job skills, and dependent on welfare or Medicaid. They are also more likely than the general population to be convicted of crimes and incarcerated, to abuse drugs and alcohol, or to have poor physical or mental health. Research has shown thatwomen who have been in foster care experience higher rates of early pregnancy and are more likely to see their own children placed in foster care.

Many of these problems are at least in part a product of problems in the classroom where foster children tend to have lower educational attainment than their peers. Foster children on average have lower scores on standardized tests and higher absenteeism, tardiness, truancy and dropout rates. Overall, a synthesis of available research evidence published by the Child

Welfare League of America found that, ''Almost all of the reviewed studies of those who were in out-of-home care revealed that the subject's level of educational attainment is below that of other citizens of comparable age.''

This is not surprising when one considers the many problems and challenges that foster children commonly experience at school. These common problems include instability, persistent low-expectations, poor adult advocacy on their behalf, inadequate life-skills training, and a failure to receive needed special education services.

Instability and Low Expectations: Root Causes of Poor Educational Outcomes

One of the biggest problems foster children face is instability. Children in long-term foster care often experience multiple out-of-home placements. For example, here in Washington, D.C., 40 percent of the children in the District's foster care system have experienced four or more placements.

Out-of-home placements often lead to school transfers since where one attends school is often tied to where one lives. For example, the Vera Institute of Justicereports that in New York City between 1995 and 1999, 42 percent of children changed schools within 30 days of entering foster care.

Research evidence suggests that frequent school transfers and disruptions in the learning process can take a toll on a student's development. For example, a study by the General Accounting Office reported that third-grade students who had experienced frequent school changes were more likely to perform below grade level inreading and math or to repeat a grade than were students who had never changed schools.

It is not surprising, therefore, that frequent school transfers would negatively affect foster children. A research synthesis reported that former foster children who experienced fewer out-of-home placements performed better in school and completed more years of education than did others in foster care. A survey of former fosterchildren found that they ''strongly believed that they had been shifted around too much while in foster care, and as a result, they suffered, especially in terms of education.''

It is clear how instability causes problems. School transfers create gaps in the learning cycle. They force children to adjust to new classroom settings, teachers, and classmates and cause children to lose social networks, peer groups, and relationships with adults—relationships that can be particularly important to foster care children with tumultuous family lives. These changes can exacerbate the emotional instability and unrest caused by the home transfers themselves. Reducing instability for foster children is identified by researchers and advocates as a way to improve the foster care system.

In addition to disruptions in their educational environment, adults formerly in foster care report that the foster system did not encourage high aspirations for their education. One survey found that older youth in foster care have high aspirations and resent others' low expectations. They also reported that they would have benefited from stronger adult encouragement.

Addressing the Need for Greater Stability, High Expectations and Better Educational Opportunities

There is no single solution to all of the challenges and problems that foster children face in school and at home. Ideally, every child in the foster care system would become a part of a stable, loving, permanent home with adults committed to nurturing their talents and skills. However, policymakers can embrace measures to alleviate some of the stresses associated with foster care that contribute to lower educational attainment and poor life outcomes.

One promising reform solution would be to provide foster children with more control and more options for where they attend school. For example, offering tuition scholarships—or school vouchers—to children in foster care would be an important step in encouraging greater stability in their education—indeed in their lives—and open the door to better educational opportunities for many students.

In 2006, Arizona Governor Janet Napolitano, a Democrat, signed legislation to create the nation's first K–12 tuition scholarship program for foster children. Under this program, approximately 500 foster children will be awarded $5,000 tuition scholarships to attend private school starting in the fall of 2007.

The Benefits of Providing Scholarships to Foster Children

A scholarship program for children in foster care, like the new program created in Arizona, could provide a number of important benefits:

- **First, a tuition scholarship could provide foster children with stability**. A scholarship or choice option could allow a child to remain in the same school (whenever geographically possible) even when placed in a new home setting. This could have educational and social benefits. Allowing a child to remain in the same school could prevent disruptions in the learning process. Importantly, it would also allow a child to maintain peer groups, friendships, and important relationships with adults.

- **Second, for other children, a tuition scholarship could allow some children to transfer into schools that offer a better educational experience.** Academic studies have reported that students participating in school voucher programs have improved academically compared to their peers who remain in public school. For example, the school voucher program in Milwaukee has been subject to two randomized-experiment studies that found that students who received vouchers through a lottery made academic gains when compared to their peers who remained in public school. Similar studies of private school choice programs in Charlotte, North Carolina, New York City, and Washington, D.C. reached similar conclusions.

- **Third, a tuition scholarship program could allow students to attend schools that offer specialized services that cater to a foster child's unique needs.** Many schools are unequipped to offer the specialized services that foster children may need. Allowing for greater choice could give families the opportunity to select the most appropriate school for their child. It could also give schools an incentive to specialize, innovate, and deliver the specialized education services that foster children may need, such as counseling, tutoring, remedial instruction, and life skills training.

- **Fourth, a tuition scholarship program could improve family satisfaction and involvement in children's education**. Most foster parents are dedicated individuals who want the best for the children in their care. However, many lack the resources needed to give that child the education that he or she deserves. They need and deserve assistance in creating an environment that will help their child thrive. A school choice program would give foster parents the ability to provide their children a quality education, which would likely improve the foster care experience for both children and parents.

How Congress Can Help Encourage School Choice for Foster Children

Providing social services and education, of course, is primarily the responsibility of state and local governments, not the federal government. Indeed states and localities are beginning to embrace the idea of school choice for children in foster care. This idea of providing tuition scholarships is gaining momentum across the country. In addition to the new program that was created in Arizona in 2006, other states are considering legislation to provide school choice scholarships to children in foster care. In 2007, state legislators in at least four states—Florida, Maryland, Tennessee, and Texas—have considered similar initiatives. The American Legislative Exchange Council has created model legislation to provide opportunity scholarships to children in foster care.

However, Congress can take a number of steps to advance this reform initiative and improve educational opportunities for children in foster care:

First, Congress should request that the GAO compile research on the frequency of foster children's school transfers and the need to improve educational opportunities for children in foster care. The federal government has the opportunity to work through the Administration for Children and Families in the Department of Health and Human Services to study this problem and highlight the need for reform.

Second, Congress should reform the Chafee Foster Care Independence Act to allow states to implement programs to improve educational opportunities for younger children. The Chafee program provides funding grants to states to assist older foster youth and former foster children in the process of attaining independence in adulthood. For example, through the program, states can award "education and training vouchers" to older youths (age 16 and older) who are aging out of the foster care system.

However, the education aid offered by the Chafee Foster Care Independence Act may come too late in many cases because it targets foster children 16 years old and older. Foster children throughout the K–12 education system have a number of unique needs. Providing education choice and flexibility to younger students could provide them with a more solid educational foundation, helping them to achieve academic success, social stability, and adult self-sufficiency. Congress should give states the flexibility to use funds allocated through the Chafee Foster Care Independence Program to promote K–12 education options for younger children in foster care if state policymakers believe that this would be the best use of funds to prepare foster children for independence in adulthood.

Third, since the federal government has oversight over the District of Columbia, Congress should provide opportunity scholarships to foster children in Washington, D.C. In 2004, Congress created a school voucher program for low-income students in Washington, D.C. This program has proven very popular with parents. All of the program's 1,800 scholarships are currently subscribed. And, in all, 6,500 children have applied for scholarships. A recent evaluation of the program conducted by Georgetown University researchers found that the parents of participating students were very satisfied with their children's experience in the program and have become more involved in their education.

There is good reason to believe that many more children would benefit from opportunity scholarships, including the approximately 1,800 school-aged children in foster care living in Washington, D.C. Congress should expand the existing Opportunity Scholarship program to allow more children to participate, and it should expand the eligibility requirements to ensure that all foster children can participate. As an alternative, Congress could create a new program that specifically focuses on providing opportunity scholarships for children in foster care in Washington, D.C.

Conclusion

It is clear that giving foster children the ability to attend a safe and high quality school of choice will not address all of the problems they face, but it can give some of our most at-risk children in our society a chance for a better life.

Consider the words of Lisa Dickson, a former foster child, who graduated from high school and went on to succeed in college and graduate school. Ms. Dickson, now an advocate for foster children, wrote an essay "What the Arizona Foster Voucher Program Would Have Meant to Me":

"As I look back on my experience in foster care, educational vouchers would have benefited me if they had made it possible for me to attend one high school, rather than five. I don't know that I would have chosen a private school, rather than a public one. I do know that I never received college preparatory counseling at any of the high schools I attended. I also know that having one teacher and one textbook, and perhaps also some individualized tutoring, would have helped me to master algebra. There was no individualized educational attention given, at home or at school, to any of the teenagers from the group homes where I resided. No special tutoring was made available to foster youth who were failing their classes."

Since foster children are charges of the state, they are, in a sense, all of our children. We should not be satisfied until every child in foster care has the opportunity to have a stable and high quality education that prepares him or her to succeed in life. I believe creating a voluntary, school choice scholarship program for children in foster care is a promising step toward accomplishing this important goal.

Mr. Chairman, I'd again like to thank you for the opportunity to testify about this important issue today. I look forward to your questions.

The Heritage Foundation is a public policy, research, and educational organization operating under Section 501(C)(3). It is privately supported, and receives no funds from any government at any level, nor does it perform any government or other contract work.

The Heritage Foundation is the most broadly supported think tank in the United States. During 2006, it had more than 283,000 individual, foundation, and corporate supporters representing every state in the U.S. Its 2006 income came from the following sources:

Individuals	64%
Foundations	19%
Corporations	3%
Investment Income	14%
Publication Sales and Other	0%

The top five corporate givers provided The Heritage Foundation with 1.3% of its 2006 income. The Heritage Foundation's books are audited annually by the national accounting firm of Deloitte & Touche. A list of major donors is available from The Heritage Foundation upon request.

Members of The Heritage Foundation staff testify as individuals discussing their own independent research. The views expressed are their own, and do not reflect an institutional position for The Heritage Foundation or its board of trustees.

Chairman McDermott. Thank you very much. I'd like to thank all the witnesses for your testimonies and they will be entered into the record. I would like to ask a couple of questions beginning with Jewel and Mr. Whitfield. You talked about living in your home, we are talking about disconnectedness, and if you are living in your car over several different periods, and you are living in a house where you did not have anybody who seemed to be running your life or trying to organize your life, who reached out to you? Or, did you reach out and were rejected by the system? Did you try to leave and go to a more stable situation? You said you were sick, how did you deal with the system out there? I would like to hear what goes through a kid's head when they are out there and looking at the system and knowing they need something, but what happened to you?

Ms. Kilcher. Go ahead.

Mr. Whitfield. Actually, I used to be a foster kid when I was younger, and I was in the system for about two years. I came home with my family because they had rehabilitated over the course of the time, the environment that I was in, like the neighborhood, so I began to hang outside with the neighborhood crew so at that particular time my family, they just started like pushing away or whatever. I went to jail for a juvenile case. When I was released, the foster care people dropped the case that they had or whatever with me, so I just felt like my friends are all I have, which makes you feel bad.

Chairman McDermott. Okay.

Jewel?

Ms. Kilcher. I was never in foster care. I did not like adults, I did not really trust adults and had never seen an adult give you something without wanting something. So, I stayed away from any institution possible. I just tried to not make friends, but just really keep to myself. I was not aware that there were programs. Hearing the congresswoman speak earlier, I wanted to camp out on her lawn, I liked her so much. I did not know people like that existed. There was a doctor when I was sick, I was turned away from all the emergency rooms, but one doctor would not see me but he gave me the card of a doctor. That doctor ended up just being a very nice man who actually did not try to have sex with me and treated me. He ended up being the one that helped to get medicine that I could not afford.

I think had I known about programs, there is sort of this stigma that there are kids out there and they are just tough. Well, kids do not want to be tough, kids want to be loved. If you give any of us a shot, we will respond. Looking back and being able to come through what I have come through, I think I am a much stronger and more dependable, more loyal person than most people who I know who have been through less, but it was because I was sort of given a shot by one or two people that actually had kindness. I had a song called "Hands," and the line in it is, "In the end, only kindness matters" because institutions did not change my life, but kindness did.

Chairman McDermott. How do we set up the situation for adults to go out looking for youngsters in a way that they can get them in?

Dr. Mincy. Thank you for the question. I think the big picture is that I deal with college students all the time. They are protected in a way, they are there for an academic purpose, but they have personal glitches and when they do, there are counselors, there are health care providers, there is a system to care for them, to keep them not only on their academic track but also to help them when they get off track.

I think the big thing we need to hear about disconnected youth is that there is no system because they are out of school and out of the workplace, they are not on any basic track but when they encounter problems, there is no track for them. The whole field of youth development, the field that is working to reconnect them, has to rely upon funding streams that come from very different agencies with very different rules. It also has to rely upon funding from sometimes public donors, sometimes private donors and all of that funding is fickle. So, what you are hearing is a non-system. Whether we happen to encounter disconnected youth in homelessness or incarceration, that is not the real answer.

The point is that when young people are out of school and out of work, there is a non-system for them, and we need to figure out how to reconnect and how to create something that feels comprehensive and seamless when young people are off track, and there are a lot of them. It is not only a social justice, antipoverty purpose, it is that we need these young people as workers and how can we work together to make sure that there is a more coherent system for them?

Chairman McDermott. With the goal to return them to their families?

Dr. Mincy. Not necessarily. We are talking about young people who are between 18 and 24 years old with a goal to help them transition to adulthood like your children and mine.

Chairman McDermott. When do you stop trying to send them home, how old?

Ms. Kilcher. I did not want to be sent home, I think most children, would be home otherwise. If their homes were great, they would be there. I would not suggest sending them home in general but that is just me.

Ms. Shore. I would like to say though that the programs that do exist are very effective, although small. We see 1,500 young people a year and when you say, "How do we make that connection," we do it in all kinds of ways. There is an outreach van, there is the Safe Place Program that we participate in also, so that every single firehouse in the city has a sign and urges young people to go in. We go to high schools, but this is a constant process because you are talking about every year there are 10 and 11 year olds that have not heard about the programs. So, you continually need to be reaching out and making those connections.

There certainly are not enough services and there certainly is a lot of disconnection. I do want to say that I think that the nascent services that exist in the Runaway and Homeless Youth Act programs are very good, they are solid. There is a lot of effort, at least I know in our program, to identify the kids that can go home and do the necessary work with the families so that they can in fact return or to identify when that really is not a likely possibility because families have come apart in many cases. We have to recognize that there is another whole set of young people here that are older, that the foster care system is not interested in taking in and whose families are dying or so sick that they really cannot take care of them or in jail. There is a whole group of young people that I think have not really been touched on yet but need to get added as well.

Chairman McDermott. We may not get it all done today. That is what you are telling me, right?

Ms. Shore. No, but I think that we should recognize that there is some hope in that there are things that are working, that we already know about, we have the technology for, we just need to really have the will to expand them, to say this is essential.

Chairman McDermott. I move to Mr. Weller. Mr. Weller?

Mr. Weller. Thank you, Mr. Chairman. This is an important hearing, and I appreciate your organizing this. I think we have heard some very helpful testimony from a variety of people before the Subcommittee this morning. I have a number of questions. To begin, I am very uncomfortable calling someone by their first name.

Ms. Kilcher. Kilcher is my last name.

Mr. Weller. Ms. Kilcher, just to be polite, one of our witnesses in a previous hearing when we were looking at child poverty, Isabelle Sawhill with the Brookings Institution, which is a research institution here—a respected one here in Washington, testified that those who finish high school, work full time, and only have children after getting married are more likely to live out of poverty and in the middle class. That is a common message we see as we study lifting families, and particularly kids, out of poverty. You have achieved success, clearly in listening to your story, the hard way. I admire you and your ability and the challenges you have had to achieve the success that you have had.

Mr. Weller. Do you have a high school diploma?

Ms. Kilcher. Yes, sir.

Mr. Weller. After you moved out of your family household, did you continue your education even though you were living outside of the house?

Ms. Kilcher. I did not continue my education. It was really difficult going to high school. I was still paying for tuition to go to the school I was going to.

Mr. Weller. You were going to a special academy?

Ms. Kilcher. Yes, I had a partial scholarship.

Mr. Weller. Okay, so while you were living out?

Ms. Kilcher. While I was homeless, yes, I went to a private art school.

Mr. Weller. While you were homeless, you went to a private school. Your peers, your friends, you talked about some of the other girls, were they still in school?

Ms. Kilcher. As I mentioned, I probably went to nine or 10 different schools in my life so I did not really have normal friends. I moved on every three to six months. While I was homeless and working, I did not really make friendships but I tried to stick up for people if I could. I remember getting fired from one job, my boss asked me to pose for a nude calendar, and he did not mind that I would not, but then he tried to get a girlfriend of mine to pose for it and she was just scared. He could see that weakness in her eyes, and he kept pushing her, and I just stuck up for her and he ended up firing both of us.

Mr. Weller. Were they still in high school?

Ms. Kilcher. She was trying to go to school. Yes, most kids I have seen really are trying. They really want to. They are trying to hold jobs or trying to——

Mr. Weller. Who influences, obviously there is a culture at this age, the values?

Ms. Kilcher. It is random.

Mr. Weller. Do they receive them from entertainment, do they receive them from reading the paper or where do they receive their general values, whether it is pro-education or attending school or working or trying to better themselves?

Ms. Kilcher. It is a really random thing to see whatever is able to come into your life that gives you hope. Some days it would just be something like the kindness of a stranger giving me $5. I did not know anybody that was telling me about these programs. If I had, I would have been very interested but I just did not happen to come across any kind of grassroots, word of mouth thing that spread the worth.

Mr. Weller. Now, you are an entertainer, right?

Ms. Kilcher. Of the singing variety.

Mr. Weller. You are a songwriter, you sing, and you do a lot of things but do you feel that for young people that the message that is coming from entertainment, whether it is music or going to the movies or watching movies or video, is pro-education, is encouraging them to further their education?

Ms. Kilcher. Oh, there are all kinds. The reason I think I was able to be successful was people identified with certain kind of longing I had and a certain kind of passion and it helped other people feel better, but that was just my music.

Mr. Weller. Are they listening—when they are listening to music, are they receiving a message that is pro-education and encourage them to go back to school?

Ms. Kilcher. It depends on the artist. For some it is an aphrodisiac, some it is an escape. There are different purposes for different styles of music.

Mr. Weller. For young people, entertainers do have a significant influence. We can all admit to that.

Ms. Kilcher. Yes, I would say——

Mr. Weller. Do you think they have a responsibility to encourage education?

Ms. Kilcher. Every person has the responsibility to try and be the best person they can be. You cannot put that to bear on any one person better than they can bear it.

Mr. Weller. Thank you. Mr. Lips, you were here for Congresswoman Bachmann's testimony and she was talking about the challenge with the 23 foster children that she had and the experiences of trying to ensure they had a good education and the experience of children changing schools and the rules of existing programs. Even though her children were attending, I believe, a parochial school or a private school, the rules prohibited them, if they could afford it, from enrolling the foster kids in the same school as their biological kids. Can you outline some of your thoughts about what some solutions are to maybe help give those young people more of an opportunity?

Mr. Lips. Thank you, Congressman Weller. I was really impressed by Congresswoman Bachmann's remarks. The idea of providing every child with the opportunity to attend a school of choice is a really simple way I think to improve their lives. Last year, Arizona created a program to offer school vouchers to children who have been placed in foster care. It was signed into law by Governor Janet Napolitano, a Democrat, and it is going to begin serving children this fall, about 500 kids will receive scholarships. If Ms. Bachmann had lived in Arizona, she would have been able to apply this program and choose the right school for her child. It could be a public school, it could be a charter school or it could be a private school. I think that this is a very simple and small way to make a difference in these children's lives, either by keeping them in the same school, a focus of stability, or by offering a new opportunity that would improve their lives.

Mr. Weller. I have read where it takes children months to readjust if they go from one school to another, to make new friends, develop peers, and hopefully end up in the right crowd. Would this type of program, say if someone is in a foster program in the same city and there is a family providing them a home but they are on the other side of town, would this type of program allow them to continue to go to the school elsewhere in the city they were previously attending so they could continue to be around their friends and the relationships they currently have?

Mr. Lips. Absolutely, that is the purpose. We see that school transfers can lead to learning setbacks and emotional setbacks. A scholarship program like this would allow a child to remain in the same school, whether it is a public or charter or private school as one focus of stability in an otherwise often unstable life.

Mr. Weller. Last, Congresswoman Bachmann referred to the situation when she and her husband were interested in enrolling their foster children in the same private school where their children attend and their foster kids were asking for that opportunity but the rules of their program prohibited them. Can you explain what those rules are, are you familiar with those?

Mr. Lips. I am not familiar with the exact laws in Minnesota. I would suspect, I believe that that State had an open enrollment law, which would require the child to attend any public school in the area but it would certainly limit the option of choosing between a public and private school, which it sounds like Congresswoman Bachmann was looking to do. I think that this is why we should offer a full range of choices. These kids are so at risk. Anything we can do to give them a leg up would be really important and beneficial, I believe.

Mr. Weller. Thank you. You have been generous with time, Mr. Chairman, thank you.

Chairman McDermott. Thank you. Mr. Meek?

Mr. Meek. Thank you, Mr. Chairman. I had to step out for a moment, but I did get an opportunity to hear from most of our witnesses that are here. It is interesting because in my district back in Miami, I represent Miami and South Broward County and South Beach on the weekends, I would admit to that.

[Laughter.]

Mr. Meek. Anything to help the economy, but, in all seriousness, I had an opportunity to hear from all of you. I am glad that you recognized the increase in funding, that we are trying to move in that direction here in this new Congress.

I wanted to ask, and this is a general question for the panel, as it relates to at-risk youth and the funding that we are talking about and the programs that are on shoe-string budgets, working with what they have, in this time of pay-as-you-go, as we are looking to bring the budget into balance, what are some of the arguments we can use as Members of Congress? We do not have a day like this everyday in Congress where we have real people that come and share real experience with us and for us to make real decisions and follow through on it several months down the road.

What are some of the reasons why Congress should invest even further in making sure that not only young people have options where their lives have not been what you may read in a storybook or you may see a usual kind of situation, you go through a K through 12 experience and then you move on to higher education and then you get a post-graduate degree and then you move on to this great, wonderful job, it is not like that for everyone, and we do understand that. How do we tell that story beyond this Subcommittee on the reason we should not only increase funding but also target the very young adults, when we talk about young adults, those that are over 18, how do we target them, how do we carry this story forward?

Ms. Kilcher. I would say three things spring to my mind, if I may. One is it saves money in the long run. There have been a lot of studies done on if you can help kids get an education now, that they are going to stay out of the system later. If you can give them help now, we would like to stay out of being arrested and those things if you can give us a legitimate way to make money and many of us were willing. I forget what the numbers are, but I do know it saves money in the long run to try and help kids at a younger age stay out of the system.

Also, throughout history, some of the greatest achievers of any society have come from unlikely places. I think that homeless kids have a lot to give if you can see what treasures their minds are. They are not disposable and often can contribute more than a lot of what I would call somewhat—kids that were well off that sometimes became lazy in the system because of the luxury of being lazy. Then, thirdly, I would say that it is—I forgot my third point, I am sure someone else will have a good one.

[Laughter.]

Mr. Meek. As we start to go down answering my question, Mr. Whitfield, I know that you were sharing with us, and, Dr. Burt, I want to make sure that we get to you next, but, Mr. Whitfield, I want you thinking about some of your experiences and how you deal with these issues because I will tell you that I have family members that have had similar events in their lives, maybe not just the same, but similar events where they were challenged and fell into this whole unemployable, folks do not want to take the risk or take the chance and giving someone an opportunity, what are some things that we need to what we call in Washington "stay the course" on these issues? All of you on the panel and, Mr. Chairman, "you had me at 'hello'" on this issue, but I think it is important that we are able to give life to it beyond this Committee. Obviously, we sit on this Subcommittee, we have some interest in this subject area. So, I am going to get to you, Mr. Whitfield, because I thought you had a very revealing testimony, and I am glad that you are here today.

Dr. Burt?

Dr. Burt. Oh, thank you. Well, I just wanted to say that the basic argument is that you cannot afford not to in two senses, one is that, as Dr. Mincy had said, and I am sure he has a lot more statistics on it than I do, basically right now we are throwing away about a quarter of every youth cohort that comes along. Twenty-five percent at least do not graduate from high school and many of those that do, do not have any real functional capacity to be operating at the level of jobs that will allow them to actually be self-sufficient. A little bit fewer than those but still a very significant number who drop out and so on, we cannot afford to throw those people away as workers. Number two, we cannot afford what happens to them and what we need to pay for when they end up in the criminal justice system, when they end up in the mental health system, when they end up in such so-called substance abuse systems. We just cannot afford it. We are paying one way or we are paying the other, and it makes much more sense to be investing in them to be productive citizens than not.

That gets me back to a point that I wanted to make an earlier question, which is really in addition to investing in those who we have already failed in a lot of ways, it is really, really important to recognize that you can often tell who is going to be in trouble when you look at first graders and you realize that they are not being taught to read.

So, we just had a story in The Washington Post a couple of days ago about Philadelphia turning its schools around and really focusing on making sure that nobody gets out of first grade without knowing how to read. We have evaluation reports on very, very large mechanisms, such as Success for All, Comer Schools. We know how to make sure that kids get off on the right track when they are in school, and especially focusing on the ones who are least likely to succeed because of their home environments. So, both that very early investment is really important as well as the argument that you cannot afford not to.

Mr. Meek. Mr. Whitfield?

Chairman McDermott. Mr. Whitfield, do you have anything to add to this?

Mr. Whitfield. I think that there should be more summer jobs out there like something to keep the youth occupied and things to do during the school year too, after school or whatever, so it would give people less time to just loiter around, to keep them occupied 24/7.

My second one is the youth out there with a lack of education, I think that it should be GED programs, more ways for them to get some type of education, and for them to be able to have some type of financing for themselves or whatever so they can really support themselves and do not have to look toward the street corner to make money. I think that stops a lot of people from going to school right there because when you are in high school, you want to dress properly. If you do not have the type of money to dress properly, people ''clown'' you or whatever, do things like that, so I think there should be more ways for them to be able to finance themselves, have financing.

Chairman Mcdermott. Thank you. Mr. Lewis?

Mr. Lewis. Thank you very much, Mr. Chairman. Mr. Chairman, let me thank you so much for holding this hearing. I think a hearing of this nature is needed now more than ever before. I want to thank all of the witnesses for being here. Jewel, as someone who knows what it is to be young, homeless, you never gave up, you never gave in, what pushed you? I missed the earlier part of your testimony, but I read it and do you have a message that you can send to other young people through your music or through your words?

Ms. Kilcher. Yes, I have tried to always let my lyrics represent what I have tried to struggle for in my own life in hopes that it helps people. I think that every child feels innately that there is a special spark in them, and you should not be thinking about that, you should just be thinking about having fun.

At the most fundamental levels, when you are so concerned with surviving to the point where you are trying to figure out where your food and where your sleep and your shelter is going to come from, the thing I tried to foster most was just to try not to let that little spark die, whatever that is in every child. Every child really feels they have. The only time I saw kids lose the battle on the streets is when they stopped feeling that spark. Sometimes the smallest act would help me feel good about humanity and other times it was genuine large acts of kindness, like a doctor helping you for no reason when you have no money.

I cannot say what inspires some kids to find help and others not. I cannot tell you the difference in what that is, I just know that I met more kids that were willing to do anything for the words ''I love you'' than not. I have never really honestly met a ''bad seed,'' maybe one, that you would genuinely call somebody that was genuinely hard to even get through to. So, it is hard for me to answer your question, I am not sure why I continued, but I know that the resilience of youth has shocked me perpetually.

Mr. Lewis. So, you are suggesting to the Committee and to all of us that there is something within all human beings, young, whatever, that ''spark'' you call it, the ''spirit'' or whatever that is there, I am not going to let it fade away or go away and will continue to push?

Ms. Kilcher. I think ultimately that is what we are all trying to nurture through education, through trying to give you a support system for money, all of that, you are trying to—that is why we are all here, it is humanity.

Mr. Lewis. So, since we have you here, there is a little gospel song that says something like, "We fall down but we get up," but we do not get up alone, we need help. We need Youth Build, we need Job Corps, we need the intervention of the Federal Government.

Mr. Whitfield, coming in contact with jail, jail is not a pleasant place to go. Some of my colleagues know that when I was much younger, I went to jail a few times but it was fighting for civil rights. I got arrested and went to jail 40 times. This weekend, I went to visit a young man that was in jail in Georgia, 21 years old, probably one of the smartest human beings I ever met.

Did you learn something, do you have a message for your peers and for others that you can say jail is not a good place, prison is not a good place and that you can do better, you can come out whole?

Mr. Whitfield. My personal experience with jail, it kind of like—I do not prefer, I do not suggest no one to go to jail.

Mr. Lewis. I would not, either, it is not a pleasant place, it is not a good place.

[Laughter.]

Mr. Whitfield. I prefer telling them, "Stay away from it" because it just builds up inside of you like you are not able to do your everyday routine. It is like you are under a time schedule. A lot of stuff going in between the time schedule, your peers, the staff that run the facility, it just builds up in the inside of you and just makes you mad. So, I do not know how to break it down to the smallest terms.

Mr. Lewis. I think you are breaking it down just fine. Do you have a relationship with your grandmother today, do you talk with her?

Mr. Whitfield. Oh, most definitely.

Mr. Lewis. She is encouraging and telling you to go——

Mr. Whitfield. Most definitely. Now that my family pretty much sees me in this path of straight success, they are pulling into me, they are coming into me. First, I think they did not have too much faith in me when I was coming up because of the places that I chose to go and people I chose to hang around, so they kind of like pushed me away. So, now that they see I am doing something positive with myself, it is like they are coming into me now. The family stopped using drugs, things are pretty much getting better now that they see me doing something positive on myself.

Mr. Lewis. Thank you very much. Thank you, Mr. Chairman.

Chairman McDermott. Thank you. Mr. Herger will inquire?

Mr. Herger. Thank you. Mr. Whitfield, we are proud of you.

Mr. Whitfield. Thank you.

Mr. Herger. Needless to say, you can see how proud we are of you, Jewel. You are really in a position, really both of you are in positions to be role models for others. It is great to see what you have done, the fact that you have rolled up your sleeves and gone after it and made good decisions. We all make some not-so-good decisions periodically during our lives, what is important is that we can correct them.

Mr. Lips, I am interested particularly in some of what we heard. We also heard from Congresswoman Bachmann on the importance of education and how people get stereotyped in these classes where they go. I forget the term she used, the "dumb math class," for the "dumb kids" or whatever, how easy that is to have that happen. Could you tell me how foster children are impacted—a little bit different, but I would like to get around to that also—by the special education system and are students receiving the services they deserve or are they being under-served?

Mr. Lips. Thank you, Congressman Herger. On that first issue, this is a problem, low expectations is a problem that we hear a lot about. There have been many focus groups of youth—of adults who were formerly in foster care, and that is one of the problems that they commonly identify, that people did not expect much of them, and they were shuffled into the back of the class and were not given the right opportunities. This is a really important question— important problem that we should consider as we are designing policies and try to address.

On that second issue that you mentioned of special education, this is really important for foster children. Research shows that between 30 to 40 percent of the children in foster care also are eligible for special education services. I believe Congresswoman Bachmann mentioned that all of the kids that she took in had IEPs. If you are being shuffled around from school to school, transferred, your paperwork gets lost, you get shuffled through the system, and there are many stories of kids either being under-served, not receiving the special education services that they deserve or being over-served, kids who could otherwise be benefited by being in the mainstream, being shuffled into special education classes.

This is a reason, again, why we could benefit by providing foster children with school choice options. There is a great program in Florida called the McKay Scholarship Program that is specifically tailored for special needs students. It is helping 16,000 kids, the approval rating or I should say satisfaction rates among parents is above 90 percent. It is a great thing and it is getting these kids the services that they need. It is a model that we should look to, and thank you.

Mr. Herger. Thank you, Mr. Lips. Mr. Whitfield, I am sorry I had to step out for a while, but I did hear your testimony and I am sure it is so very characteristic of so many. I believe you mentioned how you were in school, you had fallen behind, you were going to classes, you really did not feel good at classes because you did not know how to answer the questions.

I remember an experience I had myself when I was a junior in high school. I was in a math class, a higher math class, and I had the flu for a couple of weeks, and I was out and I was never able to catch up again. I had a very bright teacher who probably should have been teaching at Berkeley rather than at our high school, but I was not able to catch up and, boy, that feeling of being lost and hating to come to class when you just do not seem to be able to get it.

Yet, it is amazing with assistance, with help, somebody working with you, that you can catch up, you can do what you need to do and you can do well. So, again, I want to commend you.

Mr. Chairman, I want to thank you and the ranking member for putting this hearing together. This is so incredibly important. We have so many young people that are being lost between the cracks, great lives that are just so lost out there and if there is anything we can do, we should be doing. There are many role models, we are seeing here today, with the two of you who have been involved, and also, again, I am so touched with our new Member of Congress, Michele Bachmann, on the story with 28 or 29 that she has raised. We raised nine that were ours, and we thought that was a lot, I cannot even imagine 28 or 29, but yet there are people who are doing that. I know another family out where I live in Chico, California that has done the same type of thing. These are very gifted people to be able to do that, but yet we need to do it in every way we can. So, again, I thank you very much.

Chairman McDermott. I cut Mr. Meek off from his time, I give you one minute.

Mr. Meek. Mr. Chairman, I just wanted to make a last closing comment, and I want to thank not only you, Mr. Chairman, but also the full Committee Chairman, Mr. Rangel, because I know this is something that we have talked about in closed quarters, about what we should do now that we have the opportunity to do it. I just want to give words of encouragement to not only Jewel but Mr. Whitfield, who came and opened their lives up in a way that I know they have done before but probably never before Congress. Being one, I have dyslexia, and being able to talk with people, Charles Schwab and Danny Glover and I did some of the similar things that you are doing now, talking about our learning disability and how it affected us as we grew up and how we deal with it as professionals.

I want to let you know that your purpose here today, both of your purposes, your story of talking about your indiscretions, what you have done, your story of being homeless and washing your hair and how people judge you, but I say to both of you how do they like you now that you're here, that you are sharing not only before the greatest democracy on the face of the earth, your personal story to help others. So, I want to commend both of you for holding the ladder in place to allow others to climb up.

Mr. Chairman, I think this is a good day to be in Congress and to be in this room to see these two very great Americans share their stories and open their lives and to the professionals that are working in the field helping people, I want to let you know if it was not for you, there would be no us, those of us who need the assistance, and we appreciate you for being in the field. That is all I wanted to stay, Mr. Chairman. I look forward to working and for progress on this issue as we continue to tackle issues that come before this Committee.

Thank you.

Chairman McDermott. Mr. Weller has a unanimous consent.

Mr. Weller. Thank you, Mr. Chairman. This has been an interesting hearing, and I just want to ask unanimous consent to include in the record some additional information from several respected groups. The first is a summary of how many youth drop out of high school titled, ''Every Nine Seconds in America a Student Becomes a Dropout.'' This was prepared by the non-partisan American Youth Policy Forum based on a number of studies. The second is a fact sheet put together by the Casey Family Programs based in Seattle, Washington about educational outcomes specifically for children in foster care. Third and last is a statement about the need to promote educational success for young people in foster care, which was put together by the National Foster Youth Advisory Council. I ask unanimous consent to include these as part of the record.

Chairman McDermott. Without objection, so ordered.

[The provided material follows:]

Every Nine Seconds in America a Student Becomes a Dropout

The Dropout Problem in Numbers*

Millions of students leave school before high school graduation.

■ In School Year 2002-2003, US public schools awarded 2.7 million diplomas and the National Center for Education Statistics calculated the graduation rate to be 73.9%. Graduation rates varied greatly by state, from 87% in New Jersey to under 60% in the District of Columbia and South Carolina. Thirty-nine states increased their graduation rates from 2001 to 2003 while most southern states, plus Alaska, the District of Columbia, and New York, experienced declines.[1] Other authoritative research found the 2002 graduation rate to be 71%, little changed from 1991's 72%.[2]

■ In 2004, there were 27,819,000 18-24-year-olds in the United States. Of these, 21,542,000 (78%) had either graduated from high school, earned a GED, completed some college, or earned an associate's or bachelor's degree. The balance, 6,277,000 (22%), had not yet completed high school.[3] Some scholars exclude GED holders, resulting in a much higher noncompletion figure. Similarly, if researchers count the adult population over age 24, the high school noncompletion rate would be higher still.[4]

■ An estimated 3.8 million youth ages 18-24 are neither employed nor in school—15% of all young adults. From 2000 to 2004, the ranks of these disconnected young adults grew by 700,000.[5]

■ From 1990 to 2000, high school completion rates declined in all but seven states and the rate of students dropping out between 9th and 10th grades increased.[6]

Members of some demographic groups are at much greater risk of dropping out of school.

■ Nationally, only about two-thirds of all students who enter 9th grade graduate with regular high school diplomas four years later. For minority males, these figures are far lower.[7] In 2001, on average, 72% of female students, but only 64% of male students graduated. African American students had a graduation rate of 50%, the lowest of racial and ethnic groups identified; the other student groups graduated at the following rates: American Indian, 51%; Latino, 53%; White, 75%; and Asian and Pacific Islander, 77%. But there were enormous disparities among state graduation levels, and even larger disparities by ethnicity and gender within the same states.[8]

■ In SY 2000-2001, high school students from low-income families (the lowest 20%) dropped out of school at six times the rate of their peers from higher-income families.[9]

■ In SY 2000-2001, only 47.6% of persons with disabilities ages 14 and older graduated with standard diplomas while 41.1% dropped out.[10]

When young people drop out of school, they—and American society at large—face multiple negative consequences.

■ Of those who fail to graduate with their peers, one-quarter eventually earn a diploma, one-quarter earn the GED, and about one-half do not earn a high school credential.[11]

---

* There is no generally-accepted definition of a dropout. Some use school enrollment figures; others rely on US Census population surveys. Some include GED recipients; others do not. Some keep records of transfer students; many do not.

- Three-quarters of state prison inmates are dropouts, as are 59% of federal inmates.[12] In fact, dropouts are 3.5 times more likely than high school graduates to be incarcerated in their lifetime.[13] African American men are disproportionately incarcerated. Of all African American male dropouts in their early 30s, 52% have been imprisoned.[14] 90% of the 11,000 youth in adult detention facilities have no more than a 9th grade education.[15]

- The earning power of dropouts has been in almost continuous decline over the past three decades. In 1971, male dropouts earned $35,087 (in 2002 dollars), but this fell 35% to $23,903 in 2002. Earnings for female dropouts fell from $19,888 to $17,114.[16] The mean earnings of Latino young adults who finish high school are 43% higher than those who dropout.[17]

- The earnings gap widens with years of schooling and formal training. In 2003, annual earnings of male dropouts fell to $21,447. High school graduates earned an average of $32,266; those with associate's degrees earned $43,462; bachelor's degree holders earned $63,084—about triple that of dropouts.[18]

- In 2001, only 55% of young adult dropouts were employed, compared with 74% of high school graduates and 87% of four-year college graduates.[19]

- Between 1997 and 2001, more than one-quarter of all dropouts were unemployed for one year or longer, compared with 11% of those with a high school diploma or GED.[20] In 2003, more than one-half of African American young adult male dropouts in Chicago were unemployed.[21]

- The US death rate for persons with fewer than 12 years of education is 2.5 times higher than for those with 13 or more years of education.[22]

- Dropouts are substantially more likely to rely on public assistance than those with a high school diploma.[23] The estimated lifetime revenue loss for male dropouts ages 25-34 is $944 billion. The cost

to the public of their crime and welfare benefits is estimated to total $24 billion annually.[24]

- Dropouts contribute to state and federal tax coffers at only about one-half the rate of high school graduates; over a working lifetime about $60,000 less, or $50 billion annually for the 23 million high school non-completers, ages 18-67.[25]

- The US would save $41.8 billion in health care costs if the 600,000 young people who dropped out in 2004 were to complete one additional year of education. If only one-third of high school dropouts were to earn a high school diploma, federal savings in reduced costs for food stamps, housing assistance, and Temporary Assistance for Needy Families would amount to $10.8 billion annually.[26]

- Increasing the high school completion rate by 1% for all men ages 20-60 would save the United States $1.4 billion annually in reduced costs associated with crime.[27]

- Federal investments in second-chance education and training programs fell from $15 billion in the late 1970s to $3 billion (inflation-adjusted) today.[28]

- Dropouts "cost our nation more than $260 billion dollars...That's in lost wages, lost taxes, and lost productivity over their lifetimes. In federal dollars, that will buy you ten years of research at the National Institutes of Health."[29]

- The statistic bears repeating: every nine seconds in America a student becomes a dropout.[30]

Sources

1 Seastrom, M., et al. (2005). *The averaged freshman graduation rate for public high schools from the Common Core of Data: School years 2001-03.* Washington, DC: US Department of Education, National Center for Education Statistics.

2 Greene, J.P., & Winters M.A. (2005, February), p. 1.

3 National Center for Education Statistics. (2004). *Digest of education statistics 2004.* Washington, DC, Table 9; Greene, J.P., & Winters, M.A. (2005, February). "Public high school graduation and college readiness rates: 1991-2002." *Education Working Paper No. 8.* New York, NY: Manhattan Institute for Policy Research.

4 Hood, L. (2004). *High school students at risk: The challenge of dropouts and pushouts.* New York, NY: Carnegie Corporation of New York; US Department of Education, National Center for Education Statistics. (2005). *The condition of education 2005.* Washington, DC: US Government Printing Office, pp. 55-57; Reimer, M., & Smink, J. (2005). *Information about the school dropout issue.* Clemson, SC: National Dropout Prevention Center/Network at Clemson University.

5 Annie E. Casey Foundation. (2004). *Kids count data book.* Baltimore, MD: Author.

6 Barton, P. E. (2005). *One-third of a nation: Rising dropout rates and declining opportunities.* Princeton, NJ: Policy Information Center, Educational Testing Service, p. 3.

7 Orfield, G. (Ed.). (2004). *Dropouts in America: confronting the graduation rate crisis.* Cambridge, MA: Harvard Education Press, p. 1. See also: Swanson, C.B. (2004). *Who graduates? Who doesn't? A statistical portrait of public high-school graduation.* Washington, DC: The Urban Institute.

8 Orfield, G., Losen, D.J., Wald, J., & Swanson, C. B. (2004). *Losing our future: How minority youth are being left behind by the graduation rate crisis.* Cambridge, MA: The Civil Rights Project at Harvard University. See also: Losen, D.J. (2005, December). *Racial inequity in graduation rates.* Research presented during Connect for Kids and National Education Association conference call on the Dropout Crisis. Greene, J.P., & Winters, M.A. (2005, February) find the African American graduation rate in 2002 to be 56%, Latinos 52%, and Whites 78%.

9 US Department of Education, National Center for Education Statistics. (2004). *The condition of education 2004.* Washington, DC: US Government Printing Office, Indicator 10, p. 11.

10 US Department of Education. (2003). *Twenty-fifth annual report to Congress on the implementation of the Individuals with Disabilities Education Act.* Washington, DC.

11 Alliance for Excellent Education. (2004). *A framework for an excellent education for all high school students.* Washington, DC: Author.

12 Harlow, C.W. (2003). *Education and correctional populations, bureau of justice statistics special report.* Washington, DC: US Department of Justice.

13 Catterall, J.S. (1985). *On the social cost of dropping out.* Stanford, CA: Center for Education Research, cited in Alliance for Excellent Education. (2004, December). *Measuring graduation to measure success.* Washington, DC: Author.

14 Western, B., Schiraldi, V., & Ziedenberg, J. (2004). *Education and incarceration.* Washington, DC: Justice Policy Institute, p. 1.

15 Coalition for Juvenile Justice. (2001). *From the prison track to the college track.* Washington, DC: Author.

16 Barton, P.E. (2005), p. 5.

17 US Bureau of the Census. (2002). *Educational attainment in the United States.* Washington, DC, Table 9.

18 Center on Education Policy and American Youth Policy Forum. (2001). *Higher learning = higher earnings.* Washington, DC: Center on Education Policy and American Youth Policy Forum.

19 Sum, Andrew et al. (2002). *Left behind in the labor market: labor market problems of the nation's out-of-school, young adult populations.* Chicago, IL: Alternative Schools Network. Retrieved December 27, 2005 from http://www.nupr.neu.edu/2-03/left_behind.pdf

20 Wald, M., & Martinez, T. (2003). *Connected by 25: Improving life chances of the country's most vulnerable 14-24-year-olds.* William and Flora Hewlett Foundation Working Paper. Stanford, CA: Stanford University. Retrieved December 27, 2005 from www.youthtransitions.org

21 Center for Labor Market Studies, Northeastern University. (2003). *Youth labor market and education indicators for the state of Illinois.* Chicago, IL: Alternative Schools Network.

22 Alliance for Excellent Education. (2003). *Fact sheet: The impact of education on health and well-being.* Washington, DC: Author.

23 Adair, V.C. (2001). Poverty and the (broken) promise of education. *Harvard Educational Review,* 71(2), pp. 217-239.

24 Thorstensen, B. I. *If you build it, they will come: Investing in public education.* Retrieved December 27, 2005 from http://abec.unm.edu/resources/gallery/present/invest_in_ed.pdf

25 Rouse, C.E. (2005, October). *The labor market consequences of an inadequate education.* Paper presented at the symposium on the social costs of inadequate education, Teachers College, Columbia University, New York, NY. Retrieved December 27, 2005 from http://www.tc.columbia.edu/centers/Equity Campaign/symposium/speakers.asp?SpeakerId=11

26 Muennig, P. (2005, October). *Health returns to education interventions.* Paper presented at the symposium on the social costs of inadequate education, Teachers College, Columbia University, New York, NY. Retrieved December 27, 2005 from http://www.tc.columbia.edu/centers/EquityCampaign/symposium/resourceDetails.asp?PresId=5

27 Moretti, E. (2005, October). *Does education reduce participation in criminal activities?* Paper presented at the symposium on the social costs of inadequate education, Teachers College, Columbia University, New York, NY. Retrieved December 27, 2005 from http://www.tc.columbia.edu/centers/Equity Campaign/symposium/speakers.asp?SpeakerId=9

28 Barton, P.E. (2005), p. 4.

29 *Closing the achievement gap in American schools: The No Child Left Behind Act: Hearing before the Committee on Education and the Workforce, House of Representatives,* 109th Cong. (2005, September 29) (testimony of Margaret Spellings). Retrieved December 27, 2005 from (http://edworkforce.house.gov/hearings/109th/fc/spellingsnclb092905/spellings.htm

30 Lehr, C.A. et al. (2004). *Essential tools: Increasing rates of school completion.* Minneapolis, MN: National Center on Secondary Education and Transition. [Full text available online from Education Commission of the States at: http://www.ecs.org/html/Document.asp?chouseid=6649)

National Working Group on Foster Care and Education

Educational Outcomes for Children and Youth in Foster and Out-of-Home Care
Fact Sheet
December 2006

For the over 800,000 children and youth served in foster care each year in the United States, educational success is a potential positive counterweight to abuse, neglect, separation, and impermanence. Positive school experiences enhance their well-being, help them make more successful transitions to adulthood, and increase their chances for personal fulfillment and economic self-sufficiency, as well as their ability to contribute to society.

Unfortunately, the educational outcomes for children and youth in foster care are dismal. As this current research summary reveals, young people in foster care are in educational crises. Although data are limited, particularly national data, research makes it clear that there are serious issues that must be addressed to ensure the educational success of children and youth in foster care.

SCHOOL PLACEMENT STABILITY/ENROLLMENT ISSUES

School Mobility Rates of Children and Youth in Foster Care
- Children and youth have an average of one to two home placement changes per year while in out-of-home care.[1]
- A 2001 study of more than 4,500 children and youth in foster care in Washington State found that at both the elementary and secondary levels, twice as many youth in foster care as youth not in care had changed schools during the year.[2]
- In a New York study of 70 children and youth in foster care, more than 75% did not remain in their school once placed in foster care, and almost 65% had been transferred in the middle of the school year.[3]
- A three-state study of youth aging out of care (the Midwest Study) by Chapin Hall revealed substantial levels of school mobility associated with placement in out-of-home care. Over a third of young adults reported having had five or more school changes.[4]
- School mobility rates are highest for those entering care for the first time. According to another Chapin Hall study of almost 16,000 children and youth in the Chicago Public School system, over two-thirds switched schools shortly after their initial placement in out-of-home care.[5]

Negative Effects of School Mobility
- A 1996 study students in Chicago Public Schools found that students who had changed schools four or more times had lost approximately one year of educational growth by their sixth year.
- A 1999 study found that California high school students who changed schools even once were less than half as likely to graduate as those who did not change schools, even when controlling for other variables that affect high school completion.[7]
- In a national study of 1,087 foster care alumni, youth who had had one fewer placement change per year were almost twice as likely to graduate from high school before leaving care.[8]

Suspensions/Expulsions
- 66.8% of youth in out-of-home care in the Midwest Study had been suspended at least once from school (compared to a national sample of 27.8%). About one
4.6% of the national sample.[9]

Enrollment Issues
- In the New York study, 42% of the children and youth did not begin school immediately upon entering foster care. Nearly half of these young people said that they were kept out of school because of lost or misplaced school records.[10]
- A 2001 Bay Area study of over 300 foster parents found that "missing information from prior schools increased the odds of enrollment delays by 6.5 times".[11]

This product was produced and developed by Casey Family Programs, 1300 Dexter Ave N #300 Seattle, WA 98109 www.casey.org

ACADEMIC OUTCOMES

Academic Achievement

- The 2001 Washington State study found that children and youth in foster care attending public schools scored 16 to 20 percentile points below non-foster youth in statewide standardized tests at grades three, six and nine.[12]
- Youth in foster care in the Midwest Study, interviewed primarily after completing 10th or 11th grade, on average read at only a seventh grade level. Approximately 44% read at high school level or higher. Few excelled in academic subjects, especially relative to a comparable national sample. Less than one in five received an "A" in English, math, history, or science.[13]
- Chapin Hall's research on Chicago Public School children and youth in out-of-home care indicates they lag at least half a school year behind demographically similar students in the same schools. (There is an overall achievement gap of upwards of one year. However, some of this is attributed to the low-performing schools that many of them attend). Almost 50% of third to eighth grade students in out-of-home care scored in the bottom quartile on the reading section of the Iowa Tests of Basic Skills (ITBS) test.[14]

Grade Retention/Old for Grade

- In the Washington State study, twice as many youth in foster care at both the elementary and secondary levels repeated a grade compared to youth not in care.[15]
- Nearly 45% of youth in care in the New York State study reported being retained at least once in school.[16]
- In the Midwest Study, 37.2% of youth in foster care (compared with 21.5% of a comparable national sample) reported repeating a grade.[17]
- Chicago Public School students in out-of-home care were almost twice as likely as other students to be old for their grade, by at least a year, even after demographic factors were taken into account and comparisons made to other students attending the same schools.[18]

SPECIAL EDUCATION ISSUES

Number of Youth in Special Education

- Numerous studies indicate anywhere between one-quarter and almost one-half (23%–47%) of children and youth in out-of-home care in the U.S. receive special education services at some point in their schooling.[19]
- At both the elementary and secondary levels, more than twice as many foster youth as non-foster youth in the Washington State study had enrolled in special education programs.[20]
- Nearly half of the youth in foster care in the Midwest Study had been placed in special education at least once during the course of their education.[21]
- Chicago Public School students in out-of-home care between sixth and eighth grades were classified as eligible for special education nearly three times more frequently than other students.[22]

Advocacy Regarding Special Education Services

- In research done in 2000 by Advocates for Children of New York, Inc.:
  - 90% of biological parents of children in foster care surveyed did not participate in any special education processes concerning their child.[23]
  - 60% of caseworkers/social workers surveyed "were not aware of existing laws when referring children to special education" and over 50% said "that their clients did not receive appropriate services very often while in foster care".[24]
- A 1990 study in Oregon found that children who had multiple foster care placements and who needed special education were less likely to receive those services than children in more stable placements.

SOCIAL-BEHAVIORAL ISSUES

Mental Health

- In a recent study of foster care alumni in Oregon and Washington (Northwest Alumni Study), 54.4% of alumni had one or more mental health disorders in the past 12 months, such as depression, social phobia or panic syndrome (compared with 22.1% of general population).[25]
- In the same study, 25.2% had post-traumatic stress disorder within the past 12 months (compared with 4.0% of general population), which is twice the rate of U.S. war veterans.[26]

Social-Behavioral
- Several studies have found that children and youth in foster care are significantly more likely to have school behavior problems and that they have higher rates of suspensions and expulsions from school.[27]
- Recent research in Chicago confirmed previous statewide research findings that children in foster care are significantly more likely than children in the general population to have a special education classification of an emotional or behavioral disturbance.[28]
- In the Midwest Study, by about 19 years of age, almost half of the young women had been pregnant, a significantly higher percentage than the 20% in a comparative national sample.[29]

HIGH SCHOOL COMPLETION RATES

High School Completion Rates/Drop-Out Rates
- A recent report by the EPE Research Center indicates that the nationwide high school completion rate for **all** students is 70%. More are lost in ninth grade than in any other grade (9th: 35%; 10th: 28%; 11th: 20%; 12th: 17%).[30]
- Studies have found differing rates of high school completion (through a degree or GED) though the measures have been defined somewhat differently:
  - In the Washington State study, 59% of youth in foster care enrolled in 11th grade completed high school by the end of 12th grade.[31]
  - The young adults in the Northwest Alumni Study completed high school **(via diploma or GED)** at 84.8% which is close to the general population rate of 87.3%.[32]
  - Over one-third of the young people the Midwest Study had received neither a high school diploma nor a GED by age 19, compared to fewer than 10% of their same-age peers in a comparable national sample.[33]
  - A national study in 1994 of young adults who had been discharged from foster care found that 54% had completed high school.[34]
  - In the Chapin Hall study of Chicago Public School youth, fifteen-year-old students in out-of-home care were about half as likely as other students to have graduated 5 years later, with significantly higher percentages of students in care having dropped out (55%) or incarcerated (10%).[35]

Factors Contributing to Dropping Out
- Multiple studies suggest that being retained in a grade significantly increases the likelihood of dropping out.[36] For example, one study found that being retained even once between first and eighth grade makes a student four times more likely to drop out than a classmate who was never held back, even after controlling for multiple factors.[37]
- The recent report by the EPE Research Center indicates that repeating a grade, changing schools, and behavior problems are among the host of signals that a student is likely to leave school without a traditional diploma.[38]
- The book, Drop Outs in America reports research that shows the following students are at-risk for dropping out: students of color, students who had been held back, students who are older than others in their grade, and English-language learners.[39]

POST-SECONDARY ENTRANCE/COMPLETION RATES

Post-secondary Entrance/Completion Rates
- The Northwest Alumni Study found that of the foster care alumni who were interviewed,
  - 42.7% completed some education beyond high school
  - 20.6% completed any degree/certificate beyond high school
  - 16.1% completed a vocational degree (21.9% among those age 25 or older)
  - 1.8% completed a bachelor's degree: (2.7% among those age 25 or older) (24% is the completion rate among the general population of same age)[40]
- Recent longitudinal data (from the general population) suggests that 39% of students who enrolled in a public two-year institution received a credential within six years (28%--associate degree or certificate, 11%--baccalaureate).[41]

College Preparation/Aspiration
- The majority of those youth in out-of-home care interviewed in the Midwest Study at age 17-18 hoped and expected to graduate from college eventually.[42]

- Another study indicates that only 15% of youth in foster care are likely to be enrolled in college preparatory classes versus 32% of students not in foster care.[43]
- Strong academic preparation has been found to be the single most important factor in enrolling and succeeding in a postsecondary program. However, in the United States, studies of the general population have found that:
  - Only 32% of all students leave high school qualified to attend a four-year college.[44]
  - Only 20% of all African American and 16% of all Hispanic students leave high school college-ready.[45]
  - Between 30-60% of students "now require remedial education upon entry to college, depending on the type of institution they attend".[46]

Endnotes

Visit www.casey.org/friendsandfamilies/partners for fact sheet citations.

[1] National AFCARS data, 2002
[2] Burley & Halpern, 2001, p. 1
[3] Advocates for Children of New York, Inc., 2000, p. 5
[4] Courtney, et al., 2004, p. 42
[5] Smithgall et al., 2004, p.46
[6] Kerbow, University of Chicago, 1996, p.20
[7] Rumberger, et al., 1999, p. 37
[8] Pecora et al., 2003, p. 44
[9] Courtney, et al., 2004, pg. 42
[10] Advocates for Children of New York, Inc., 2000, p. 4
[11] Choice, et al., 2001, p. 44
[12] Burley & Halpern, 2001, p. 13
[13] Courtney, et al., 2004, pp. 43, 45
[14] Smithgall et. al. 2004, pp. 14, 17
[15] Burley & Halpern, 2001, p. 1
[16] Advocates for Children of New York, inc., 2000, p. 45
[17] Courtney, et al., 2004, p. 42
[18] Smithgall et. al. 2004, p. 22
[19] Courtney, et al., 2004 (47% of 732); Smithgall, et al., 2004 (45% of 1,216 sixth through eighth graders); Burley and Halpern, 2001 (23% of 1,423 third graders, 29% of 1,539 six graders, 24% of 1,597 ninth graders); Choice, et al., 2001 (36% of 303); Advocates for Children of New York Inc., 2000 (30% of 70); Zanghi, 1999 (41% of 134); Jones, et. al., 1998 (23% of 249); Goerge, et al., 1992 (29.1% of 14,714)
[20] Burley & Halpern, 2001, p. 16
[21] Courtney, et al., 2004, p. 40
[22] Smithgall et. al. 2004, p. 58
[23] Advocates for Children of New York, Inc., 2000, p. 6
[24] Advocates for Children of New York, Inc., 2000, p. 6.
[25] Pecora et al., 2005, p. 34
[26] Ibid.
[27] Courtney, et al., 2004, pg. 42; Barber & Delfabbro, 2003, pp. 6, 7; McMillen et al., 2003, p. 475; Zima et al., 2000, pp. 98, 99
[28] Goerge et al., 1992, p. 3; Smithgall et al., 2004, p. 58
[29] Courtney, et al., 2005, p. 54
[30] EPE Research Center, 2006
[31] Burley & Halpern, 2001, p. 1
[32] Pecora, et al., 2005, p. 35
[33] Courtney, et al., 2005, p. 22
[34] Cook, 1994, p. 218
[35] Smithgall et. al. 2004, p. 23
[36] Studies quoted in Rumberger, 2000, p. 14
[37] Rumberger, 1995, p. 601
[38] EPE Research Center, 2006
[39] Orfield, G., Ed., 2004, p. 157
[40] Pecora, et al., 2005, p. 36
[41] ACE Center for Policy Analysis, 2003, p.3
[42] Courtney, et al., 2004, p. 39
[43] Blome, 1997 cited in Sheehy et al., 2001, p. 9
[44] Greene, 2005, p. 9
[45] Ibid.
[46] Conley, 2005, p. xi

Promoting Educational Success for Young People in Foster Care
National Foster Youth Advisory Council

We, the members of the National Foster Youth Advisory Council (NFYAC), believe that every child and young person in foster care is entitled to the wide range of supports, services, and opportunities that promote our educational success.

We believe that all children and youth in foster care need:

- Caring and involved adults who *know* us, understand our experiences in foster care, and can assist us with educational planning and achievement;
- Safety, stability, and permanency, and the ability to attend our "home school" without disruption;
- Confidentiality of records and respect for our right to privacy;
- Support in accessing opportunities that promote our well-being and the ability to reach our full potential;
- The ability to pursue an educational or training program of our own choosing;
- Immediate enrollment in a new school, timely transfer of school credits, and continuity with regard to educational records when moves to other schools occur;
- Access to information, resources, and strategies that promote positive educational experiences;

"What Worked" - Key Components of Our Success

Members of the National Foster Youth Advisory Council convened on two occasions during 2003, to address the many challenges facing young people in foster care with regard to education. To move beyond a focus on the problems that youth encounter, group members were asked to identify *What Worked* and the range of supports that facilitated their educational success. The group articulated the following key components:

1. NFYAC members identified caring people, those individuals who comprise our "circle of support," as the most critical support. For some, foster parents, siblings, mentors, "homework buddies" (peers who support completion of assignments), coaches, guidance counselors, and teachers were the individuals who made a difference. Others identified educational advocates and tutors – those individuals charged with supporting the educational achievement of the youth with whom they work.

2. Overwhelmingly, NFYAC members stressed the importance of having permanency and a sense of safety and stability. One Council member expressed, "young people need permanent homes and need to know that they're not going to be randomly moved from place to place." Having a safe place to live and call "home" makes it easier to build relationships with caring adults, and to ultimately develop a circle of support that facilitates success across the board, especially around education. Members felt strongly

1

The National Foster Youth Advisory Council is supported by the Jim Casey Youth Opportunities Initiative and the Child Welfare League of America.

about the custodial agency's responsibility to maintain the youth's school placement, even if the young person is attending private school.

On the issue of safety, a number of young people raised the issue of bullying in schools. For many who struggled with "always being the new kid in school," not having a group of close friends, and not having the resources to wear the "latest fashions," school often represented a place where they were misunderstood, ridiculed, and singled out as different. Efforts to address bullying in school settings and its root causes are critical to ensuring safety and an affirming learning environment for all young people, but especially for those in foster care.

3. Financial assistance was also an important component of the 'recipe' for educational success. Many NFYAC members identified resources that support the pursuit of post-secondary education, such as tuition waivers, support for room and board, cash assistance and scholarships. A number of members also highlighted the importance of having assistance with college visits and tours and the completion of applications, especially for federal financial aid. There was also quite a bit of discussion around health care and obtaining insurance if you leave the state where you were in care to attend college. Lastly, other supports, such as free breakfast and lunch programs, having a dress code and school uniforms (to defray the costs of clothing for school), providing school supplies, and transportation assistance were helpful to young people struggling to be successful in elementary through high school.

4. Flexibility with educational planning, such as the ability to choose classes and deal with multiple absences, credit recovery programs, and summer school were helpful to young people trying to stay on track with their education. Because the timely recovery of credits and transfer of school records pose major challenges to young people attempting to enroll in new schools, the aforementioned supports were essential to promoting academic continuity and success. NFYAC members also expressed that having teachers who understood their experiences in foster care made a big difference.

5. Programs promoting child and youth development were particularly supportive of young people in foster care. Many NFYAC members remembered being involved with Head Start programs and reflected on the important role that extracurricular and after school programs had on their educational success.

Recommendations for Improving Educational Outcomes

Given the list of challenges and corresponding supports that the group identified, NFYAC members were asked to generate a list of recommendations for improving educational outcomes for young people in foster care. As the discussions took place, it was evident that these recommendations were not solely limited to improving educational outcomes, but spoke to a much broader need to revisit the way in which success is defined and pursued for America's foster youth.

The National Foster Youth Advisory Council is supported by the Jim Casey Youth Opportunities Initiative and the Child Welfare League of America.

The issue of educational underachievement is related to many of the other negative outcomes experienced by young people leaving foster care. With limited supports and resources, young people are forced to focus on day-to-day survival. As one member said, "If all aspects of your life are unbalanced and you need to figure out where you're going to spend the night, it's going to be difficult to think about your education."

Members of NFYAC believe in the strengths, talents, and potential of all young people in foster care. Our central message is that young people in foster care require what all young people need to become contributing members of society - unconditional love, care, and support and a strong connection to caring adults and communities that are willing to invest in our well-being and success.

NYFAC's Top Ten Recommendations for Improving Educational Outcomes for Youth in Foster Care:

Help me create my circle of support.

Everyone needs to feel loved and cared for! Young people in foster care need to experience a sense of belonging - they need to have someone to rely on when things get tough and also need to have someone to call upon when it's time to celebrate. Parents, caregivers, peers, teachers and other supportive adults need to be engaged in supporting young people in a variety of ways, especially when it comes to educational decisions and planning. To improve educational outcomes, we need to revisit the broad range of youth outcomes that we articulate for young people involved with the child welfare system. Having access and connections to "people resources" as well as opportunities to create one's own "circle of support" are critical components of facilitating the positive development of youth in care.

Make sure I have a place to call home.

A "home" is much more than just having a place to live -- it's knowing that you're safe, feeling "wanted," and having a permanent place to be. Having a home means having a place to go for the holidays and summer vacations. It means you don't have to take all of your belongings with you when you leave. The research shows that placement instability negatively impacts the educational achievement of young people in foster care. When youth are moved from place to place -- it's challenging to focus on anything beyond immediate day-to-day survival. All young people, regardless of what their experiences are or where they come from, need a place to call home.

Let me be involved in making decisions about my life.

Young people learn to make good decisions by having opportunities to make choices and be held accountable. Sometimes that involves making mistakes. Because of the way in which the child welfare system works, adults often presume that they know what's best without really understanding the experiences, hopes, and dreams of the young people with whom they work. Young people should be involved in making decisions about their educational future -- we have a right to have our voices heard.

The National Foster Youth Advisory Council is supported by the Jim Casey Youth Opportunities Initiative and the Child Welfare League of America.

Get to know me for who I am, NOT what I'm in.

The stigma of foster care has negatively impacted the lives of many young people who have spent time in out-of-home care. Many young people who are involved with the foster care system grow up believing that they are incapable of achieving success. One NFYAC member remembers a school policy that prevented her from being allowed to bring school textbooks home *simply because she was in foster care.* The messages inherent in these types of policies and practices send damaging and discouraging messages to young people about their value and their potential for success. Negative assumptions about and low expectations for foster youth are so pervasive in our society. We need to "raise the bar" for young people in foster care, refrain from labeling them, and make sure that we're communicating belief and confidence in their ability to accomplish great things and fulfill their dreams. As one NFYAC member exclaimed, "Talk to me about getting a PhD., not just a GED!"

Focus on what's "right" about me, not just what's wrong.

Many young people in foster care have experienced abuse and neglect, and as a result, may be dealing with a range of issues. While young people need to be supported in accessing treatment and/or counseling when necessary, the child welfare system tends to focus on the problems and challenges and does little to highlight the strengths of individuals and families. Members of NFYAC call for a shift in deficits or failure focused thinking when dealing with young people. Young people need support in identifying their strengths, thinking about their potential, and highlighting their interests and aspirations. When caring adults focus on what's right with young people, the possibilities are endless.

Help adults in my life, especially my teachers and guidance counselors, understand the system with which I'm involved.

The general public does not have an understanding of foster care and the young people that are involved with the system. We need to build awareness and educate the public about the unique strengths of and challenges facing youth in care. It is especially important to provide information, resources, and training to educators – and to involve young people and foster parents in the design and delivery of such staff development opportunities. Young people in foster care possess a wealth of information about the system. Their knowledge, insights, and expertise represent an untapped resource that is invaluable to the adults who work with them.

Connect me with information.

Young people need to have access to information and support in navigating many of the resources that exist. Whether it's information about scholarship opportunities, health insurance, college tours, or community programs that support educational success, young people also need to develop their own strategies for managing multiple sources of information. Members of NFYAC articulated the importance of ensuring that young people have opportunities to manage information about themselves and specifically highlighted "educational passports" as an effective tool. Lastly, young people need to be connected with information about state and federal

4

The National Foster Youth Advisory Council is supported by the Jim Casey Youth Opportunities Initiative and the Child Welfare League of America.

policies that have the potential to impact their foster care and educational experiences – the Foster Care Independence Act of 1999 and the Education and Training Vouchers programs are examples of key federal policies.

Respect our privacy.

"Would _____ please come to the office? Your social worker is here." Many of the members of NFYAC remember hearing their names called over the intercom system at school and these announcements often included pieces of personal information that didn't need to be shared with the entire school. Others recall that sensitive information about their circumstances was unnecessarily accessible to students and administrative personnel working in school offices.

The issue of confidentiality is a sensitive one for many young people in foster care, particularly in school settings. While members of NFYAC understand that there are times when information about the lives and families of young people in care needs to be shared, there is also a sense that the information sharing is not always conducted in a manner that prioritizes the privacy of the young people involved. NFYAC members highlighted the fact that many young people in foster care do not want information about their family history or living situation shared with their peers or other adults not involved with their educational planning. In school settings, administrators, teachers, social workers, and counselors can support young people by using discretion with sensitive and personal information, maintaining confidentiality of records, and respecting their right to privacy.

Teach me to take care of myself.

"Life skills development begins with learning to tie your own shoes – it's not something that starts when you turn 16!" Developing the skills needed to take care of oneself occurs over time. This process begins in childhood and continues throughout the lifespan. Young people in foster care need both formal and informal learning opportunities to acquire, practice, and utilize basic living skills. These skills include "tangible" or competency-based skills like completion of high school and the pursuit of post-secondary education as well as "intangible" skills such as a sense of self confidence and purpose and the ability to make good decisions.

Develop federal and state policies that promote our success.

While there has been much legislative activity benefiting young people in foster care during the last five years, much remains to be done. Members of NFYAC are committed to supporting and partnering with decision makers at the local, state, and federal levels to craft legislation that prioritizes the health and well-being of foster youth in our country.

Mr. Weller. Thank you.

Chairman McDermott. I want to thank you all for coming and spending the time as you have sat here for a couple of hours. As Mr. Meek said, the most important thing we miss is personal testimonials. We hear experts come in and talk to us but it is really good to have a couple of people come and tell us what really happens to them. That puts a public face on it that makes it very powerful, so thank you very much for both of you coming and exposing yourself, talking about tough things in life. We appreciate it.

Thank you all. The meeting is adjourned.

[Whereupon, at 3:00 p.m., the hearing was adjourned.]

[Submissions for the Record follow:]

STATEMENT OF CENTER FOR LAW AND SOCIAL POLICY

Thank you for focusing attention on this most important challenge related to our youth and thank you for the opportunity to submit testimony to the subcommittee. I am the Director for Youth Policy at the Center for Law and Social Policy (CLASP). CLASP is a nonprofit organization engaged in research, analysis, technical assistance, and advocacy on a range of issues affecting low-income families. Our youth policy work at CLASP has focused attention on the dimensions of the disconnected youth challenge in our nation and on the need to look more strategically at how our youth serving systems—education, workforce, juvenile justice, child welfare—can come together and in tandem with the business community and community based organizations create the infrastructure and support to connect our youth to positive pathways to adult success.

The desperate situation in many of our poor urban, rural, and minority communities where fewer than half of the youth that start high school complete four years later necessitates bold, strategic thinking and comprehensive interventions.

I am submitting for the record an article "What's a Youngster to Do? The Education and Labor Market Plight of Youth in High Poverty Communities" that I authored and that was published in the July 2005 issue of the Clearinghouse REVIEW Journal of Poverty Law and Policy. The challenges and solutions outlined in this article are very relevant to the subject matter of this hearing and the work of the subcommittee. This article draws attention to the dimensions of the youth challenge in several high poverty communities. It also points out that we know a great deal about what works to transform the pathways for these youth. It suggests the need for a new paradigm. One that recognizes that if this issue is to be solved it will require all systems and sectors to participate at the ground level building the system connections, supports, programs and pathways that will be needed to upgrade the skills of these youth and to secure their economic future. It will require the collective will, the resources, and an investment in building the capacity and the programming in these communities to address this problem at the scale necessary to produce measurable and sustainable improvements in the education and labor market outcomes for these young people who, absent intervention, will have extreme difficulty with adult labor market, family, and civic responsibilities.

What's a Youngster To Do? The Education and Labor Market Plight of Youth in High Poverty Communities
Linda Harris, Director, Youth Policy
Center for Law and Social Policy

Published in The Clearinghouse REVIEW Journal of Poverty Law and Policy
July/August 2005

"Our economy, national security, and social cohesion face a precarious future if our nation fails to develop now the comprehensive policies and programs needed to help all youth. In developing these polices and programs, it is crucial to recognize the growing gap between more fortunate youth and those with far fewer advantages. . . . Unless we are motivated, at least in part, by our belief in young people and our sense of obligation to them,

we risk losing more than we can ever hope to win." **William T. Grant Foundation Commission on Work, Family and Citizenship, The** *Forgotten Half: Non-College Youth in America,* **1988**

For almost two decades researchers and economists warned about an impendingcrisis for the young and the unskilled in the labor market. Those tracking the demographic trends, the labor market shifts, the immigration patterns, and the global influences predicted that, absent substantial intervention, youth, especially youth in the urban core, would face perilous times coming into the 21st century. Economist in the 1987 publication *Workforce 2000* noted that most new jobs created in the nineties and beyond would require some level of post-secondary education. Theycautioned that without substantial adjustment in policies and without investments being made in education and training, the problems of minority unemployment, crime and dependency would be worse in the year 2000.[9] The National Center on Education and the Economy in their 1990 report *America's Choice: High Skills or Low Wages* noted that 1 in 5 young people in this country grow up in third world surroundings and start out with severe learning disadvantages from which theynever recover. They recommended the investment in a dropout recovery system that would build the connection between education and work for youth without high school certification.[10] Despite these admonitions, federal investment in employment, training and second chance programs decreased dramatically over the ensuing 15 years.

The future that these studies predicted is upon us, with the attending consequences. While the national graduation rate for youth in public school is an appalling 68%, the rate for youth in high poverty urban districts is below 50%. The lack of attention and public will around this issue is attributable in part to the fact that the aggregate statistics on graduation rates and employment rates for the nation's youth masks the stark reality of the problem for youth in poor urban, rural, or minority communities. This situation goes largely unattended because this is aninvisible constituency. When young people drop out, or disconnect, or stop looking for work they are no longer counted in any system or any statistic unless they find their way to the public welfare system or the criminal justice system as many of them do. No public institution or system is called upon to account for the preparation and transition of youth to the labor market.

Prevailing sentiment would rest that responsibility with the parent and studentand that would be quite appropriate if we were talking about a small minority of students falling by the wayside. However, when more than half of the young people attending public school in a community leave school before graduating, the problem is beyond that of parental and personal responsibility. It is evidence of the breakdown of the education, community, and economic infrastructure that in healthy communities prepares and supports youth as they transition to adulthood. In economically distressed communities these institutions are overburdened, under-resourced, broken, or simply incapable of providing the level of support needed to prepare these youth for successful transition to adulthood and the labor market.

This article focuses a lens on the situation for youth in selected large cities with poverty rates above 30% and with school districts that have more than 60% of their students eligible for free or reduced lunches. Twelve cities were selected to amplifythe challenges faced by young people growing up in these urban areas: Atlanta, Baltimore, Buffalo, Cleveland, Detroit, Fresno, Los Angeles, Miami, Milwaukee, New York, Philadelphia, and Washington,

DC. Totally, just over 3 million students were enrolled in these districts, 86.1% of them minority. Table 1 displays the general profile of distress in these communities.

Table 1. Profile of High Poverty Cities

City	School Enrollment[1]	% Minority[1]	%below poverty line[2]			Violent crime rate[3]	Juvenile arrest rate (100,000)[4]	Teen births[5]	Graduation rate[1]	%Teens[6] employed
			Total	Black	Hispanic					
Atlanta	58,320	93.2	39.3	47.0	29.0	2,289	607	100	39.6	30.9
Baltimore	99,859	89.2	31.0	35.8	22.9	2,054	1,281	86	47.9	28.4
Buffalo	45,721	71.5	38.7	45.0	56.7	1,271	327	72	47.3	34.2
Cleveland	75,684	80.7	38.0	45.6	40.6	1,322	NA	99	30.0	32.4
Detroit	162,194	96.3	34.8	35.2	31.9	2,072	200	78	57.0	28.8
Fresno	79,007	79.8	36.8	44.6	40.5	853	423	86	55.8	28.3
Los Angeles	721,346	90.1	30.7	38.5	36.6	1,349	304	61	46.4	27.2
Miami [7]	368,265	88.7	38.5	52.4	34.6	1,906	NA	174	52.1	26.0
Milwaukee	97,985	81.3	32.0	43.7	33.2	956	892	88	45.8	39.2
New York	1,066,515	84.7	30.3	33.9	39.9	955	332	41	38.2	19.7
Philadelphia	201,190	83.3	31.6	37.2	50.4	1,524	1,008	64	41.9	25.8
Washington	68,925	95.5	31.7	37.6	25.6	1,596	NA	53	65.2	239
Average for High poverty cities	Total 3,045,011	86.2	34.4	41.38	36.8	1,512	537.4	83.5	47.3	28.7
For US			16.6	33.1	27.8	495	276	48	68	41.2
Ratio of High Pov Cities to US			2.08	1.25	1.32	3.06	1.95	1.74	.695	59.9

[1] Orfield, G., Losen, D., Wald, J., & Swanson, C., (2004). *Losing Our Future: How Minority Youth are Being Left Behind by the Graduation Rate Crisis,* Cambridge, MA: The Civil RightsProject at Harvard University. Statistics are for the public school district.

[2] Kids Count—Census Data Online—2000 Census-Income and Poverty, http://aecf.org/cgi-bin.

[3] Crime in the United States: 2003, Uniform Crime Reports, table 8, United States Department of Justice.

[4] Snyder, H., Puzzanchera, C., Kang, W. (2005) "Easy Access to FBI Arrest Statistics 1994–2002" Online, Available: http://ojjdp.ncjrs.org/ojstatbb/ezaucr/. Arrest Statistics are for the county in which the city is located.

[5] Births per thousand females aged 15–19 from Kids Count, "Teen Births in America's Largest Cities 1990 and 2000" Annie E. Casey Foundation, 2000.

[6] Extracted from the 2000 Census PUMS—5% file.

[7] Enrollment and Graduation rates are for the Miami-Dade County district.

Consider the prospects for these youth. One in three resides in a household that is below the poverty level, twice the national average. They live in communities where the rate of violent crime is 3 times the national average. Youth are twice as likely to be arrested and almost twice as likely to be a teen parent. Only one in two youth entering high school will graduate and only 14% of minority youth will complete 4 years of college (compared to 49.7% of White youth). This environment of low achievement, low expectations, early exposure to violent and illicit activity, and lack of exposure to positive pathways out, constrains the life options for young people. It is a daunting landscape for an adolescent to navigate. There are youth who will graduate and go on to post-secondary success. They will do so against considerable odds.

Equally bleak are the labor market prospects for youth who don't complete high school in these communities. The chart below presents a few labor market statistics from the 2000 Decennial Census. While this profile is as of the last census, recent analysis by the Center for Labor Market Studies at Northeastern University shows a worsening situation for teens in the labor market with teen employment being at its lowest level in 57 years. [11]

According to the decennial census just over a quarter of youth 16 to 19 in these communities were working. That compares to 41% nationally for the same age group. Young people in high poverty cities do not have the same early access to the labor market. Transportation poses a barrier to access to employment in the suburban hubs and in the central city labor market youth are competing with immigrants and a growing number of older workers who are taking the jobs traditionally held by teenaged workers. Studies show that there is a direct benefit to early work experience for teens. Work experience in the junior/senior year adds to wages in the later teen years and to increased annual earnings through age 26 especially for those not attending four-year colleges.[12] Youngsters in high poverty communities are disadvantaged by their lack of early work exposure during the critical years when they should be building their labor market attachment, their workplace skills, and a portfolio of experiences that would allow them to progress.

Among these high poverty cities, there are districts that fail to graduate 60 to 70 percent of their students. These students without access to quality "second chance" options are destined to remain without academic credentials. Census statistics for various age categories showed that those without a high school diploma were intermittently employed throughout their early and late twenties. The employment rate for dropouts in their early twenties was only 44% compared to 60.9% for those with a high school diploma. The attachment to the labor market for dropouts in their early twenties was tenuous with only 50 percent having worked more than 3 months during the entire year of 1999.[13] For those in their late twenties without a high school diploma, the percent working remained below 50%.

The chart also highlights the disparity in employment between White and minority youth. In the chart above minority refers to Black and Hispanic youth. In general the percentage of minority youth working at the time of census in these communities was approximately 78% of that for White youth. The disparity gap narrows for youth with bachelor's degrees. However, only 14% of minority youth in these cities had graduated from a 4 year college compared to 49% of White youth. It is fairly clear that if the employment gap among the races is to be closed significant effort and resources must be directed at greatly improving the participation in post-secondary education and career training for minority youth of color.

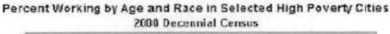

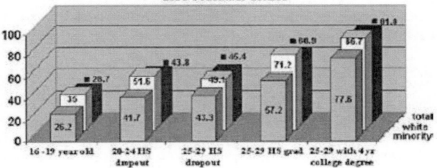

Source: Extracted from the 2000 Census PUMS 5% file. Working includes those in the military.

Chart 1

The question, "**what's a youngster to do?**" is more than a rhetorical question. In communities with large minority populations, where fewer than 50% of the youth graduate, where only 42% of minority 20 to 24 year old dropouts find employment, and where resources for safety net and second chance programs have been dramatically reduced, how will they survive economically, form families, and participate constructively in civic life. The simple answer is that too many will be unsuccessful.Unless the education and labor market status of these youth dramatically improve, they will spend their adult years on the fringes of the labor market marginalized in their ability to adequately provide for their economic wellbeing or that of their families. More young people will find avenues for economic survival through illicit activity, thus reinforcing the pipeline to prison and the accompanying stigma that will exacerbate their labor market situation upon re-entry.

In 2004, CLASP surveyed nearly 200 young people from 15 high poverty cities who had dropped out of school and who were eventually re-connected to supportive alternative programs. They were asked, among other things, what they did with their time after dropping out of school and before engaging in the alternative program. Most youth were idle, unemployed, simply hanging out. Twenty eight percent (28%) were engaged in criminal or gang activity. Only 24% reported working mostof the time. Fortunately, these young people found their way to comprehensive alternative programs. They responded that what they found most valuable was the caring adult support and guidance and the ability to reconnect to education. Once reconnected, 47% responded that they had post-secondary ambitions most with very specific majors in mind. Many of the youth who fall by the wayside have hopes and aspirations and their paths can be positively redirected with the appropriate guidance and support.[14] However, sustaining the funding streams to support the transformations of youth delivery systems in economically distressed communities has proven challenging for those communities engaging in such transformation efforts. Department of Labor investment in youth programming declined from $15 billion (in current dollars) in 1979 to just over $2.6 billion today.[15] The most recent federal Youth Opportunity Grant funding to high poverty urban and rural communities is being discontinued.

So, **what's a Nation to do?** For almost 2 decades, the first chance education systems in these communities have been neglected and the second chance programs have been greatly impacted by the continual retrenchment in funding. Relying solely on the slow pace of systemic education reform will almost certainly guarantee that a decade hence we will be facing greater challenges of social isolation, disparate labor market outcomes and we will be posing the same questions. To make a difference for youth in these communities several things must happen:

1. Systemic education reform and aggressive youth recovery efforts must occur in tandem. These efforts must draw from the strength and resources of the broader community to provide rich alternative learning environments, advocacy and mentoring support, and horizon extending exposure to careers and experiences that will heighten aspirations. Many communities have discovered that the State and local education dollar can be deployed to re-engage dropouts and struggling students in smaller, more supportive community-based learning environments. Communities must engage with their local districts to spark innovation in developing multiple high quality options that will keep struggling students engaged and provide "on ramps" for those who have dropped out.

2. All youth serving systems should be mandated to collaborate on the solution set and put in place accountability systems and supports such that no youth falls through the cracks. The public must demand better accountability for outcomes from youth serving systems. In communities with high levels of youth distress the education, workforce, child welfare, juvenile justice, and mental health systems should be required to collaborate on a transition support system that tracks and supports the movement of youth through the various systems and prepares them for post-secondary success. Youth aging out of foster care and youth re-entering from incarceration should have transition plans that connect them with the services from all relevant systems. Youth councils, such as those currently mandated in the Workforce Investment Act, should serve to keep the focus on the problem and solutions and to engage stakeholders in the process.

3. Federal and State resources must flow in support of such scaled efforts creating a policy, legislative, and regulatory environment that affirms a commitment to not leave these youth behind and provides the incentives and resources, at scale, to stand behind the commitment. Efforts like the Youth Opportunity Grant which provided substantial funding to high poverty communities to build capacity and engage thousands of in-school and out-of-school youth in sustained activity, should be extended not ended.

4. The realities of the job market, the workplace and the 21st century skill set needed to be competitive must factor heavily in the redesign of high schools and alternative programming. Business must play a prominent role in this redesign and in opening up the workplace to provide rich career exposure. Jobs today and in the near future are more knowledge and technology based. Success in the workplace will require the ability to analyze, quickly adapt, continually upgrade, and develop transferable skills. A dramatic shift in the secondary/post-secondary education paradigm will be required to shift from 50% dropping out to 100% graduating with these skills. Actively engaging business, secondary, post-secondary, and alternative education leaders in the school reform process can provide the impetus and support for such change.

5. Work experience, internships, and community service/service learning opportunities must be greatly expanded in these communities to provide for theseyouth the same level of exposure to work environments and civic opportunities as experienced by youth in more advantaged jurisdictions. Up until the passage of the Workforce Investment Act in 1998, which eliminated the summer youth program, thousands of 14 and 15 year old youth received their first exposure to work and community service through this federal funding. Over the years the summer jobs program provided communities with a vehicle for impartingwork skills, college and career exposure, leadership skills, and work ethic in the early teen years. With the elimination of the summer jobs program and the constricting opportunities in the job market, young people are not developing the skills and work ethic that will be essential for labor market success in later years.

6. A national youth policy must be advanced that has among its principles thereconnection of the approximately 5 million youth[16] who are out of school and out of work and out of the labor market and societal mainstream. There is no overarching national youth policy that embraces all youth including those who have been ''disconnected''. Nor is there policy that frames our values, beliefs, promises and actions to be taken on behalf of all youth. National attention on this issue tends to focus on specific pieces of legislation or special target groups—gang prevention, foster care, young offenders. While this attention is much needed, these problems are vestiges of continued neglect of the larger disconnected youth problem. A more comprehensive national youth policy is needed to move the country from siloed fragmented interventions to more systemic, integrated solutions.

What's a community to do? What is happening to young people in high poverty communities, many of which are also predominantly minority communities, should be unacceptable to all segments of the community. When viewed simply as a failureof public schools, it is easy for one to point the finger and disengage from the solution. However, when viewed as a failure of the collective community to provide for the future for its youth it should serve as a call to action. Those working in the youth field are well aware of the amazing transformations that take place when young people are reconnected to supportive alternative environments. There is a growing body of evidence about effective practice and what works to restore the education and labor market pathways. Caring adult support, integrated learning environments, high quality work experience and civic engagement, in combination, have been demonstrated effective in restoring the pathways to success for youth.[17] The technology, and experience exist, but the delivery infrastructure is fragmented and fragile after years of funding decline.

High school reform and the growing pressure for accountability should serve asthe impetus to community activism around these unacceptable educational and labor market outcomes in high poverty communities. The growing exposure of the educational and labor market disparities for youth of color should also sound the alarm. The community has an important role to play in creating the public will to elevate the much neglected plight of youth in poverty communities for priority attention. Community leaders and parents will need to be informed and vigilant as the high school reform efforts unfold. Reform efforts that cater to the letter of the law, instead of the intent and spirit of leaving no youth behind, may in fact exacerbate the dropout problem. Attempts to comply with high standards, high stakes testing, and making average yearly progress could easily lead to the less abled andmore difficult youth being pushed out or tracked to less desirable alternatives. The challenge is to deliver **all** youth to graduation with a skill set that allows them to compete on equal footing for the opportunities in the labor market. Communities, if they are to thrive, can not continue to allow the loss of young talent, potential, and energy.

What is needed is a vision for youth that is anchored in the belief that all youth should have equitable access to the promise and prosperity that America has to offer. This belief should guide our priorities, our policies and our actions as individuals in a caring community and as a Nation. It should resonate across all levels of government and at the grass roots of community service delivery. There must be a commitment to actualize that vision by making the investments at the scale needed until the education and labor market disparities for poor and minority youth dissipate. It is not just about funding. It is about rethinking systems, policies, relationships, and collective responsibility. Leadership on this issue begins with the acknowledgement that the situation that exists for youth in high poverty communities is unacceptable and that solutions must be bold, systemic, and collaborative. Every sector of the community and every youth serving system should be coalesced to be part of the solution. A solution that is two decades overdue!

STATEMENT OF GREATER MIAMI SERVICE CORPS

As the Executive Director of the Greater Miami Service Corps (GMSC), I am pleased to submit testimony and success stories for consideration by the House Ways and Means Subcommittee on Income Security and Family Support as you consider best practices for engaging disconnected and disadvantaged youth and young people.

PROGRAM BACKGROUND

Established in 1989, Greater Miami Service Corps is a non-profit youth service organization, based in Miami-Dade County that provides out-of-school young people with the resources and services necessary to transition to independence and self-sufficiency. Program emphasis is placed on preparing young people to enter the workforce through education, paid work experience, internships, job placement and post-program follow-up and support services to ensure placement retention. A profile ofour population includes youth who are either unemployed or underemployed; high school dropouts; basic skills deficient; single parents; non-custodial parents; youth with prior criminal histories and youth aged out of foster care.

GMSC, is one of 115 Service and Conservation Corps currently operating in 41 states and the District of Columbia. Corps annually enroll more than 23,000 young men and women who contribute 13 million hours of service every year. The CorpsNetwork and its member Corps have a long and successful history in addressing the needs of disconnected and disadvantaged youth between the ages of 16 and 25.

GMSC was one of eleven programs created through a national demonstration project called the Urban Corps Expansion Project (UCEP), a joint project between The Corps Network (formerly National Association of Service and Conservation Corps) and

Public/Private Ventures. The UCEP project was sought to address several unmet community needs, specifically: the need for increased community service and volunteerism; the need for involvement of young adults in addressing the physical and social conditions of their community; the need for structured, meaningful work experiences for young adults; and the need for ''comprehensive educational'' opportunities for disadvantaged youth.

SERVICE STRATEGY

The Greater Miami Service Corps and The Corps Network member programs use the ''Corps Works'' model which incorporates service as a strategy to engaging youth. This service model was research validated by Abt, Associates and Brandeis University in 1997. The model incorporates subsidized community based work experience, which simulates a real-world work environment. Specifically, in order to prepare for future work and success in family and community life, youth enter a 6– 12 month, comprehensive work-based learning program. Youth spend the bulk of each week, Monday through Thursday working in crews on service projects under the guidance of trained adult supervisors. Service projects provide numerous work-based learning opportunities rooted in reading and language comprehension, mathematics and critical thinking. These activities not only provide valuable work experience but also enhance literacy levels among youth. Projects also provide opportunities for teamwork, communication as well as good safety practices. Projects may be production based and as such carry deadline-driven services creating an environment similar to what youth will experience in other employment settings. The skills attained by youth are varied by region but may include building and lawn maintenance, child development, construction, clerical/office support and experience in the health care industry. These projects save taxpayers money and provide meaningful work for young people who will graduate our program with marketable skills.

To address employment barriers directly (in addition to the crew-based work experience), youth devote time (at least six hours per week or more) to individualized education in pursuit of a high school diploma, GED or remediation for those who have diplomas. Whenever possible, youth are enrolled in community college classes to build the habits and expectations of post-secondary education.

In addition to providing help with academics and work experience, youth have numerous opportunities to demonstrate leadership. Leadership opportunities offered include attendance at Board meetings, community presentations, team captain, Corps Senate, leadership development and business training.

In return for their efforts, Corpsmembers receive a living allowance, classroom training to improve basic competencies, a chance to earn a GED or high school diploma, experiential and environmental service-learning-based education, generic and technical skills training, a wide range of support services, and, in many cases, an AmeriCorps post-service educational award of up to $4,725.

This best practice model informs the community that the Greater Miami Service Corps develops young people to succeed. More than 70% of Corpsmembers who complete the rigorous program are placed in jobs. An additional group of Corpsmembers, return to school or go on to college and an additional group join the military.

FUNDING PICTURE

The services provided by GMSC remain as critical today as they did in 1989. Continuing articles published by the Miami-Herald and the Sun-Sentinel on youth violence, low graduation rates, increased poverty and the continuing dilemma of babies having babies demonstrate the need for increased funding of youth programs that target disadvantaged youth. However, funding for services locally remains unstable. Continued decreases in state Workforce Investment Act funding as well as the impact to revenue generated through property taxes to the County and local municipalities creates a tremendous impact to the number of youth that can receive services.

Since 2002, we have seen a decline in the number of youth our program serves annually, from 425 to approximately 200. At the same time, the number of youth eligible for services continues to increase. A June 13th article in the Miami Herald indicates that "fewer than 50% of students in Miami-Dade earned a high school diploma." Overall, Florida's 60.5% graduation rate is 45th in the country, out of 50 states and the District of Columbia. Without the resources for programs like the Greater Miami Service Corps, many of these young people will face a dismal future of low wages due to low education and skill levels.

In order to ensure that our youth and young people receive basic services, many programs have formed collaborations to address youth barriers to employment such as transportation, childcare, housing, tutoring, etc. But so much more is needed. Attached are success stories of local youth who were formerly considered "disadvantaged and disconnected." In order to engage the increased number of youth that are unable to access services due to limited funding, federal and state funds must be increased to make it possible for youth to participate in drop-out reconnection programs. Funding sources to consider include Youth Opportunity Grants, Public Land Corps and Department of Labor Offender Re-entry and Youthbuild funding. It is important that foundations are part of the conversation for funding support in to developing a pathway to youth for industry specific jobs.

Received via email January 11, 2007

Ms Dorsett:

First of all I wanted to let you know how nice was to see you last Tuesday; it's been a while since I graduate from the GMSC and all the memories I have from you guys are nothing but good ones.

Thanks to all your staff and your attention to detail has changed many lives in the community; I'm the living example that if you believe in yourself and take the opportunities that you offer you will be able to success in life.

While I was in the program I had the opportunity to work with Miami Dade housing agency and six months later I was a full time employee for the county, I've could stop right there but then I thought that if I got that far I could've go even furtherand I did.

I decided to join the Navy so I can have a back up to complete my education. It worked.

It's not easy to be away from family and friends but at the same time I've become a better person, a stronger leader, a warrior. I've been in more than 15 countries in less than two years!!!

Thank you for all the opportunities that you gave me; I have no words to explain how much I appreciate all your help, I couldn't get this far If I wouldn't go to GMSC.

God bless you for giving people a new hope and a new way to see the real world, it is never to late to study some of us wasted time but thanks to programs like the one you offer helps communities to put young people in the right track for their future.

Once again thank you for show me that there's a future if you really fight for your goals, now I'm able not just to support myself but my family as well; I'm even in the process to buy a house.

GOD BLESS YOU AND ALL THE STAFF!!!

Very respectfully

Petty Officer Hernandez, U.S NAVY
PS3 HERNANDEZ, EMILIO
EXECUTIVE DEPARTMENT
USS LEYTE GULF (CG–55)

FPO AE 09570–1175

Received via email 3/20/2007

I use to be in the Greater Miami Service Corp, a long time ago. I am glad to see that it is still around. The corps helped me get my High School Diploma from Lindsay Technical school. I am 32 years old now, so a lot has happen since, but if it was not for the corps setting my sails right, I would have not been on my way.

After I left the corps I moved into my own apt and got a permanent job with the Dade County providing subsidized housing for low income families. I had great aspirations, I wanted greater things in life so I left that job and joined the U.S.A.F. in September of 1996. Since then I have traveled to Spain, Ireland, Oman, Iraq, Afghanistan, Guam, Hawaii, 23 of the 48 contiguous states, and just recently Japan. I have driven a 800 horsepower car down a drag strip, eaten culturally unique cuisine from every country I visited, met more celebrities then I can remember and own a driveway full of cars that makes my dad jealous. Now I am a Staff Sergeant in the Air Force and my job is to monitor my Squadron of 100 people ensuring persons, equipment and aircraft move on time off the airfield. I am writing this letter to you so maybe you can read it to those young people maybe it can inspire them to stick with the program just a little bit longer.

Thank you

SSgt Juan D. Hernandez
Kadena Air Base Japan, U.S.A.F.

Greater Miami Service Corps

Elmer Garcia is the third member of his family to attend and graduate from GMSC. After relocating from Guatemala, he was uncertain of what he should do. When he first arrived, his Mom told him about the Greater Miami Service Corps. However, he decided to work for an oriental trading company. After three years without opportunities for advancement, he decided to try the Corps. While enrolled, he earned his general education diploma, increased his English literacy and obtained full-time employment through an internship placement with Energy Programs Division of Miami-Dade County Community Action Agency. He states, "As a result of the program, I am now enrolled in Miami-Dade

College to pursue an Associates Degree in Business Administration. The Corps helped put me on the path to achieve my goals.''

Success Stories

Linda Eugene came to the Greater Miami Service Corps six months after relocating from Haiti. She states, ''My primary reason for joining was to benefit from the scholarships.'' After completing her twelve month tenure, she continued in school full-time and worked on a part-time basis. In 1999, she earned her Associate in Arts; in 2002 she attained her Bachelor of Arts in Public Administration. She did not stop there . . . in 2004 she earned a Masters in Business Administration with a concentration in Accounting. She now works full-time with the Tax Collectors Office and teaches English as a Second Language (ESOL) on a part-time basis.

When **Gladis Chacon's** grandfather died, her world changed. She and her siblings found themselves on the verge of homelessness. Due to the age of her siblings, they were placed in foster care. Since she was twenty and too old for foster care, Gladis moved into a shelter. That's when a counselor referred her to the Greater Miami Service Corps. She states, ''It was my first real job situation and I could not believe that I was accepted, it was like oh my God they want me?'' After twelve months Gladis graduated. She is now gainfully employed with the Miami-Dade County Community Action Agency; she has an apartment and is now working toward obtaining her general education diploma. She states, ''The most important thing I learned is that it's important to be strong and never give up.''

Willie Scott, a young father of three, wanted to make a difference in his life and that of his children. A family friend referred him to the Greater Miami Service Corps. After joining the Corps, Willie quickly demonstrated his leadership ability through his designation as Team Captain. In his role as Team Captain, he was able to learn managerial and administrative skills. Upon program completion, Willie obtained full-time employment with South Miami Hospital, a Baptist Health South Florida affiliate. Willie states, ''Greater Miami Service Corps. . . .''

Born in Port au Prince Haiti, **Sophonie Slaughter** came to the United States with her mother at a young age. Her Mom worked hard to make a life for the two of them; however, shortly after arriving in the United States; ''Sophie'' as she is affectionately known, found out her Mom was gravely ill. When she was in the fourth grade, her Mom passed away and she was placed in foster care.

Over the years, she would move from foster home to foster home; until she was finally adopted while in the seventh grade. Even at a young age, Sophie never allowed her personal situation to stop her from pursuing her dreams. She enjoyed helping people and always dreamed of one day becoming a nurse.

When she turned 18, she decided to move into her own apartment. During that period she continued working on her education and received her High School Diploma from Miami Jackson Senior High School. She also became the mother of two children.

One day, Sophie observed some young people in the community in orange and khaki uniforms. She walked up to one of them and queried about the program they were working with. They shared with her the opportunities at the Community Action Agency/Greater

Miami Service Corps. She was excited about what she heard and spoke with her case manager at the Children's Home Society. Her case manager provided her a referral and she enrolled in the Community Action Agency/Greater Miami Service Corps (CAA/GMSC).

While enrolled in the program, she completed her education at Nursing Unlimited; receiving certificates as a Home Health Aide and Nursing Assistant. She also received numerous certificates for leadership, attendance and ethics from CAA/ GMSC. As a result of her desire to become a nurse, she was placed on internship at Baptist Health South Florida-South Miami Hospital where she received CPR and Basic Life Support training and work experience in patient care transportation. Sophie recently commenced the employment process with the Hospital. Sophie states, "Without the help from the Corps and the Hospital, I would not be able to attain my dreams."

Sophie's story is a testament to many young people who are just looking for an opportunity to improve their lives.

STATEMENT OF THE HONORABLE RUBÉN HINOJOSA, A REPRESENTATIVE IN CONGRESS FROM THE STATE OF TEXAS

Chairman McDermott, Ranking Member Weller, and Colleagues:

I appreciate the opportunity to submit a statement into the record of your hearing on disconnected and disadvantaged youth. I congratulate the Subcommittee for shining a light on the challenges facing our nation's disconnected and disadvantaged youth. In my position as Chairman of the Higher Education, Lifelong Learning, and Competitiveness Subcommittee of the Education and Labor Committee, the segment of our nation's youth and young adult population that is disconnected from school and work is also of great concern to me.

I am pleased to focus my statement today on youth experiencing homelessness. I congratulate the Chairman for including this population of young people within the scope of your hearing, as they are often overlooked in the national conversation taking place about "disconnected youth." In my opinion, there is no more obvious indicator of disconnection than the lack of a safe place to live.

Our nation's homeless youth are exposed to some of the harshest elements imaginable. They are exposed to the harsh elements of hot and cold weather. They are exposed to the harsh elements of crime, abuse, and exploitation on the street. They are vulnerable to illness and physical trauma. They are deprived of the protective and nurturing elements that come with a home and a strong, supportive family. They are robbed of the supports necessary for productive adulthood.

The National Network for Youth has launched a nation campaign called "A Place to Call Home Campaign." This bold initiative is of critical importance to our nation. It asserts that no young person should have to suffer the fate of being "thrown away" by society—cast out and cast aside without a place to call home. It calls upon all sectors of society to assure permanency—lasting connections to people, places to live and opportunities and supports—for our nation's homeless youth.

Congress must do its part. That is why I have am planning to introduce the Place to Call Home Act, which will ensure that federal policy creates solutions rather than barriers for homeless youth.

I am working with the National Network for Youth to convert the goals of the Campaign into policies that we can enact through federal legislation. We need a comprehensive approach—one that identifies all of our agencies and congressional committees that can help mend the social safety net that is torn for homeless youth. Our bill will improve programs and remove barriers to services for homeless and other disconnected youth in permanent housing, in healthcare, in secondary education, higher education, job training, juvenile justice, and child welfare. It will be called the Place to Call Home Act. I plan to introduce it in July, in time for the commemoration of the 20th Anniversary of the enactment of the Stewart B. McKinney Homeless Assistance Act, Congress's first comprehensive responsive to mass homelessness in our nation.

Among the bill's provisions of interest to the Ways and Means Committee, the Place to Call Home Act will:

- Expand eligibility for federal foster care and adoption assistance to youth through age 20.
- Expand eligibility for the Chafee Foster Care Independence Program, including room and board and education and training vouchers, to youth under the age of 25.
- Increase the mandatory spending levels of the Promoting Safe and Stable Families program to $505 million, and the Chafee program to $200 million.
- Eliminate the income eligibility requirement for federal foster care and adoption assistance.
- Authorize maintenance payments for kinship guardianship assistance to foster care children and youth.
- Prohibit states from enacting policies or practices to place a family within the child welfare system on the sole or primary basis that the family is experiencing homelessness.
- Require states, as a condition of receiving foster care maintenance payments, to have policies and procedures designed to reduce children and youth in their custody from running from their placement.
- Require states, as a condition of receiving foster care maintenance payments, to have policies and procedures designed to ensure that children and youth in their custody are discharged in such a manner that ensures the child or youth is placed in stable and appropriate housing.
- Add homeless youth as a target group for eligibility for the Work Opportunity Tax Credit.
- Permit states to establish a "transitional compliance period" in the Temporary Assistance for Needy Families (TANF) program, whereby income-eligible minor parents who at the time of application are having trouble meeting the complex rules and eligibility conditions related to education and living arrangements (such as school dropouts and homeless youth) of the TANF program are nevertheless allowed to receive assistance on the condition that they comply with the minor parent rules within an established period after enrollment.
- Ensure that states provide alternative living arrangements for minor parents seeking TANF assistance and unable to live at home, and to consult with minor parents about their preferred living arrangement.

- End restrictions on states' ability to count participation in vocational and post-secondary training as a strategy for helping parents, including teen parents, attain access to better jobs. Allow 24 months for such participation.
- Commence the lifetime limit on TANF assistance for teen parents completing their education and training programs when they turn age 20, rather than when they turn age 19, in order to allow these older youth to complete their education/training without the lifetime limit clock ticking.
- Establish sanctions protections procedures that help teen parents understand, avoid, and/or end sanctions.
- Require the identification of the extent and strategies to address the unmet service and living arrangement needs of teen parents in state TANF plans.
- Require the Secretary of Health and Human Services to conduct studies of: teen parents receiving TANF assistance and to identify state and community best practices related to teen parent enrollment and tracking; teen parents not receiving TANF assistance to identify reasons for non-participation and to measure indicators of family well-being; the effects of paternity establishment policies; and, the nature, extent, and impact of sanctions imposed on parents who have not attained age 20.

The very estimate that as many as three million of our nation's youth and young adults do not have a home at some point in time each year is an obvious indication that our social safety net has begun to unravel. We need to mend that net and make it strong again. It will take all of our efforts, including that of the Ways and Means Committee, the Education and Labor Committee, and others.

I urge this Subcommittee to help me move the Place to Call Home Act forward. I hope that members of the Subcommittee will join as co-sponsors of the legislation and advance its income security and family support provisions as part of other legislation you may move through Congress this session.

This hearing is a signal of the 110th Congress's commitment to preventing and ending youth homelessness. I trust it will serve as an opportunity to mobilize the nation to make sure that every young person has a place to call home.

STATEMENT OF NATIONAL COUNCIL FOR ADOPTION

The National Council For Adoption thanks you for the opportunity to submit this written statement for your June 19, 2007 hearing's record, on the subject of disconnected, disadvantaged and homeless youth. The National Council For Adoption (NCFA) applauds the subcommittee's focus on this vulnerable segment of American society. The chairman's and subcommittee's leadership in addressing this sad issue creates an excellent opportunity for both political parties to enact changes that will positively impact millions of Americans.

We at NCFA are aware of the myriad of ways in which early childhood difficulties and a poor environment work to undermine the personal development of hundreds of thousands of children, thus placing them at risk of growing into disconnected and disadvantaged youth. We also know of the role that funding restrictions under Title IV–E of the Social Security Act play in keeping thousands of children in foster care environments, cut off from those caretakers and role models who could provide them with the emotional and personal connections all children and youths need to become well-adjusted, contributing members of society.

In 2005, the most recent year for which statistics are available, a record 24,407 youths aged out of this nation's foster care system, never having experienced the loving, permanent family that is every child's birthright.[18] In 1998, that number was 17,310.[19] This increase is troubling. Not only is emancipation the least desirable outcome for a child entering the child welfare system, as it presupposes that the child will never be matched to a loving, permanent family. It also correlates with increased risk of poverty, homelessness, and incarceration among those exiting the system. Given these correlations, a reversal of the current trend in the numbers emancipated from foster care should be among the goals of any national strategy to reduce the number of disconnected and disadvantaged youths.

Effects of the Child Welfare System on Foster Children

Nearly all studies of children in foster care show that they experience higher than average rates of behavioral, emotional, academic, mental and physical difficulties. This pattern is observed even when children in the child welfare system are compared to demographically similar children who have remained outside the system. For example, the first national overview of the well-being of children in the child welfare system, which drew on data from the 1997 and 1999 National Surveys of America's Families, found that 27 percent of children involved with the child welfare system ages 6 through 17 had "high levels of behavioral and emotional problems." This compares to 7 percent of all children ages 6 through 17, and 13 percent of children in "high-risk parent care." This same overview found that 28 percent of all children involved with the child welfare system had "limiting physical, learning, or mental health conditions," relative to 7 percent of all children and 14 percent of children in "high-risk parent care." [20]

There are two obvious, and by no means mutually exclusive, explanations for this. One is that whatever incident of abuse or neglect precipitates the child's entry into the foster care system negatively affects the development of that child for years afterward. The other is that the individual's stay in the child welfare system, oftentimes moving from one foster home or foster care facility to another with little opportunity to form lasting personal bonds, is detrimental to his or her development. Both these factors are most likely at work in the majority of cases.

A foster child who is ultimately reunited with his or her original and rehabilitated family, or placed in a permanent, loving adoptive family, can be said to have received a second chance at life—complete with the opportunity to heal, which only a loving, stable family can provide. This is not the case for those who age out, however. The difficulties reported above, disproportionately common among all children involved with child welfare services, persist among those who are neither reunited with their original families nor adopted.

Socioeconomic Outcomes for Children Who Age Out of Foster Care

A three-state study of former foster youths, aged 19, who had been emancipated from the system found significant deficits in education, poorer economic situations, and rates of delinquent or violent behavior compared to a nationally representative sample of youths, aged 19, studied as a part of the most recent National Longitudinal Study of Adolescent Health (NLSAH).[21]

Thirty-seven percent of former foster youth had neither a high school diploma nor a GED at the time of the study, compared to 9 percent of the NLSAH sample. Also, 24 percent of former foster youth were enrolled at the time of their study in a two or four year college program, compared to 56 percent of those surveyed in the NLSAH sample.

Ten percent of former foster youths who reported any income from employment in the past year earned $10,000 or more, versus 21 percent of those in the NLSAH sample who reported earning any income from employment in the previous year. Furthermore, former foster youths were significantly more likely than those in the NLSAH sample to report having been unable to pay their rent or mortgage (12 percent vs. 6 percent) and utilities (12 percent vs. 7 percent), as well as to having been evicted (4 percent versus .8 percent) in the previous year. Perhaps most telling is the fact that 31 percent of former foster youths reported not being in school and not having a job at the time of the study, compared to 12 percent of those in the NLSAH sample.

In regard to delinquent and violent behavior, both males and females in the former foster youth sample were significantly more likely to report having pulled a knife or gun on someone (8 percent of males, 4 percent of females) than those in the NLSAH sample (3 percent of males, less than 1 percent of females). In addition, 28 percent of former foster youths reported having been arrested, and 19 percent reported having been incarcerated during the past year. This compares dismally to the 0.6 percent of all Americans aged 18–19 who have *ever* been incarcerated, as estimated by the U.S. Department of Justice.[22] Finally, nearly 50 percent of young women formerly in foster care reported having been pregnant at least once by age 19, compared to 20 percent of young women in the NLSAH sample.

In short, young men and women who age out of the foster care system work less, earn less, are undereducated, and are more likely to engage in criminal and delinquent behavior, relative to their peers. These facts speak to a continuing disconnection from society among youths who age out of the foster care system.

Flexible Funding under Title IV–E of the Social Security Act: Necessary to Successful Reform

Current federal funding legislation prevents the type of reform needed to reduce the number of emancipated youths. Title IV–E federal dollars are, by far, the largest source of child welfare services funding. Sixty-one percent of this funding, however, is earmarked for foster care maintenance services at the expense of other crucial child welfare services that would allow these youths to find the permanency the deserve. States therefore have a clear financial incentive to move children into foster care, and no such incentive to move them out.

As a result, the system falls asleep on the foster care button, and children in need of loving, permanent families are left in a government-financed limbo instead.

With this in mind, National Council For Adoption would like to make the following recommendations to Congress aimed at increasing the flexibility of federal child welfare funds to better provide for America's neglected and abused children.

- Reassess the child welfare priorities and reallocate resources so as to give more emphasis and funding to the crucial, but neglected strategy of adoptive and foster parent recruitment;
- Extend the flexibility of the Promoting Safe & Stable Families (Title IV–B, Subpart 2) funding to Title IV–E funding. This would allow states to decide how best to use federal dollars on community-based family support services, family preservation services, time-limited family reunification services, adoptive and foster parent recruitment and training, post-placement services for adoptive and foster families, and adoption promotion and support services, to meet the needs of children in their care;
- Allow states to project their annual expenditures for foster care maintenance (Title IV–E) over a specified period of time. The difference between the state's projected expenditures and the state's actual expenditures are the savings that states may consolidate with their Title IV–B funding to use for other child welfare purposes such as those stated above. States would continue to be required to match their federal savings at their foster care matching rates to ensure that states continue their share of spending for child welfare purposes; and
- Reauthorize the federal child welfare waivers allowing HHS to grant new waivers to 10 states to allow them to use their Title IV–E dollars for other child welfare services not covered by Title IV–E such as post-permanency services to support and strengthen adoptive families. Successful Title IV–E waiver demonstrations in North Carolina, Indiana, Oregon and other states have proven that programs allowing states to use previously restricted, foster care maintenance dollars to underwrite other child welfare services can and do work.

There are currently 114,000 children in foster care whose parental rights have been terminated. Under the current federal financing system, a substantial portion of these children will simply age out of foster care. However, a shift in child welfare funding away from foster care maintenance and toward the placement of these children with loving, permanent families would work to decrease the numbers aging out of foster care and, by extension, the number of disconnected and disadvantaged youths.

In conclusion, Chairman McDermott and other members of the subcommittee, National Council For Adoption would like to thank you for the opportunity to present this proposal to reduce the numbers of disconnected and disadvantaged youths in the United States. We offer our continued assistance in advancing this crucial mission.

STATEMENT OF NATIONAL HUMAN SERVICES ASSEMBLY

We, members of the National Human Services Assembly and the National Collaboration for Youth, commend this Subcommittee for the work it does on behalf of our nation's most vulnerable, and for seeking solutions by holding this hearing on disconnected youth.

The National Human Services Assembly, founded in 1923, is an association of the nation's leading national non-profits in the fields of community and youth development, and human services. Many of the member organizations are national offices of direct human service providers. Others conduct research or provide technical assistance.

The National Collaboration for Youth (NCY), a 33-year old affinity group, is a coalition of the National Assembly member organizations that have a significant interest in youth development. Members of NCY include 50 national, non-profit, youth development organizations that collectively serve more than 40 million young people; employ over 100,000 paid staff; utilize more than six million volunteers; and have a physical presence in virtually every community in America. Its mission is to provide a united voice as advocates for youth to improve the conditions of young people in America, and to help young people reach their full potential.

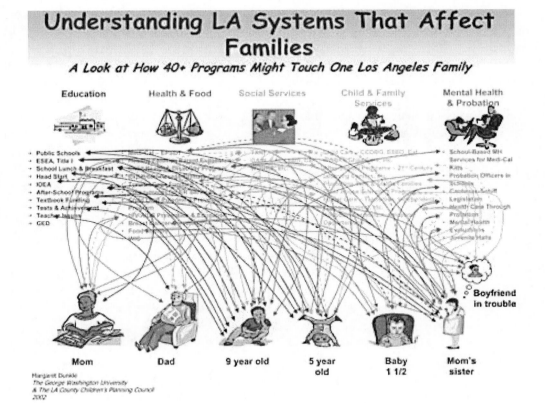

While many NCY members look to serve all young people, many of our organizations have a focus on reaching the most at-risk youth. As research demonstrates, and the graphic [23] included in this testimony indicates, children, youth, their families and caregivers often have multiple needs and are eligible for a variety of services funded through existing federal programs. It is often difficult, however, for service providers, young people and their families to access opportunities provided by different agencies.

For more than 3 years, NCY members have been working on a piece of legislation specifically designed to untangle this mass of services and create a seamless web of support for at-risk young people. The Tom Osborne Federal Youth Coordination Act (PL 109–365, Title VIII), passed at the end of the 109th Congress, but has yet to receive the modest $1 million in funding necessary to begin the work of the Federal Youth Development Council.

The original legislation, H.R. 856, passed the House in November 2005 by anoverwhelming bipartisan vote of 353 to 62, with 163 Republicans supporting it, and no Democrats opposing. In fact, we remain grateful for the support of both the Chair and Ranking Member of this subcommittee for their votes that day.

If implemented, the Federal Youth Development Council would play a vital role in increasing the coordination, cooperation, and efficiency among the twelve federal departments and myriad agencies that provide services to disadvantaged youth.This new interagency Council, and its focus on youth development, will result in considerable benefits for young people by providing youth with a more accessible and comprehensive array of services.

In addition to ensuring improved communication and coordination among federal departments and agencies, the Council will

- Assess the needs of youth and those who work with youth; and the quantity and quality of federal programs offering services, supports and opportunities to help meet these needs.
- Recommend objectives and quantifiable goals for federal youth programs and recommend allocation of resources to support the goals.
- Identify overlap or duplication and recommend ways to better facilitate coordination, improve efficiency and effectiveness of such programs.
- Identify target populations of youth and focus additional resources or develop demonstration projects and model programs to target those groups.
- Conduct research and evaluation, identify and replicate model programs and promising practices, provide technical assistance relating to the needs of youth, and coordinate the collection and dissemination of youth-services related data and research.
- Provide technical assistance to states to support state-funded youth coordinating councils.

Additionally, the Council will report to Congress with an assessment of the needs of youth and those who serve them, including recommendations for better integration and coordination of federal, state, and local policies affecting youth.

The composition of the Council is unique—it acknowledges that government alone cannot provide all the solutions needed. Membership on the Council includes nongovernmental youth development organizations and disadvantaged youth. The importance of this design, inclusive of all representative stakeholders and expressly authorized in the Act, cannot be overstated.

Organizations, such as ours, are essential partners in providing programming to at-risk youth, and can provide valuable insight as to how increased communication and coordination at the federal level will have a direct impact toward improved services at the local and state level. Furthermore, our nation's young people are more than capable of articulating the efficacy of policies and programs. As recipients of services provided by the federal government they are in the ideal position to assist the Council as it moves forward, and by serving on the council, youth members might also gain the propensity toward a future career in public service.

While certainly the Federal Youth Development Council cannot provide all the solutions that this Subcommittee is seeking, we do believe that it is an integral and important part of a system to better serve and engage our nation's future leaders.

Thank you for your time and attention. Any of the undersigned would be happy to answer questions you might have, and assist your Subcommittee as it works towards finding solutions.

Afterschool Alliance, Jodi Grant, Executive Director
Alliance for Children and Families, Peter Goldberg, President and CEO
America's Promise Alliance, Marguerite Kondracke, President and CEO
Big Brothers Big Sisters of America, Judy Vredenburgh, President and CEO
Camp Fire USA, Jill Pasewalk, President and CEO
Child Welfare League of America, Christine James-Brown, President and CEO
Communities In Schools, Inc., Daniel J. Cardinali, President
First Focus, Bruce Lesley, President
Forum for Youth Investment, Karen J. Pittman, Executive Director
MENTOR/National Mentoring Partnership, Gail Manza, Executive Director
National Collaboration for Youth, Irv Katz, President and CEO
National Network for Youth, Victoria Wagner, President and CEO
National Recreation and Park Association, John A. Thorner, Executive Director
The Salvation Army, USA, Commissioner Israel L. Gaither
Search Institute, Peter Benson, President
United Neighborhood Centers of America, Ian Bautista, President
YMCA of the USA, Neil Nicoll, President and CEO
Youth Service America, Steven A. Culbertson, President and CEO

STATEMENT OF THE NATIONAL NETWORK FOR YOUTH

Introduction

The National Network for Youth (NN4Y), founded in 1974, is a national nonprofit membership organization that champions the needs of runaway, homeless, and other disconnected youth through advocacy, innovation and member services. NN4Y is committed to ensuring that opportunities for development and permanency be made available to youth who face greater odds due to abuse, neglect, exploitation, homelessness, lack of resources, community prejudice, differing abilities, barriers to learning, and other life challenges. NN4Y provides its members and the general public education, networking, training, materials and policy advocacy with federal, state, and local lawmakers. NN4Y maintains offices in Seattle, Washington, and in Washington, DC.

Today our membership includes more than 500 community-based, faith-based, and public organizations that provide an array of services to youth and families in the United States and territories as well as some international locations. Many of our members receive funding through the Federal Runaway and Homeless Youth Act. NN4Y's organization members provide the full gamut of preventive, interventive, and developmental supports to youth and families in high-risk situations, including street-based crisis intervention, emergency shelter, transitional and independent housing, permanent housing, individual and family counseling, lifeskills, parenting, and health and wellness education, physical and mental health treatment and care, supplemental educational, workforce development, arts, and recreation services. Collectively, NN4Y member organizations serve over 2.5 million youth annually. In addition, youth, youth workers, and regional and state networks of youth-serving organizations belong to NN4Y.

By any measure of disconnection, runaway and homeless youth certainly fall within its scope. It is this group of young people about which this statement is focused.

Runaway and Homeless Youth Basics

Runaway and homeless youth are the most vulnerable of our nation's "disconnected" youth. The National Network for Youth refers to these two populations collectively as "unaccompanied youth." Like other disconnected youth, unaccompanied youth experience separation from one or more of the key societal institutions of family, school, community, and the workplace. Their disconnection is accentuated by their lack of a permanent place to live, which is not only disruptive in and of itself, but also indicative of the larger socioeconomic instability they are experiencing.

Between one million and three million of our nation's youth experience an unaccompanied situation annually, according to various estimates derived from government studies and data sets. Some of these estimates do not include young adults ages 18 and older within their scope.

Unaccompanied youth become detached from parents, guardians and other caring adults—legally, economically, and emotionally—due to a combination of family and community stressors.

Family Stressors—Many of our nation's unaccompanied youth are compelled to leave their home environments prematurely due to severe family conflict, physical, sexual, or emotional abuse by an adult in the home, parental neglect, parental substance abuse, or parental mental illness. For other youth, the values and traditions with which their families operate prescribe that the young person separate economically from the family unit upon reaching the legal age of majority or after graduation, in some cases regardless of whether the youth is actually prepared for independent adulthood. Others are expelled from the home due to parental inability to accept the sexual orientation, parenting status, mental or addictive disability, or normal adolescent behavior of their child. For still other young people, their families are simply too poor to continue to bear the financial burden of providing for the youth's basic needs. Youth in families that are experiencing homelessness may be separated from the family unit—and become homeless on their own—so that emergency shelter or domestic violence services can be secured for the remaining family members, or to squeeze most of the family into means of habitation that are too small for all of its members.

Community Stressors—State custodial systems—including child welfare, juvenile justice, mental health, addiction treatment, and developmental disabilities—which have responsibility for ensuring the safety and protection of children and youth who are not properly cared for by parents and guardians—are failing in general to accept older youth into their custody due to financial limitations and policy disincentives. Many of the young people who do come in contact with public custodial systems are not adequately prepared for independence and residential stability during their period of custody nor provided an aftercare arrangement to support them after the custodial relationship has ended. Many of these young people have no home environment to which to return. Youth with mental illness, addiction, and other disabilities face discrimination when searching for an independent living arrangement.

Many unaccompanied youth who are psychosocially prepared for independent adulthood are not economically ready for self-sufficiency. Inadequate educational preparation, lack of employment skills, short or non-existent work histories, language barriers, and undocumented immigration status all contribute to the relegation of many youth to unemployment or to low-wage jobs—neither of which generate income sufficient for acquiring affordable housing.

Policy barriers also stand in the way of permanency for unaccompanied youth. In some jurisdictions, youth below the age of majority are prohibited from entering into leases or other contracts on their own behalf. "One strike" laws prohibit individuals with criminal histories from residency in public and assisted housing and prohibit juvenile ex-offenders from returning to their families. And, federal, state, and local public and assisted housing programs rank young people low, if at all, among their priority populations for assistance.

Regardless of the causal factor, unaccompanied youth, when left to fend for themselves without support, experience poor health, educational, and workforce outcomes which imperil their prospects for positive adulthood. This results in their long-term dependency on or involvement in public health, social service, emergency assistance, and corrections systems.

National Network for Youth Public Policy

The National Network for Youth was founded as the National Network of Runaway and Youth Services to be the membership association of community-based organizations that had emerged in the 1970s to focus on the needs of youth in runaway and homeless situations. NN4Y was the architect of the Federal Runaway and Homeless Youth Act (RHYA) and still considers that law today as our primary public policy accomplishment. We remain vigilant over the RHYA and are the leading national organization dedicated to ensuring the Act's continuation (through the reauthorization process) and its annual federal appropriation, $103 million in federal FY 2007. **We urge Congress to increase appropriations for RHYA programs to $140 million annual. We also call on Congress to reauthorize the Runaway and Homeless Youth Act, which is set to expire in 2008.**

Our public policy work reaches far beyond the RHYA, however. We also devote attention to ensuring that runaway, homeless, and other disconnected youth receive full and fair access to child welfare, juvenile justice, physical health, mental health, education, workforce investment, positive youth development, and housing opportunities and supports.

Place to Call Home *and* Place to Call Home Act

In February 2007, the National Network for Youth announced a long-term campaign to end youth homelessness at the NN4Y annual Symposium in Washington, DC in February 2007. *A Place to Call Home: The National Network for Youth's Permanency Plan for Unaccompanied Youth* seeks to build the conditions, structures, and supports to ensure permanency for unaccompanied youth, where permanency is understood to include a lasting connection to loving families, caring adults, and supportive peers; a safe place to live; and the youth's possession of skills and resources necessary for a life of physical and mental wellness, continuous asset-building, dignity, and joy.

The Place to Call Home Campaign will guide NN4Y's strategy and actions for the future. The Campaign involves activities in four work areas: public policy advancement and system change; practice improvement and professional development; public awareness and stakeholder education; and research and knowledge development.

The signature public policy component of the Place to Call Home Campaign is the **Place to Call Home Act,** comprehensive legislation to prevent, respond to, and end runaway and homeless situations among youth. We are currently working with Representative Rube'n Hinojosa (D–TX) to develop the Place to Call Home Act. We expect the bill to be introduced in July.

The **Place to Call Home Act addresses the causal factors of and offers ultimate solutions to unaccompanied situations among youth.** The bill includes provisions in the homeless assistance, housing, child welfare, juvenile justice, public health, education, workforce investment, teen parenting, and immigration areas.

Income Security and Family Support Provisions Within Place to Call HomeAct

The Place to Call Home Act includes many provisions that address income security and family support issues within the jurisdiction of the Ways and Means Committee. **We urge the Subcommittee to act on the recommendations below either by bringing up the Place to Call Home Act for consideration once itis introduced, by bringing up the provisions independently, or by attachingthem to other income security and family support legislative vehicles.**

Child Welfare

State child welfare systems have the purpose of ensuring the safety and protection of children and youth who are not properly cared for by parents and guardians.We must strengthen these systems so that they provide better access by, and supports for longer periods, to homeless and other disconnected youth.

We urge Congress to **expand eligibility for federal foster care and adoption assistance to youth through age 20.** Terminating such assistance at age 18 is not in keeping with what we now know about adolescent brain development, which is that the brain does not mature to its adult capacity until the mid-20s. So essentially, by terminating assistance at age 18, we are abandoning youth at a time when they are still in great need of supervision and support.

Concurrent to an extension of eligibility for foster care to youth through age 20, we recommend Congress to **extend eligibility for the Chafee Foster Care Independence Program to youth under age 25.** Included in this age extension should be eligibility for room and board and for education and training vouchers.We recommend at **least a $200 million annual spending level ($60 millionabove current law) for the Chafee program.** We also recommend the addition of a requirement to evaluate use of Chafee room and board services and how they improve housing outcomes for youth.

We recommend that Congress **authorize maintenance payments for kinshipguardianship assistance to foster care children.** Guardianship is a particularlyattractive permanency option for older youth in care. Uniform federal policy and funding to states is needed in this important area.

We recommend that Congress **require states, as a condition of receiving foster care maintenance payments, to have established and functioning policies and procedures designed to reduce the numbers of children and youthin their custody from running from their placement.** Analysis of state datauncovers that 21 percent of foster youth run from placement. This places a burden on both the child welfare and youth homeless assistance systems and may lead to disciplinary action against the youth.

We urge Congress to **require states, as a condition of receiving foster caremaintenance payments, to have established and functioning policies and procedures designed to ensure that children and youth in their custody are discharged in such a manner that ensures the child or youth is placed instable and appropriate housing.** We must block the path from child welfare to homelessness for far too many of our nation's youth exiting care.

We recommend that Congress **increase from $305 million to $505 million the mandatory funding level for the Promoting Safe and Stable Families Program.** This is a vital account that states use to establish prevention and early intervention supports for families at risk of child removal from the home, and support to homeless families. Our nation's children and youth deserve better than to have to scrape annually for discretionary dollars for the Promoting Safe and Stable Families Program, especially when Congress has already designated a portion of PSSF funds as mandatory spending.

We recommend that Congress **eliminate the income eligibility requirement for access to foster care and adoption assistance.** Income should not be a determining factor in a young person and their family's ability to access federal child welfare assistance. Child abuse and neglect are by no means limited to low-income families.

We urge Congress to **prohibit states from enacting policies or practices to place a family within the child welfare system on the sole or primary basis that the family is experiencing homelessness.** Lingering state practices in this regard continue to lead children and youth being separated from their family when the core issue is the family's inability to obtain a safe living arrangement for all its members. There are more pro-social responses to the housing crisis among families than to separate children from their caregivers.

Finally, we request Congress to **authorize the Government Accountability Office to conduct a study on state policies and practices with regard to access of unaccompanied youth to child protective services and to foster care and adoption assistance.** We need to understand better why when homeless youth service providers turn to the child welfare system for assistance in caring for a homeless youth, the door is too often closed.

Temporary Assistance for Needy Families—Teen Parent Protections

The Temporary Assistance for Needy Families (TANF) program is an essential source of income and supportive services for families in poverty, including young families. Teen parents face special barriers to accessing and utilizing the TANF program—barriers that must be dismantled.

We urge Congress to permit states to establish a "transitional compliance period," **whereby income-eligible minor parents** who at the time of application are having trouble meeting the complex rules and eligibility conditions related to education and living arrangements (such as school dropouts and homeless youth) of the TANF program are nevertheless **allowed to receive assistance on the condition that they comply with the minor parent rules within an established period after enrollment.**

We recommend Congress to **ensure that states consult with minor parents about their preferred living arrangement. We urge Congress to ensure the appropriate provision of alternative living arrangements for minor parents unable to live at home.** This should include identifying transitional living youth projects for older homeless youth funded through the Runaway and Homeless Youth Act (RHYA) as a type of alternative living arrangement.

We recommend that Congress **end restrictions on states' ability to count participation in vocational and post-secondary training as a strategy for helping parents, including teen parents, attain access to better jobs.** Twenty-four months should be allowed for such participation.

While we oppose the lifetime ban on TANF assistance, given that it is part of current law, we at least ask Congress to **commence the lifetime limit on TANF assistance for teen parents completing their education and training programs when they turn age 20, rather than when they turn age 19,** in order to allow these older youth to complete their education/training without the lifetime limit clock ticking.

We recommend that Congress **establish procedures that help teen parents understand, avoid, and/or end sanctions.**

States should be required to identify the extent of and strategies to address the unmet service and living arrangement needs of teen parents in state TANF plans.

And the **Secretary of Health and Human Services should be required to conduct studies of: teen parents** receiving TANF assistance and to identify state and community best practices related to teen parent enrollment and tracking; teen parents not receiving TANF assistance to identify reasons for non-participation and to measure indicators of family well-being; the effects of paternity establishment policies; and, the nature, extent, and impact of sanctions imposed on parents who have not attained age 20.

Work Opportunity Tax Credit

Congress should **add homeless youth as a target group for eligibility for the Work Opportunity Tax Credit.** Currently, youth living in Enterprise Communities and Empowerment Zones are eligible for the WOTC. This category needs to be expanded. "Homeless youth" for purposes of WOTC should be defined as an individual not less than age 16 and not more than age 24 and otherwise having the same meaning as "homeless child and youth" under federal education law.

Conclusion

Thank you for considering our views and recommendations. We hope the Committee on Ways and Means and the Subcommittee on Income Security and Family Support will join us in our campaign to ensure a Place to Call Home for all our nation's youth.

STATEMENT OF NATIONAL YOUTHBUILD COALITION

Introduction

Thank you, Mr. Chairman and members of the Committee for allowing me to submit this statement for the record. Thank you for holding this important hearing.

I belong to various organizations and task forces that have developed and will submit broad sets of policy and funding recommendations to address the range of issues affecting disconnected youth. Therefore, knowing that you will receive such recommendations from elsewhere, in this testimony submitted as chairperson of theNational YouthBuild Coalition, I will focus simply on the powerful potential role of the federal YouthBuild program as part of the solution to the crisis of disconnected youth.

We recommend that Congress seize the leadership role in taking YouthBuild to full scale: Bring it to every community that is calling for it, open the doors to all the young people who are knocking, eliminate waiting lists of both youth and ofcommunity-based organizations eager to implement YouthBuild in America's poorest communities. Within five years YouthBuild could grow from 8,000 youth per year in 226 communities to 50,000 youth in

850 communities, producing beautiful housing and proud young leaders, eager to make a difference, rebuilding their own lives and their own communities.

YouthBuild Description and History

YouthBuild is a national youth and community development program that simultaneously addresses the key issues facing low-income communities: housing, education, employment, crime prevention, community service, and leadership development.

In YouthBuild programs, sponsored primarily by community-based non-profit organizations, low-income disconnected young people ages 16–24 enroll full-time for 6 to 24 months. They work toward their GEDs or high school diplomas while learning construction job skills by building affordable housing for homeless and low-income people. A strong emphasis is placed on leadership development, personal counseling, positive values, community service, and personal responsibility. The members belong to a positive mini-community in which students and teachers are committed to each other's success. They take pride in the housing they produce.

YouthBuild students go through a process of personal transformation that has been documented by independent researchers to result in a radical change in the students' attitudes and future aspirations, coupled with acquisition of skills that enable them to move on to careers and post-secondary education. We also see graduates getting married, buying homes, and caring well for their children.

YouthBuild began in Chairman Rangel's East Harlem district in 1978. It was replicated in New York City and across the country before being authorized as a federal program in 1992 under the jurisdiction of the US Department of Housing and Urban Development. Since 1994, when HUD YouthBuild funds first reached communities, more than 68,000 YouthBuild students have produced 16,000 units of low-income housing. Today, there are 226 YouthBuild programs in 42 states, engaging approximately 8,000 young adults each year in America's poorest urban, rural and tribal communities.

In September, 2006, at the recommendation of the Bush Administration, YouthBuild was transferred by unanimous consent in Congress to the jurisdiction of the US Department of Labor. The National YouthBuild Coalition of nearly 1,000 organizations cooperated with this move in the hope that it was the precursor to a major expansion that would use YouthBuild's proven approach to reconnect more of America's lost youth.

Need

I don't need to belabor just how dire is the need to reconnect America's under-educated and unemployed youth. A few statistics released recently at a national summit on dropouts tell the grim story:

- More than one million American high school students leave high school every year without a diploma.

- Nearly half of all African Americans, Hispanics and Native Americans fail to graduate with their high school classes.
- 1.7 million low income youth are both out of school and out of work, likely to be the parents of the next generation raised in poverty and despair.
- Another 225,000 are in prison.

A major federal intervention is desperately needed. Every effective programshould be immediately taken to full scale; and every community should be mobilized to address this problem in a cohesive fashion. The problem is finite and can be solved. YouthBuild is ready with a track record and the infrastructure to grow quickly as part of a national mobilization.

YouthBuild Demographics and Outcomes

YouthBuild students are the very disconnected and disadvantaged youth who are the focus of this hearing. They are detached from school and work. 91 percent are high school dropouts; 72 percent are young men; 48% are African American, 22% Latino, 22% White, 3% Native American; 33% have been adjudicated, 10% in foster care; 30% have been homeless. They are both urban and rural. Twenty-six percentare already young parents themselves.

YouthBuild programs have demonstrated the principles and practices that work to reconnect most youth and to create pathways to higher education, careers, and citizenship. What we have learned is that every disconnected youth is yearning to become somebody that other people will welcome and respect, and if given the right conditions they will transform their own lives and play a constructive role in society.

The 226 existing YouthBuild programs, all based on the same philosophy and model, have been highly successful. Although 91 percent of the students were previously high school dropouts and all of them are poor, nearly 70 percent complete the program, and 71 percent of graduates go on to college or jobs earning an average of nearly $9 an hour. The recidivism rate for graduates previously convicted of a felony is less than 24 percent, compared to 67 percent nationwide.

Imagine the social and economic impact across the country of simultaneously helping 70 percent of high school dropouts complete their GED or diploma while drastically reducing the recidivism rate of youthful offenders to just 24 percent!

Demand

The challenge for the YouthBuild network is quite simply this: We have only enough resources to serve a fraction of the young people who seek a second chance, in this nation that believes in second chances. Each year YouthBuild programs turn away 14,000 youth for lack of funds: 800 in North Philadelphia, 500 in Harlem, 400 in Newark, 800 in Madison, and so on. Furthermore, over 1,000 community-based organizations have applied to HUD since 1994 to bring this proven and inspiringprogram to their neighborhoods. Over 600 traveled to DC for DOL's first YouthBuild bidders' conference this month. DOL only has funds for 100.

Recommendation

Congress should establish a five-year plan in partnership with DOL andYouthBuild USA, to expand the federal YouthBuild program to full scale. This successful network could grow through a planned five year growth process from 8,000 low-income, disadvantaged youth in 226 communities to 50,000 youth in 850 communities.

The federal YouthBuild program has developed a public/private partnership that has coupled the long-term commitment, knowledge, and leveraged resources of YouthBuild USA with the know-how and capacity of several federal agencies. The federal government has built the infrastructure with an investment of $650M; YouthBuild USA has brought $114M into the mix; and local YouthBuild programs have raised over $1B of matching funds. Together we have the knowledge, infrastructure, commitment, capacity, and demand to do this within five years. It would take a steady annual increase to an appropriation of $1B in the fifth year, at an annual cost per full-time youth participant of $20,000. This includes a $5,000 stipend for each youth to compensate for their hard work and service producing affordable housing.

Part of this growth plan should include a federal incentive for states to join in, by offering a 50% federal match for every adjudicated young person funded by any state government to participate in YouthBuild programs as a diversion or re-entry program. In Wisconsin, California, and Newark state governments have already noticed YouthBuild and begun to invest in it as a re-entry program. States could save millions by lowering the recidivism rates through YouthBuild.

How YouthBuild Works: The Formula to "Flip the Script"

YouthBuild is not the only program that works. It is, however, the only national program that reaches a highly disadvantaged population with a comprehensive community-based program that puts equal emphasis and commits equal time to education and job training, that offers job training in the form of creating a profoundly valuable community service, and that is committed to teaching leadership skills and values through engaging the young people in helping to develop the policies that affect them. There are precious few pipelines for low-income youth to become good citizens, to take on active leadership roles in their communities.

The formula to do what the young people call "flip the script" of their lives, taking them from a negative direction to a positive direction, includes all of the following elements:

- a way for young adults to resume their **education** toward a high school diploma and college
- **skills training** toward decent-paying jobs
- an **immediate visible role contributing to the community** that earns respect from family and neighbors
- **stipends or wages** to support themselves and their children
- **personal counseling** from admired, deeply-caring role models who are committed to these young adults and who also firmly challenge self-defeating attitudes from a basis of love

- **positive peer support with a clear value system** strong enough to compete with the streets
- **a mini-community that offers a sense of belonging** and a foundation young people can believe in—with everyone committed to everyone else's success
- **a role in governance** and the ability to participate in important decisionsabout staff and policies in their own programs
- **leadership development and civic education** offering a vision of the important role young adults can play in their neighborhoods and society to change conditions that have harmed them and the people they love—and the skills to do so
- **assistance in managing money and building assets** such as individual development accounts, scholarships, financial literacy training, and budgeting
- **placements with colleges and employers**
- **support after graduation** with continued counseling and the opportunity to belong to a supportive community.

This is the YouthBuild model. If caring, competent adults offer those elements in an environment of profound respect for the intelligence and value of the young people, you will see dramatic changes. Young people will define new goals for their lives and will gain the skills and confidence to take real steps toward achieving their goals.

The Voice and Experience of Disconnected Youth, One Story Representing Hundreds of Thousands

Listen to what Mike Dean has to say:

When he was just 11 years old in Columbus, Ohio, Mike cut hair to put food on the table for his four younger siblings—often just Ramen noodles. Their mom was hooked on drugs and alcohol and was gone frequently for a day or two at a time. Mike had to get his sisters and brothers ready for school. He often was embarrassed at school because roaches would crawl out of his clothes or notebooks. An average student, he lettered in basketball, a sport that kept him in high school.

At age 16, he fled his home life and spent the next few years crashing at different friends' homes. He often skipped school for weeks at a time. He wasn't a gangster or a bad kid—just one without direction. At age 17, he got his 15-year-old girlfriend pregnant. When the basketball coach found out Mike was a runaway, he was cut from the team. Behind academically, Mike dropped out of school completely and hung out with the wrong crowd, drinking and getting high. He tried working at McDonalds but saw how much his drug dealer friends were earning so he joined their ranks. He was arrested and went to the workhouse for a few weeks. But when he got out, he returned to his old ways again.

Mike's girlfriend saw an ad for YouthBuild, and they both applied. In YouthBuild, Mike suddenly found people who showed him genuine love, a new experience for him. "Eventually, YouthBuild became my family, and I let a lot of my old friends go," he says. "These people really gave me a chance, despite all that had transpired. There were people who actually showed they cared."

Today, Mike is 30. He earned his GED through YouthBuild. He earned more than $10 an hour at union construction jobs. Today, he is a program manager/construction manager at YouthBuild, helping other young people who were once like him. He is vice president of the national YouthBuild alumni council. He's starting his own construction business.

He married his girlfriend, and they have three children with a fourth on the way. He owns his own home. He is an ordained minister and vice president of a nonprofit that mentors young men. He would like to start his own nonprofit to help juveniles successfully return to their neighborhoods after they have been in juvenile detention facilities. He wants to create the nonprofit to honor the memory of his younger brother who was shot to death after he left a juvenile detention facility.

In your own states, your own communities, you have young men—and women— who were just like Mike Dean. Adrift. Floundering. Heading downhill fast. You can play a major role in determining whether they turn their lives around.

In Closing

Let me just say again: We know what works. We simply need the resources to expand so we can engage tens of thousands more young people in programs such as YouthBuild. All the programs with waiting lists should be supported to open their doors to all the youth who are knocking. They are leaving the public schools and lining up outside the doors of programs that offer them a sense of belonging to a caring community, skills for jobs and college, and clear pathways to a hope-filled and meaningful future.

I am convinced that if we do this, we can solve one of America's most pressing domestic policy challenges. In fact, if we build up a head of steam so that young people all across the country see the doors opening for their friends and former street buddies, I believe they would all want to follow their friends, creating a great movement in the right direction. We have seen this often: for example, after Trevor Daniels joined Youth Action YouthBuild in East Harlem, and found a pathway to college, the next year **sixteen of his friends from his housing project followed right behind him,** and joined YouthBuild, with new hope in their hearts.

Thank you very much for this opportunity to submit this statement to this subcommittee.

Dorothy Stoneman
Chairperson of the National YouthBuild Coalition

End Notes

[1] V.J. Hotz et al., "The Impacts of Teenage Childbearing on the Mothers and the Consequences of those Impacts for Government," in R. Maynard (Ed.), *Kids Having Kids* (Washington, DC: Urban Institute Press, 1997), pp. 55–94.

[2] J. Jacobson and R. Maynard, *Unwed Mothers and Long-Term Dependency* (Washington, DC: American Enterprise Institute for Public Policy Research).

[3] Maynard, R.A., (Ed.). (1996). *Kids Having Kids: A Robin Hood Foundation Special Report on the Costs of Adolescent Childbearing*, New York: Robin Hood Foundation.

[4] R.M. George and B.J. Lee, "Abuse and Neglect of the Children," in R. Maynard (Ed.), *Kids Having Kids* (Washington, DC: Urban Institute Press, 1997), pp. 205–230.

[5] Annie E. Casey Foundation, *Kids Count Special Report: When Teens Have Sex: Issues and Trends* (Baltimore, MD: Annie E. Casey Foundation, 1998).

[6] This testimony draws on my own and other researchers' published and unpublished work. The views expressed are mine alone and do not necessarily reflect the views of any organization with which I am affiliated.

[7] For a recent comprehensive overview of youth homelessness, see Paul Toro, Amy Dworsky, and Patrick Fowler, "Homeless Youth in the United States: Recent Research Findings and Intervention Approaches." Paper presented at the Second National Homelessness Research Symposium, March 1–2, Washington, D.C., sponsored by Department of Health and Human Services (DHHS) and the Department of Housing and Urban Development (DHUD).

[8] A slightly higher proportion of youth who were in foster care at age 16 "exit" foster care by running away (21 percent) as leave care because they reach age 18 (18 percent). Another group comprising 18 percent of those in care at age 16 leave under "other" circumstances, including transfer to juvenile corrections and other institutions (Orlebeke, 2007). These approximately 50,000 additional youth once in the custody of foster care systems are at very high risk of homelessness; they probably also overlap to an unknown degree with the 200,000 leaving correctional facilities each year.

[9] Johnson, W., Packer, A., Workforce 2000: Work and Workers for the 21st Century, Hudson Institute, U.S. Department of Labor, 1987.

[10] National Center on Education and the Economy, America's Choice: High Skills or Low Wages!, 1990, pg. 44.

[11] Sum, A., Khatiwada, I., McLaughlin, J., Palma, S. The Paradox of Rising Teen Joblessness in an Expanding Labor Market: The Absence of Teen Employment Growth in the National Jobs Recovery of 2003–2004, Center For Labor Market Studies, Northeastern University, January 2005.

[12] "The Summer Job Market for U.S. Teens 2000–2003 and the Projected Job Outlook for the Summer of 2004," power point presentation by Andrew Sum, Ph.D. & Iswar Khatiwada, Center for Labor Market Studies, Northeastern University, to the U.S. Conference of Mayors, June 2004.

[13] All references in this document to census statistics not otherwise cited are from extracts from the 2000 PUMS 5% file from the Decennial Census, U.S. Bureau of the Census.

[14] CLASP conducted a survey of 196 dropouts enrolled in the Youth Opportunity Program in 13 cities. The report is forthcoming in the summer 2000.

[15] Estimate provided by David Brown, National Youth Employment Coalition.

[16] Sum, A., Khatiwada, I., Pond, N., & Trub'skyy, M., with Fogg, N., Palma, S. (2003, January). *Left Behind in the Labor Market: Labor Market Problems of the Nation's Out-of-School, Young Adult Populations*. Boston, MA: Center for Labor Market Studies, Northeastern University, p. 7.

[17] James, Donna Walker (ed) (1997). *Some Things DO Make a Difference for Youth: A Compendium of Evaluations of Youth Programs and Practices*. Washington, DC: American Youth Policy Forum.

[18] *The AFCARS Report (#13): Preliminary Estimates for FY 2005*, Administration of Children and Families, Department of Health and Human Services. December, 2006. Available online at http://www.acf.hhs.gov/programs/cb/statslresearch/afcars/tar/report13.htm

[19] *The AFCARS Report (#12): Final Estimates for FY 1998 through FY 2005*, Administration of Children and Families, Department of Health and Human Services. October, 2006. Available online at http://www.acf.hhs.gov/programs/cb/statslresearch/afcars/tar/report12.htm

[20] Kortenkamp, J. & Ehrle, J. *The Well-Being of Children Involved with the Child Welfare System,* January 2002, The Urban Institute. Available online at http://www.urban.org/ UploadedPDF/310413lanflb43.pdf

[21] Courtney, Mark E. et al, *Midwest Evaluation of the Adult Functioning of Former Foster Youth: Outcomes at Age 19,* May 2005, Chapin Hall. Available online at http:// www.chapinhall.org/articlelabstract.aspx?ar=1355

[22] Bonczar, Thomas P., *Prevalence of Imprisonment in the U.S. Population: 1974–2001*, August, 2003, Bureau of Justice Statistics, U.S. Department of Justice. Available online at http:// www.ojp.usdoj.gov/bjs/pub/pdf/piusp01.pdf

[23] Dunkle, M. (2002). *Understanding LA Systems That Affect Families: A Look at How 40+ Programs Might Touch One Los Angeles Family*. The George Washington University and The LA County Children's Planning Council.

In: Vulnerable and Disconnected Youth: Background...   ISBN: 978-1-60741-488-9
Editor: Dierk Neumann   © 2010 Nova Science Publishers, Inc.

Chapter 2

DISCONNECTED YOUTH: FEDERAL ACTION COULD ADDRESS SOME OF THE CHALLENGES FACED BY LOCAL PROGRAMS THAT RECONNECT YOUTH TO EDUCATION AND EMPLOYMENT

United States Government Accountability Office

WHY GAO DID THIS STUDY

While most young people successfully transition to adulthood, a significant number of youth are disconnected from school and employment. These youth are more likely than others to engage in crime, become incarcerated, and rely on public systems of support. Several federal agencies oversee a number of programs and grants that assist local programs in serving this population at the local level. GAO reviewed the following: (1) characteristics of locally operated programs that serve disconnected youth, (2) the key elements of locally operated programs to which directors attribute their success in reconnecting youth to education and employment, and (3) challenges involved in operating these programs and how federal agencies are helping to address these challenges. GAO interviewed officials from four federal agencies, experts, and directors of 39 local programs identified by agencies and experts as helping youth meet educational and employment goals.

WHAT GAO RECOMMENDS

GAO recommends that the Department of Labor (Labor) work with states and workforce investment boards to better ensure they have the information and guidance needed to develop and implement contracts that allow local programs to serve youth who are in need of more assistance than others while still achieving performance goals. Labor agreed with our recommendation and identified several steps it plans to take to implement it.

WHAT GAO FOUND

The 39 local programs GAO reviewed differed in their funding sources and program structure, yet shared some characteristics, such as years of experience serving youth. These programs received funding from multiple sources: federal, state, local, and private, although most relied on some federal funds. They were structured differently—for example, some were community-based organizations that provided services on a daily basis, some were charter schools, and some offered residential living. Most of the programs were created to address local concerns such as youth homelessness or dropout rates, and many had at least 10 years of experience serving youth.

Program directors GAO interviewed attributed their success in reconnecting youth to education and employment to several key elements of their programs. These included effective staff and leadership; a holistic approach to serving youth that addresses the youth's multiple needs; specific program design components, such as experiential learning opportunities and self-paced curricula; and a focus on empowering youth.

Many of the 39 local program directors reported common challenges in operating their programs—the complex circumstances of their participants, service gaps, funding constraints, and management of federal grants—that increased federal coordination efforts under way may help address. Most of the 15 directors that relied on Labor's Workforce Investment Act Youth funds reported that meeting performance goals within 1-year time frames that workforce investment boards often write into contracts hinders their ability to serve youth with great challenges, who may need more time to obtain skills. Labor officials reported that they intend for workforce investment boards to develop longer-term contracts to help programs serve hard-to-employ youth. Labor has provided limited technical assistance and is considering issuing guidance on this issue, but has not established a time frame to do so. Federal agencies have recently intensified their coordination efforts, which may help local programs faced with challenges managing across multiple federal grants.

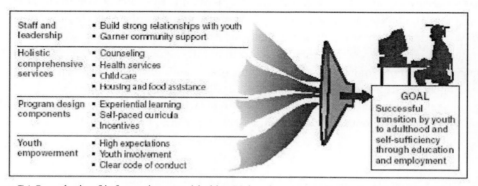

Source: GAO analysis of information provided by 39 local program directors; Images (Art Explosion).

Key Elements of Local Programs Cited by 39 Program Directors in Reconnecting Youth to Education and Employment

ABBREVIATIONS

CCJJDP	Coordinating Council on Juvenile Justice and Delinquency Prevention
GED	General Educational Development
HHS	Department of Health and Human Services
WIA	Workforce Investment Act
YO	Youth Opportunity

February 28, 2008
The Honorable George Miller
Chairman
Committee on Education and Labor

Dear Mr. Chairman:

A significant number of American youth are not in school and not working. Some of these young people may have become disconnected from education and employment through incarceration, aging out of foster care, dropping out of high school, or homelessness. As a result, these "disconnected" youth may face difficulties in successfully transitioning to adulthood and self-sufficiency.[1] Not only does this lead to negative outcomes for the youth themselves, but for communities and the nation as a whole. Disconnected youth are more likely than other youth to engage in criminal activities, become incarcerated, and rely on public systems of support.

Federal, state, and local governments as well as private entities are involved in helping to put these youth on a path to self-sufficiency through education and/or employment. Several federal departments oversee a number of federal grant programs in the areas of education, employment, foster care, juvenile justice, and homelessness that can serve this population at the local level. State and local governments assist in the delivery of services to youth at this local entry point. In addition, federal, state, and local collaborations exist that bring together various agencies and programs with the aim of better coordinating services to help these youth.

To respond to your interest in the federal role in improving outcomes for disconnected youth, we looked at the following questions: (1) What are some characteristics of locally operated programs that serve disconnected youth? (2) What are the key elements of locally operated programs to which program directors attribute their success in reconnecting youth to education and employment? (3) What challenges are involved in implementing and operating these programs and how are federal agencies helping to address these challenges?

To conduct this work, we asked federal agency officials and 11 experts on youth issues to identify local entities that are operating programs or initiatives with federal or other funding that have been successful in helping disconnected youth reach educational or employment goals. We asked the experts and agency officials, on the basis of their experience and expertise, to identify local programs that could serve as examples or models for expansion or replication; rigorous program evaluations were generally not available. The experts were selected for their understanding of and range of perspectives on youth issues as well as their knowledge of efforts under way at the local level. We identified and interviewed officials from four primary federal agencies that support programs working with this population: the Departments of Labor, Health and Human Services (HHS), Justice, and Education. We selected these agencies based on their legislative mandate to administer relevant federal programs, our previous work, reports from the Congressional Research Service and the White House Task Force for Disadvantaged Youth,[2] and discussions with federal officials. We reviewed relevant appropriation and other laws, regulations, and documents pertaining to the key federal programs and coordinating bodies involved with assisting disconnected youth, and synthesized information from interviews with appropriate federal officials.

Out of 100 programs that were identified, we interviewed 39 directors of locally operated programs using a standard set of questions. We selected programs that were geographically diverse, and that represented both urban and rural locations. We also selected programs with a range of approaches to working with disconnected youth, such as employment skills training programs, alternative education programs, transitional living programs, and programs that targeted different subpopulations of disconnected youth in 16 states and the District of Columbia. See appendix I for a complete list of the 39 programs. We conducted in-person interviews with directors and youth participants in 19 of these programs, and completed the remaining interviews with directors by phone. See appendix II for more information on our scope and methodology. We conducted this performance audit from May 2007 to February 2008 in accordance with generally accepted government auditing standards. Those standards require that we plan and perform the audit to obtain sufficient, appropriate evidence to provide a reasonable basis for our findings and conclusions based on our audit objectives. We believe that the evidence obtained provides a reasonable basis for our findings and conclusions based on our audit objectives.

RESULTS IN BRIEF

The 39 local programs we reviewed received funding from a range of government and private sources, and differed in their program structure, yet shared some characteristics. These youth-serving programs received funding from federal, state, local, and private sources. Nearly half of the 39 local youth-serving programs we reviewed received a combination of funding from these sources, and all but 6 of the programs received some federal funding. Some federal funding sources required programs to follow a specific model or offer a standard set of services, while others allowed programs to use funding more flexibly. The programs also varied in their program structure. For example, several programs were community organizations that provided specific training for the youth at their organization during the day. Some were established as charter schools, and others were residential programs, most often providing transitional housing to runaway and homeless youth. Some of the programs were a combination of these different approaches. Within these different program structures, select programs also targeted their efforts to specific youth subpopulations, such as court-involved youth. Yet despite differences, these programs shared some specific characteristics. For example, all of the programs we reviewed were created to meet the needs of local youth such as addressing youth homelessness and high school dropout rates. Most of the programs had also operated for several years and provided ancillary services, such as counseling, in addition to employment and education assistance, to address the multiple needs of their youth participants.

While varying types of local programs serve disconnected youth, program directors we interviewed reported similar elements of their programs that are key in reconnecting youth to education and employment, including effective staff and leadership, a holistic approach to serving youth that addresses their multiple needs, specific program design components, and a focus on empowering youth. Nearly all 39 program directors cited effective staff as a key element in building supportive relationships with the youth in their programs. Many of the youth we spoke with told us that they continued to participate in their programs because the staff helped establish goals and provided a positive and supportive environment. In addition, program leadership also played a key role in maintaining successful programs and garnering community support. To address the multiple needs of the youth participants, to the extent possible, many programs approached the youth's needs holistically, incorporating support services, such as counseling, either on-site or in collaboration with other service providers in the community. Many program directors also attributed their success in working with youth to specific program design components, such as experiential learning, which helps to engage and retain youth by emphasizing concepts taught in the classroom with hands-on learning opportunities through community service projects and on-site training. Finally, program directors told us that their staff empowers youth participants by setting high expectations, establishing a clear code of conduct, and strengthening their leadership skills through various program operation activities, such as outreach and recruitment efforts.

Many program directors also reported common challenges in implementing and operating their programs, specifically addressing the complex circumstances of their programs' participants, gaps in services at the community level, constraints on funding, and managing federal grants. The complex issues experienced by the youth—such as mental health issues and low academic skills—were frequently cited by program directors as challenges they face in reconnecting youth to educational and employment goals. For example, one program director told us the youth in her program on average test at or below a sixth grade level in reading and math, a fact that affects the program's ability to help these youth achieve educational and employment outcomes. Program directors we interviewed, regardless of their geographic location, cited service gaps for disconnected youth in their communities, particularly in the areas of mental health treatment, housing, and transportation. Local programs we reviewed also reported that funding constraints from all sources as well as unpredictable funding levels have created significant challenges for them to keep pace with demand for services and to plan for the future. Funding for many of the key federal programs we reviewed that serve disconnected youth has remained the same or declined since 2000. In addition, many of the directors of programs receiving Workforce Investment Act (WIA) Youth funding—one of the larger federal funding sources that can be used to assist disconnected youth—noted that meeting certain youth performance goals within contract time frames discouraged them from serving youth who may need additional time and assistance to achieve specified outcomes. Labor officials acknowledged that the workforce investment boards—entities that contract with and oversee local programs—often issue 1-year contracts that may unintentionally discourage programs from working with lower-skilled youth to meet performance goals. Labor officials noted that in most cases there is no requirement to achieve performance goals within 1 year, and Labor's intent is for workforce investment boards to develop longer-term contracts to help programs serve hard-to-employ youth. Labor has provided limited technical assistance and is considering issuing guidance on this issue, but has not established a time frame to do so. Labor officials also said that anticipated changes in federal performance goals may help to address this issue by better capturing improvements made by youth at all skill levels. Last, many local programs faced challenges managing multiple federal funding sources, such as working across varying eligibility and reporting requirements. In recent years, at the federal level, existing and new federal initiatives have intensified efforts to coordinate federal youth programs and provide assistance to state and local youth-serving programs, which may help to address some of the challenges faced by local programs.

This report contains a recommendation to Labor to improve implementation of the WIA Youth program by working with workforce investment boards to better ensure they have the information and guidance needed to develop and implement contracts that allow local programs to serve youth who are in need of more assistance than others while still achieving performance goals. We provided a draft of this report to Labor, HHS, Justice, and Education for review and comment. Labor agreed with our recommendation, indicating it will work with workforce investment boards to identify constraints, issue guidance in the spring of 2008 for the workforce investment system on developing contracts with local service providers, and provide technical assistance to support the implementation of the guidance. HHS provided information about a Web site available to communities that we added to the report. Labor, HHS, and Education provided technical comments that we incorporated where appropriate. Justice had no comments on the draft report.

BACKGROUND

While most youth successfully transition to adulthood, many youth become disconnected from school and work, or social supports,[3] and experience challenges in making this transition. Some of these youth are more likely than others to remain low-income, to lose jobs during economic downturns, and to engage in criminal activities, antisocial behavior, and teenage parenting. No single estimate exists on the total number of disconnected youth because of varying definitions, distinct time periods from which data are drawn, and the use of different data sources. However, researchers' estimates of the number of disconnected youth range from 2.3 million to 5.2 million.[4]

Disconnected youth encompass a broad population that may include high school dropouts, homeless and runaway youth, incarcerated youth, or youth who have aged out of the foster care system. Youth of different races and ethnicities are represented among this youth population. However, research studies show that African-American males constitute a disproportionate share of the population. For example, many young African-American males experience high incarceration rates, and African-Americans are generally overrepresented in the child welfare and juvenile justice systems.[5] Many young women also become disconnected to assume parenting responsibilities. In addition, the risk of disconnection is particularly high among youth with emotional disturbances and learning disabilities, many of whom have not mastered basic literacy skills. These youth have higher dropout rates and poorer employment outcomes than other youth.

To assist youth transitioning to adulthood, direct services are provided at the local level with the support of federal, state, local, and private funding sources. A range of local entities, such as community-based organizations and charter schools, in urban and rural communities nationwide, provide services to reconnect these youth to education and employment.

Role of Federal Agencies in Assisting Local Efforts

Multiple federal agencies play a role in providing funding and assistance to local programs that serve disconnected youth. The White House Task Force for Disadvantaged Youth identified 12 federal agencies that fund over 300 programs that assist local communities in serving disadvantaged youth in some capacity. However, four agencies—the Departments of Labor, HHS, Education, and Justice—play a primary role and contain some of the largest youth-serving grant programs in terms of funding.[6]

Despite having distinct missions, these four agencies share the common goal of reconnecting youth to education and the workforce, and each works to accomplish this goal by administering multiple programs. (See table 1 for a listing of key federal grant programs that serve disconnected youth.)

- Labor's workforce programs provide funding for both workforce training and education services for youth up to age 24, including youth involved in the juvenile justice and criminal justice systems, school dropouts, and homeless youth.
- HHS's grant programs serve runaway and homeless youth up to age 21 or youth who have aged out of foster care or are likely to age out. These grants fund local programs that have education and workforce components, and also assist youth in connecting to housing and long-term support networks.
- Education's various related grant programs focus on youth who are homeless; neglected, delinquent, or at risk; out of school; or incarcerated in a state prison within 5 years of release or parole eligibility. The programs facilitate youths' enrollment and success in school and vocational programs.
- Justice's grant programs serve those youth 17 and under who are involved in or at risk of becoming involved in the juvenile justice system. Grant programs administered by Justice aim to help youth make the successful transition out of the juvenile justice system and on to education and workforce pathways.

In total, these programs received over $3.7 billion in appropriated funds in 2006. Labor's Job Corps program accounted for almost half—$1.6 billion—of these appropriations, and its WIA Youth Activities accounted for nearly $1 billion. Some of the programs serve a broad subsection of youth, including some who may not be disconnected per our definition, such as young adults over 24 and in-school youth. See appendix III for more information on key federal grant programs' eligibility criteria and purposes.

Table 1. Key Federal Grant Programs That Serve Disconnected Youth

Agency or office	Federal grant	Appropriated funds, in millions of dollars (2006)
Department of Labor		
Office of the Secretary	Job Corps	$1,573.3
Employment and Training Administration	WIA Youth Activities	$940.5
Employment and Training Administration	YouthBuild	$49.5
Employment and Training Administration	Youth Offender Grants	$49.1
Employment and Training Administration	Youth Opportunity (Funding ended in 2003)	Not applicable
Department of HHS		
Children's Bureau	Chafee Foster Care Independence Program	$140
Family and Youth Services Bureau	Runaway and Homeless Youth Program	$102.9
Department of Education		
Office of Vocational and Adult Education	Adult Education Basic Grants to States[a]	$564
Office of Safe and Drug-Free Schools	Grants to States for Workplace and Community Transition Training for Incarcerated Youth	$22.8
Office of Elementary and Secondary Education	Education for Homeless Children and Youth—Grants for States and Local Activities	$61.9
Office of Elementary and Secondary Education	Title I-D Prevention and Intervention Programs for Children and Youth Who Are Neglected, Delinquent, or at Risk—Grants for States and Localities	$49.8
Department of Justice		
Office of Juvenile Justice and Delinquency Prevention	Part E Developing, Testing, and Demonstrating Promi-sing New Initiatives and Programs	$106
Office of Juvenile Justice and Delinquency Prevention	Title II B—State Formula Grants	$74.3
Office of Juvenile Justice and Delinquency Prevention	Juvenile Accountability Block Grant	$46.4
Office of Juvenile Justice and Delinquency Prevention	Title V Community Prevention Block Grants	$4.6

Source: GAO analysis of agency data.

[a]The Adult Education Basic Grants to States serves adults and out-of-school youth ages 16 and older.

Federal youth-serving agencies distribute funds to locally operated programs through varying mechanisms. Some programs first provide funds to states, which are then passed to local units of government or programs. For example, Justice awards formula grants to states that can be used to fund projects for the development of more effective juvenile delinquency programs and improved juvenile justice systems. Juvenile justice specialists in each state administer the funding through subgrants to units of local government or local private agencies in accordance with legislative requirements. Similarly, Education, through the Adult Education and Family Literacy Act, Title II of WIA, awards funds to local eligible providers through state education or labor agencies. Much in the same way, Labor allocates WIA Title I funds to states, which in turn distribute much of this money to their local workforce investment boards.[7] These boards then award competitive contracts to youth providers. Other federal grants, such as Labor's YouthBuild program and HHS's Transitional Living Program[8] are awarded through a competitive process in which local organizations submit grant proposals directly to the federal agencies.

Federal agencies also provide technical assistance and guidance to local programs. For example, to support programs that receive WIA funds, Labor provides online training courses through a contractor, including Web-based, interactive seminars and tutorials. Labor also provides targeted technical assistance to help local areas most in need by assisting them in identifying and correcting issues that are negatively affecting performance outcomes. Similarly, a training provider and a technical assistance provider assist HHS's Transitional Living Program grantees nationally by helping them to develop new approaches to serving youth, access new sources of funding, and establish linkages with other grantees that have similar issues and concerns. These providers also track trends, identify and share best practices, and sponsor conferences and workshops. To assist local programs in identifying successful program models, Justice maintains a database with information on evidence-based prevention programs that serve at-risk and court-involved youth across the country.

All four federal agencies require local programs to report on their progress with youth by collecting data on youth outcomes, such as attainment of their General Educational Development (GED) credential or job placement, and some of these outcomes are tied to financial sanctions and incentives. For example, HHS requires Transitional Living Program grantees to record each youth's living situation, physical and mental health, and grade completed when the youth exits from the program, among other data elements. Sometimes data must pass through an intermediary agency such as a state education agency or local workforce investment board, and these entities may require additional data from programs for their own monitoring purposes. The federal programs collect this information to monitor the progress toward goals, and to ensure that local programs are serving the targeted population and spending money appropriately. Federal agencies may also affect local programs by setting specific penalties for programs or states that do not meet certain goals or benchmarks. These mechanisms are intended to encourage a high level of performance and accountability. For example, Labor negotiates performance goals with states for WIA Youth Activities, and if states do not meet 80 percent of those goals for more than 2 years in a row, monetary sanctions may be imposed. However, Labor offers states technical assistance after the first year when requested by states, and relatively few states have actually been financially penalized. States are also eligible to receive performance incentives if they exceed certain performance levels.

LOCAL PROGRAMS WE REVIEWED DIFFERED IN THEIR FUNDING SOURCES AND PROGRAM STRUCTURE, YET SHARED SOME CHARACTERISTICS

The 39 local programs we reviewed received funding from a range of government and private sources, and differed in their program structure, yet shared some specific characteristics.[9] The programs we reviewed received funding from federal, state, local, and private sources, and all but 6 programs received some federal funding. Some federal funding sources required programs to follow a specific model or offer a standard set of services, while others allowed programs to use funding more flexibly. The programs also varied in their program structure. For example, some were community-based organizations that provided services on a daily basis, some were charter schools, and some offered residential living. Within these different program structures, some programs also targeted their efforts to specific youth subpopulations, such as court-involved youth. Yet despite these differences, programs shared some characteristics. For example, all of the programs we reviewed were created to meet the needs of local youth such as addressing youth homelessness and high school dropout rates. Most of the programs had also operated for several years, and provided ancillary services in addition to employment and educational assistance to address the multiple needs of their youth participants.

Programs Received Funding from Federal, State, Local, and Private Sources

The 39 programs we reviewed received funding from a variety of sources, including federal, state, local, and private sources. Eleven of these programs reported that their funding primarily comes from federal sources, and nearly half received a combination of federal, state, local, and private funding. All but 6 of the programs in our review received some federal funding. Figure 1 summarizes the sources of funding for the local programs we reviewed.

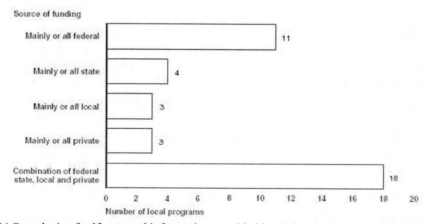

Source: GAO analysis of self-reported information provided by 39 local program directors.

Figure 1. Primary Sources of Funding for the 39 Programs We Reviewed

---

Youth Opportunity Boston (Boston, Massachusetts)

Established in 1997, Youth Opportunity (YO) Boston is a community-based organization that helps court-involved youth between the ages of 14 and 24. With multiple challenges and many barriers to helping youth achieve immediate success, YO Boston's service population is among the most difficult to serve. Many of the youth are high school dropouts, have spent time in detention facilities, and lack the basic skills needed for entry-level employment, and more than 80 percent are involved with gangs. The program was initially funded by Labor's Youth Opportunity demonstration grant. However, this grant ended in 2005. Currently, the program is funded by state and local funding sources. At the time of our review, the program served about 600 court-involved youth on an annual basis and employed 15 permanent staff and 17 temporary staff.

Staff meet with youth while they are still in detention facilities to develop a relationship and make a plan for their re-entry back into the community. Youth admitted in the program are provided with a range of services, including employment training, case management, and educational preparation. Youth also participate in YO Boston's Transitional Employment Services program—a multitiered, subsidized employment program—that places youth in group "team-based work" with various community partners. Youth are then placed in internships with nonprofits and small companies that may hire the youth and pay their wages. Some of the group projects that youth have participated in include working at a nonprofit that provides clothing and goods to children in foster care, painting a stadium, landscaping public land, and producing a newspaper for the program. During our visit to the program, we observed a cardiopulmonary resuscitation (CPR) course taught to youth by the city's emergency medical services and police departments. These youth were being trained in this because they are often the first individuals at a violent crime scene. This also gives youth the opportunity to positively contribute in the community. Most youth stay in the program for a minimum of 18 to 24 months. Though challenging because of the transient population served, the program does follow up quarterly with youth for up to 2 years after they exit the program through phone calls and home visits.

Source: GAO based on information from Youth Opportunity Boston.

Figure 2. Illustration of a Community Organization in Boston, Massachusetts

In some cases, federal funding sources may require programs to follow a specific model or offer a standard set of services, and in other cases federal funding can be used more flexibly. For example, all of Labor's Job Corps centers feature campus-like settings with youth housed in dormitories and a similar model for guidance and support at all sites to help youth achieve long-term employment. Similarly, HHS's Transitional Living Program grantees are required to offer a specific set of services, either directly or by referral, to youth in their programs, including instruction in budgeting, housekeeping, menu planning, food preparation, and parenting. By contrast, Education's Adult Education Grants, which serve both adults and out-of-school youth ages 16 and older, support workplace literacy services, GED instruction, family literacy services, or English-language learning programs and can be delivered by public schools, community colleges, libraries, or other providers.

The 39 Programs We Reviewed Were Structured Differently to Provide Employment and Educational Services to Youth

The 39 programs we reviewed structured their services to youth in different ways. For example, some programs were community organizations that provided specific training for youth at their organization during the day. Some were established as charter schools, and some were residential programs, most often providing transitional housing to homeless and/or runaway youth. Many of the programs were a combination of these different approaches. For example, one charter school also provided residential facilities for youth. Another program with a primary focus on providing employment opportunities to youth also had a charter school on the premises. Depending in part on the structure of the program, the programs varied in size, length of involvement for youth, and the extent of follow-up they conducted with exiting participants.

Several of the programs we reviewed were community organizations that worked to improve the employment outcomes of youth by helping them to gain the skills needed to be successful in the workplace. They generally provided a range of employment training opportunities to youth during the day, such as teaching youth interviewing techniques, and how to develop a résumé and work in a team environment. Some programs provided vocational training to youth participants in certain industries, such as construction or health care, to teach work skills. To the extent possible, some programs also provided youth with on-the-job training by placing them in internships and employment opportunities. In addition to employment training and placement, several of the programs also assisted youth in meeting their educational goals by providing them with opportunities to earn a GED credential or high school diploma either on-site or in collaboration with other organizations in the community. Figure 2 describes a community organization we visited in Boston that works to improve employment outcomes for youth.

See Forever Foundation's Maya Angelou Public Charter School (Washington, D.C.)

The See Forever Foundation was founded in 1997, and a year later it established the Maya Angelou Public Charter School for youth between the ages of 14 and 17 who have not succeeded in traditional schools. In particular, Maya Angelou Public Charter School helps to develop the academic, social, and employment skills youth need to build rewarding lives and promote positive change in their communities. The school, funded by local government and private funding sources, has four campuses—two for high school students, one for middle school students, and one at the Oak Hill Academy, a long-term secure facility for adjudicated youth. For the 2007-2008 school year, Maya Angelou Public Charter School serves approximately 475 students at its four campuses and employs 125 staff to work with these youth. At least half of these youth may be low-income, involved in the juvenile justice or foster care systems, in need of special education services, or may have failed school at one point in time.

The formal school day begins at 9:00 a.m. and runs until 4:30 p.m. The program offers after-school academic enrichment activities, vocational programs, and recreational programs until 7:15 p.m. 4 days a week. Over 200 tutors in the community come to the school campuses 3 days a week to provide one-on-one tutoring to students. Maya Angelou Public Charter School high school campuses release students early on Wednesdays to allow them to participate in paid internships. The school provides students with a minimum of 1 hour of group counseling each week to help them address barriers to their academic success. Gender-segregated, group-based residences are available during the school week to approximately 23 students who have experienced obstacles in their school attendance, including chronic truancy and difficult situations at home. The length of enrollment varies, but as of this year, youth can be admitted to the school as young as 6th grade, and attend classes on the various campuses for up to 7 years. Last year, 80 percent of 9th to 12th graders at the high school operated at the 6th grade level or below. While students work at their own pace, the school aims to accelerate performance with the hope of moving students through as many as two grade levels each year. Advancement is based on academic proficiency and the speed at which the students are able to achieve their objectives.

Source: GAO based on information from Maya Angelou Public Charter School.

Figure 3. Illustration of a Charter School in Washington, D.C.

Janus Youth Programs Willamette Bridge House (Portland, Oregon)

Janus Youth Programs created the Willamette Bridge House, a transitional living program, in 1987 to provide stable housing for homeless youth between the ages 16 and 20 who were not in foster care or some other system. The program is funded through grants provided by HHS and the U.S. Department of Housing and Urban Development, in addition to other federal, state, local, and private funding sources. The program works with 7 youth at any given time, and employs 6 full-time staff working with these youth. In addition to the 7 youth residing in the Willamette Bridge House, the program also works with 15 to 20 youth at any given time who are transitioning into their own apartments and need the program's help with basic fees, such as security and utility deposits. The youth served by the program include court and/or gang-involved youth, high school dropouts, pregnant or parenting youth, and other youth subpopulations.

To determine which youth will be accepted into the program, staff assess each young person's motivation to get off the streets. Once in the program, youth are required to fulfill 42 hours of work each week, which can include basic education, GED preparation, employment, or any other activities agreed to with their case manager. The program provides a range of services: individualized case management, parenting classes, budgeting assistance, job and life skills training, basic food shopping and preparation, and a savings plan. Youth can stay in the program up to 18 months. While in the program, youth and staff work together to secure stable, permanent housing options upon exit from the program. The program conducts formal follow-up with participants 6 and 12 months after they exit.

Source: GAO based on information from Janus Youth Programs.

Figure 4. Illustration of a Transitional Living Program in Portland, Oregon

Several of the programs were established as charter schools or nontraditional schools, often referred to as "alternative education schools," to assist youth who have dropped out of traditional public schools. These programs typically allowed youth to learn in a small classroom-based setting. Some of these programs were selective and required youth to test at certain grade levels or have a certain amount of credits earned before they can be admitted into the program, and generally had a focus on academic and vocational education. Youth typically spent part of their time attending academic classes, such as math or reading classes, to achieve basic academic skills so they can pass the GED exam or earn a high school diploma. In addition to these academic classes, youth typically attended vocational classes to learn work skills and specific trades. To facilitate learning outside of the classroom, some of these schools provided youth with internships or employment opportunities in the community, or allowed youth to participate in service projects. Figure 3 describes a charter school we visited in Washington, D.C.

Many of the programs we reviewed provided residential living accommodations and services to youth to help them develop the skills necessary to transition to independence. Many of these programs were transitional living programs that served runaway and/or homeless youth. Living accommodations for youth in transitional living programs typically vary and can include group homes, maternity group homes, or apartments that are supervised by staff. Several of these programs were small, with fewer than 20 youth residents. Some programs were structured and established ground rules that participants must follow. To address the multiple needs of these youth, these programs generally offered a range of services, including educational opportunities, such as GED preparation, postsecondary training, or vocational education; and basic life skills building, such as budgeting and housekeeping. The length of time youth participants stayed in a program varied; some youth stayed on average 4 months, while others stayed a year and a half or longer, depending on their needs and certain eligibility criteria.[10] Figure 4 describes a transitional living program we visited in Portland, Oregon. In addition, one residential program we reviewed was targeted to court-involved youth. Labor's Job Corps program also provided residential facilities to youth in that program.

Within these different program structures, some of the programs we reviewed targeted their efforts to specific youth subpopulations. For example, a few programs provided support to youth aging out of the foster care system, who typically lack social supports, to help them make a successful transition to adulthood and self-sufficiency. These programs may offer a range of support services, such as food and housing assistance, educational opportunities, and advocacy. Other programs worked to improve the outcomes of court-involved youth. Some of these programs varied in structure and approach to working with youth. For example, one program operating a juvenile residential facility offered youth vocational education and life skills training, as well as a full range of academic courses and diploma options. Other programs provided court-involved youth with on-the-job training through their vocational curricula and service projects.

Despite Different Approaches to Serving Youth, Local Programs Shared Some Specific Characteristics

Despite these differences, the 39 local programs we reviewed shared some characteristics. All of the programs we reviewed were created to meet the needs of local youth, such as addressing youth homelessness and high school dropout rates. For example, one program was started by an individual seeking to assist high school dropouts in her community by allowing youth to complete their GED while acquiring construction skills. Another program providing employment training and placement to youth was started by a local police officer who wanted to help young men returning to the community from jail obtain support services and the skills needed to achieve self-sufficiency. Most of these programs were well established, with many providing services to youth for at least 10 years. Slightly less than half of the programs had 20 years or more of experience in assisting youth, and relatively few were newly established with less than 5 years of experience. In addition, most programs provided services, such as counseling or housing assistance, to their youth participants directly or through referrals to community service providers.

DIRECTORS OF THE 39 LOCAL PROGRAMS CITED SIMILAR KEY ELEMENTS IN RECONNECTING YOUTH TO EDUCATIONAL AND EMPLOYMENT GOALS

While varying types of programs serve disconnected youth, directors of the 39 local programs we reviewed identified similar key elements of their programs that assist them in reconnecting youth to educational and employment goals. These include employing effective staff and leadership to build strong relationships with youth and the community, addressing youth needs in a holistic manner, incorporating a variety of specific program design components, and empowering youth to achieve their goals. Our findings on key elements in reconnecting youth are generally in line with those cited in literature on youth and by other experts on youth issues whom we interviewed. These elements and key components are shown in figure 5 and are discussed in more detail in the following sections.

Staff and Leadership Are Key in Building Relationships with Youth and Community Partners

Nearly all of the 39 directors cited the importance of staff in building strong relationships with youth to help them achieve their goals. For some youth, their interactions with staff may be among the first positive experiences they had with adults. Many youth we spoke with across programs agreed that staff were a primary reason they continued in the program. For example, one youth we spoke with told us she continued to participate in her program because the staff helped her establish goals and provided a supportive environment. In many cases, the relationships between staff and youth participants continue well after these youth complete the program, providing an ongoing source of support to the participants. Figure 6 depicts photos of staff working with youth participants at two programs we visited. Directors reported that they have developed a range of strategies to retain staff, which included providing competitive pay and benefits. One director provides training to reduce burnout and help her staff feel more confident and competent. Others said that they maintain a low caseload for case managers, allow staff to have input in program development, and conduct recognition ceremonies to award staff for their accomplishments.

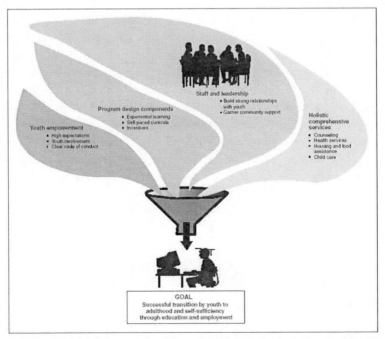

Source: GAO analysis of key elements of the 39 local programs; Images (Art Explosion).

Figure 5. Key Elements of Local Programs Cited by Program Directors in Reconnecting Youth to Education and Employment

Project CRAFT/Nashville (Nashville,Tennessee)   Civicorps Schools (Oakland, California)

Source: GAO.

Figure 6. Staff Working with Youth Participants at Various Work Sites

Program leadership also played a key role in maintaining successful programs and garnering community support that leads to funding and other resources. The vision of certain program directors helped programs to continually innovate to meet the needs of youth in their communities. For some programs, the same leadership had been in place since their inception, a fact that has contributed toward their continued stability. Directors had built strong relationships with a range of community stakeholders, including mayors, city departments, local businesses, employers, and clergy. For example, two youth-serving programs reported that they received funding from their mayor and city after the federal Youth Opportunity grants were eliminated, a fact that enabled them to continue to provide services to youth. Additionally, programs established relationships with service providers in the community to gain access to a range of educational or employment opportunities for youth. For example, one program partnered with a local community college program to provide skills training and certification for entry-level jobs. Other programs partnered with employers to provide their youth participants with employment placements, internships, and job shadowing opportunities. One director working with court-involved youth noted that these relationships were critical to finding employment for their youth participants with criminal records. Program reputation, longevity of the program and its staff, and ability of the management to plan for the future and attract relevant stakeholders were cited as factors helping programs to coordinate efforts within their communities.

Directors Emphasized the Importance of Addressing Youth Needs in a Holistic Manner

To address the multiple needs of participants, many program directors told us that, to the extent possible, their programs took a holistic approach to providing comprehensive support services to youth either on-site or in collaboration with other service providers in the community. (Figure 7 illustrates the range of services one local Job Corps center offers youth participants in addition to educational and employment assistance.) In one program, on-site case managers provided individual counseling to youth and referred these youth to providers in the community for additional services, such as substance abuse and mental health services, if needed. Another director of a program working with runaway and homeless youth said the program provides a continuum of services, including on-site health services, such as psychological assessments and human immunodeficiency virus testing. Other medical services were provided through a partnership with the local public health department.

Specific Program Design Components Help Programs to Engage and Retain Young People

Program directors incorporated a variety of specific design components to help engage and retain youth, such as experiential learning opportunities, engagement in civic activities, self-paced curricula and flexible schedules, and financial and nonfinancial incentives. Many program directors told us that they incorporated experiential learning opportunities, which provide youth with hands-on learning opportunities and on-site training, to emphasize concepts used in the classroom or to teach work skills. For example, one director of a program that teaches various trades to court-involved youth allows young people to apply their academic skills to real world situations. Youth receiving training in construction, for example, can apply math concepts they learn in the classroom to construction projects in the community. One young person participating in this program said that he appreciated this applied setting and is more motivated to learn math skills. Through such on-the-job training, youth also learn how to take directions from supervisors and work as part of a team, skills that are necessary in the work environment. Figure 8 depicts a photo of a local program's workshop that trains out-of-school youth in construction.

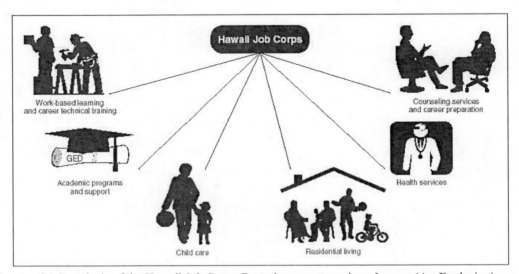

Source: GAO analysis of the Hawaii Job Corps Center's support services; Images (Art Explosion).

Figure 7. Example of a Local Job Corps Center's Holistic Approach to Providing Comprehensive Support Services

Youth Employment Partnership, Inc. (Oakland, California)

Source: GAO.

Figure 8.Workshop at a Local Program That Trains Out-of-School Youth in Construction

Directors reported that civic engagement provides youth with an opportunity to give back to the community and learn how to get involved with government and community activities. One director of a program serving court-involved youth said that his curriculum incorporated a restorative justice framework whereby youth participate in community activities to make up for their negative behavior. Some of these community service activities included building a deck for a local youth-serving organization or constructing homes for low-income families. Other programs arranged local field trips to expose youth to government and community activities. For example, one educational and occupational training program organized field trips to city hall, cultural events, and museums to teach youth about various community activities. A young person who attended such an event at the local city hall said the experience taught him about public hearings and how to be an advocate for issues that affect him.

To accommodate the various needs of their youth participants, many programs employed an individualized or self-paced curriculum and a flexible class schedule. For example, one educational and occupational training program reported that it tailored students' academic course of study to their skill level through more individualized attention. One young person, who dropped out of school because the slow pace had left him unchallenged, told us that he became re-engaged in school work through the program's self-paced curriculum. To further accommodate the needs of their youth participants, such as parenting or employment, programs provided flexibility to their youth in developing class schedules.

Over half of the 39 programs used incentives to retain youth or encourage positive behavior. These incentives may include industry-related certifications upon graduation, transportation vouchers, rent subsidies, and educational scholarships to attend college. In particular, a few housing or foster care programs provide youth with housing subsidies and help them to set up personal savings accounts to save for future expenses, such as buying a car or placing a deposit on an apartment. A few programs had coordinated with the federal AmeriCorps program to provide educational scholarships to reward youth for their service in the program.[11] Other programs have established a behavioral management system that incorporates incentives to reward youth for positive behavior. For example, one program allowed youth to earn points for maintaining a clean room, arriving on time to school, and not being involved in negative incidents. These points can then be traded in for items valuable to the youth participants, such as compact discs.

Programs Empower Youth by Setting Expectations and Strengthening Their Leadership Skills

Program directors reported that they empower youth by setting high expectations, establishing a clear code of conduct, and strengthening their leadership skills. Many directors told us that they use an approach that focuses on youths' capacities, strengths, and developmental needs rather than solely on their problems and risks—often referred to as the "youth development approach" by researchers and practitioners. According to one director, youth have been accustomed to interacting with people and systems that focus on their deficits rather than their talents and strengths, leading them to lack confidence in their abilities. By setting high expectations, staff demonstrate confidence in youth, and in turn some youth will rise to those expectations. Many programs told us that they balance these high expectations with a clear code of conduct that provides youth with guidelines about the consequences of their behaviors.

YOUTH DEVELOPMENT APPROACH

According to HHS's National Clearinghouse on Families and Youth, the youth development approach, developed over 30 years ago by researchers and practitioners, emphasizes providing services and opportunities to support young people to succeed and contribute as adults by incorporating four components:

- a sense of competence
- a sense of usefulness
- a sense of belonging, and
- a sense of power.

A number of federal agencies, foundations, and national organizations utilize this framework in their initiatives. For example, HHS's Family and Youth Services Bureau, one of the federal agencies in our review, has funded demonstration projects at the state level to encourage collaborative approaches to youth development. For more information, see National Clearinghouse on Families and YouthWeb site at http://www.ncfy.com.

To strengthen youths' leadership skills and improve program services, many program directors reported involving youth in a variety of program operation activities. Many programs involved youth in the process to hire new staff or their outreach and recruitment efforts for new participants. One program encouraged youth to attend advisory board meetings once a quarter to talk about what is working and additional needs. Other programs have established youth councils to help set goals for the program and solicit input from other youth participants. In addition, several directors noted that they hired former youth participants as staff. One director from a program that serves foster care youth said that these youth workers are key because they can relate to other youths' circumstances and can teach them conflict resolution and coping skills.

DIRECTORS WE INTERVIEWED CITED SERVICE GAPS, FUNDING CONSTRAINTS, AND FEDERAL GRANT MANAGEMENT CHALLENGES THAT HINDERED THEIR EFFORTS; FEDERAL COORDINATION EFFORTS UNDER WAY MAY HELP ADDRESS SOME OF THESE ISSUES

Program directors reported challenges addressing some of the issues faced by youth in their programs as well as gaps in certain services, such as housing and employment opportunities for youth. Most directors reported that funding constraints from federal and other sources challenge program stability and efforts to serve more youth. Funding for many of the key federal programs we reviewed that serve disconnected youth has remained the same or declined since 2000. In addition, many of the 15 directors with federal WIA Youth funding noted that the need to meet certain WIA Youth performance goals within short-term time frames discouraged them from serving youth that may need more time and assistance to achieve specified outcomes. Labor officials acknowledged that states and workforce investment boards sometimes issue 1-year contracts with local programs that unintentionally discourage the programs from working with lower-skilled youth and that the boards may need more assistance from Labor to address this issue. Regarding local programs receiving funding from more than one federal source, several directors cited varying grant requirements that pose a challenge for local programs to reconcile. In recent years at the federal level, existing and new federal initiatives have intensified efforts to coordinate federal youth programs and provide assistance to state and local youth-serving efforts, which may help to address some challenges faced by local programs.

Programs Constrained by Circumstances and Needs of Some Youth and Gaps in Services at the Community Level

Most directors cited the complex nature of the youth populations they serve and issues facing youth at the community level as key challenges to successfully reconnecting youth to education and employment.[12] These challenges are further complicated by a gap in needed services at the local level.[13] Figure 9 identifies the top gaps in services most frequently cited by local program directors.

A large number of the program directors reported that their youth have mental health issues, and several said these issues may be undiagnosed or untreated before entering the program, and that their communities lack adequate mental health services. Directors cited trauma, depression, and attachment disorders as examples of the mental health issues faced by some of the youth. Several directors said that these mental health issues were undiagnosed prior to the youths' involvement with their programs. As one director stated, the complex family and living situations many of these youth come from and the long-term effects of abuse and neglect experienced by some of these youth need to be addressed in order for youth to have success in reaching employment or educational goals. However, more than half of the program directors cited a lack of mental health treatment as a major gap in their communities. Most often, directors attributed this gap in mental health services to inadequate funds. Some directors also attributed the gap to a misperception of the need for mental health treatment. For example, one director believed that the mental health services these youth need to transition to self-sufficiency have not been adequately understood or addressed by policymakers. At the same time, a few of the program directors also noted that youth themselves are unaware that they need intensive counseling and resist pursuing mental health treatment due to the associated stigma.

Some programs also reported that a number of their youth have learning disabilities, and that these may have been undiagnosed by the school system. For example, one alternative education program stated that in 2002, nearly 45 percent of its students were diagnosed with learning or emotional disabilities. Of these students, only half had been diagnosed before coming to their program. Many programs reported that the low educational attainment of the youth slow their efforts to achieve educational and employment outcomes. According to one director, high school-aged youth are frustrated when they test at a seventh grade level. Another director reported that, on average, her youth test at a fifth to sixth grade level in reading and a fourth to fifth grade level in math. She noted that her program's staff must work with youth who are at a tremendous skills deficit to achieve outcomes.

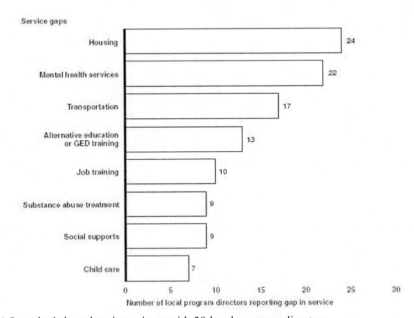

Source: GAO analysis based on interviews with 39 local program directors.
Note: Directors identified the top three services they believed were insufficient or lacking in their communities. These data only include services that were mentioned by more than three directors.

Figure 9.Gaps in Services for Disconnected Youth Reported by 39 Program Directors

Violence and drugs at the community level create additional challenges to youth efforts to successfully complete their programs. A large number of programs we reviewed reported that their communities struggled with gangs, violence, or drugs, which may affect youths' success. Due to gangs and violence, one director reported that young people in the program face peer pressure that may detract from their efforts to remain in the program. Additionally, youth may not feel safe traveling to the program, or may have trouble focusing when violence affects their family or friends. One program that works predominantly with youth involved in gangs reported that in a 2½-year time frame, 26 of their youth participants were murdered. This program and other programs have developed close relationships with law enforcement officials to keep abreast of gang activity to ensure the youths' safety and generally to serve youth in such communities better. A number of directors also reported high levels of drug activity in their communities, and many reported substance abuse issues among the youth they serve. However, program directors also cited gaps in substance abuse services. One program director said that 80 percent of youth in his program are in need of substance abuse services, and that these services were less available for his participants than in previous years.

A majority of the 39 directors cited a lack of affordable housing as a top challenge for youth who are trying to become self-sufficient. Many directors discussed a lack of affordable long-term housing, and several referred to a lack of temporary housing or shelters for youth. Some directors attributed the high cost of housing to revitalization efforts in certain areas, and some believed that policymakers lack the political will to focus on affordable housing needs. Directors reported that wages for this population are low, which creates challenges for their youth participants to afford housing. In one community, the program director reported a 3-year waiting list for low-income housing. Certain restrictions that affect specific subpopulations of disconnected youth further limit housing options. For example, landlords are reluctant to lease apartments to youth who are unemployed, have been involved in the criminal justice system, or do not have a parent to cosign a lease. In addition, some programs also expressed concern that there are not enough shelters available for homeless youth.

The affordable housing challenge is further complicated by employment challenges. Several directors cited a lack of jobs that pay a sufficient wage and a reluctance by employers to hire certain subpopulations of youth as major challenges facing youth in their community. According to one transitional living program, the lack of low-skilled jobs that pay enough to meet living expenses, coupled with rising housing costs, makes it nearly impossible for a young person to transition to a stable living situation upon leaving the program. In addition, a number of programs working with court-involved youth discussed the challenge these youth face obtaining employment because they have a criminal record. One program director working with ex-offender youth said these youth are aware of the limited employment opportunities they face and some of them lose hope in their ability to secure a job. He further noted that it is hard to keep them motivated and feeling positive given these constraints, even with stipends for academic and employment training.[14]

Job opportunities for youth may also be limited by transportation challenges. Many program directors in both rural communities and urban centers cited challenges with the accessibility or affordability of transportation that affect youth access to opportunities, especially employment. Directors cited the high cost of public transportation as a barrier for the youth in their programs. One director of a program in an urban community that places youth in employment said some jobs require youth to go on multiple interviews and the youth do not have the money to pay for transportation to and from these interviews. The program tries to help youth with the transportation barrier, but the amount of funding it can allocate toward transportation is determined by its funders. Another program that trains youth for jobs in the construction field noted that a lot of the construction jobs are in suburban areas, which are not well serviced by public transportation. We were told of young people taking multiple buses and many hours to travel to a workplace, impeding their ability to sustain employment.

Funding Constraints from Government and Other Sources Challenge Program Stability and Efforts to Serve More Youth

Local programs told us that funding constraints from all sources have created significant challenges in working with their disconnected youth populations. Difficulty with funding was rated as the number one overall challenge faced by local programs, and some program directors noted that their funding was either declining or not keeping pace with inflation or with demand for their services. Funding for 10 of the 15 key federal programs we reviewed has remained the same or declined since 2000. WIA Youth funds have been reduced from a high of $1.13 billion in fiscal year 2001 to $940 million in fiscal year 2007. This represents a decline of about 27 percent in inflation-adjusted dollars. While overall Transitional Living Program funding increased in fiscal year 2002 to support a greater number of programs, the amount available each year to individual local programs —capped at $200,000—has not changed since 1992. One program director explained that considering increases in the costs of operation, this amount funds only part of one staff rather than three as in previous years. Despite these reductions, many of the programs we spoke with emphasized that the demand for their services has continued. For example, more than half of the programs reported having a waiting list of youth in need of their services ranging from 10 to 1,000 youth, and high school dropout rates in many communities remain high. The Annie E. Casey Foundation found that between 2000 and 2005, an additional 626,000 youth between the ages of 18 and 24 became disconnected from school and work, based on U.S. Census Bureau statistics.

Program directors also stressed that the unpredictability of federal grant money has made it difficult to run their programs. In particular, most of the program directors who received Transitional Living Program funds told us that one of their greatest concerns for this grant source was its unpredictability and a perception that HHS does not take into consideration enough the experience of current grantees. HHS officials said that the agency used to award extra points to current grantees of the program, a practice it stopped a few years ago to allow new organizations to have greater opportunity. They also acknowledged that this is a highly competitive grant and that there are likely many deserving programs they are unable to support, given the budget. Other programs noted that the short-term nature of some grants made it difficult to predict how long they could sustain some of their programming and plan for the long term. Program directors we interviewed stressed the importance of predictable and long-term funding commitments for working with disconnected youth who in particular require sustained services and support during precarious transitional years. While most of the programs we reviewed received some federal dollars, those that relied more heavily on private, state, or local funding expressed similar concerns with the limited amount, as well as the consistency, of funds available for the populations of youth with which they work.

In response to these funding constraints, program directors reported that they had modified or limited their services. One program eliminated its GED instruction in response to decreases in WIA Youth funds, and another reduced youth served from 1,500 participants in 2000 to a current capacity of 300 because of similar reductions. Some program directors told us that the amount of funding they received limited their ability to follow up with youth after they complete the program or to conduct program evaluations to improve services. Program directors told us that funding levels also affected their ability to attract and retain staff. In fact, one Transitional Living Program director told us that upon leaving the program, some of the youth the program serves found jobs that paid higher wages than those of the program staff, a fact that affected the program's ability to retain staff.

Performance Contracts Associated with Some Federal Funding May Have Unintended Consequences

Many of the 15 local program directors who received WIA Youth funding reported that meeting the performance goals for which they were held accountable within short-term contracts discouraged them from working with low-skilled youth who may need increased time and assistance to reach specified outcomes, such as employment or educational gains.[15] Several local program directors said their WIA contracts are for 1 year, and that the need to achieve outcome measures often based on only 12 months of service provided a disincentive to serve those youth with the greatest challenges.[16] Program directors explained that youth entering their programs may have multiple barriers, such as criminal backgrounds, limited reading abilities, and lack of social support, and require a longer investment in order to achieve positive outcomes than other youth. In order to meet current federal performance goals, such as employment outcome goals, within a 1-year period, some directors of the WIA-funded programs reported that they only accept youth who test at least at a certain grade level. One director explained that many employers will not consider hiring young people who cannot read at least at a specific grade level. In some areas, this can mean leaving behind a significant number of youth who are out of school. One program director in Baltimore told us that because of its policy to accept youth that test at least at a seventh grade level, the program has to turn away 80 percent of youth who seek its services even though it has the capacity to serve some of these youth.

Labor officials said they were aware that workforce investment boards, which award contracts to local programs, have implemented local program contracts in a way that may unintentionally discourage programs from working with lower-skilled youth and have taken some initial steps to address this issue. The officials acknowledged that 12 months is often an inadequate time frame within which to ensure that youth will fulfill education- and employment-related outcomes. Labor officials explained that for all but one of the measures there is no requirement to achieve performance goals within 1 year and workforce investment boards often develop 1-year contracts despite Labor's intent for them to develop longer-term contracts. Labor has taken some steps to address this problem. For example, it is currently conducting some training for workforce investment boards to explain the importance of a longer-term investment in youth in order to reach outcomes. It has also, through a national contractor, provided technical assistance on this issue to some state and local workforce investment boards and youth programs. However, it has not provided technical assistance more broadly on this issue. Labor officials also told us they were considering issuing guidance at some point in the future to help boards understand ways to establish contracts to better ensure programs have incentives to work with hard-to-employ youth, a population group Labor acknowledges is important to serve. Labor officials said they have not yet established a time frame for developing and issuing guidance on this.

Labor officials noted another development that may provide local youth-serving programs more flexibility to serve youth at all skill levels. As part of an Office of Management and Budget requirement for programs across multiple agencies to report on uniform evaluation metrics, Labor has adopted and implemented the three common performance measures for youth employment and training programs developed by the Office of Management and Budget. It asserts that these measures may better capture improvements made by youth at all skill levels, instead of the seven measures currently in statute, reducing the incentive for some programs to select only higher-skilled youth. The three new performance measures, referred to as the common measures, apply to youth of all ages, and focus on literacy or numeracy gains as well as placement in employment and education as outcomes, which may give more flexibility to programs to work with youth at different levels. By contrast, the current measures for older youth (aged 19 to 21) emphasize employment outcomes, such as employment retention after 6 months. (See table 2.) Labor uses data on performance measures that states collect from service providers to track states' progress in meeting performance goals. Labor officials told us that states must collect data for both sets of measures until the new measures are established through law, although some states have already started to work with the new measures.[17] For program year 2007, Labor reported that 22 states had waivers in place that allowed them to collect data for only the three new common measures; 10 of these states were granted waivers recently in program year 2006 and two of them in program year 2005. While the new measures may give states more flexibility in how they measure youths' progress, it may be too early to assess whether these new measures have been incorporated into contracts with local programs in ways that result in reduced incentives for programs to select higher-performing youth.

Table 2. Existing and New Common Measures for WIA Youth Program

	WIA measures currently in statute	Common measures
Youth (ages 19 to 21)	• Entered Employment Rate • Average earnings change in 6 months • Employment retention rate at 6 months • Entered employment/education/ training and credential rate	• Placement in employment and education • Attainment of a degree or certificate • Literacy or numeracy gains
Youth (ages 14 to 18)	• Skill attainment rate • Diploma or equivalent attainment rate • Placement and retention in postsecondary education, advanced training, or employment rate	

Source: U.S. Department of Labor.

Federal Grant Requirements That Vary across Programs Can Pose Challenges

Local program directors that received multiple federal grants from different agencies expressed difficulty in working across varying reporting requirements, funding cycles, and eligibility requirements. (See figure 10.) To a lesser extent, these program directors also experienced challenges working across varying program goals and sharing information about their clients that participate in multiple federal grants.

- *Varying reporting requirements.* Directors of 17 of the 19 local programs we reviewed that received more than one federal grant stated that reconciling varying reporting requirements presented at least some challenge.[18] One program director explained that each of the program's federal funding sources has its own management information system, but they all require similar information, causing staff to spend a significant amount of time inputting nearly identical data elements into separate data collection systems.

- *Varying funding cycles.* Fifteen program directors reported at least some challenge in managing grants that span different funding cycles. Even within the same federal agency, grants can have different fiscal year schedules and different grant durations. For example, among the large workforce programs, workforce investment boards often award 1-year WIA contracts to local programs, and YouthBuild is now a 3-year grant.[19] Working across differing funding cycles and grant years can make it difficult for programs to plan for the future.

- *Differing eligibility requirements.* Directors of 13 local programs reported that they face challenges reconciling differing eligibility requirements. For example, grants from HHS and the Department of Housing and Urban Development to support and house homeless youth use different definitions of homelessness and varying age criteria, which can make it difficult for a local program that depends on both sources of funding. Some workforce grants fund youth less than 21 years of age and others fund up to 24 years of age, making it especially challenging for local programs to combine funding sources.

To Address the Various Needs of Disconnected Youth, Federal Agencies Have Intensified Efforts to Coordinate across Youth-Serving Programs

Recognizing that services addressing the various needs of disconnected youth fall under the jurisdictions of multiple agencies, federal agencies have intensified efforts to coordinate across the array of youth-serving programs. Our past work has highlighted the need for federal collaboration given the multiple demands and limited resources of the federal government.[20] As we noted in our previous work on multiple youth programs, enhanced coordination at the federal level can lead to more efficient use of resources and a more integrated service delivery approach at the local program level.[21] Related to disconnected youth in particular, the federal officials we spoke with highlighted the ongoing coordination efforts of the Coordinating Council on Juvenile Justice and Delinquency Prevention (CCJJDP), led by Justice, and the Shared Youth Vision initiative, led by Labor, among other collaborative efforts.

- The CCJJDP, which was authorized in 1974 by the Juvenile Justice and Delinquency Prevention Act, coordinates federal juvenile delinquency programs. Among its responsibilities, the council examines how programs can be coordinated among federal, state, and local governments to better serve at-risk youth. The CCJJDP, which meets on a quarterly basis, is composed of nine federal agency members, including those from Education, Labor, and HHS, and nine nonfederal members, who are juvenile justice practitioners. In recent years, the council has broadened its focus to other at-risk youth and is seeking to implement some of the 2003 White House Task Force recommendations, including the following: (1) improving coordination of mentoring programs, (2) developing a unified protocol for federal best practices clearinghouses, (3) building a rigorous and unified disadvantaged youth research agenda, (4) improving data collection on the well-being of families, (5) increasing parents' involvement in federal youth programs, (6) targeting youth in public care, (7) targeting youth with multiple risk factors, and (8) expanding mentoring programs to special target groups. A Justice official said one project under way involves researching best practices for federal collaborative efforts to prepare a tool kit to assist federal agencies in their ongoing youth coordination efforts.
- The Shared Youth Vision initiative emerged in response to the 2003 White House Task Force recommendations, which cited a lack of communication, coordination, and collaboration among federal agencies that provide services to the nation's neediest youth, and out of the CCJJDP. It involves officials from Labor, Education, HHS, Justice; the Departments of Transportation, Agriculture, Housing and Urban Development; the Corporation for National and Community Service; and the Social Security Administration. Its mission is to serve as a catalyst at the national, state, and local levels to strengthen coordination, communication, and collaboration among youth-serving agencies to support the neediest youth in their healthy transition to adult roles. Labor officials we spoke with see this initiative as a way to more holistically support youth who come to the attention of various related social service systems, in order to reinforce the effectiveness of each intervention. They also said that the initiative can help make local youth programs more aware of other services available in their communities, such as mental health or substance abuse treatment services that youth may need. One senior HHS official noted that the initiative can be a powerful way to extend federal partnerships into communities, and another official observed that the initiative has led to better coordination of resources among agencies for juvenile justice programming, mentoring, and youth aging out of foster care. To date, the initiative has sponsored several regional forums convening state- and local-level officials from various agencies to share information and discuss better ways to work together to serve youth. In response to state interest in continuing these efforts, Labor awarded grants ranging from $27,500 to $116,000 to 16 competitively selected states to help the states develop strategic plans to connect their systems that serve youth at the state and local levels. For example, Florida is using this initiative

to bring together the state Department of Juvenile Justice, local school districts, and community-based organizations to create a one-stop prevention and intervention system for court-involved youth on probation.

- Several federal agencies have undertaken initiatives to improve coordination among specific programs or programs serving specific subpopulations. For example, Education and HHS are cosponsoring a 4-year program to offer long-term support to youth with serious emotional disorders and emerging serious mental illness. Through the Safe Schools/Healthy Students Initiative, HHS, Education, and Justice are collaborating to reduce violence and drug abuse in schools and communities. Working through the CCJJDP, HHS's Family and Youth Services Bureau and the Corporation for National and Community Service (an independent federal agency) have instituted the Federal Mentoring Council to coordinate mentoring efforts for disadvantaged youth across eight federal agencies. In addition, since 2005, in an effort to provide stronger support to local partnerships working with youth, several federal agencies, including HHS, Labor, Education, and Justice, have created a Web site that provides interactive tools to assist communities to form effective partnerships, assess community assets, map local and federal resources, and search for evidence-based programs to meet the needs of youth, including disconnected youth.[22]

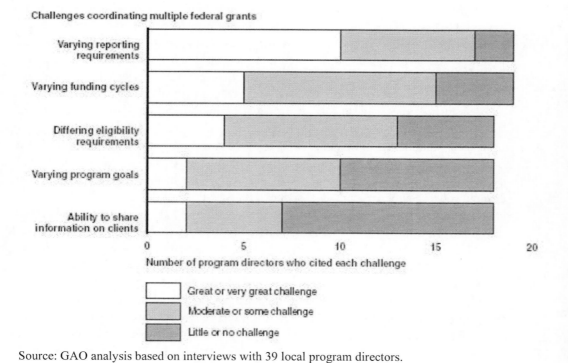

Source: GAO analysis based on interviews with 39 local program directors.

Figure 10. Programs Cite Multiple Challenges in Coordinating across Federal Grant Programs

In addition to these ongoing efforts, Congress in 2006 enacted legislation creating the Federal Youth Development Council with the task—within 2 years—of issuing final recommendations designed to lead to improved coordination and assessment of federal youth programs. However, the council has not been convened. The council is to include members from HHS, Education, Labor, Justice, and several other federal entities, as well as other members as appointed by the President, with the Secretary of HHS serving as the chairperson. The authorizing legislation provides for the council to terminate after meeting at least quarterly for 2 years and issuing a final report. Council duties include several related to finding ways to better facilitate the coordination, efficiency, and effectiveness of federal programs and promote high-quality research and evaluation of youth services and supports. The final report is to include, among other items, an assessment of the needs of youth, especially those in disadvantaged situations, and of those who work with youth; a summary of a plan for quantifiable goals and objectives for federal programs that assist disadvantaged youth; and recommendations for ways to coordinate and improve information sharing among the various federal programs and agencies serving youth, as well as for ways to better integrate and coordinate youth policies at all levels of government. The legislation also specified that the council should coordinate its efforts with existing interagency coordination entities in order to complement and not duplicate efforts. Some assert that the council could reduce duplication of effort by agencies and working at cross-purposes and lead to a stronger emphasis at the federal level on youth development. Funding was not appropriated to the council for fiscal years 2007 and 2008. HHS did not seek funding for the council in the fiscal year 2008 President's budget.[23] HHS has said that the CCJJDP, of which HHS is a member, has begun to address some of the objectives and goals proposed for the council. In addition, on February 7, 2008, the President issued an executive order to establish an Interagency Working Group on Youth Programs. Under the order, HHS would lead this effort to coordinate among relevant federal, private, and nongovernment entities; facilitate the development of a federal Web site on youth; and encourage high standards for assessing program impact.

Due to the relationships established through some of these ongoing formal efforts, officials told us that they now more routinely talk to their counterparts in other agencies. For example, Labor officials told us that they now contact stakeholders in other agencies as a matter of course and as issues arise, and that this practice marks a change from prior years. Similarly, a Justice official stated that Justice staff now consider contacting officials in other agencies to get their expertise and input when awarding grants, recognizing that they are serving some of the same populations. While officials spoke highly of these coordination efforts, some officials pointed to the importance of sustained attention at the appropriate levels to help ensure the longevity of these efforts. More specifically, one official noted that turnover in agency staff, especially among political appointees, can hinder long-term progress and suggested that assigning high-level career officials as point persons at each agency could be a way to facilitate this coordination and strengthening existing coordinating bodies.

CONCLUSIONS

Preparing disconnected youth to become self-sufficient adults is an important responsibility for all levels of government. The government bears some of the costs for youth who have difficulty becoming self-sufficient, and who may instead commit crimes, become incarcerated, and utilize public systems for assistance. However, with adequate support, disconnected youth may be able to obtain the skills needed to make the transition to adulthood and ultimately participate fully in society, including in the workforce. Our research found that many successful locally operated programs serving disconnected youth still struggle to access services and opportunities for youth in their communities that can help these young people meet their needs and achieve educational and employment goals. While all levels of government can help to assist this population, the federal government plays an important role by providing funding, oversight, and technical assistance to support locally operated programs serving disconnected youth. In addition, ongoing and relatively new coordination efforts at the federal level hold potential for promoting more holistic service delivery to youth while also ensuring more efficient use of federal resources, although it is too early to know the impact these efforts may have on local programs serving youth. Sustained attention and leadership from agencies at appropriate levels will be needed to support such coordination efforts and help them endure, while at the same time minimizing unwarranted duplication among the coordination efforts themselves.

Federal agencies also play an important role in holding programs accountable for meeting performance goals, although the pursuit of such goals can sometimes lead to unintended consequences. As a result, it is important to understand all the ways in which rewarding and sanctioning performance can change behavior at the local program level. For example, local program directors receiving WIA Youth funds told us that meeting the seven current performance measures within 1-year contracts provides incentives for the programs to serve youth participants who may quickly achieve desired performance goals within the specified time frames, potentially leaving behind youth with the most challenges to successful outcomes. This potentially means that one of the larger federal funding sources that can be used to assist disconnected youth may discourage local efforts from serving them. While the new common measures, if enacted, may help address this issue, it is important that all workforce investment boards understand how to develop long-term contracts for local programs that avoid discouraging them from serving youth facing increased challenges. Labor has also identified this as a concern and has taken some initial steps to address this issue. However, unless Labor works more with boards to ensure they have the information they need for effective contract development, local programs may continue to lack adequate incentives to work with lower-skilled youth who could greatly benefit from their services.

RECOMMENDATION FOR EXECUTIVE ACTION

To improve implementation of the WIA Youth Activities program, we recommend that the Secretary of Labor work with states and workforce investment boards to better ensure they have the information and guidance needed to develop and implement contracts that allow local programs to serve youth who are in need of more assistance than others while still achieving performance goals. This could include (1) working with workforce investment boards to identify and understand the incentives or constraints that discourage boards from structuring contracts with local programs that would assist their efforts to serve lower-skilled youth, (2) issuing guidance—based on this input—that provides specific examples of ways to develop contracts with local service providers that allow them to serve youth at varying skill levels, and (3) providing technical assistance to support the implementation of this guidance.

AGENCY COMMENTS AND OUR EVALUATION

We provided a draft of this report to Labor, HHS, Justice, and Education for review and comment. Labor agreed with our recommendation, and indicated it will work with workforce investment boards to identify constraints, issue guidance to the workforce investment system in the spring of 2008 on ways to develop contracts that allow programs to successfully serve youth at varying skill levels, and provide technical assistance to support the implementation of the guidance. Labor's written comments are reproduced in appendix IV; we incorporated technical comments it provided where appropriate. HHS provided additional information about a Web site available to communities to provide them support for their efforts to help youth, including disconnected youth, and we have added this information to the report. HHS's written comments are reproduced in appendix V; it also provided technical comments that we incorporated where appropriate. Education provided technical comments only, which we also incorporated where appropriate. Justice had no comments on the draft report.

As agreed with your office, unless you publicly announce its contents earlier, we plan no further distribution of this report until 30 days after its issue date. At that time we will send copies of this report to the Secretaries of Labor, Health and Human Services, and Education, and the Attorney General; relevant congressional committees; and other interested parties. We will also make copies available to others upon request. In addition, the report will be made available at no charge on GAO's Web site at http://www.gao.gov. Please contact me on (202) 512-7215 if you or your staff have any questions about this report. Other contacts and major contributors are listed in appendix VI.

Sincerely yours,

Cornelia M. Ashby

Cornelia M. Ashby
Director,
Education, Workforce, and Income Security Issues

APPENDIX I: LIST OF LOCAL PROGRAMS INTERVIEWED

An asterisk indicates programs we visited in-person. In-person interviews included a tour of the facilities and meeting with youth participants.

Organization name	City	State	Brief description	Key federal funding source(s)[a]
Access Inc.—Youth Empowerment Services	San Diego	Calif.	Assists out-of-school youth to complete their high school education while exploring and preparing to enter employment in a growth industry career ladder in collaboration with a network of programs and service providers.	• WIA (Labor)
American YouthWorks	Austin	Tex.	Helps young people transition into self-sufficient adults through education, job training, and community service.	• AmeriCorps (Corporation for National and Community Service) • YouthBuild (Labor) • WIA (Labor) • Elementary and Secondary Education Act, Titles I, II, III, IV, and V (Education)
Avon Park Youth Academy	Avon Park	Fl.	Provides a residential program that focuses on vocational education and life skills training, as well as offers a full range of academic courses; diploma options, including GED; and college selection services.	• Elementary and Secondary Education Act, Title I (Education)[b]
* Career Academy at Harbor City High School	Baltimore	Md.	Provides educational and occupational training to Baltimore City youth.	• WIA (Labor)
*Civicorps Schools (formerly East Bay Conservation Corps)	Oakland	Calif.	Promotes citizenship and builds a civil society by creating educational models that incorporate service as a way of learning.	• No federal funding

(Continued)

Organization name	City	State	Brief description	Key federal funding source(s)[a]
*Civic Works	Baltimore	Md.	Engages out-of-school youth and high school students through education, community revitalization, and workforce development programs.	• AmeriCorps (Corporation for National and Community Service) • YouthBuild (Labor) • WIA (Labor)
*First Place For Youth	Oakland	Calif.	Supports youth in their transition from foster care to successful adulthood through a supportive housing program, an academic enrichment program, counseling, youth community center, and collaboration with other organizations.	• Supportive Housing Program (Department of Housing and Urban Development) • Community Development Block Grant (Department of Housing and Urban Development)
*Fostering Success	Nashville	Tenn.	Aims to help youth aging out of foster care to have access to education, employment, health care, housing, and a place to call home.	• No federal funding
Guadalupe Youth and Young Adult Programs	Guadalupe	Ariz.	Provides a nurturing environment for Guadalupe youth and young adults that combines education, life and leadership skills, and job readiness and community services.	• AmeriCorps (Corporation for National and Community Service) • YouthBuild (Labor)
Harlem Children's Zone	New York	N.Y.	Works to enhance the quality of life for children and families in some of New York City's most devastated neighborhoods.	• No federal funding
Haven House Services—Preparation for Independent Living Program	Raleigh	N.C.	Establishes transitional living program participants as the leaseholders of their own market-rate apartments in order to address the issue of housing after graduation from its transitional living programs.	• WIA (Labor) • Runaway and Homeless Youth (HHS) • Supportive Housing Program (Department of Housing and Urban Development)

(Continued)

Organization name	City	State	Brief description	Key federal funding source(s)[a]
Hawaii Job Corps Center	Waimanalo	Hawaii	Provides academic, career, technical, and life skills training resulting in long-term quality employment.	• Job Corps (Labor)
Hollywood Cinema Production Resources	Los Angeles	Calif.	Trains underserved youth and young adults in the crafts and technicians skills of the entertainment industry.	• Youth Offender Initiative (Labor)
Improved Solutions for Urban Systems Corporation	Dayton	Oh.	Teaches high school dropouts skills in one of four fields: construction technology, health care, manufacturing technology, and computer technology.	• AmeriCorps (Corporation for National and Community Service) • YouthBuild (Labor) • Youth Offender Initiative (Labor) • Temporary Assistance to Needy Families (HHS)
*Janus Youth Programs — Willamette Bridge House Transitional Living Program	Portland	Ore.	Empowers youth who were previously homeless, pregnant, or parenting to support themselves and work on fulfilling educational and employment needs, integrating a "self-governance" model that incorporates resident participation in all program decision-making processes.	• Horizon (Department of Housing and Urban Development) • Runaway and Homeless Youth (HHS)
Jobs for Youth/Chicago	Chicago	Ill.	Helps young men and women from low-income families become a part of the economic mainstream and, in the process, provide the business community with motivated job-ready workers.	• Adult Basic Education Grants (Education) • WIA (Labor)
*Joseph L. Meek Professional Technical Campus of the Alliance High School	Portland	Ore.	Provides Portland youth with vocational and academic programs and offers opportunities for students seeking an alternative to the traditional high school model.	• Elementary and Secondary Education Act, Title I (Education) • Carl D. Perkins Vocational-Technical Education Act (Education)

(Continued)

Organization name	City	State	Brief description	Key federal funding source(s)[a]
*Larkin Street Youth Services	San Francisco	Calif.	Provides a range of housing options—from immediate emergency shelter to permanent supportive housing—in addition to essential wraparound services that offer young people the resources and skills they need to exit street life.	• McKinney-Vento Act (HHS) • Runaway and Homeless Youth (HHS) • Ryan White Care Act, Title IV (HHS)
Las Artes Arts and Educational Center	Tucson	Ariz.	Addresses the needs of out-of-school youth by providing an opportunity to create public art while earning a GED.	• WIA (Labor)
*Latin American Youth Center–Workforce Investment and Social Enterprise	Washington	D.C.	To offer clear guidance and direction toward a career path to youth who do not have marketable skills or who have dropped out of school.	• WIA (Labor)
Lighthouse Youth Services	Cincinnati	Oh.	Provides safe, secure living environments for homeless youth and adults, and assists them with developing the skills necessary to live self-sufficiently and responsibly.	• Runaway and Homeless Youth (HHS) • Shelter Plus Care Program (Department of Housing and Urban Development) • Scattered Sites Grant (Department of Housing and Urban Development)
*Maya Angelou Public Charter School	Washington	D.C.	Creates learning environments in low- income communities in which teens, particularly those who have not succeeded in traditional schools, can develop the academic, social, and employment skills they need to build rewarding lives and promote positive change in their communities.	• No federal funding[c]
*MY TURN, Inc.	Brockton	Mass.	Assists youth in the development and identification of their skills, goals, and self-confidence through career exploration, employment training, and postsecondary planning in collaboration with partnering organizations.	• WIA (Labor)

(Continued)

Organization name	City	State	Brief description	Key federal funding source(s)[a]
Northwest Piedmont Service Corps	Winston Salem	N.C.	Helps young men and women develop workplace and life skills to make them successful contributing members of the community.	• WIA (Labor)
*Oasis Center	Nashville	Tenn.	Addresses the needs of youth in crisis through housing and other support services.	• Runaway and Homeless Youth (HHS)
*Open Meadow Alternative Schools	Portland	Ore.	Aims to retain youth who have not fared well in traditional academic settings and those who have already dropped out, as well as supporting their transition to college and employment.	• WIA (Labor) • Community Development Block Grant (Department of Housing and Urban Development)
Operation Fresh Start	Madison	Wis.	Serves at-risk youth, primarily high school dropouts and offenders, through a paid opportunity to learn basic work skills, improve basic academic skills, prepare for the high school equivalency examination or complete diplomas, secure and retain employment and/or postsecondary placement at the end of training, and contribute to the community.	• AmeriCorps (Corporation for National and Community Service) • Community Development Block Grant (Department of Housing and Urban Development)
				• HOME Investment Partnerships Program (Department of Housing and Urban Development) • WIA (Labor)
*Portland Community College–Gateway to College	Portland	Ore.	Promotes student success and readiness for an adult learning environment by grouping students into learning communities for their first term, offering intensive literacy development, maintaining rigorous academic standards, and providing individualized support.	• Not applicable[d]

(Continued)

Organization name	City	State	Brief description	Key federal funding source(s)[a]
*Project CRAFT/Nashville	Nashville	Tenn.	Strives to improve educational levels, teach vocational skills, and reduce recidivism among adjudicated youth while addressing the home-building industry's need for entry-level workers by incorporating hands-on training in the construction trade with academic instruction.	• Youth Offender Grant (Labor)
Promise House–Transitional Living Services Program	Dallas	Tex.	Offers older youth who have nowhere to go, no family, no money, and nowhere to live the opportunity not only to learn how to live independently, but to finish their education, find meaningful work, and become productive citizens.	• Continuum of Care Grant (Department of Housing and Urban Development) • Runaway and Homeless Youth (HHS)
* Sasha Bruce Youthwork–Independent Living Program	Washington	D.C.	Strives to improve the lives of runaway, homeless, neglected, and at-risk youth and their families in the Washington area by providing shelter, counseling, life skills training, and positive youth development activities.	• Stewart McKinney Homeless Assistance Act (HHS)
School to Career	San Antonio	Tex.	Promotes and sustains communication among community partners to leverage resources and supportive services for young adults aging out of the foster care system.	• No federal funding
Teen Living Programs–Transitional Living Program	Chicago	Ill.	Assists youth who are homeless to permanently leave the streets, secure stable housing, and build self-sufficient, satisfying lives.	• Runaway and Homeless Youth (HHS)
Welcome New Jersey–Camden Community Connections	Camden	N.J.	Provides life skills management, job readiness skills training, edu-cation tutorial and academic pro-gress assistance, and community service and job opportunities to youth living in Camden County who are at risk of adjudication through the juvenile justice system.	• High Growth Youth Offender Initiative (Labor) • WIA (Labor)
*Youth Opportunity (YO!) Baltimore	Baltimore	M.D.	Helps City youth receive the education and career skills training needed to become successful adults.	• WIA (Labor) • Youth Opportunity (Labor)

(Continued)

Organization name	City	State	Brief description	Key federal funding source(s)[a]
*Youth Opportunity (YO) Boston	Boston	Mass.	YO Boston is a citywide program that helps young people on the wrong path make a turn toward a positive, self-sufficient future by connecting them with opportunities and employment.	• No federal funding[e]
YouthBuild McLean County	Bloomington	Ill.	Offers young people an opportunity to build their futures and their communities through education, leadership development, job training, and the rehabilitation and production of affordable housing.	• AmeriCorps (Corporation for National and Community Service) • YouthBuild (Labor) • Urban and Rural Community Economic Development Program (HHS) • Self-Help Housing Loan program (U.S. Department of Agriculture)
*Youth Employment Partnership, Inc.	Oakland	Calif.	Provides training, job placement, access to education, and comprehensive support services to enhance the employment opportunities of underserved youth.	• AmeriCorps (Corporation for National and Community Service) • WIA (Labor) • YouthBuild (Labor)
Youth In Need— Transitional Living Program	St. Charles	Mo.	Offers homeless youth opportunities to learn independent living skills, work toward completing their education, and become self-sufficient members of the community.	• Runaway and Homeless Youth (HHS)

Source: GAO analysis of data from 39 local programs.

[a] Key federal funding sources as reported by the 39 program directors. GAO did not verify this information.

[b] This funding source provides only 1 percent of the program's budget.

[c] Previously, the program reported receiving federal funding through the TRIO grant (Education); Safe Schools/Healthy Schools (HHS, Justice, and Education); and Titles I, II, and V of the Elementary and Secondary Education Act, as amended (Education).

[d] This program received less than $10,000 from the Elementary and Secondary Education Act, Title I (Education) in fiscal year 2006.

[e] Initially, this program was funded by the federal Youth Opportunity Grant. However, program authorization expired in fiscal year 2003 and funding has not been appropriated for the program.

APPENDIX II: SCOPE AND METHODOLOGY

Our review focused on (1) the characteristics of programs that provide services to disconnected youth, (2) the key elements of locally operated programs that program directors attribute to their success in reconnecting youth to education and employment, and (3) the challenges that are involved in implementing and operating these programs and how federal agencies are helping to address these challenges. For the purposes of this engagement, we defined disconnected youth as individuals between the ages of 14 and 24 who have dropped out of school and are not employed, or do not have supportive social networks, which may help youth access employment or educational opportunities. This definition is intended to include youth who are close to aging out of the foster care system, in the juvenile justice system, homeless and runaway youth, and youth who have dropped out of school. We did not focus on prevention efforts, such as school-focused dropout prevention programs, or on youth with disabilities or migrant youth, although prevention efforts may be part of programs we reviewed, and youth with disabilities and migrant youth may be among the disconnected youth these programs serve.

To obtain background information on the role the federal government plays in assisting programs that serve disconnected youth, we identified four primary federal agencies as having programs for this population: the Departments of Labor, HHS, Justice, and Education. We selected these agencies based on their legislative mandate to administer relevant federal programs, our previous work, and reports from the Congressional Research Service and the White House Task Force for Disadvantaged Youth, and discussions with federal officials. However, other federal agencies, such as the Department of Housing and Urban Development and the Corporation for National and Community Service, may also have programs that serve this population. We talked with agency officials to identify the key programs within these four agencies that serve disconnected youth. We reviewed the relevant laws, regulations, appropriations, and documents of 15 key federal programs as well as coordinating bodies involved with assisting disconnected youth, and synthesized information from interviews with appropriate federal officials.

To obtain information on the types of programs that provide services to disconnected youth and to understand the key elements that contribute to the success of locally operated programs and the challenges they face, we interviewed directors of local programs identified by agency officials and 11 experts on youth issues as successfully helping disconnected youth reach educational or employment goals. We selected experts based on their understanding of and range of perspectives on youth issues as well as their knowledge of efforts under way at the local level. Specifically, we identified them through reviews of key studies, participation in the White House Task Force for Disadvantaged Youth, and other conferences focused on youth issues. In speaking with the experts, we asked them to identify other experts in the field who were working on disconnected youth issues, and we reviewed our list with three of the experts to ensure we had a comprehensive list. We asked the experts and agency officials to identify local programs that could serve as examples or models for expansion or replication that represent various approaches or subpopulations and geographic diversity, including programs in both urban and rural locations. We also asked them to indicate the specific reasons why they were recommending the program as successful and whether evaluation results or outcome data were available for the local effort. However, many noted that rigorous program evaluations are not readily available. Likewise, when we asked programs we interviewed whether they had conducted impact evaluations of their programs, few had completed evaluations. We did not review any available evaluations in determining whether to include a program in our review.

Out of 100 programs that were identified, we selected 39 local programs to include in our review. We selected a mix of programs in 16 states and the District of Columbia that provided different types of services, such as transitional living programs, employment skills training programs, and alternative education programs; that targeted different subpopulations; and that represented geographic diversity, including a mix of urban and rural locations. (See app. I for a list of the programs we interviewed.) Most of the programs received federal funding, but some relied primarily on state, local, or private funding sources. For organizations with multiple programs focused on disadvantaged youth, we asked the executive director to identify the single program that had the most long-standing success in reconnecting youth to education and employment.

We interviewed directors of these programs using a standard set of questions. We asked directors to provide information on the key elements they thought made the program successful, implementing and operating challenges, gaps in services provided in their community, funding sources, and federal grants and policies. Prior to the interviews, we reviewed our list of closed-ended and open-ended questions with internal and external experts and conducted two pretests to ensure the questions were appropriate and clear. To use resources most efficiently, we conducted in-person interviews with 19 programs in six locations where there were a number of programs to visit, that enabled us to have broad geographic coverage, and where we could see examples of the different types of programs assisting disconnected youth. Site visit locations included Baltimore, Maryland; Boston and Brockton, Massachusetts; Nashville, Tennessee; Portland, Oregon; San Francisco and Oakland, California; and Washington, D.C. On our site visits, we toured facilities and met with youth at the programs we visited to learn about their experiences in the program. In addition, we spoke with representatives from various citywide initiatives in Baltimore, Boston, and San Francisco to gain an understanding of their efforts at cross-system collaboration to serve disconnected youth. We completed the remaining interviews by phone. We conducted this performance audit from May 2007 to February 2008 in accordance with generally accepted government auditing standards. Those standards require that we plan and perform the audit to obtain sufficient, appropriate evidence to provide a reasonable basis for our findings and conclusions based on our audit objectives. We believe that the evidence obtained provides a reasonable basis for our findings and conclusions based on our audit objectives.

APPENDIX III: KEY FEDERAL GRANT PROGRAMS THAT SERVE DISCONNECTED YOUTH

Agency or office	Federal grant	Eligible youth	Purpose
Department of Labor			
Office of the Secretary	Job Corps	Low-income youth ages 16 to 24	To assist eligible youth who need and can benefit from an intensive program, operated in a group setting in residential and nonresidential centers, to become more responsible, employable, and productive citizens.
Employment and Training Administration	Workforce Investment Act Youth Activities	Low-income Individuals ages 14 to 21 who have a barrier to completing an educational program or securing or holding employment	To make available to youth activities in workforce training, education attainment, community involvement, leadership development, and supports while in the program and for follow-up services not less than 12 months after program completion.
Employment and Training Administration	YouthBuild	School dropouts ages 16 to 24, who are members of a low- income family, in foster care, or are youth offenders, disabled, migrant, or children of incarcerated parents.	To provide disadvantaged youth with opportunities for employment, education, leadership development, and training through the rehabilitation or construction of housing for homeless individuals and low-income families, and of public facilities
Employment and Training Administration	Youth Offender Grants	14 to 24-year-old youth offenders, gang members, and youth at risk of court or gang involveement	To increase employability and employment of youth offenders, gang members, and youth at risk of court or gang involvement.
Employment and Training Administration	Youth Opportunity Grants (Program authorization expired in fiscal year 2003 and funding has not been appropriated for the program)	All 14 to 21-year-olds residing in designated impoverished areas	To provide education, employment, and leadership development activities and supports for youth in high-poverty neighborhoods to increase their long-term employment.

(Continued)

Agency or office	Federal grant	Eligible youth	Purpose
Department of Health and Human Services			
Children's Bureau	Chafee Foster Care Independence Program	Children who are likely to remain in foster care as well as youth 18 to 21 who have aged out of the foster care system	To identify youth likely to remain in foster care until age 18 and assist these youth up to age 21 to make the transition to self-sufficiency by providing housing and educational and vocational services, among other services.
Family and Youth Services Bureau	Runaway and Homeless Youth Program	Emergency services for homeless and runaway youth under 18 years of age. Transitional housing services for homeless youth ages 16 to 21	To provide comprehensive services for youth in at-risk situations and their families. The program supports emergency shelter and services and street-based education and outreach to young people, and provides older homeless youth with longer-term housing and assistance to develop the skills and resources to live independently.
Department of Education			
Office of Vocational and Adult Education	Adult Education Basic Grants to States	Adults and out-of-school youth ages 16 and older	To provide adult education and literacy services, including workplace literacy services, family literacy services, and English literacy and civic education programs.
Office of Safe and Drug-Free Schools	Grants to States for Workplace and Community Transition Training for Incarcerated Youth	A person age 25 or younger who is incarcerated in a state prison and is within 5 years of release or parole	To assist and encourage incarcerated youth to acquire functional literacy, and life and job skills through the pursuit of postsecondary education certificates, associate of arts degrees, and bachelor's degrees.
Office of Elementary and Secondary Education	Education for Homeless Children and Youth—Grants for States and Local Activities	Homeless children, including preschoolers and youth	To ensure that homeless children, including preschoolers and youth, have equal access to free and appropriate public education. Among other things, this grant also supports an office for the coordination of the education of homeless children and youth in each state.

(Continued)

Agency or office	Federal grant	Eligible youth	Purpose
Office of Elementary and Secondary Education	Title I-D Prevention and Intervention Programs for Children and Youth Who are Neglected, Delinquent, or At Risk — Grants for States and Localities	Children and youths in state-run institutions for juveniles and in adult correctional institutions	To improve educational services for neglected and delinquent children and youth in state-run institutions for juveniles and in adult correctional institutions.
Department of Justice			
Office of Juvenile Justice and Delinquency Prevention	Part E Developing, Testing, and Demonstrating Promising New Initiatives and Programs	Individuals 17 and under involved in the juvenile justice system; some states may provide services until their 24th birthday	To support programs that will develop, test, or demonstrate promising new initiatives that may prevent, control, or reduce juvenile delinquency.
Office of Juvenile Justice and Delinquency Prevention	Title II B—State Formula Grants	Individuals 17 and under involved in the juvenile justice system; some states may provide services until their 24th birthday	To support the planning, establishment, operation, coordination, and evaluation of projects for the development of more effective juvenile delinquency programs and improved juvenile justice systems.
Office of Juvenile Justice and Delinquency Prevention	Juvenile Accountability Block Grant	Individuals 17 and under involved in the juvenile justice system; some states may provide services until their 24th birthday	To strengthen their juvenile justice systems and encourage juveniles to be accountable for their actions.
Office of Juvenile Justice and Delinquency Prevention	Title V Community Prevention Block Grants	Individuals under age 17 involved in the juvenile justice system; some states may provide services until their 24th birthday	To support local projects and activities for youth who have had contact with the juvenile justice system or who are likely to have contact with the juvenile justice system.

Source: GAO analysis of agency data.

APPENDIX IV: COMMENTS FROM THE DEPARTMENT OF LABOR

U.S. Department of Labor   Employment and Training Administration
200 Constitution Avenue, N.W.
Washington, D.C. 20210

FEB   5 2008

Ms. Cornelia M. Ashby
Director
Education, Workforce, and Income Security Issues
U.S. Government Accountability Office
441 G Street, N.W.
Washington, D.C. 20548

Dear Ms. Ashby:

Thank you for sharing the Government Accountability Office (GAO) draft report
entitled, DISCONNECTED YOUTH: *Federal Action Could Address Some of the
Challenges Faced by Local Programs That Reconnect Youth to Education and
Employment* with the Department. The Department found the report to be very
informative. In the report, GAO provides guidance on improving the
implementation of the Workforce Investment Act, Youth Activities program.
GAO recommends the Department "...work with states and Workforce
Investment Boards to better ensure they have the information and guidance
needed to develop and implement contracts that allow local programs to serve
youth who are in need of more assistance than others while still achieving
performance goals."

The Department agrees with this recommendation and intends to work with
Workforce Investment Boards to identify constraints and plans to issue guidance
to the Workforce Investment system in the spring of 2008 that will provide
specific examples of ways to develop contracts with local service providers that
allow them to successfully serve youth at varying skill levels. In addition, the
Department will provide technical assistance to support the implementation of
this guidance.

Sincerely,

Thomas M. Dowd
Administrator
Office of Policy Development and Research

APPENDIX V: COMMENTS FROM THE DEPARTMENT OF HEALTH AND HUMAN SERVICES

DEPARTMENT OF HEALTH & HUMAN SERVICES

Office of the Assistant Secretary
for Legislation

Washington, D.C. 20201

FEB 8 2008

Ms. Cornelia M. Ashby
Director
Education, Workforce, and
    Income Security Issues
U.S. Government Accountability Office
Washington, DC 20548

Dear Ms. Ashby:

Enclosed are the Department's comments on the U.S. Government Accountability
Office's (GAO) draft report entitled: Disconnected Youth: Federal Action Could Address
Some of the Challenges Faced by Local Programs that Reconnect Youth to Education
and Employment (GAO 08-313).

The Department appreciates the opportunity to review and comment on this report before
its publication.

Sincerely,

Vince Ventimiglia
Assistant Secretary for Legislation

COMMENTS OF THE DEPARMENT OF HEALTH AND HUMAN SERVICES
ON THE GOVERMENT ACCOUNTABILITY OFFICE'S (GAO) DRAFT
REPORT ENTITLED, "DISCONNECTED YOUTH: FEDERAL ACTION
COULD ADDRESS SOME OF THE CHALLENGES FACED BY LOCAL
PROGRAMS THAT RECONNECT YOUTH TO EDUCATION AND
EMPLOYMENT (GAO-08-313)

GAO Recommendation

To improve implementation of the WIA Youth Activities program, we recommend that
the Secretary of Labor work with states and Workforce Investment Boards to better
ensure they have the information and guidance needed to develop and implement
contracts that allow local programs to serve youth who are in need of more assistance
than others while still achieving performance goals. This could include (1) working with
Workforce Investment Boards to identify and understand the incentives or constraints
that discourage boards from structuring contracts with local programs that would assist
their efforts to serve lower-skilled youth, (2) issuing guidance—based on this input—that
provides specific examples of ways to develop contracts with local service providers that
allow them to serve youth at varying skill levels, and (3) providing technical assistance to
support the implementation of this guidance.

Response to Recommendation

Since 2005, in an effort to provide stronger support to local partnerships as they work to
support youth, several Federal agencies, including the Department of Health and Human
Services, the Department of Labor, the Department of Education, and the Department of
Justice, have created a website called the Community Guide to Helping America's Youth
(www.helpingamericasyouth.gov). This website provides interactive tools to assist
communities as they seek to form effective partnerships, assess community assets, map
local and Federal resources, and search for evidence-based programs to meet the needs of
youth, including disconnected youth.

End Notes

[1] There is not a commonly accepted definition of disconnected youth. For the purposes of this study, we define disconnected youth as youth aged 14 to 24 who are not in school and not working, or who lack family or other support networks.

[2] In December 2002, the President of the United States established the White House Task Force for Disadvantaged Youth to develop for his consideration a comprehensive federal response to the problems of youth failure, under existing authorities and programs, with a focus on enhanced agency accountability and effectiveness.

[3] Social networks of family, friends, and communities can provide assistance in the form of employment connections, health insurance coverage, tuition, and other supports such as housing and financial assistance. See Adrienne Fernandes, *Vulnerable Youth: Background and Policies*, Congressional Research Service, Washington, D.C.: April 24, 2007.

[4] The 2.3 million figure is based on data from March 2006 cited in *Vulnerable Youth: Background and Policies*. The 5.2 million figure is based on 2001 data, cited in Andrew Sum, Ishwar Khatiwada, Nathan Pond, and Mykhaylo Trub'skyy, *Left Behind in the Labor Market: Labor Market Problems of the Nation's Out-of-School, Young Adult Populations*, Center for Labor Market Studies (Northeastern University: November 2002). These estimates refer to youth aged 16 to 24, which differs from the definition for youth (aged 14 to 24) used in this report, and are derived from a dataset that includes the civilian, non-institutionalized population.

[5] See GAO, *African American Children in Foster Care: Additional HHS Assistance Needed to Help States Reduce the Proportion in Care, GAO-07-816* (Washington, D.C.: July 11, 2007), for more information on overrepresentation of African-American children in foster care.

[6] Other federal agencies also play an important role in funding programs that serve disconnected youth, including the Department of Housing and Urban Development and the Corporation for National and Community Service, among others.

[7] Local workforce investment boards are composed of representatives of businesses, local educational entities, labor organizations, community-based organizations, economic development agencies, and one-stop partners. WIA required states and localities to bring together federally funded employment and training programs into a single comprehensive workforce system, called the one-stop system.

[8] The Transitional Living Program is one of three programs that constitute HHS's Runaway and Homeless Youth program.

[9] The programs we reviewed are not a representative sample of the range of programs that serve disconnected youth. See appendix II for more information on the selection criteria we used.

[10] Average length of stay is longer for transitional living programs than for emergency shelters for youth.

[11] The AmeriCorps program, administered within the Corporation for National and Community Service, provides financial awards for education to individuals upon completion of intensive public service that meets educational, public safety, health, and environmental needs.

[12] In 2005, GAO surveyed 36 grantees that received Labor's Youth Opportunity funding. The grantees also identified obstacles faced by their clients—homelessness, lack of family support, mental health problems, and low levels of academic achievement—as a major implementation challenge. See GAO, *Youth Opportunity Grants: Lessons Can be Learned from Program, but Labor Needs to Make Data Available, GAO-06-53* (Washington, D.C.: Dec. 9, 2005).

[13] In a 2006 report on challenges faced by child welfare agencies, GAO reported that in 2006 more than half of state child welfare agencies said that they were dissatisfied with mental health services, substance abuse services, transportation services, and housing for parents of at-risk families. States interviewed for the report cited that funding constraints were among the reasons maintaining an adequate level of services was difficult. See GAO, *Child Welfare: Improving Social Service Program, Training, and Technical Assistance Information Would Help Address Longstanding Service-Level and Workforce Challenges, GAO-07-75* (Washington, D.C.: Oct. 6, 2006).

[14] Similarly, 28 out of 36 of the Youth Opportunity grantees interviewed for GAO's 2005 report also cited a lack of jobs in the community as an implementation challenge.

[15] We have documented a similar effect of performance benchmarks on local programs' selection criteria in the WIA Adult and Dislocated Workers programs. See GAO, *Workforce Investment Act: Improvements Needed in Performance Measures to Provide a More Accurate Picture of WIA's Effectiveness*, GAO-02-275 (Washington, D.C.: Feb. 1, 2002).

[16] We have similarly found in a prior report that programs receiving WIA funds preferred to focus on in-school youth because serving out-of-school youth was much more difficult and expensive, and less effective. See GAO, *Workforce Investment Act: Labor Actions Can Help States Improve Quality of Performance Outcome Data and Delivery of Youth Services*, GAO-04-308 (Washington, D.C.: Feb. 23, 2004).

[17] The Workforce Investment Act, initially authorized through fiscal year 2003 may be one legislative vehicle for establishing new measures. Congress has not yet reauthorized WIA, although it has continued to appropriate funds for WIA programs each year.

[18] Program directors responded on the severity of these challenges using a five-point scale as follows: very great challenge, great challenge, moderate challenge, some challenge, and little or no challenge.

[19] Labor officials explained that 95 percent of the funds for the 3-year YouthBuild grant are spent on program operations in the first 2 years, with the remaining 5 percent allowed for follow-up with participants during the third grant year.

[20] GAO, *Results-Oriented Government: Practices That Can Help Enhance and Sustain Collaboration among Federal Agencies*, GAO-06-15 (Washington, D.C.: Oct. 21, 2005).

[21] GAO, *At Risk and Delinquent Youth: Multiple Programs Lack Coordinated Federal Effort*, GAO/T-HEHS-98-38 (Washington, D.C.: Nov. 5, 1997).

[22] For more information, see the Community Guide to Helping America's Youth at www.helpingamericasyouth.gov.

[23] Pub. L. No.109-365, title VIII, which established the council, authorized appropriations of $1,000,000 for each of the fiscal years 2007 and 2008 to carry out the title, although funds were not appropriated.

In: Vulnerable and Disconnected Youth: Background...   ISBN: 978-1-60741-488-9
Editor: Dierk Neumann   © 2010 Nova Science Publishers, Inc.

Chapter 3

VULNERABLE YOUTH: BACKGROUND AND POLICIES

Adrienne L. Fernandes

SUMMARY

The majority of young people in the United States grow up healthy and safe in their communities. Most of those of school age live with parents who provide for their well-being, and they attend schools that prepare them for advanced education or vocational training and, ultimately, self-sufficiency. Many youth also receive assistance from their families during the transition to adulthood. During this period, young adults cycle between attending school, living independently, and staying with their families. On average, parents give their children an estimated $38,000, or about $2,200 a year, while they are between the ages of 18 and 34 to supplement wages, pay for college tuition, and assist with down payments on a house, among other types of financial help. Even with this assistance, the current move from adolescence to adulthood has become longer and increasingly complex.

For vulnerable (or "at-risk") youth populations, the transition to adulthood is further complicated by a number of challenges, including family conflict or abandonment and obstacles to securing employment that provides adequate wages and health insurance. These youth may be prone to outcomes that have negative consequences for their future development as responsible, self-sufficient adults. Risk outcomes include teenage parenthood; homelessness; drug abuse; delinquency; physical and sexual abuse; and school dropout. Detachment from the labor market and school — or disconnectedness — may be the single strongest indicator that the transition to adulthood has not been made successfully. Approximately 1.8 million noninstitutionalized civilian youth are not working or in school.

The federal government has not adopted a single overarching federal policy or legislative vehicle that addresses the challenges vulnerable youth experience in adolescence or while making the transition to adulthood. Rather, federal youth policy today has evolved from multiple programs established in the early 20th century and expanded in the years following the 1964 announcement of the War on Poverty. These programs are concentrated in six areas: workforce development, education, juvenile justice and delinquency prevention, social services, public health, and national and community service. They are intended to provide vulnerable youth with opportunities to develop skills to assist them in adulthood.

Despite the range of federal services and activities to assist disadvantaged youth, many of these programs have not developed into a coherent system of support. This is due in part to the administration of programs within several agencies and the lack of mechanisms to coordinate their activities. In response to concerns about the complex federal structure developed to assist vulnerable youth, Congress passed the Tom Osborne Federal Youth Coordination Act (P.L. 109-365) in 2006. This legislation, like predecessor legislation that was never fully implemented — the Claude Pepper Young Americans Act of 1990 (P.L. 101-501) — establishes a federal council to improve coordination of federal programs serving youth. Congress has also considered other legislation (the Younger Americans Act of 2000 and the Youth Community Development Block Grant of 1995) to improve the delivery of services to vulnerable youth and provide opportunities to these youth through policies with a "positive youth development" focus. This report will be updated periodically.

INTRODUCTION

Congress has long been concerned about the well-being of youth. The nation's future depends on young people today to leave school prepared for college or the workplace and to begin to make positive contributions to society. Some youth, however, face barriers to becoming contributing taxpayers, workers, and participants in civic life. These youth have characteristics or experiences that put them at risk of developing problem behaviors and outcomes that have the potential to harm their community, themselves, or both. Poor outcomes often develop in home and neighborhood environments that do not provide youth with adequate economic and emotional supports. Groups of vulnerable (or "at-risk") youth include emancipating foster youth, runaway and homeless youth, and youth involved in the juvenile justice system, among others. Like all youth, vulnerable youth face a difficult transition to adulthood; however, their transition is further complicated by a number of challenges, including family conflict and obstacles to securing employment that provides adequate wages, health insurance, and potential for upward mobility.

The federal government has not adopted a single overarching federal policy or legislative vehicle that addresses the challenges at-risk youth experience in adolescence or while making the transition to adulthood. Rather, federal youth policy today has evolved from multiple programs established in the early 20th century and expanded through Great Society initiatives. These programs, concentrated in six areas — workforce development, education, juvenile justice and delinquency prevention, social services, public health, and national and community service — provide vulnerable youth with opportunities to develop skills that will assist them in adulthood.

Despite the range of federal services and activities for vulnerable youth, many of the programs have not been developed into a coordinated system of support. In response, federal policymakers have periodically undertaken efforts to develop a comprehensive federal policy around youth. Congress has passed legislation (the Tom Osborne Federal Youth Coordination Act, P.L. 109-3 65) that authorizes the federal government to establish a youth council to improve coordination of federal programs serving youth. Congress has also considered other legislation in recent years (the Younger Americans Act of 2000 and the Youth Community Development Block Grant of 1995) to improve the delivery of services to vulnerable youth and provide opportunities to these youth through policies with a "positive youth development" focus.

This report first provides an overview of the youth population and the increasing complexity of transitioning to adulthood for all adolescents. It also provides a separate discussion of the concept of "disconnectedness," as well as the protective factors youth can develop during childhood and adolescence that can mitigate poor outcomes. Further, the report describes the evolution of federal youth policy, focusing on three time periods, and provides a brief overview of current federal programs targeted at vulnerable youth. (**Appendix Table A-1**, toward the end of the report, enumerates the objectives and funding levels of 51 such programs. Note that the table does not enumerate all programs that target, even in small part, vulnerable or disconnected youth.) The report then discusses the challenges of coordinating federal programs for youth, as well as federal legislation and initiatives that promote coordination among federal agencies and support programs with a positive youth development focus.

OVERVIEW

Age of Youth and the Transition to Adulthood

For the purposes of this report, "youth" refers to adolescents and young adults between the ages of 10 and 24. Under this definition, there are approximately 60 million youth (or 21% of the population) in the United States.[1] Although traditional definitions of youth include adolescents ages 12 to 18, cultural and economic shifts have protracted the period of adolescence. Children as young as 10 are included in this range because puberty begins at this age for some youth, and experiences in early adolescence often shape enduring patterns of behavior.[2] Older youth, up to age 24, are in the process of transitioning to adulthood. Many young people in their mid-20s attend school or begin to work, and some live with their parents or other relatives.

The current move from adolescence to adulthood has become longer and more complex.[3] Youth of the 1950s were more likely to follow an orderly path to adulthood. They generally completed their education and/or secured employment (for males), including military service, which was followed by marriage and parenthood in their early 20s. (This was not true for every young person; for example, African Americans and immigrants in certain parts of the country faced barriers to employment.) Unlike their postwar counterparts who had access to plentiful jobs in the industrial sector, youth today must compete in a global, information-driven economy. Many more youth now receive vocational training or enroll in colleges and universities after leaving high school. Changed expectations for women mean they attend college in greater numbers than men.[4] During the period of transition, young adults cycle between attending school, living independently, and staying with their parents. They also use this time to explore career options and relationships with potential long-term partners. The median age of first marriage has risen each decade since the 1950s, with 27 now being the median age for men and 25 the median age for women.[5] These choices enable youth to delay becoming financially independent, which can create a financial burden for their families. On average, parents give their children an estimated $38,000 — or about $2,200 a year — between the ages of 18 and 34 to supplement wages, pay for college tuition, and help with housing costs, among other types of financial assistance.[6] Parents also provide support by allowing their adult children to live with them or providing child care for their grandchildren. Approximately 23% of adults ages 23 to 27 lived with one or both of their parents in 2003.[7]

Programs that assist youth making the transition to adulthood also recognize that adolescence is no longer a finite period ending at age 18. Since FY2003, the Chafee Foster Care Education and Training Vouchers program has provided vouchers worth up to $5,000 annually per youth who is "aging out" of foster care or was adopted from foster care after 16 years of age.[8] The vouchers are available for the cost of attendance at an institution of higher education, as defined by the Higher Education Act of 1965. Youth receiving a voucher at age 21 may continue to participate in the voucher program until age 23.

Further, the changing concept of the age of adulthood is gaining currency among organizations and foundations that support and study youth development projects. The Youth Transition Funders Group is a network of grant makers whose mission is to help all adolescents make the successful transition to adulthood by age 25. Similarly, the Network on Transitions to Adulthood, a consortium of approximately 20 researchers from around the country, was created in 2000 to study the changing nature of early adulthood. The network recently published two books on this population which highlight the difficulties for youth today in becoming self- sufficient, independent adults even into their mid-20s.[9]

Defining the Vulnerable Youth Population

The majority of young people in the United States grow up healthy and safe in their communities. Those of primary and secondary school age live with parents who provide for their emotional and economic well-being and they attend schools that prepare them for continuing education or the workforce, and ultimately, self- sufficiency . Approximately one-quarter of today's youth will graduate from a four-year college or university.[10] Nonetheless, some young people do not grow up in a secure environment or with parents that provide a comprehensive system of support. These youth often live in impoverished neighborhoods and come to school unprepared to learn. Even youth who have adequate academic and emotional support may experience greater challenges as they transition to adulthood.

There is no universal definition of the terms "vulnerable" or "at-risk" youth, and some believe that these labels should not be used because of their potentially stigmatizing effects.[11] The terms have been used to denote individuals who experience emotional and adjustment problems, are at risk of dropping out, or lack the skills to succeed after graduation.[12] They have also been used to suggest that youth grow up in unstable family or community environments.[13] Researchers, policymakers, and youth advocates, however, might agree to this definition: vulnerable youth have characteristics and experiences that put them at risk of developing problem behaviors and outcomes that have the potential to hurt their community, themselves, or both.[14] "At risk" does not necessarily mean a youth has already experienced negative outcomes but it suggests that negative outcomes are more likely. Youth may also experience different levels of risk. On a risk continuum, they might have remote risk (less positive family, school, and social interaction and some stressors) to imminent risk (high-risk behaviors and many stressors).[15] Vulnerable youth may also display resiliency that mitigates negative outcomes.

Groups of Vulnerable Youth

Researchers on vulnerable youth have identified multiple groups at risk of experiencing poor outcomes as they enter adulthood.[16] These groups include, but are not limited to the following:

- youth emancipating from foster care;
- runaway and homeless youth;
- youth involved in the juvenile justice system;
- immigrant youth and youth with limited English proficiency (LEP);
- youth with physical and mental disabilities;
- youth with mental disorders; and
- youth receiving special education.

Some researchers have also classified other groups of vulnerable youth based on risk outcomes: young unmarried mothers, high school dropouts, and disconnected (e.g., not in school nor working) youth.

Among the seven groups listed above, some lack financial assistance and emotional support from their families. Former foster youth, for example, often do not have parents who can provide financial assistance while they attend college or vocational schools. Other vulnerable youth have difficulty securing employment because of their disabilities, mental illness, juvenile justice records, or other challenges. Vulnerable youth who have depended on public systems of support often lose needed assistance at the age of majority.[17] Many will lose health insurance coverage, vocational services, and supplementary income.[18] They will also face challenges in accessing adult public systems, where professionals are not always trained to address the special needs of young adults. Regardless of their specific risk factor(s), groups of vulnerable youth share many of the same barriers to successfully transitioning into their 20s.

Figure 1 (below) shows the approximate number or percentage of youth who belong to each group and their basic characteristics. Even within these groups, the population is highly diverse. For example, among youth with disabilities, individuals experience asthma, visual or hearing impairments, emotional disturbances, congenital heart disease, epilepsy, cerebral palsy, diabetes, cancer, and spina bifida. Youth in these seven groups also represent diverse socioeconomic and racial backgrounds. However, youth of color and the poor tend to be overrepresented in vulnerable populations. This is due, in part, to their exposure to poverty, and crime, racism, and lack of access to systems of care, such as health care and vocational assistance.[19]

Youth may also be members of multiple vulnerable populations. For instance, former foster youth are particularly at risk of becoming homeless. Each year about 20,000 youth "age out" of foster care, and of these youth, about two-fifths receive independent living services.[20] Emancipated youth may have inadequate housing supports.[21] Even if states made available all federal funds under the Chafee Foster Care Independence Program for housing, each emancipated youth would receive less than $800 per year.[22] Recently emancipated foster youth also tend to be less economically secure than their counterparts in the general youth population because they earn lower wages and are more likely to forego college and vocational training.[23] Their economic vulnerability can place them at risk of losing their housing. **Figure 1** shows the overlap that exists among some of the seven groups of youth. (**Note: Figure 1** does not include all possible vulnerable youth groups nor does it show all possible overlap(s) among multiple groups. The number of youth across groups should not be aggregated.)

FRAMEWORK FOR RISK

Not all vulnerable youth experience negative outcomes. However, three broad categories of factors influence whether youth face challenges in adolescence and as they transition to adulthood.[24] These categories include antecedents of risk, markers of risk, and problem behaviors. **Figure 2** summarizes the three categories and the risk outcomes vulnerable youth may experience.

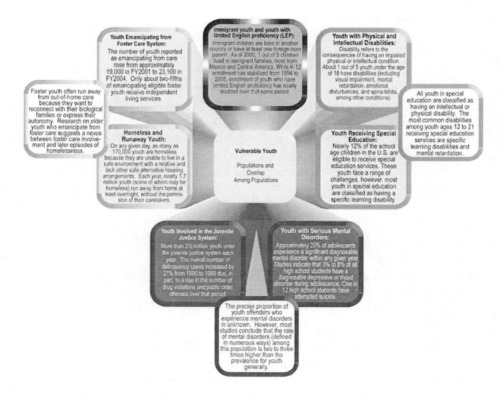

Source: Created by the Congressional Research Service (CRS).

Figure 1. Vulnerable Youth Groups and Overlap Among Groups

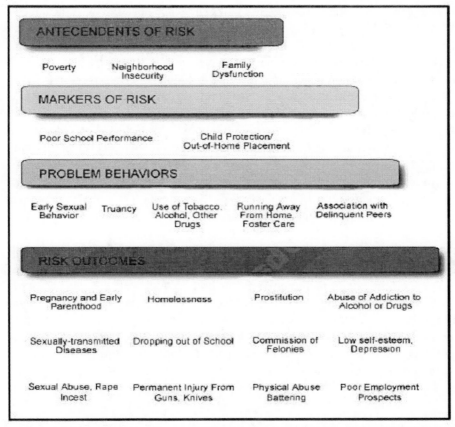

Source: Figure created by the Congressional Research Service (CRS) based on Martha Burt, Gary Resnick, and Nancy Matheson, "Comprehensive Service Integration Programs for At-Risk Youth: Final Report," The Urban Institute, 1992, Exhibit 2.2.

Figure 2. Risk Framework for Vulnerable Youth

Antecedents of risk are the social environmental conditions that influence outcomes; these factors significantly predict the overall well-being of youth. Poverty, community conditions, and family structure are three primary antecedents of risk. Poverty is linked to a number of potential future problems among youth, including low professional attainment, and meager future earnings. An analysis that utilized data from the National Longitudinal Survey of Youth and U.S. census tract information for 1980 to 1990 estimated that adolescents ages 14 to 22 who grew up in relatively high poverty metropolitan neighborhoods had a lesser likelihood as adults of being employed.[25] Other macro-level forces — the location of employers and the erosion of the manufacturing sector — can also limit the jobs available to poor youth who live in urban areas.[26] Some analyses have found that youths' place of residence in proximity to jobs affects their labor market involvement independent of other factors.[27] Jobs in the manufacturing sector have been replaced by the growth of the service and high-technology sectors, jobs requiring technical and managerial skills.[28] Youth who drop out of school or do not pursue postsecondary education cannot easily compete for available jobs.

Markers of risk also suggest that youth will experience negative outcomes in adolescence and beyond. Markers of risk are tangible indicators that can be measured or documented in public records; low school performance and involvement in the child welfare system are two such markers. Low academic performance, based on scores from a basic cognitive skills test as part of the 1994 National Longitudinal Education Survey, is associated with low employment rates. Among16-to-24 year olds who scored below the 20th percentile on the test, 74% of white youth, 47.7% of black youth, and 57.4% of Hispanic youth were employed.[29] Youth involved in the child welfare system, including out-of-home placement in the foster care system, are at-risk because of their history of abuse or neglect. Over 111,000 children and youth ages 10 to 17 (3 8.8% of all those in care) were in foster care and approximately 9% of foster youth emancipated from care on the last day of FY2005.[30] Studies show that youth who have "aged out" of foster care fare poorly relative to their counterparts in the general population on several outcome measures.[31]

Problem behaviors further define a youth's level of risk for incurring serious consequences during the transition to adulthood. Problem behaviors are activities that have the potential to hurt youth, the community, or both. Youth with these behaviors likely live under risk antecedent conditions and have displayed risk markers. Behaviors include early sexual experimentation; truancy; use of tobacco, alcohol, or other drugs; running away from home or foster care; and association with delinquent peers. Problem behaviors, coupled with poor socioeconomic and social environmental factors, can precipitate more long-term negative outcomes, described in **Figure 2** as risk outcomes. *Risk outcomes* include school dropout, low employment prospects, teen pregnancy, and alcohol and substance abuse.

Disconnectedness

Youth advocates and researchers have begun to focus on vulnerable youth who experience negative outcomes in employment and the workforce.[32] Generally characterized as "disconnected," these youth are not working or attending school. They are also not embedded in strong social networks of family, friends, and communities that provide assistance in the form of employment connections, health insurance coverage, tuition and other supports such as housing and financial assistance. However, there is no uniform definition of this term.

On the basis of the varying definitions of disconnectedness, low educational attainment and detachment from the labor market appear to be signature characteristics of the population. An analysis by the Congressional Research Service of the U.S. Census Bureau's Current Population Survey (CPS) data used a definition of disconnectedness to include noninstitutionalized youth ages 16 through 24 who did not work anytime during a previous year due primarily to a reason other than school and were presently (usually March or April of the current year) not working or in school. The definition excludes youth who are married to a connected partner *and* are parenting, on the assumption that these young people work in the home and rely on financial and social support from their spouses. Thus, young people who are married without children (to a connected or disconnected partner) or are cohabiting with or without children meet the definition of being disconnected. According to this definition, 1.8 million youth — or 4.9 percent of the general youth population ages through

24 — were disconnected in 2007.[33] **Table 1** shows that of the noninstitutionalized male population, 3.0% of whites, 9.0% of blacks, and 3.2% of Hispanics were disconnected.[34] Although black and white women had nearly the same rate of disconnection as their male counterparts (9.5% and 4.2%, respectively), Hispanic females were almost twice as likely than their male counterparts to experience disconnection.

Incarcerated Youth[35]

The definitions of disconnectedness discussed above include only the civilian noninstitutional population. They therefore omit such persons as inmates of prisons and jails, the majority of whom are minority males (non-Hispanic blacks and Hispanics).[36] An analysis of 16-to-24-year olds examined the disconnectedness (defined as out of work and school for at least one year) of both the civilian noninstitutional and incarcerated population, based on data from the 1999 CPS supplemented with summary statistics of youth incarceration rates from the Department of Justice's Bureau of Justice Statistics. When incorporating the incarcerated population, the rates of disconnection increased for white males from 3% to 4.2%; for black males from 10.5% to 17.1%; and for Hispanic males from 9% to 11.9%.[37] Another study that added residents of institutions and active-duty personnel in the Armed Forces to October 2000 CPS data found the rate of disconnection among 16 to 19 year old males rose from 8% to 10% and among 20 to 24 year old males, from 11% to 13%.[38] In contrast, inclusion of these population groups had no effect on the incidence of disconnection among females, which remained at 9% for teenagers and 18% for young adults.

A third study of incarcerated youth included those ages 18 to 24 in local jails and state or federal prisons after being convicted of a crime, as well as unmarried youth this same age with a high school degree or less who had been unemployed for one or more years. At any point during the 1997 to 2001 period, the researchers estimated that almost 1.8 million young adults (or 7% of the population ages 18 to 24) experienced long spells of unemployment (1.7 million) or were incarcerated (420,000).[39] A majority (59% or 1 million) in this group were male, who accounted for 8% of the 18-to-24 year old male population. The 728,000 disconnected females accounted for 6% of the 18-to-24 year old female population. Over one-third of the disconnected males were incarcerated compared to just 3% of females. Nearly all the disconnected mothers had their first child between 14 and 20, and half of them reported welfare receipt.

Positive Youth Development: The Importance of Resiliency and Opportunity

Although vulnerable youth overall experience more negative outcomes than their counterparts who are not considered to be at risk, some of these youth have accomplished their goals of attending college and/or securing permanent employment. Youth advocates argue that vulnerable youth can reach their goals if given adequate opportunities to develop positive behaviors during adolescence. Emphasizing that youth are in control of their future and can make contributions to their communities and society, these advocates view vulnerable youth as resources rather than victims or perpetrators.[40]

Table 1. Disconnected Civilian, Noninstitutional Youth by Race and Hispanic Origin, Ages 16 through 24 (2007)

Total (% of total 16-24 population)	Number of Men (% of 16 to 24 population)				Number of Women (% of 16 to 24 population)			
	Non-Hispanic White	Non-Hispanic Black	Hispanic	Non-Hispanic Other	Non-Hispanic White	Non-Hispanic Black	Hispanic	Non-Hispanic Other
1,827,536	355,545	231,604	111,551	54,473	478,708	258,394	269,632	67,628
(4.9)	(3.0)	(9.0)	(3.2)	(4.2)	(4.2)	(9.5)	(8.6)	(5.2)

Source: Congressional Research Service (CRS) analysis of U.S. Census Bureau, Current Population Survey (March 2007).

Note: Beginning with the March 2003 CPS, the Census Bureau allows survey respondents to identify themselves as belonging to one or more racial groups. The terms black and white refer to persons who identified with only a single racial group (i.e., non-Hispanic black or non-Hispanic white). The term Hispanic refers to individuals' ethnic, as opposed to racial, identification. Hispanics can be of any race.

What is Youth Development?

Youth development refers to the processes — physical, cognitive, and emotional — that youth undergo during adolescence. The competencies that youth begin to gain during adolescence can assist them as they transition to adulthood. Youth who master competencies across several domains will likely achieve desirable outcomes, including educational and professional success, self-confidence, connections to family and the community, and contributions to society. These areas of competency include the following:

- *Cognitive*: Knowledge of essential life skills, problem solving skills, academic adeptness;
- *Social*: Connectedness with others, perceived good relationships with peers, parents, and other adults;
- *Physical:* Good health habits, good health risk management skills;
- *Emotional:* Good mental health, including positive self-regard; good coping skills;
- *Personal:* Sense of personal autonomy and identity, sense of safety, spirituality, planning for the future and future life events, strong moral character;
- *Civic:* Commitment to community engagement, volunteering, knowledge of how to interface with government systems; and
- *Vocational:* Knowledge of essential vocational skills, perception of future in terms of jobs or careers.[41]

A primary factor that influences how well youth develop these competencies is the interaction between *individual characteristics*, or traits influenced by genetic inheritance and prenatal environment, and the *social environment* — societal conditions, community, and the family can serve to reinforce positive behaviors and promote positive outcomes for vulnerable youth.[42]

Societal conditions — economic conditions, the prevalence of discrimination, and educational institutions — affect the development of youth competencies and connectedness to others. Adolescents who perceive their future in terms of jobs or careers often achieve desirable outcomes. For vulnerable youth, poor economic conditions and fewer opportunities to work can affect how they perceive their future.

Youth's interaction with the community is another variable that shapes their development. Community culture, or the values and beliefs of a particular community, may support the positive development of youth by reinforcing cultural norms that favor academic achievement and professional success. Communities can play a role in fostering youth development by providing multiple pathways to help youth strengthen their competencies through schools and other institutions. Youth advocates argue that these pathways should involve services and long-term programs that provide opportunities for youth during the school day and in non-school hours when youth may be more susceptible to risky behaviors.[43] Within schools, the availability of resources for youth and their parents, such as programs that monitor and supervise youth, and quality youth-serving institutions and organizations can buffer youth from negative community cultures. Outside of schools, youth development programs emphasize the positive elements of growing up and engage young people in alternatives to counteract negative pressures. Approximately 17,000 organizations offer youth programs, some of which are well-known with many decades of experience (such as the Girl Scouts of the U.S.A. and 4-H), and others that are local, grassroots entities.[44] These organizations offer a variety of services that focus on the development of personal skills and critical life skills, and opportunities for youth to participate in the decisions of the organization.[45]

Finally, the family context plays a pivotal role in youth development. Parental monitoring and family structure affect how well youth transition to adulthood. Positive adolescent development is facilitated when youth express independence from their parents, yet rely on their parents for emotional support, empathy, and advice. Parenting styles and family structure play important roles in the lives of youth. Parents who discipline in a moderate and caring manner, and provide positive sanctions for prosocial behaviors can assist youth to develop a sense of control over their future. Family structures that promote positive parent-child relationships, even after divorce or times of stress (such as separation or loss of a parent), can provide youth with emotional and other support during adolescence and beyond.

The Youth Development Movement

The belief that all youth are assets has formed the basis of the youth development movement that began in the 1 980s in response to youth policies and programs that attempted to curb the specific problems facing youth (i.e., pregnancy, drug use) without focusing on how to holistically improve outcomes for youth and ease their transition to adulthood. A range of institutions have promoted this approach through their literature and programming: policy organizations (Forum for Youth Investment and National Network for Youth); national direct service organizations for youth (4-H and the Boys and Girls Clubs of America); public and private research institutions (National Research Council and Carnegie Corporation of New York), and government sub-agencies with a youth focus (the U.S. Department of Health and Human Services' Family and Youth Services Bureau and the U.S. Department of Justice's Office of Juvenile Justice and Delinquency Prevention).[46] The youth development movement has attempted to shift from an approach to youth that emphasizes problem prevention to one that addressed the types of attitudes, skills, knowledge, and behaviors young people need to develop for adulthood.[47]

Despite the endorsement of the positive youth development approach by prominent organizations, the movement has faced challenges.[48] Youth advocates within the movement point to insufficient guidance for program planners and policymakers about prioritizing which youth to serve, given the limited resources available to communities for youth programs. They have also criticized the lack of sufficient evaluation of programs and organizations using a positive development approach. According to these advocates, some youth development efforts have been built on insufficient data about demand for or supply of programs and were started without baseline data on reasonable youth indicators. Further, they argue that youth development messages have, at times, failed to generate excitement among policymakers because they did not convey how positive youth development policy and programs could respond to the challenges young people face and lead to better outcomes for youth and society at large. In turn, the movement has failed to adequately link to local and regional infrastructures that assist with funding, training, and network development.

To address these challenges, youth advocates (the same groups that have raised criticisms about the movement) have proposed a number of recommendations. For example, the Forum for Youth has urged advocates to clarify a youth development message that specifies concrete deliverables and to connect the movement to sustainable public and private resources and other youth advocacy efforts.[49] The recommendations have also called for evaluations of youth programs with a positive youth approach and improved monitoring and assessment of programs.

EVOLUTION OF THE FEDERAL ROLE IN ASSISTING VULNERABLE YOUTH

The remainder of this report describes the evolution of federal youth policy and provides an overview of current programs and initiatives that focus on vulnerable youth. Many of these initiatives promote coordination of federal youth programs and positive youth development.

The federal government has not adopted a single overarching federal policy or legislative vehicle that addresses the challenges that young people experience in adolescence or while making the transition to adulthood. Rather, federal youth policy today evolved from multiple programs and initiatives that began in the early 1900s to assist children and youth. From the turn of the twentieth century through the 1950s, youth policy was generally subsumed under a broad framework of child welfare issues. The Children's Bureau, established in 1912, focused attention on child labor and the protection of children with special needs. The age boundaries of "youth" were not clearly delineated, but based on proposed child labor reform legislation at that time, "child" referred to those individuals age 16 and under. Also during this period, work and education support programs were created to ease the financial pressures of the Great Depression for older youth (ages 16 to 23), and increasingly, federal attention focused on addressing the growing number of youth classified as delinquent. The subsequent period, spanning the 1960s and 1970s, was marked by the creation of programs that targeted youth in six policy areas: workforce development and job training, education, juvenile justice and delinquency prevention, social services, public health, and national and community service.

Finally, from the 1980s until the present, many of these programs have been expanded; others have been eliminated. The federal government has also recently adopted strategies to better serve the youth population through targeted legislation and initiatives.

1912-1950s: Children's Bureau Programs and Workforce Programs

At the turn of the twentieth century, psychologists first formally defined the concept of adolescence. American psychologist G. Stanley Hall characterized the period between childhood and adulthood as a time of "storm and stress," with youth vulnerable to risky behavior, conflict with parents, and perversion.[50] The well-being of adolescents was emerging as an area of concern during this time, albeit as part of a greater focus on child welfare by states and localities. States began to recognize the distinct legal rights of children, generally defined as age 16 and younger, and to establish laws for protecting children against physical abuse, cruelty, and neglect. Children who were abused or neglected were increasingly removed from their homes and placed in almshouses and foster homes by the state. Juvenile courts and reform schools, first created in the late 1800s, were also expanding during this period. By 1912, 22 states had passed legislation to establish juvenile courts.[51]

The year 1912 also marked the federal government's initial involvement in matters relating to child welfare with the creation of the Children's Bureau in the U.S. Department of Labor. The Bureau emerged out of the Progressive Movement, which emphasized that the stresses on family life due to industrial and urban society were having a disproportionately negative effect on children.[52] Though not a cabinet-level agency, the purpose of the Bureau was to investigate and report upon all "matters pertaining to the welfare of children and child life" for the federal government. The Bureau adopted a "whole child" philosophy, meaning that the agency was devoted to researching every aspect of the child's life throughout all stages of his or her development. In particular, the Bureau focused on infant and maternal health, child labor, and the protection of children with special needs (e.g., those who were poor, homeless, without proper guardianship, and mentally handicapped).

The concept of a "youth policy" in those early years was virtually nonexistent. However, the Bureau's efforts in combating child labor and investigating juvenile delinquency from 1912 through the early 1950s targeted youth ages 10 to 16. Bureau Chief Julia Lathrop and Progressive Era advocates pushed for laws that would prohibit the employment of children under age 16.[53] The Bureau also tracked the rising number of juvenile delinquents in the 1 930s and evaluated the causes of delinquency, citing unhappy home conditions and gang membership as a predictor of gang activity.[54] In 1954, the Bureau established a division on juvenile delinquency prevention.

Perhaps the most well known policies the Children's Bureau implemented that affected youth were through the child health and welfare programs established by the Social Security Act (P.L. 74-231) of 1935. As originally enacted, the law authorized indefinite annual funding of $1.5 million for states to establish, extend, and strengthen public child welfare services in "predominately rural" or "special needs" areas. For purposes of this program (now at Title IV-B, Subpart 1 of the Social Security Act), these were described as services "for the protection and care of homeless, dependent, and neglected children, and children in danger of becoming delinquent."[55] The Aid to Dependent Children Program (now Temporary

Assistance for Needy Families Block Grant) was also created under the act to provide financial assistance to impoverished children. "Dependent" children were defined as children under age 16 who had been deprived of parental support or care due to a parent's death, continued absence from the home, or physical or mental incapacity, and was living with a relative. Amendments to the program extended the age of children to 18.[56]

Separately in the 1930s, the federal government addressed youth poverty triggered by the Great Depression. The Federal Transient Relief Act of 1933 established a Transient Division within the Federal Transient Relief Administration to provide relief services through state grants. Also in 1933, the Civilian Conservation Corps (CCC) opened camps and shelters for more than one million low-income older youth. Two years later, in 1935, President Franklin Roosevelt created the National Youth Administration (NYA) by executive order to open employment bureaus and provide cash assistance to poor college and high school students. The Transient Division was disbanded shortly thereafter. From 1936 to 1940, legislation was proposed to provide for comprehensive educational and vocational support for older youth. As introduced in 1938, the American Youth Act (S. 1463), if passed, would have established a federal National Youth Administration to administer a system of public-works projects that would employ young persons who were not employed or full-time students. The act would have also provided unemployed youth with vocational advisors to assist them in securing apprentice training. Further, young people enrolled in school and unable to continue their studies without financial support would have been eligible to receive financial assistance to pay school fees and school materials, and personal expenses.[57] The act, however, was never brought to a full vote by the House or Senate. The Roosevelt Administration raised concerns in hearings on the bill that it was too expensive and would have provided some of the same services already administered through the CCC and NYA.[58] (The two programs were eliminated in the early 1940s.)

By the late 1940s, the Children's Bureau no longer had jurisdiction to address "all matters" concerning children and youth because of federal government reorganizations that prioritized agency function over a particular constituency (i.e., children, poor families, etc.). The bureau was moved in 1949 from the U.S. Department of Labor to the Federal Security Agency (FSA), and child health policy issues were transferred to the Public Health Service. The Bureau's philosophy of the "whole child" diminished further when the FSA was moved to the newly organized Department of Health, Education, and Welfare (HEW) in 1953.[59]

1960s-1970s: War on Poverty Initiatives and Expansion of Programs

The 1960s and 1970s marked a period of federal efforts to assist poor and disadvantaged children, adolescents, and their families. President Lyndon B. Johnson's War on Poverty initiatives and subsequent social legislation established youth-targeted programs in the areas of workforce development and job training, education, delinquency prevention, social services, and health. The major legislation during this period included:

- Economic Opportunity Act (EOA) of 1964 (P.L. 88-452): As the centerpiece of the War on Poverty, the EOA established the Office of Economic Opportunity. The office administered programs to promote the well-being of poor youth and other low-income individuals, including Job Corps, Upward Bound, Volunteers in Service to America (VISTA), Head Start, and Neighborhood Youth Corps, among others. The mission of the Job Corps was (and still is) to promote the vocational and educational opportunities of older, low-income youth. Similarly, Upward Bound was created to assist disadvantaged high school students who went on to attend college.

- Elementary and Secondary Education Act (ESEA) of 1965 (P.L. 89-10): The purpose of the ESEA was to provide federal funding to low-income schools. Amendments to the act in1966 (P.L 89-750) created the Migrant Education Program and Migrant High School Equivalency Program to assist states in providing education to children of migrant workers.

- Higher Education Act (HEA) of 1965 (P.L. 89-329): The HEA increased federal funding to universities and created scholarships and low interest loans for students. The act also created the Talent Search Program to identify older, low-income youth with potential for postsecondary education. The act was amended in 1968 (P.L. 90-575) to include two programs: Student Support Services and Upward Bound (which was transferred from the Office of Economic Opportunity to the Office of Education, and later to the U.S. Department of Education). Student Support Services was created to improve disadvantaged (defined as disabled, low-income, or first in their family to attend college) college students' retention and graduation rates.

- Youth Conservation Corps Act of 1970 (P.L. 91-378): The legislation permanently established the Youth Conservation Pilot Program to employ youth of all backgrounds to perform work on federal lands.

- Comprehensive Employment and Training Activities Act (CETA) of 1973 (P.L. 93-203): The program established federal funding for the Youth Employment and Training Program and the Summer Youth Employment Program. The programs financed employment training activities and on-the-job training.

- Juvenile Justice and Delinquency Prevention Act (JJDPA) of 1974 (P.L. 93-415): The act extended federal support to states and local governments for rehabilitative and preventative juvenile justice delinquency projects, as established under the Juvenile Delinquency Prevention and Control Act (P.L. 90-445). The major provisions of the JJDPA funded preventative programs in local communities outside of the juvenile justice system. The act's Title III established the Runaway Youth Program to provide temporary shelter, counseling, and after-care services to runaway youth and their families. Congress later amended (P.L. 95-115) Title III to include homeless youth.

- Education for All Handicapped Children of 1975 (P.L. 94-142): The act required all public schools accepting federal funds to provide equal access to education for children with physical and mental disabilities. Public schools were also required to create an educational plan for these students, with parental input, that would emulate as closely as possible the educational experiences of able-bodied children. (This legislation is now known as the Individuals with Disabilities Education Act.)

White House Conferences on Children and Youth: 1960s and 1970s

Since 1909, the executive branch has organized a White House Conference on Children (and youth, in later decades). The White House conferences of 1960 and 1971 focused on efforts to promote opportunities for youth. The recommendations from the 1960 conference's forum on adolescents discussed the need for community agencies to assist parents in addressing the concerns of youth, as well as improved social services to adolescents and young adults.[60] The recommendations called for the federal government to establish a unit devoted to youth and to support public and private research regarding the issues facing this population, including their employment, education, military service, marriage, mobility, and community involvement. The 1971 conference had a broader focus on issues that were important to youth at the time. Recommendations from the conference included a suspension of the draft, less punitive measures for drug possession, and income guarantees for poor families.[61]

Family and Youth Services Bureau

The Family and Youth Services Bureau (FYSB) was created in 1970 to provide leadership on youth issues in the federal government.[62] At that time, it was held that young people were placed inappropriately in the juvenile justice system, while others were not receiving needed social services. Known then as the Youth Development and Delinquency Prevention Administration, the sub-agency proposed a new service delivery strategy (similar to the contemporary positive youth development approach) that emphasized youth's competence, usefulness, and belonging.[63] The Juvenile Justice and Delinquency Prevention Act (JJDPA) of 1974 emphasized that youth committing status offenses (behaviors considered offenses only if carried out by a juvenile, such as truancy or running away) were more in need of care and guidance than they were of punishment. Passage of the JJDPA laid the foundation for much of FYSB's work today with runaway and homeless youth and other vulnerable youth groups.

1980s-Present: Current Youth Programs

Current federal youth policy has resulted from the piecemeal creation of programs across several areas of social policy. Many of the youth-focused programs that trace their history to the War on Poverty continue today, and several new programs, spread across several agencies, have been created. (While the Family and Youth Services Bureau was created to provide leadership on youth issues, it administers a small number of youth programs: the Runaway and Homeless Youth program, the Mentoring Children of Prisoners program, and the Abstinence Education program.) Federal youth policy today also includes recent initiatives to promote positive youth development and increase coordination between federal agencies that administer youth-focused programs.

Appendix Table A-1 provides an overview of 51 major federal programs for youth in six policy areas discussed above — job training and workforce development, education, juvenile justice and delinquency prevention, social services, public health, and national and community service. The table includes the programs' authorizing legislation and US code section; objectives; FY2006, FY2007, and FY2008 funding levels and the requested FY2009 funding levels; agency with jurisdiction; and targeted at-risk youth population.[64] The 45 programs were selected based upon their objectives to serve vulnerable youth primarily between the ages of 10 to 24, or to research this population. The CRS contributors to **Table**

A-1, their contact information, and CRS reports on some of the programs are listed in **Table A-2.**

As enacted, the programs are intended to provide vulnerable youth with the opportunities to develop skills and abilities that will assist them in adolescence and during the transition to adulthood. Congress has allocated funding to these programs for a number of services and activities, including conflict resolution; counseling; crime/violence prevention; gang intervention; job training assistance; mentoring; parental/family intervention; planning and program development; and research and evaluation. The programs differ in size, scope, and funding authorization levels and type (mandatory vs. discretionary).

The list is not exhaustive and may omit programs that serve the targeted youth population. Two major block grant programs — the Temporary Assistance for Needy Families Program (TANF) and the Social Services Block Grant (SSBG) — are not included because they do not provide dedicated funding for youth activities. However, states can choose to use TANF and SSBG funds for such purposes. TANF law permits states to use block grant fund to provide services to recipient families and other "needy" families (defined by the state) so long as the services are expected to help lead to independence from government services or enable needy families to care for children at home. States may also provide services to non-needy families if they are directed at the goals of preventing and reducing out-of-wedlock pregnancies or encouraging the formation of two-parent families. SSBG provides funding to assist states to provide a range of social services to adults and children, and each state determines what services are provided and who is eligible. Youth-focused categories of services that can be funded through the SSBG include education and training services to improve knowledge or daily living skills and to enhance cultural opportunities; foster care services for children and older youth; independent and transitional living services; pregnancy and parenting services for young parents; and special services for youth involved in or at risk of involvement with criminal activity.[65]

Job Training and Workforce Development

The federal government funds four major job training and workforce development programs for youth: Job Corps, Workforce Investment Act (WIA) Youth Activities, YouthBuild, and Youth Conservation Corps.[66] These programs (except for the Youth Conservation Corps) are administered by the Department of Labor and target low-income youth ages 16 to 24 who require additional assistance in meeting their vocational goals. Job Corps is the largest of these programs, with centers in all 50 states and Puerto Rico. Program training consists of career preparation, development, and transition; academic initiatives; and character building. Job Corps has been evaluated positively by Mathematica, in 1982 and 2001.[67] The Workforce Investment Act (WIA) of 1998 (P.L. 105-220) reauthorized the program through FY2003, although annual appropriations have continued funding through FY2008.

The Workforce Investment Act also established WIA Youth Activities to fund employment training and academic support services for both youth in school and school dropouts ages 14 to 21. Eligible youth must be low-income and either deficient in basic literacy skills, a school dropout, homeless, a runaway, foster child, a parent, an offender, or an individual who needs additional assistance to complete an educational program or secure employment. Youth councils of local Workforce Investment Boards (WIBs) advise the boards about youth activities. WIBs are certified by the state to coordinate the workforce development activities of a particular area through a local workforce investment system.[68]

Created by the Cranston-Gonzalez National Affordable Housing Act of 1990 (P.L. 101-625), YouthBuild has many of the same educational and vocational objectives as those established under Job Corps and WIA Youth Activities. YouthBuild participants ages 16 to 24 work toward their GED or high school diploma while learning job skills by building affordable housing. The program, formerly in the U.S. Department of Housing and Urban Development, was made part of WIA, administered by DOL, under the YouthBuild Transfer Act of 2006 (P.L. 109-281). Finally, the Youth Conservation Corps, established in 1970 by the Youth Conservation Corps Act (P.L. 9 1-378) and administered by the Departments of Agriculture and Interior, targets youth ages 15 to 18 of all backgrounds to work on projects that conserve natural resources.

Education

Most federal education programs for vulnerable youth are authorized by the Elementary and Secondary Education Act (ESEA) of 1965 and the Higher Education Act (HEA) of 1965, administered by the U.S. Department of Education. The ESEA provides the primary source of federal funds to K-12 education programs. The legislation's purpose, from its original enactment in 1965 to the present, is, in part, to provide supplementary educational and related services to educationally disadvantaged children who attend schools serving relatively low-income areas. The Higher Education Act is the source of grant, loan, and work-study assistance to help meet the costs of postsecondary education. The act also supports programs by providing incentives and services to disadvantaged youth to help increase their secondary or postsecondary educational attainment. Separate legislation authorizes additional education programs serving youth with disabilities and homeless youth.

Programs Authorized by Title I of the ESEA

Title I of ESEA provides most of the funding for programs that serve disadvantaged youth, and was most recently reauthorized and amended by the No Child Left Behind Act (NCLBA) of 2001 (P.L. 107-110).

Title I-A (Education for the Disadvantaged Program) is the largest federal elementary and secondary education program, with funds provided to approximately 15.8 million (34% of all) pupils.[69] Title I-A grants fund supplementary educational and related services to low-achieving and other pupils attending schools with relatively high concentrations of pupils from low-income families. The NCLBA expanded Title I-A provisions requiring participating states to adopt content and pupil performance standards, and assessments linked to these; and to take specified actions with respect to low-performing schools and local education agencies (LEAs). Title I-C (Migrant Education Program) provides formula grants to state education agencies (SEAs) for the development of programs targeted to migrant students and Title I-D (Neglected, Delinquent, or at Risk of Dropping Out Program) gives funding to LEAs and SEAs to meet the special educational needs of youth in institutions and correctional facilities for neglected and delinquent youth, as well as youth at risk of dropping out. Finally, Title I-H (High School Dropout Program) targets grants to schools that serve grades 6 to 12 and have annual dropout rates that are above the state average as well as middle schools that feed students into such schools.

Other ESEA Programs

Titles III and IV of the ESEA also target disadvantaged youth. Title III (English Language Acquisition Program) provides grant funding to states to ensure that limited English proficient (LEP) children and youth, including immigrant children and youth, attain English proficiency. The NCLBA has given SEAs and LEAs great flexibility in designing and administering instructional programs, while at the same time foocusing greater attention on the achievement of English proficiency. Title IV-A (Safe and Drug-Free Schools Program) supports the efforts of SEAs and LEAs to prevent student violence in and around schools and the illegal use of alcohol, tobacco, and drugs. Program activities include education and counseling; training of school personnel; and family, community, and emergency activities.

Title IV-B (21st Century Community Learning Centers program) provides competitive grants to LEAs for academic and other after-school programs. The purpose of the program is to provide opportunities for academic enrichment to help students, particularly those from low-income backgrounds, meet local and state academic achievement standards and reinforce their regular academic instruction.

Programs Authorized Under HEA

Foremost among Higher Education Act programs targeted to low-income, college-bound youth are Trio and GEAR UP.[70] The Migrant High School Equivalency program is another key component of the HEA.

Trio Programs. Trio programs are designed to assist students from disadvantaged backgrounds to pursue higher education and to complete their postsecondary studies.[71] Five Trio programs provide direct services to students and two provide indirect services.[72] The five primary programs are: Talent Search, Upward Bound, Educational Opportunity Centers, Student Support Services, Ronald E. McNair Postbaccalaureate Achievement, and. Each of these programs is designed to intervene at various points along the education continuum.

Talent Search, authorized under the original HEA legislation, encourages youth who have completed at least five years of elementary education with college potential to complete high school and enter postsecondary education; to encourage dropouts to reenter school; and to disseminate information about available postsecondary educational assistance. *Upward Bound* projects seek to motivate middle school and high school students to succeed in postsecondary education through instruction and counseling, among other activities.

Educational Opportunity Centers provide information to prospective postsecondary students regarding available financial aid and academic assistance, and help them apply to college. *Student Support Services* projects are intended to improve college students' retention and graduation rates, and improve transfer rates from two-year to four-year colleges through instruction; exposure to career options; mentoring; and assistance in graduate admissions and financial aid processes. In selecting grantees, the Secretary of Education considers an institution's efforts to provide participants with aid sufficient to meet full financial needs and to constrain student debt. Finally, the *Robert E. McNair Postbaccalaureate Achievement* program prepares disadvantaged students for post-doctoral study through seminars, research opportunities, summer internships, tutoring, mentoring, and exposure to cultural events and academic programs.

GEAR UP. Gaining Early Awareness and Readiness for Undergraduate Program (GEAR UP), a program not part of the TRIO array of programs, was added to the HEA by the Higher

Education Act Amendments of 1998 (P.L. 105-244). GEAR UP seeks to increase disadvantaged students' secondary school completion and postsecondary enrollment by providing support services. GEAR UP differs from Trio in two key aspects: the program (1) serves a cohort of students from seventh grade to their first year of college and (2) assures students of the availability of financial aid to meet college costs. States or partnerships (schools and at least two other entities, such as community organizations and state agencies) are eligible for funding. Any funded state or partnership must provide comprehensive mentoring, tutoring, counseling, outreach, and support services to participating students. Participating states are also required to establish or maintain a postsecondary college scholarship for participants; partnerships are permitted to include a scholarship component.

Migrant High School Equivalency Program. The Migrant High School Equivalency Program, authorized under HEA, funds institutions of higher education (or private nonprofits in cooperation with institutions of higher education) to recruit and provide academic and support services to students who lack a high school diploma and whose parents are engaged in migrant and other seasonal farmwork. The purpose of the program is to assist students to obtain a high school equivalency diploma and gain employment, or to attend college or another postsecondary education or training program.

Individuals with Disabilities Education Act

The Individuals with Disabilities Education Act (IDEA), as amended by the No Child Left Behind Act, is the major statute that provides federal funding for the education of children and youth with disabilities.[73] Part B of the act includes provisions for the education of school- aged children. As a condition for the receipt of funds states must provide "free appropriate public education" to youth as old as 21 (age may vary depending on state law). This term refers to the right of all children with disabilities to receive an education and related services that meet state curriculum requirements, at no costs to parents. Appropriateness is defined according to the child's individualized education plan (IEP) which delineates the special instruction the child should receive and his or her educational goals.

Education of Homeless Children

The McKinney-Vento Act (P.L 100-77), as amended by the No Child Left Behind Act, authorizes the Department of Education to fund LEAs to provide homeless children and youth comparable educational services. With certain exceptions for health and safety emergencies (and for schools permitted under a "grandfather" clause), states are prohibited from using funds for either a separate school or separate program within the school.

Juvenile Justice and Delinquency Prevention

The Office of Juvenile Justice and Delinquency Prevention (OJJDP) in the Department of Justice coordinates federal activities and administers programs relating to the treatment of juvenile offenders and the prevention of juvenile delinquency. These programs include those enacted under the Juvenile Justice and Delinquency Prevention Act of 1974.

Juvenile Justice and Delinquency Prevention Act[74]

The Juvenile Justice and Delinquency Prevention Act (JJDPA) was first enacted in 1974 (P.L. 90- 415) and was most recently reauthorized in 2002 by the 21st Century Department of

Justice Appropriations Authorization Act (P.L. 107-273). Its provisions were authorized through FY2007. The JJDPA as originally enacted had three main components: it created a set of institutions within the federal government that were dedicated to coordinating and administering federal juvenile justice efforts; it established grant programs to assist the states with setting up and running their juvenile justice systems; and it promulgated core mandates that states had to adhere to in order to be eligible to receive grant funding. While the JJDPA has been amended several times over the past thirty years, it continues to feature the same three components. The major components of the JJDPA are discussed below.

State Formula Grants. The JJDPA authorizes OJJDP to make formula grants to states which can be used to fund the planning, establishment, operation, coordination, and evaluation of projects for the development of more effective juvenile delinquency programs and improved juvenile justice systems. Funds are allocated annually among the states on the basis of relative population of people under the age of eighteen, and states must adhere to certain core mandates in order to be eligible for funding.

Juvenile Delinquency Prevention Block Grants. This is a discretionary grant program and funding can be used to carry out projects designed to prevent juvenile delinquency. Grant funding is allocated to eligible states based on the proportion of their population that is under the age of 18. Funding for this grant program has not been appropriated to date.

Juvenile Mentoring Program. This grant program was repealed in 2002 by the 21st Century Department of Justice Reauthorization Act (P.L. 107-273); however, it has continued to receive appropriations each subsequent fiscal year.[75] These grants could be awarded to local educational agencies (in partnership with public or private agencies) to establish and support mentoring programs.

Part E: Developing, Testing, and Demonstrating Promising New Initiatives and Programs (Challenge Grants). The Challenge Grants program authorizes OJJDP to make grants to state, local, and Indian governments and private entities in order to carry out programs that will develop, test, or demonstrate promising new initiatives that may prevent, control, or reduce juvenile delinquency.

Title V Community Prevention Block Grants. The Community Prevention Block Grant program authorizes OJJDP to make grants to states, that are then transmitted to units of local government, in order to carry out delinquency prevention programs for juveniles who have come into contact with, or are likely to come into contact with, the juvenile justice system.

Social Services

The major social service programs to assist at-risk youth are authorized under the Social Security Act, as amended, and are administered by the U.S. Department of Health and Human Services.[76]

Foster Care Program and Chafee Foster Care Independence Program (CFCIP)

Title IV-E of the Social Security Act authorizes the federal foster care program.[77] Under this program, a state may seek federal funds for partial reimbursement of the room and board costs needed to support eligible children who are neglected, abused, or who, for some other reason, cannot remain in their own homes. More than half a million children are in foster care in the United States on any given day of the year and a little less than half of these (roughly 46% of the daily caseload) are estimated as eligible for federal or Title IV-E foster care support. To be eligible for Title IV-E, a child must be in the care and responsibility of the state and 1) the child must meet income/assets tests and family structure rules in the home he/she was removed from;[78] 2) have specific judicial determinations made related to reasons for the removal and other aspects of his/her removal and placement; and 3) be placed in an eligible licensed setting with an eligible provider(s).

The federal government has established certain requirements related to state provision of foster care that are applicable to all children and youth in foster care. These include that a state has a written case plan detailing, among other things, where the child is placed and what services are to be provided to ensure that a permanent home is re-established for the child. Further, for each child in foster care, this plan must be reviewed on a regular basis, including a review by a judge no less often than every 12 months. For many youth who enter foster care, returning to their parents is the way permanence is re-established. For some youth, however, it is not safe or possible to reunite with their parents. In those cases states must work to find adoptive parents or legal guardians who can provide a permanent home for these youth.

Foster youth who reach the "age of majority" (18 years in most states) and who have not been reunited with their parents or placed with adoptive parents or guardians are said to "emancipate" or "age out" of foster care. The Chafee Foster Care Independence Program, created in 1999 (P.L. 106-169), required states to provide independent living services for youth until their 21st birthday and those of any age in foster care who are expected to leave care without placement in a permanent family.[79] Services may consist of educational assistance, vocational training, mentoring, preventive health activities, and counseling. States may dedicate as much as 30% of their program funding toward room and board for youth ages 18 through 20. A separate component of the CFCIP — the Education and Training Vouchers program — was established in 2002 (P.L. 107-133) to provide vouchers to youth eligible for the CFCIP and youth adopted from foster care after 16 years of age. The vouchers are available for the cost of attendance at an institution of higher education, as defined by the Higher Education Act of 1965.[80] Only youth receiving a voucher at age 21 may continue to participate in the voucher program until age 23.

Mentoring Children of Prisoners Program

The Mentoring Children of Prisoners Program was authorized in 2002 (P.L. 107-133) to provide children and youth whose parents are imprisoned with free mentoring and support services.[81] The purpose of the program is to give guidance to youth and to help youth reconnect with their parents after they are released. Public and private entities (including state or local governments, tribal governments, and community and faith-based groups) are eligible to apply for three-year grants to establish or expand and operate mentoring programs. The Child and Family Services Improvement Act of 2006 (P.L. 109-288) also authorized HHS to enter into an agreement with a national mentoring support organization to operate a demonstration project that will test the efficacy of vouchers as a method for delivering mentoring services.

Runaway and Homeless Youth Program

The Runaway and Homeless Youth Program, established in 1974 under Title III of the Juvenile Justice and Delinquency Prevention Act, contains three components: the Basic

Center Program (BCP), Transitional Living Program (TLP), and Street Outreach Program (SOP).[82] These programs are designed to provide services to runaway and homeless youth outside of the law enforcement, juvenile justice, child welfare, and mental health systems. Services include temporary and long-term shelter, counseling services, and referrals to social service agencies, among other supports. The funding streams for the Basic Center Program and Transitional Living Program were separate until Congress consolidated them in 1999 (P.L. 106-71). Together, the two programs, along with other program activities, are known as the Consolidated Runaway and Homeless Youth Program.[83] Although the Street Outreach Program is a separately funded component, SOP services are coordinated with those provided by the BCP and TLP.

Public Health

Public health programs for vulnerable youth are concentrated in the U.S. Department of Health and Human Services, Administration for Children and Families (ACF) and Substance Abuse and Mental Health Services Administration (SAMHSA).[84] These programs address youth mental health, substance abuse, teen pregnancy prevention, and support for pregnant and parenting teens.

Mental Health and Substance Abuse Services

SAMSHA is organized into three units: the Center for Mental Health Services (CMHS), the Center for Substance Abuse Treatment (C SAT), and the Center for Substance Abuse Prevention (CSAP). Collectively, the centers administer approximately 13 programs (not all discussed here or in **Table A-1**) for youth ages 10 to 21 (and up to 25 for some programs). The programs primarily target youth with serious emotional disturbances (SED) and youth at-risk of abusing drugs and alcohol.

CMHS. Suicide prevention activities are funded by SAMHSA's Campus Suicide Prevention Grant Program and State-Sponsored Youth Suicide Prevention and Early Intervention Program (collectively known as the Garrett Lee Smith Memorial Act Suicide Prevention Program). The campus grant program funds services for all students (including those with mental health problems and substance abuse that makes them vulnerable to suicide), while the state-sponsored program supports statewide and tribal activities to develop and implement youth suicide prevention and intervention strategies.[85]

The Comprehensive Mental Health Services for Children with SED program provides community-based systems of care for children and adolescents with serious emotional disturbances and their families. The program aims to ensure that services are provided collaboratively across youth-serving systems (such as schools and foster care placements) and that each youth receives an individual service plan developed with the participation of the family (and, where appropriate, the youth) to meet the mental health needs of that youth. A second program, the National Child Traumatic Stress Initiative, was created to establish a national network that provides services and referrals for children and adolescents who have experienced traumatic events.

CSAT. The Assertive Adolescent and Family Treatment Program provides grants to states to address gaps in substance abuse services for youth. The purpose of the program is to use proven family-centered practices to treat drug addicted youth. This treatment model focuses on making families and primary caregivers part of the treatment process based on the belief that their inclusion increases the likelihood of successful treatment and reintegration of adolescents into their communities. Another program that provides treatment for youth who are drug dependent is the Juvenile Treatment Drug Courts. This program targets juvenile offenders (pre-adjudicated or adjudicated status, or post-detention), and provides substance abuse treatment, wrap-around services supporting substance abuse treatment, and case management. A judge oversees the drug treatment program and may allow the youth to avoid (further) penalties for their delinquent behavior.

CSAP. The Strategic Prevention Framework State Infrastructure Grant provides funding to states to implement strategies for preventing substance and alcohol abuse among adolescents and adults. The grant implements a five-step process: 1) conduct a community needs assessment; 2) mobilize and/or build capacity; 3) develop a comprehensive strategic plan; 4) implement evidence-based prevention programs and infrastructure development activities; and 5) monitor process and evaluate effectiveness. CSAP also administers, in cooperation with the White House Office of National Drug Control Policy, the Drug-Free Communities Support program (see below).

Teen Pregnancy Prevention and Support Programs

The U.S. Department of Health and Human Services administers research and education programs to reduce teen pregnancy or to provide care services for pregnant and parenting adolescents.[86] Two education programs — Abstinence Education Grants and Community-Based Abstinence Education — promote abstinence until marriage in schools. States may request funding for the Abstinence Education Grants program when they solicit Maternal and Child Health block grant funds (used for a variety of health services for women and children, including adolescent pregnancy prevention activities); this funding must be used exclusively for the teaching of abstinence. Since FY2000, abstinence-only education for youth ages 12 to 18 has also been funded through HHS's Community-Based Abstinence Education program (formerly known as Special Programs of Regional and National Significance, SPRANS).

In addition to the education programs, HHS sponsors projects to increase awareness about teen pregnancy and abstinence. The Adolescent Family Life Demonstration Projects and Research Grants were designed to promote family involvement in the delivery of services, adolescent premarital sexual abstinence, adoption as an alternative to early parenting, parenting and child development education, and comprehensive health, education, and social services geared toward the healthy development for mother and child. The project program provides services to youth and the research and evaluation program evaluates the delivery of those services.

National and Community Service[87]

The Corporation for National and Community Service (CNCS) is an independent federal agency that administers programs authorized by two statutes: the National and Community Service Act (NCSA, P.L. 101-610) of 1990, as amended, and the Domestic Volunteer Service Act (DVSA, P.L. 93-113) of 1973, as amended.[88] The focus of these programs is to provide public service to communities in need through multiple service activities. Although CNCS works to involve a diverse range of individuals in their programs, the agency makes particular efforts to engage disadvantaged youth, either because they enroll these youth to help to carry out the programs (i.e., members or volunteers) or provide services to them through the programs (i.e., beneficiaries). CNCS's strategic plan for 2006 through 2010 emphasizes the agency's focus on improving the lives of disadvantaged and other youth by leveraging national service programs to meet their most pressing academic, health related, environmental, and social needs.[89] The strategic plan also lays out the agency's commitment to involving disadvantaged youth in their communities through service, citing that these youth are less likely to participate in volunteer activities than their counterparts who are not disadvantaged.

CNCS defines disadvantaged children and youth are those up to age 25 with exceptional or special needs (as defined in part 2552.81 of the DVSA regulations), or who are economically disadvantaged and for whom one or more of the following apply: 1) out-of-school, including out-of-school youth who are unemployed; 2) in or aging out of foster care; 3) limited English proficiency; 4) homeless or have run away from home; 5) at risk of leaving school without a diploma; and 6) former juvenile offenders or at risk of delinquency.

The major CNCS programs are organized into three service streams: AmeriCorps, Learn and Serve America, and Senior Corps.

AmeriCorps

AmeriCorps identifies and address critical community needs by tutoring and mentoring disadvantaged youth, managing or operating after-school programs, helping communities respond to disasters, improving health services, building affordable housing, and cleaning parks and streams, among other services. For providing these types of services full-time for a term of service (up to one year), AmeriCorps members earn an education award of $4,725 (and proportionally less if they provide services for half-time, reduced half-time, etc.). CNCS classifies programs as AmeriCorps programs if members are eligible to earn the education award. Three CNCS programs meet this criteria: AmeriCorps State and National, Volunteers in Service to America (VISTA), and National Civilian Community Corps (NCCC).

AmeriCorps State and National program[90] provides state formula and competitive grant funding to governor-appointed state service commissions, which award grants to non-profit groups that recruit AmeriCorps members to respond to local needs (AmeriCorps State). The balance of grant funding is distributed competitively by CNCS to multi-state and national organizations (AmeriCorps National), such as Teach for America, and to Indian tribes and territories. Some grantees enroll members who are disadvantaged, such as YouthBuild USA, which recruits at-risk youth ages 17 to 24 as members, to meet the housing and technology needs of their communities. Other grantees place members in organizations and schools to serve disadvantaged youth in grades K through 12 in after-school, before school, and enrichment programs.

The focus of VISTA[91] is to strengthen efforts to eliminate poverty through volunteer service. VISTA provides full-time members to non-profit community organizations and public agencies through a non-competitive application process managed locally by CNCS State Offices. VISTA supports projects that focus on serving disadvantaged youth beneficiaries, some of whom are younger than age 12. These projects include mentoring, as well as after school, tutoring, and job skills development programs. Although VISTA does not target any one population of youth, the program has recently placed an emphasis on serving children of prisoners and youth aging out of foster care.

Finally, NCCC[92] is a residential program for youth 18 through 24. Members live and train at five campuses[93] and are deployed to serve communities in every state. Like the other two

AmeriCorps programs, members work closely with non-profit organizations and public agencies to meet community needs.

Learn and Serve America

Learn and Serve America emphasizes service-learning, which is intended to engage students in using what they learn in the classroom to solve real-life problems. Learn and Serve America makes formula grants to state education agencies (SEAs) and makes competitive grants to SEAs, Indian tribes, and non-profit organizations to support service by students, including youth from disadvantaged circumstances, during school as well as after school and in the summer months.[94] The program also provides grants to support community service projects by students, faculty, and staff on college campuses. Learn and Serve projects provided assistance to youth beneficiaries from disadvantaged circumstances through mentoring and tutoring. Several of the projects also focused on substance abuse prevention, special education, and dropout prevention, among other activities targeted to youth generally.

Senior Corps

Senior Corps is composed of volunteers over the age of 55 who help to meet a wide range of community challenges through three programs: Foster Grandparents Program (FGP), Retired and Senior Volunteer Program (RSVP), and Senior Companion program. The first two provide assistance in the community by working with children and youth with a variety of needs, among other populations and activities. The FGP provides aid to children and youth with exceptional needs, including children who have been abused or neglected or are otherwise at risk; mentors troubled teenagers and young mothers; cares for premature infants and children with physical disabilities; and teaches reading instruction to children who are falling behind their grade level. RSVP provides a variety of services to communities. These services include tutoring children and teenagers, renovating homes, and serving as museum docents. Grants for Senior Corps program are awarded to non-profit organizations and public agencies. Upon successful completion of a three-year grant cycle, the organization or agency is eligible to renew the grant for another cycle without competition from other entities.

FEDERAL EFFORTS TO IMPROVE COORDINATION AMONG PROGRAMS FOR VULNERABLE YOUTH

Overview

Despite the range of services and activities programs for vulnerable youth, many of these programs appear to have developed with little attempt to coordinate them in a policy area or across policy areas. Policymakers and youth advocates argue that federal agencies must develop mechanisms to improve coordination — defined, at minimum, as communication and consultation. They argue that coordination is necessary because of the expansion of programs that serve youth, the increasing complexity and interrelated nature of public policies that affect youth, the fragmentation of policy-making among agencies, and the establishment of new policy priorities that cross older institutional boundaries.[95] To address concerns about the coordination of federal programs, Congress has passed the Tom Osborne Federal Youth

Coordination Act (P.L. 109-365), the YouthBuild Transfer Act (P.L. 109-281), and the Claude Pepper Young Americans Act (P.L. 101-501); however, of the three, only the YouthBuild Transfer Act has been funded. The Administration has also undertaken efforts to coordinate programs around youth topic areas and youth populations.

Concerns about Coordination of Youth Programs

In addition to the 51 programs described in **Table A-1**, dozens of other programs in multiple federal agencies target, even in small part, vulnerable youth. The U.S. Government Accountability Office (GAO) cataloged 131 programs for at- risk or delinquent youth across 16 agencies in FY1996. GAO defined these youth as individuals age five to 24 who, due to certain characteristics or experiences, were statistically more likely than other youth to encounter certain problems — legal, social, financial, educational, emotional, and health — in the future.[96] The White House Task Force for Disadvantaged Youth, convened in 2002, compiled a similar list of over 300 programs for disadvantaged youth (using nearly the same definition as GAO) in 12 agencies for FY2003 targeting vulnerable youth and youth generally.[97] In its October 2003 final report, the task force identified concerns with coordinating youth programs:

- *Mission Fragmentation*: The federal response to disadvantaged youth is an example of "mission fragmentation" because dozens of youth programs appear to provide many of the same services and share similar goals. For example, academic support was identified as a service provided by 92 programs and mentoring was identified as a service provided by 123 such programs, in FY2003.
- *Poor Coordination for Sub-Groups of Youth:* According to the task force, the federal government does not coordinate services for specific groups of youth (i.e., abused/neglected youth, current or former foster youth, immigrant youth, minority youth, obese youth, urban youth, and youth with disabilities, among others). The task force report listed 30 sub-groups of vulnerable youth, with each subgroup receiving services through at least 50 programs administered by 12 agencies. The report cited that each agency operates their programs autonomously and is not required to coordinate services with other agencies.
- *Mission Creep:* Known as "mission creep," multiple agencies are authorized by broadly-written statute to provide similar services to the same groups of youth despite having distinct agency goals and missions. Though youth programs are concentrated in the U.S. Departments of Education, Health and Human Service, and Justice, nine other agencies administer at least two youth-focused programs: Agriculture, Housing and Urban Development, Interior, Labor, Transportation, Corporation for National and Community Service, Defense, Office of Drug Control Policy, and Environmental Protection Agency.
- *Limited Program Accountability:* The extent of overlap among youth programs and the efficacy of these programs are difficult to determine because some of them have not been recently assessed through the Office of Management and Budget's Program Assessment and Rating Tool (PART) or by an independent program evaluation. As

of FY2003, more than half of the 339 youth-related programs identified by the task force had not been evaluated within the last five years. Of those programs that were evaluated, 75% were evaluated independently and the remaining programs were self-evaluated by the grantees. According to the task force, the quality of the evaluations was low because most did not randomly assign some youth to the programs and track their progress against similarly-situated youth not in the program.

- *Funding Streams that Reduce Accountability:* The funding streams for youth programs affect their oversight. More than 300 youth projects received earmarked appropriations (not necessarily from an account in a federal youth program) in FY2003, totaling $206.2 million. According to the report, earmarked projects do not have the same level of accountability as discretionary and mandatory programs. The report also raised concerns that programs in needy communities may be overlooked through the earmark process.

Congress has also examined challenges to coordinating programs targeted to certain groups of youth. In a May 2004 hearing, the Government Reform Committee examined redundancy and duplication in federal child welfare programs.[98]

Tom Osborne Federal Youth Coordination Act (P.L. 109-365)

In response to the concerns raised by the White House Task Force for Disadvantaged Youth, Congress passed the Tom Osborne Federal Youth Coordination Act (Title VIII of the Older Americans Act, P.L. 109-365) creating the Federal Youth Coordination Council, to be chaired by the Secretary of the U.S. Department of Health and Human Services. Although not explicitly stated in P.L. 109-365, the purpose of the council is twofold: to improve coordination across federal agencies that administer programs for vulnerable youth and to assist federal agencies with evaluating these programs. **Table 2** describes the duties established by the council to meet these two goals. Policymakers and advocates assert that the council can help to improve policy effectiveness by reducing the duplication of effort and working at cross-purposes, while integrating distinct but reinforcing responsibilities among relatively autonomous agencies.[99] They argue that the council can improve accountability of various federal components by consolidating review and reporting requirements.

Other duties of the council include providing technical assistance to states to support a state-funded council for coordinating state youth efforts, at a state's request, and coordinating with other federal, state, and local coordinating efforts to carry out its duties.

The law specifies that the council coordinate with three existing interagency bodies: the Federal Interagency Forum on Child and Family Statistics, the Interagency Council on Homelessness, and the Coordinating Council on Juvenile Justice and Delinquency Prevention. (The legislation does not describe how the council should coordinate with these other bodies.) Further, the law requires that the council provide Congress with an interim report within one year after the council's first meeting, as well as a final report not later than two years after the council's first meeting. The final report must include 1) a comprehensive list of recent research and statistical reporting by various federal agencies on the overall well-being of youth; 2) the assessment of the needs of youth and those who serve youth; 3) a summary of the plan in coordinating to achieve the goals and objectives for federal youth programs; 4) recommendations to coordinate and improve federal training and technical assistance, information sharing, and communication among federal programs and agencies; 5) recommendations to better integrate and coordinate policies across federal, state, and local levels of government, including any recommendations the chair determines appropriate for legislation and administrative actions; 6) a summary of the actions taken by the council at the request of federal agencies to facilitate collaboration and coordination on youth serving programs and the results of those collaborations, if available; 7) a summary of the action the council has taken at the request of states to provide technical assistance; and 8) a summary of the input and recommendations by disadvantaged youth, community-based organizations, among others.

Table 2. Duties of the Federal Youth Council, by Goal

Goal: To Improve Coordination	Goal: To Assess Youth Programs
• Ensure communication among agencies administering programs for disadvantaged youth; • Identify possible areas of overlap or duplication in the purpose and operation of programs serving youth and recommending ways to better facilitate the coordination and consultation among such programs; • Identify target populations of youth who are disproportionately at risk and assist agencies in focusing additional resources on such youth; • Assist federal agencies, at the request of one or more agencies, in collaborating on a) model programs and demonstration projects focusing on special populations, including youth in foster care and migrant youth; b) projects to promote parental involvement; and c) projects that work to involve young people in service programs; • Solicit and document ongoing input and recommendations from a) youth, especially youth in disadvantaged situations; b) national youth development experts, researchers, parents,community-based organizations, foundations, business leaders, youth service providers, and teachers; and c) state and local government agencies.	• In coordination with the Federal Interagency Forum on Child and Family Statistics, assess a) the needs of youth, especially those in disadvantaged situations, and those who work with youth; and b) the quality and quantity of federal programs offering services, supports, and opportunities to help youth in their development; • Recommend quantifiable goals and objectives for federal programs to assist disadvantaged youth; • Make recommendations for the allocation of resources in support of such goals and objectives; • Develop a plan (that is consistent with the common indicators of youth well-being tracked by the Federal Interagency Forum on Child and Family Statistics) to assist federal agencies (at the request of one or more such agencies) coordinate to achieve quantifiable goals and objectives; • Work with federal agencies a) to promote high-quality research and evaluation, identify and replicate model programs and promising practices, and provide technical assistance relating to the needs of youth; and b) to coordinate the collection and dissemination of youth services-related data and research.

Source: Created by the Congressional Research Service (CRS), on the basis of language in P.L. 109-365.

Funds were not appropriated for the council for FY2007 or FY2008, and the President's FY2009 budget does not request funding for the council. However, on February 7, 2008, President Bush signed Executive Order 13459 to establish an Interagency Working Group on Youth Programs, discussed below.[100]

Executive Order 13459

In Executive Order 13459, President Bush cited the success of the interagency collaboration that resulted from the Helping America's Youth (HAY) initiative as the impetus for creating an Interagency Working Group on Youth Programs. See below for additional information on HAY. The working group is to consist of the Departments of Agriculture, Commerce, Defense, Education, Health and Human Services, Housing and Urban Development Justice, and Labor; the Office of National Drug Control Policy; and the Corporation for National and Community Service. The HHS Secretary is to serve as chair and the Attorney General as vice chair for the two years following the date of the executive order. Subsequent chairs and vice chairs will be designated by the HHS Secretary on a biennial basis. The primary functions of the working group are as follows:

- identify and engage key government and private or nonprofit organizations that can play a role in improving the coordination and effectiveness of programs serving and engaging youth, such as faith-based and other community organizations, businesses, volunteers, and other key constituencies;
- develop a new federal website on youth, built upon the Community Guide to Helping America's Youth, with the first phase of the website to be launched within 10 months of the date of the executive order; develop strategies to ensure that the website is routinely updated, improved, and publicized; provide for training to youth-serving entities to enable effective use of the website; and identify and assess the strengths and weaknesses of existing federal web sites focusing on youth-serving entities in order to improve access to the most useful content;
- encourage all youth-serving federal and state agencies, communities, grantees, and organizations to adopt high standards for assessing program results, including through the use of rigorous impact evaluations, as appropriate, so that the most effective practices can be identified and replicated, and ineffective or duplicative programs can be eliminated or reformed;
- identify and promote initiatives and activities that merit strong interagency collaboration because of their potential to offer cost-effective solutions to achieve better results for at-risk youth, including volunteer service in concern with the USA Freedom Corps and mentoring in concert with the Federal Mentoring Council; and
- annually report to the President on its work and on the implementation of any recommendations arising from its work, with the first report submitted no later than six months after the date of the executive order.

The website is to be funded by contributions from executive departments and agencies.

Claude Pepper Young Americans Act of 1990 (P.L 101-501)

The Claude Pepper Young Americans Act of 1990 (Title IX of the August F. Hawkins Human Services Reauthorization Act, P.L. 101-501) shares some of the same objectives as the Youth Coordination Act, and like that legislation, it was not funded. The act sought to increase federal coordination among agencies that administer programs for children and youth, while also enhancing the delivery of social services to children, youth, and their families through improved coordination at the state and local levels.[101] In its report supporting the act's coordinating provisions, the Senate Labor and Human Resources Committee noted:[102]

> The Committee is concerned that the current system of service is fragmented and disjointed, making it difficult, if not impossible for children and families who are being served in one system to access needed services from another. This creates a situation in which problems of children and families not only go unmet but undetected and unresolved. Through the inclusion of these proposals, the Committee hopes to articulate a national commitment to our nation's children, youth, and families and to encourage greater cooperation at federal, state, and local levels.

Federal Council on Children, Youth, and Families

The Federal Council on Children, Youth, and Families was authorized by the Young Americans Act to address concerns about the fragmentation and duplication of services for youth at the federal and local levels. The act provided that the council comprise representatives from federal agencies and state or local agencies that serve youth, rural and urban populations; and national organizations with an interest in young individuals, families, and early childhood. The duties of the council were to include 1) advising and assisting the president on matters relating to the special needs of young individuals (and submitting a report to the president in FY1992 through FY1998); 2) reviewing and evaluating federal policies, programs, or other activities affecting youth and identifying duplication of services for these youth; and 3) making recommendations to the President and Congress to streamline services, reduce duplication of services, and encourage coordination of services for youth and their families at the state and local levels. The act was amended in 1994 (P.L. 103-252) to require that the council also identify program regulations, practices, and eligibility requirements that impede coordination and collaboration and make recommendations for their modifications or elimination.

Though the council was to be funded through FY1998, funding was never appropriated.

Grants for States and Community Programs

The Young Americans Act also established grant funding for coordinating resources and providing comprehensive services to children, youth, and families at the state and local levels. For states to receive funding, the act required each state to submit a plan discussing how state and local entities would coordinate developmental, preventative, and remedial services, among other provisions.

This grant program was never funded.

Youth Build Transfer Act (P.L. 109-281)

The Task Force for Disadvantaged Youth identified several programs, including YouthBuild, that were located in a federal department whose mission does not provide a clear and compelling reason for locating them within that agency. As such, the task force recommended that YouthBuild be transferred from the U.S. Department of Housing and Urban Development to the U.S. Department of Labor because of DOL's mission of administering workforce and training programs.[103] As discussed above, the YouthBuild program provides educational services and job training in construction for low-income youth ages 16 to 24 who are not enrolled in school. On September 22, 2006 the YouthBuild Transfer Act (P.L. 109-28 1), authorizing the transfer of the program from HUD to DOL, was signed into law. The program is now funded as part of the WIA Youth Activities program.

Federal Initiatives to Improve Coordination

Coordinating Council on Juvenile Justice and Delinquency Prevention

The Coordinating Council (Council) on Juvenile Justice and Delinquency Prevention was established by the Juvenile Justice and Delinquency Prevention Act of 1974 (P.L. 93-415) and is administered by the Department of Justice's Office of Juvenile Justice and Delinquency Prevention. The Council's primary functions are to coordinate federal programs and policies concerning juvenile delinquency prevention, unaccompanied juveniles, and missing and exploited children. The Council is led by the Attorney General and the Administrator of OJJDP and includes the heads of all the federal agencies that touch on these broad areas, including the Secretary of Health and Human Services; the Secretary of Labor; the Secretary of Education; the Secretary of Housing and Urban Development; the Director of the Office of National Drug Control Policy; the Chief Executive Officer of the Corporation for National and Community Service; and the Commissioner of Immigration and Naturalization (now the Commissioner of Immigration and Customs Enforcement).

In recent years, the Council has broadened its focus to other at-risk youth. The Council is seeking to implement some of the recommendations made by the Task Force for Disadvantaged Youth, including (1) improve coordination of mentoring programs; (2) develop a unified protocol for federal best practices clearinghouses; (3) build a rigorous and unified disadvantaged youth research agenda; (4) improve data collection on the well-being of families; (5) increase parents' involvement in federal youth programs; (6) target youth in public care; (7) target youth with many risk factors; and (8) expand mentoring programs to special target groups, among other recommendations.[104] The Council has formed the Federal Mentoring Council around the issue of mentoring to best determine how agencies can combine resources to provide training and technical assistance to federally administered mentoring programs.[105] Chaired by the Corporation for National and Community Service and Commissioner of FYSB, the Federal Mentoring Council has held a public forum on mentoring and is now developing a mentoring initiative for young people aging out of foster care.[106]

Shared Youth Vision Initiative

In response to the recommendations made by the Task Force for Disadvantaged Youth, the U.S. Departments of Education (ED), Health and Human Services (HHS), Justice (DOJ), and Labor (DOL), and the Social Security Administration partnered to improve communication and collaboration across programs that target at-risk youth groups under an initiative called the "Shared Youth Vision."

Together, the agencies have convened an Interagency Work Group and conducted regional forums in 16 states to develop and coordinate policies and research on the vulnerable youth population. Representatives from federal and state agencies in workforce development, education, social services, and juvenile justice have participated in the forums. The purpose of these forums was to create and implement plans to improve communication and collaboration between local organizations that serve at-risk youth. The department competitively awarded grants totaling $1.6 million to these states to assist them in developing strategic plans to link their systems that serve youth. For example, Arizona is using this initiative to bring together state and county agencies that can assist youth exiting foster care or the juvenile justice system in two counties connect to education and employment services and supports.[107] The Department of Health and Human Services has funded a solutions desk, administered by the National Child Welfare Resource Center for Youth Development, to provide the 16 states a single point of access to information on federal resources available to assist them in implementing Shared Youth Vision activities.

Partnerships for Youth Transition

HHS's Substance Abuse and Mental Healthy Services Administration (SAMHSA) and ED's Office of Special Education are cosponsoring a four-year program, that began in FY2003, to offer long-term support to young people between the ages of 14 and 25 with serious emotional disorders and emerging serious mental illnesses. The program is intended to assist youth transitioning to the adult system of medical care, while continuing to receive educational services. One of the program's goals is to develop models of comprehensive youth transition services that can be evaluated for their effectiveness.[108]

Safe Schools/Healthy Students (SS/HS) Initiative

From FY1999 to FY2006, HHS, ED, and DOJ have provided joint grant funding for the Safe Schools/Healthy Students Initiative to reduce violence and drug abuse at schools (K12) and in communities. Local education agencies — in partnership with local law enforcement, public mental health, and juvenile justice entities — apply for SS/HS funding. The initiative sponsors projects in schools and communities that 1) provide a safe school environment; 2) offer alcohol-, other drug -, and violence-prevention activities and early intervention for troubled students; 3) offer school and community mental health preventative and treatment intervention programs; 4) offer early childhood psychosocial and emotional development programs; 5) support and connect schools and communities; and 6) support safe-school policies.

Examples of programs for youth K through 12th grade include after-school and summer tutoring programs; recreational activities such as chess club; volunteering; and coordinated social service and academic activities for youth at risk of engaging in delinquent behavior, including mental health care services, peer mentoring, and parent workshops.

Drug-Free Communities Support Program

The Drug-Free Communities Support Program is administered by SAMSHA and the White House Office of National Drug Control Policy (which has entered into an agreement with OJJDP to manage the program on behalf of the sub-agency).[109] The program awards grants to community coalitions through a competitive grant award process. The program is intended to strengthen the capacity of the coalitions to reduce substance abuse among youth (and adults) and to disseminate timely information on best practices for reducing substance abuse.

Coordination around Specific Youth Populations

Federal agencies have partnered to address the concerns raised in the Task Force for Disadvantaged Youth report about the uncoordinated response to assisting certain sub-groups of youth.[110] According to congressional testimony in 2005 by the HHS Secretary, the U.S. Departments of Education and Labor are working together to assist youth who have dropped out of school. The agencies work to coordinate alternative education, adolescent literacy and numeracy, and enhanced GED programs funded through WIA to ensure that they comply with the No Child Left Behind requirements.

The Secretary also stated that ED and DOL, along with HHS and the USDA, have formed an interagency team to address the educational needs of migrant youth. The team has developed a proposal for a demonstration project that would provide educational assistance for migrant youth at various locations along the migrant stream (The migrant stream refers to the locations migrants frequent during particular seasons. For instance, migrants along the east coast might work in Florida and North Carolina in the winter, and Pennsylvania in the summer.) ED, HHS, DOJ, and DOL have also partnered to improve education and employment outcomes for youth offenders.

POLICIES TO PROMOTE POSITIVE YOUTH DEVELOPMENT

Overview

Some youth advocates argue that expanding programs for youth and providing mechanisms to coordinate these programs should be part of a larger effort to improve youth outcomes. This effort builds on the positive youth development approach (discussed above) that views youth as assets, in contrast to deficit-based models which focus primarily on specific youth problems.

Federal legislation and initiatives have been framed through the youth development philosophy with the goal of providing resources and guidance to communities and youth-focused programs that engage young people in roles as full participants in the work place, community, and society at large. Major legislation with a positive youth approach has included the Youth Development Community Block Grant of 1995 (H.R. 2807/S. 673) and the Younger Americans Act of 2001 (H.R. 17/S. 1005), both of which did not pass out of committee. The Administration has promoted the Helping America's Youth (HAY) initiative to raise awareness about issues affecting youth and to address these challenges through current federal programs and an online community action guide. Finally, America's Promise, a federally-sponsored program operated by the nonprofit Alliance for Youth, conducts and commissions research around positive youth development and recognizes communities and organizations that promote this philosophy.

Youth Development Community Block Grant of 1995 (H.R. 2807/S. 673)

The Youth Development Community Block Grant (YDCBG) of 1995 (H.R. 2807/S. 673) proposed to consolidate nearly two dozen federal youth programs administered by the U.S. Departments of Education, Health and Human Services, and Justice. The purpose of the legislation was to shift from a system of categorical programs that targeted the problems of certain sub-populations of youth (i.e., pregnant youth, youth abusing drugs) to one that promoted all aspects of youth development. At hearings on the legislation in the House and Senate, Members of Congress, community leaders, and youth advocates discussed the need to support comprehensive community services for youth. J.C. Watts, a co-sponsor of the legislation, testified:

> Because high risk behaviors are often interrelated, programs must consider the overall development of individual youngsters rather than focusing on one problem in isolation. Our current system of narrowly defined, categorical programs is rather like the pieces of a jigsaw puzzle scattered over a card table. The YDCBG puts these pieces together.[111]

The YDBCG Act did not prescribe specific activities or program types for which the funds were to be used. Rather, the legislation would have required states to submit a plan to HHS that outlined their youth development priorities. Funding would have flowed to local community boards, which would have tailored local YDCBG programs to community needs, consistent with the goals of these plans. Funding from the block grant could only supplement, and not supplant, existing funds for youth development programs and activities.

The block grant was to be based on three equally weighted formula factors: the proportion of the nation's total youth (defined as ages 6 to 17) that reside in each state; proportion of the nation's poor youth (defined as youth from low-income families) that reside in each state; and the average incidence of juvenile crime during the most recent four-year period. This $900 million proposed grant would have been funded through the programs that were be eliminated, with a 10% overall reduction.

The legislation was referred out of committee in both the House and Senate, but was not taken up again.

Younger Americans Act of 2001 (H.R. 17/S. 1005)

The goal of the Younger Americans Act of 2001 (H.R. 17/S. 1005) was to create a national youth policy that would have funded a network of youth programs through a central funding source, based loosely on the framework of the Older Americans Act.[112] Similar to its predecessor, the YDCBGA, the Younger Americans Act sought to provide resources to youth consisting of (1) ongoing relationships with caring adults; (2) safe places with structured activities; (3) access to services that promote healthy lifestyles, including those designed to improve physical and mental health; (4) opportunities to acquire marketable skills and competencies; and (5) opportunities for community service and civic participation.

If passed, HHS would have distributed block grant funds to states based on a formula that accounted for their proportion of the nation's youth ages 10 to 19 and the proportion of youth receiving a free or reduced-price school lunch. States would have then distributed funds to local area agencies on youth, which were to be supervised by community boards comprised of youth, representatives of youth- serving organizations, representatives of local elected officials, parents, and leaders of social and educational institutions in the community. Local youth organizations could apply to the community service board for funding to carry out program activities such as character development and ethical enrichment activities; mentoring activities; provision and support of community youth centers; and nonschool hours, weekend, and summer programs and camps, among other activities. HHS would have also set aside funding for evaluations of these programs.

The Younger Americans Act proposed to fund the program at $500 million the first year, increasing to $2 billion in its fifth year. The legislation did not pass committee in the House or Senate.

Helping America's Youth

Helping America's Youth is a national initiative, led by Laura Bush, that grew from four National Youth Summits that were coordinated and facilitated by HHS's Family and Youth Services Bureau. These summits were designed to convene policymakers, program operators, and youth in disadvantaged situations to explore national activities across ten federal agencies.

The mission of HAY is to promote positive youth development by raising awareness about the challenges facing youth and motivating caring adults to connect with youth.[113] The Administration has promoted the initiative through national and regional forums and online resources. The 2005 White House Conference on Helping America's Youth convened researchers, federal youth-serving agencies, and community and state leaders to discuss challenges facing youth and promote successful youth programs. Regional forums in six states and the District of Columbia have also brought together local civic leaders, researchers, and youth to discuss the goals of the initiative. (Laura Bush has also promoted the initiative through site visits to successful youth programs, such as Father Flanagan's Boys and Girls Town in Nebraska and Colonie Youth Court in New York.) In addition to these forums, HAY provides online assistance to communities. The Community Action Guide is an online resource to help communities assess their needs and resources and link them to effective programs to help youth.[114] Guide users can input their community locations and learn about federal resources (i.e., HUD-funded housing units or SAMSHA-funded programs), local resources (i.e., Boys and Girls Clubs), and the presence of businesses that sell tobacco and alcohol. The Guide also provides a primer on tenets of positive youth development (including guidance on how adult mentors can get involved in the lives of youth) and building community partnerships between government agencies and community organizations. This tool was created in partnership with nine federal agencies (HHS, Justice, ED, USDA, Interior,

HUD, Labor, Office of National Drug Control Policy, and the Corporation for National and Community Service).

As part of HAY, the Administration's Communities Empowering Youth (CEY) program works to reduce youth violence and to promote positive youth development. Created in 2005, CEY is administered through HHS's Compassion Capital Fund. The Compassion Capital Fund is the key element of the Administration's faith-based initiative, announced in January 2001, to expand the use of faith-based and community group as providers of social services.[115] It was created as a discretionary program in 2002 appropriations law (P.L. 107-116). CEY and other Compassion Capital Fund initiatives increase the service capacity and skills among faith-based and community-organizations, and encourage replication of effective service approaches. These organizations have a record of addressing youth violence and directing youth to resources that promote positive youth development. As CEY recipients, they assist other faith-based and community organizations that do not receive CEY funding, in four areas: (1) leadership development, (2) organizational development, (3) program development, and (4) community engagement.

In response to the federal coordination that HAY has promoted, President Bush signed an executive order to create an interagency working group on youth programs, discussed above.

Alliance for Youth: America's Promise

America's Promise is the national program established by the nonprofit organization, Alliance for Youth, to promote the Five Promises that attendees at the Presidents' Summit for America's Future (held in Philadelphia in 1997)[116] determined to be essential for the success of young people:

- Caring adults who are actively involved in their lives (i.e., parents, mentors, teachers, coaches);
- Safe places in which to learn and grow;
- Healthy start toward adulthood;
- Effective education that builds marketable skills; and
- Opportunities to help others.[117]

America's Promise is funded through a combination of federal and private funds. The Corporation for National and Community Service, the agency that administers federal community service programs, provides the federal portion of the funds. In FY2006, the organization received $4.5 million from CNCS. Congress did not appropriate funds for America's Promise for FY2007 and FY2008.[118]

The focus of the Alliance for Youth is to fund research that tracks youth outcomes, recognize communities that implement best practices in youth development, and provide financial and other resources to organizations that serve young people. The organization's 2006 report, "Every Child, Every Promise: a Report on America's Young People," correlated the presence of the Five Promises in young people's lives with success in adolescence and adulthood. The report concludes that children who have at least four of the Five Promises are more likely to be academically successful, civically engaged, and socially competent, regardless of their race or family income.[119]

Positive Youth Development State and Local Collaboration Demonstration Projects

The Family and Youth Services Bureau administers demonstration projects that promote its mission of providing positive youth development programming. From FY1998 to FY2003, 13 states received demonstration grants to assess how positive youth development principles could be integrated into state policies and procedures; provide training on the positive youth development approach; and identify data to measure positive youth outcomes. The Bureau has since awarded $3 million in grants to nine (Iowa, Illinois, Iowa, Kentucky, Louisiana, Massachusetts, Nebraska, New York, and Oregon) of the original 13 states in FY2005 to fund collaborative projects between those states and local jurisdictions and Indian tribes. The purpose of the projects is to facilitate communication and cooperation among different levels of government and the nonprofit sector that provide services to young people and to energize local constituencies around the issue of youth development. For example, one of the projects — in Chicago, Illinois — has forged a community partnership between the Illinois Department of Social Service, a local youth council, community center, a local park district, and other community service groups around the issues of quality education and youth employment.[120] The project has planned, raised funds for, and marketed a career day and a forum for youth and police.

CONCLUSION

This report provided an overview of the vulnerable youth population and examined the federal role in supporting these youth. Although a precise number of vulnerable youth cannot be aggregated (and should not be, due to data constraints), these youth are generally concentrated among seven groups: youth "aging out" of foster care, runaways and homeless youth, juvenile justice-involved youth, immigrant youth and youth with limited English proficiency (LEP), youth with physical and mental disabilities, youth with mental disorders, and youth receiving special education. Each of these categories is comprised of youth with distinct challenges and backgrounds; however, many of these youth share common experiences, such as unstable home and neighborhood environments, coupled with challenges in school. Without protective factors in place, vulnerable youth may have difficulty transitioning to adulthood. Detachment from the labor market and school — or disconnectedness — is perhaps the single strongest indicator that the transition has not been made adequately. Despite the negative forecast for the employment and education prospects of vulnerable youth, some youth experience positive outcomes in adulthood. Youth who develop strong cognitive, emotional, and vocational skills, among other types of competencies, have greater opportunities to reach their goals. Advocates for youth promote the belief that all youth have assets and can make valuable contributions to their communities despite their challenges.

The federal government has not developed a single overarching policy or program to assist vulnerable youth, like the Older Americans Act program for the elderly. Since the 1960s, a number of programs, many operating in isolation from others, have worked to address the specific needs (i.e., vocational, educational, social services, juvenile justice and delinquency prevention, and health) of these youth. More recently, policymakers have taken steps toward a more comprehensive federal response to the population. The YouthBuild Transfer Act of 2006 moved the YouthBuild program from HUD to DOL because the program is more aligned with DOL's mission of administering workforce and training programs. Also in 2006, the Tom Obsborne Youth Coordination Act was passed to improve coordination across federal agencies that administer programs for vulnerable youth and to assist federal agencies with evaluating these programs. In February 2008, President Bush signed an executive order establishing a federal Interagency Working Group on Youth Programs. Other coordinating efforts, such as the Juvenile Justice and Delinquency Prevention Council and Shared Youth Vision initiative, may have the resources and leadership to create a more unified federal youth policy, albeit the JJDPC has a primary focus on juvenile justice involved youth.

In addition to the Federal Youth Coordination Act, the few youth-targeted acts over the past ten years have not passed or have passed without full implementation. The unfunded Claude Pepper Young Americans Act of 1990 sought to increase coordination among federal children and youth agencies by creating a Federal Council on Children, Youth, and Families that would have streamlined federal youth programs and advised the president on youth issues. Similarly, federal legislation reflecting a youth development philosophy, with the goal of providing resources to youth and engaging young people in their communities, has not been reported out of committee. The 1995 Youth Development Community Block Grant and 2001 Younger Americans Act would have provided grant funding to the states with the greatest concentrations of low-income youth to provide resources, such as mentors and opportunities for community service and civic participation.

Though federal legislation targeted at vulnerable young people has not been passed or implemented in recent years, current initiatives (Shared Youth Vision, Helping America's Youth, and America's Promise) and collaborations (Safe Schools/Healthy Students Initiative and the JJDPC) appear to have begun addressing, even in small measure, the needs of this population.

APPENDIX: FEDERAL YOUTH PROGRAMS AND RELEVANT CRS REPORTS AND EXPERTS

Table A-1. Federal Programs for Vulnerable Youth

Program	Authorizing Legislation and U.S. Code Citation	Objective(s) of Program	FY2006–FY2008 Appropriations and President's FY2009 Request (rounded)	Agency with Jurisdiction	Target At-Risk Youth Population
Job Training and Workforce Development					
Job Corps	Workforce Investment Act of 1998, as amended 29 U.S.C. §2881 et seq.	To assist eligible youth who need and can benefit from an intensive workforce development program, operated in a group setting in residential and nonresidential centers, to become more responsible, employable, and productive citizens.	FY2006: $1.6 billion FY2007: $1.6 billion FY2008: $1.6 billion FY2009: $1.5 billion	U.S. Department of Labor	Youth ages 16 to 21 (with exceptions) who are either low-income, basic skills deficient, a school dropout, homeless, a run-away, or a foster child, a parent or an individual who requires additionnal education, vocational training, or inte-nsive counseling and related assis-tance to participate successfully in regular schoolwork or to se-cure and Hold employment.
WIA Youth Activities	Workforce Investment Act of 1998, as amended 29 U.S.C. §2851 et seq.	To provide services to eligible youth seeking assistance in achieving acade-mic and employment success, inclu-ding the provision of mentoring, support services, training, and incentives.	FY2006: $941 million FY2007: $941 million FY2008: $924 million FY2009: $821 million	U.S. Department of Labor	Youth ages 14 to 21 who are low-income and either deficient in basic literacy skills, a school dropout, homeless, a runaway, a foster child, pregnant, a parent, an offender, or an individual who requires additional assistance to complete an educational program, or to secure and hold employment.
Youth Build	Cranston-Gonzalez National Affordable Housing Act of 1990, as amen-ded 29 U.S.C. §2918a	To enable disadvantaged youth to obtain the education and employment skills while expaning the supply of permanent affordable housing for homeless individuals and low-income families.	FY2006: $50 million FY2007: $50 million FY2008: $59 million FY2009: $50 million	U.S. Department of Labor	Youth ages 16 to 24 who are a Member of a low-income family, in foster care, a youth offender, have a disability, are a child of incarcerated parents, or a migrant you-th or a school dropout (with exceptions).
Youth Conser-vation Corps	Youth Conser-vation Corps Act of 1970, as amended	To further the development and maintenance of the natural resources by America's youth, and in so doing to	No specific amount appropriated or req-uested. The Appro-priations Subcommittee	U.S. Department of the Interior (Bureau of Land	All youth 15 to 18 years of age (targets economically disadvantaged, at-risk).

Table A-1. (Continued)

Program	Authorizing Legislation and U.S. Code Citation	Objective(s) of Program	FY2006-FY2008 Appropriations and President's FY2009 Request (rounded)	Agency with Jurisdiction	Target At-Risk Youth Population
	16 U.S.C. §1701 et seq.	prepare them for the ultimate responsibility of maintaining and managing these resources for the American people.	on Interior, Environment, and Related Agencies generally directs the four agencies to allocate no less than a particular amount to Youth Conservation Corps activities (funding generally ranges from $1.5 million to $2 million per agency).	Management, Fish and Wildlife Agency, and the National Park Service) and U.S. Department of Agriculture (Forest Service)	
Education					
Title I-A: Education for the Disadvantaged	Elementary and Secondary Education Act of 1965, as amended 20 U.S.C. §6301 et. seq.	To improve the educational achievement of educationally disadvantaged children and youth, and to reduce achievement gaps between such pupils and their more advantaged peers.	FY2006: $13 billion FY2007: $13 billion FY2008: $14 billion FY2009: $14 billion	U.S. Department of Education	Educationally disadvantaged children and youth, in areas with concentrations of children and youth in low-income families.
Title I-C: Migrant Education	Elementary and Secondary Education Act of 1965, as amended 20 U.S.C. §6391	To support high quality and comprehensive educational programs for migrant children and youth.	FY2006: $387 million FY2007: $387 million FY2008: $380 million FY2009: $400 million	U.S. Department of Education	Migrant children and youth.
Title I-D: Preven-tion and Intervention Programs for Children and Youths Who Are Negl-ected, De-linquent, or At Risk	Elementary and Secondary Education Act of 1965, as amended 20U.S.C. §6421-6472 et seq.	To meet the special educational needs of children in institutions and community day school programs for neglected and delinquent children and children in adult correctional institutions.	FY2006: $50 million FY2007: $50 million FY2008: $49 million FY2009: $52 million	U.S. Department of Education	Abused/neglected youth, delinquent youth, and juvenile offenders.

Table A-1. (Continued)

Program	Authorizing Legislation and U.S. Code Citation	Objective(s) of Program	FY2006 -FY2008 Appropriations and President's FY2009 Request (rounded)	Agency with Jurisdiction	Target At-Risk Youth Population
Title I-H: School Dropout Prevention	Elementary and Secondary Education Act of 1965, as amended 20 U.S.C. §6551 et seq.	To provide for school dropout prevention and reentry and to raise academic achievement levels.	FY2006: $5 million FY2007: $0 FY2008: $0 FY2009: $0	U.S. Department of Education	Youth at risk of dropping out of school districts with dropout rates higher than their state's average.
Title III: English Language Acquisition	Elementary and Secondary Education Act of 1965, as amended 20 U.S.C. §6801 et seq.	To ensure that limited English proficient children (LEP) and youth, including immigrant children and youth, attain English proficiency.	FY2006: $669 million FY2007: $669 million FY2008: $700 million FY2009: $730 million	U.S. Department of Education	Children and youth with limited English proficiency.
Title IV-A: Safe and Drug Free Schools, Part A, Subpart 1, State Grants for Drug and Violence Prevention	Elementary and Secondary Education Act of 1965, as amended 20 U.S.C. §§7111-7118	To prevent violence in and around schools and to strengthen programs that prevent the illegal use of alcohol, tobacco, and drugs, involve parents, and are coordinated with related federal, state, and community efforts and resources.	FY2006: $347 million FY2007: $347 million FY2008: $295 million FY2009: $100 million	U.S. Department of Education	All youth; at-risk youth; school dropouts.
Title IV-B: 21st Century Learning Centers	Elementary and Secondary Education Act of 1965, as amended 20 U.S.C. §8241 et seq.	To create community learning Centers that help students meet state and local educational standards, to provide supplementary educational assistance, and to offer literacy and other services to the families of participating youth.	FY2006: $981 million FY2007: $981 million FY2008: $1.1 billion FY2009: $800 million	U.S. Department of Education	Students who attend high-poverty and low-performing schools.
Title VII: Education of Homeless Children	McKinney-Vento Homeless Assistance Act of 1987, as amended 42 U.S.C. §§11431-11435	To provide activities for and services to ensure that homeless children enroll in, attend, and achieve success in school.	FY2006: $62 million (plus $5 million for hurricane supple-mental) FY2007: $62 Million FY2008: $64 million FY2009: $64 million	U.S. Department of Education	Homeless children and youth in elementary and secondary schools, homeless preschool children, and the parents of homeless children.

Table A-1. (Continued)

Program	Authorizing Legislation and U.S. Code Citation	Objective(s) of Program	FY2006 -FY2008 Appropriations and President's FY2009 Request (rounded)	Agency with Jurisdiction	Target At-Risk Youth Population
Migrant High School Equivalency Program and College Assistance Programs	Higher Education Act, as amended 20 U.S.C. §1070d-2	To provide academic and support services to help eligible migrant youth obtain their high school equivalency certificate and move on to employment or enrollment in higher education.	FY2006: $34 million FY2007: $34 million FY2008: $34 million FY2009: $34 million	U.S. Department of Education	Migrant youth ages 16 to 21.
Upward Bound	Higher Education Act of 1965, as amended 20 U.S.C. §1070a-13	To increase the academic performance of eligible enrollees so that such persons may complete secondary school and pursue postsecondary educational programs.	FY2006: $310 million FY2007: $314 million FY2008: $361 million FY2009: $360 million	U.S. Department of Education	Low-income individuals and potential first generation college students between ages 13 and 19, and have completed the 8th grade but have not entered the 12th grade (with exceptions).
Educational Opportunity Centers	Higher Education Act of 1965, as amended 20 U.S.C. §1070a-16	To provide information to prospective postsecondary students regarding available financial aid and academic assistance, and help them apply for admission and financial aid.	FY2006: $48 million FY2007: $47 million FY2008: $47 million FY2009: $47 million	U.S. Department of Education	At least two-thirds of participants in any project must be low-income students who would be first-generation college goers. They must also be at least 19 years old.
Ronald E. McNair Postbaccalaurete Achievement	Higher ducation Act of 1965, as amended 20 U.S.C. §1070a-15	To provide grants to institutions of higher education to prepare participants for doctoral studies through involvement in research and other scholarly activities.	FY2006: $42 million FY2007: $45 million FY2008: $44 million FY2009: $44 million	U.S. Department of Education	Low-income college students or underrepresented students enrolled in an institution of higher education.
Student Support Services	Higher Education Act of 1965, as amended 20 U.S.C. §1070a-14	To improve college students' retention and graduation rates, and improve the transfer rates of students from two-year to four-year colleges.	FY2006: $271 million FY2007: $272 million FY2008: $281 million FY2009: $282 million	U.S. Department of Education	At least two-thirds of participants in any project must be either disabled individuals or low-income, first-generation college goers. The remaining participants must be low-income, or first-generation college goers, or disabled. Not less than one-third of the disabled participants must be low-income as well.

Table A-1. (Continued)

Program	Authorizing Legislation and U.S. Code Citation	Objective(s) of Program	FY2006 -FY2008 Appropriations and President's FY2009 Request (rounded)	Agency with Jurisdiction	Target At-Risk Youth Population
Talent Search	Higher Education Act of 1965, as amended 20 U.S.C. §1070a-12	To identify disadvantaged youth with potential for postsecondary education; to encourage them in continuing in and graduating from secondary school and in enrolling in programs of postsecondary education; to publicize the avai-lability of student financial aid; and to increase the number of secondary and postsecondary school dropouts who reenter an educati-onal program.	FY2006: $150 million FY2007: $143 million FY2008: $143 million FY2009: $143 million	U.S. Department of Education	Project participants must be between 11 and 27 years old (exceptions allowed), and two-thirds must be low-income individuals who are also potential first-generation college students.
Gaining Early Awareness and Readiness for Undergra-duate Programs (GEAR-UP)	Higher Educat-ion Act of 1965, as amended 20 U.S.C. §1070a-21-1070a-28	To provide financial assistance to low-income individuals to attend an institu-tion of higher education and support eligible entities in providing counseling, mentoring, academic support, outreach, and supportive services to students at risk of dropping out of school.	FY2006: $303 million FY2007: $303 million FY2008: $303 million FY2009: $303 million	U.S. Department of Education	Low-income students and students in high-poverty schools.
Individuals with Disabilities Education Act, Part B Grant to States	Education for All Handicapped Children Act of 1975, as amended (curr-ently known as the Individuals with Disabilities Education Act) 20 U.S.C. §1400 et seq.	To provide a free appropriate education to all children with disabilities.	FY2006: $10.6 billion FY2007: $10.8 billion FY2008: $11.0 billion FY2009: $11.3 billion	U.S. Department of Education	School-aged children and youth with disabilities, up to age 21 (pursuant to state law).
Juvenile Justice					
State Formula Grants	Juvenile Justice and Delinquency Prevention Act of 1974, as amended 42 U.S.C. §5631-33	To increase the capacity of state and local governme-nts to support the development of more effective education, training, research, and other programs in the area of juvenile delinquency and programs to improve the juvenile justice system	FY2006: $80 million FY2007: $79 million FY2008: $74 million FY2009: The U.S. DOJ FY2009 Performance Budget proposes to consolidate this program	U.S. Department of Justice	Delinquent youth, juvenile offenders, and at-risk youth.

Table A-1. (Continued)

Program	Authorizing Legislation and U.S. Code Citation	Objective(s) of Program	FY2006 -FY2008 Appropriations and President's FY2009 Request (rounded)	Agency with Jurisdiction	Target At-Risk Youth Population
		(e.g., community-based services for the prevention and control of juvenile delinquency, group homes, and halfway houses).	with other juvenile justice and child abuse programs into a single discretionary block grant under a program known as the Child Safety and Juvenile Justice Program.)		
Juvenile Delinquency Prevention Block Grant Program	21st Century Department of Justice Reauthorization Act of 2002 42 U.S.C. 5651-5656	To provide funding for programs that prevent juvenile delinquency, including, but not limited to: treatment for at-risk youth; educational projects and supportive services; counseling, training, and mentoring projects; community-based programs; and dependency treatment programs.	FY2006: $0 FY2007: $0 FY2008: $0 FY2009: The U.S. DOJ FY2008 Performance Budget proposes to consolidate this program with other juvenile justice and child abuse programs into a single discretionary block grant under a program known as the Child Safety and Juvenile Justice Program.	U.S. Department of Justice	Delinquent youth, juvenile offenders, gang members, and at-risk youth.
Gang Free Schools and Communities - Community Based Gang Interve-tion	*Currently Unauthorized.* This program was repealed by P.L. 107-273 but continues to be appropriated.	To prevent and reduce the partici-ation of juveniles in the activities of gan-s that commit crimes (e.g., programs to prevent youth from entering gangs and to prevent high school students from dropping out of school and joining gangs).	FY2006: $25 million FY2007: $25 million FY2008: $19 million FY2009: The U.S. DOJ FY2008 Perfomance Budget propoes to consolidate this program with other juvenile justice and child abuse programs into a single discretionary block grant	U.S. Deparent of Justice	At-risk youth, delinquent youth, juvenile offenders, gang members, and youth under age 22.

Table A-1. (Continued)

Program	Authorizing Legislation and U.S. Code Citation	Objective(s) of Program	FY2006 -FY2008 Appropriations and President's FY2009 Request (rounded)	Agency with Jurisdiction	Target At-Risk Youth Population
			under a program known as the Child Safety and Juvenile Justice Program.		
Juvenile Mentoring Program (JUMP)	*Currently Unauthorized.* This program was repealed by P.L. 107-273 but funding continues to be appropriated.	To develop, implement, and pilot test mentoring strategies and/or programs targeted for youth in the juvenile justice system and in foster care, and youth who have reentered the juvenile justice system (e.g., Big Brothers/Big Sisters program).	FY2006: $10 million FY2007: $10 million FY2008: $70 million FY2009: The U.S. DOJ FY2009 Performance Budget proposes to onsolid-te this program with other juvenile justice and child abuse programs into a single discretionary block grant under a program known as the Child Safety and Juvenile Justice Program.	U.S. Department of Justice	Delinquent youth, juvenile offenders, and foster youth.
State Challenge Activities, Part E	Juvenile Justice and Delinquency Prevention Act of 1974, as amended 42 U.S.C. §5665	To provide states with funding to carry out programs that will develop, test, or demonstrate promising new initiatives that may prevent, control, or reduce juvenile delinquency.	FY2006: $106 million FY2007: $105 million FY2008: $94 million FY2009: The U.S. DOJ FY2009 Performance Budget proposes to consolidate this program with other juvenile justice and child abuse programs into a single discretionary block grant under a program known as the Child Safety and Juvenile Justice Program.)	U.S. Department of Justice	At-risk youth, delinquent youth, juvenile offenders, gang members, and at-risk youth.

Table A-1. (Continued)

Program	Authorizing Legislation and U.S. Code Citation	Objective(s) of Program	FY2006 -FY2008 Appropriations and President's FY2009 Request (rounded)	Agency with Jurisdiction	Target At-Risk Youth Population
Title V Incentive Grants for Local Delinquency Prevention Program	Juvenile Justice and Delinquency Prevention Act of 1974, as amended 42 U.S.C. §4781-85	To fund delinquency prevention programs and activities for at-risk youth and juvenile delinquents, including, among other things: substa-nce abuse prevention services; child and adolescent health and mental health services; leadership and youth development services; and job skills training.	FY2006: $65 million FY2007: $64 million FY2008: $61 million FY2009: The U.S. DOJ FY2009 Performance Budget proposes to consolidate this program with other juvenile justice and child abuse programs into a single discretionary block grant under a program known as the Child Safety and Juvenile Justice Program.)	U.S. Department of Justice	Delinquent youth, juvenile offenders, at-risk youth.
Social Services					
Foster Care	Social Security Act of 1935 (Sections 471 and 472), as amended 42 USC §§671, 672	To assist states in providing foster care for eligible children, including maintenance payments (i.e. room and board) and case planning and management for children and youth in out-of-home placements.	FY2006: $4.7 billion FY2007: $4.8 billion (Based on HHS, ACF Justification of Estimtes for FY2008, and reflects expected "lapse" of funds which were expected to be necessary in the FY2007 budget justifications). FY2008: $4.6 million FY2009: $4.5 million	U.S. Department of Health and Human Services	Federal support available for children and youth who are removed from low-income families (meeting specific criteria) for their own protection. (However, federal protections related to case planning and management are available to all children/youth who are in foster care.)
Chafee Foster Care Independence Program	Social Security Act of 1935 (Section 477), as amended 42 U.S.C. §677	To assist states and localities in establishing and carrying out programs designed to assist foster youth likely to remain in foster care until age 18 and youth ages 18 - 21 who have left the foster care system in making the transition to self-sufficiency.	FY2006: $140 million FY2007: $140 million FY2008: $140 million FY2009: $140 million	U.S. Department of Health and Human Services	Current or former foster care youth under age 21.

Table A-1. (Continued)

Program	Authorizing Legislation and U.S. Code Citation	Objective(s) of Program	FY2006-FY2008 Appropriations and President's FY2009 Request (rounded)	Agency with Jurisdiction	Target At-Risk Youth Population
Chafee Foster Care Independence Program Education and Training Vouchers	Social Security Act of 1935, (Section 477), as amended 42 U.S.C. §677	To make education and training vouchers available for youth who have aged out of foster care or who have been adopted from the public foster care system after age 16.	FY2006: $46 million FY2007: $46 million FY2008: $45 million FY2009: $45 million	U.S. Department of Health and Human Services	Older foster care youth and youth adopted from foster care at age 16 or older.
Basic Center Program	Runaway and Homeless Youth Act of 1974, as Amended 42 U.S.C.§5701 et seq.	To establish or strengthen locally controlled community-based programs outside of the law enforcement, child welfare, mental health, and juvenile justice systems that address the immediate needs of runaway and homeless youth and their families	FY2006: $48 million FY2007: $48 million FY2008: $53 million FY2009: $53 million	U.S. Department of Health and Human Services	Runaway and homeless youth and their families.
Transitional Living Program for Older Homeless Youth	Runaway and Homeless Youth Act of 1974, as amended 42 U.S.C. §5701 et seq.	To establish and operate transitional living projects for homeless youth, including pregnant and parenting youth.	FY2006: $40 million FY2007: $40 million FY2008: $43 million FY2009: $43 million	U.S. Department of Health and Human Services	Runaway and homeless youth ages 16-21.
Street Outreach Program	Runaway and Homeless Youth Act of 1974, as amended 42 U.S.C. §5701 et seq.	To provide grants to nonprofit agencies to provide street-based services to runaway, homeless, and street youth, who have been subjected to, or are at risk of being subjected to sexual abuse, prostitution, or sexual exploita-ion.	FY2006: $15 million FY2007: $15 million FY2008: $17 million F72009: $17 million	U.S. Department of Health and Human Services	Runaway and homeless youth who live on or frequent the streets.
Mentoring Children of Prisoners	Social Security Act of 1935 (Section 439), as amended 42 U.S.C. §629i	To make competitive grants to applicants in areas with significant numbers of children of prisoners to support the establishment and operation of programs that provide mentoring services for these children, and to demonstrate the potential effectiveness of vouchers as delivery mechanisms for these mentoring services.	FY2006: $50 million FY2007: $50 million FY2008: $49 million FY2009: $50 million	U.S. Department of Health and Human Services	Youth of imprisoned parents.

Table A-1. (Continued)

Program	Authorizing Legislation and U.S. Code Citation	Objective(s) of Program	FY2006 -FY2008 Appropriations and President's FY2009 Request (rounded)	Agency with Jurisdiction	Target At-Risk Youth Population
Court Appointed Special Advocates	Victims of Child Abuse Act of 1990, as amended 42 U.S.C. §13011-13014	To ensure every victim of child abuse and neglect receives the services of a court appointed advocate.	FY2006: $12 million FY2007: $12 million FY2008: $13 million FY2009: The U.S. DOJ FY2009 Performance Budget proposes to consolidate this program with other juvenile justice and child abuse programs into a single discretionary block grant under a program known as the Child Safety and Juvenile Justice Program.	U.S. Department of Justice	Abused and neglected children and youth.
Children's Advocacy Centers	Victims of Child Abuse Act of 1990, as amended 42 U.S.C. §13001-13004	To establish advocacy centers to coordinate multi-disciplinary responses to child abuse and to provide training and technical assistance to professionals involved in investigating, prosecuting, and training child abuse, and to support the development of Children's Advocacy Centers on multi-disciplinary teams.	FY2006: $15 million FY2007: $15 million FY2008: $17 million F72009: The U.S. DOJ FY2009: The FY2009 Performance Budget proposes to consolidate this program with other juvenile justice and child abuse programs into a single discretionary block grant under a program known as the Child Safety and Juvenile Justice Program.	U.S. Department of Justice	Abused and neglected youth.
Public Health					
Garrett Lee Smith Memorial Act Youth Suicide Prevention Program	Public Health Service Act of 1974, as amended 42 USC § §290aa et seq., 290bb et seq.	To provide grants to states and college campuses for youth suicide prevention activities.	FY2006: $23 million FY2007: $23 million FY2008: $34 million FY2009: $23 million	U.S. Department of Health and Human Services	Youth under age 25.

Table A-1. (Continued)

Program	Authorizing Legislation and U.S. Code Citation	Objective(s) of Program	FY2006 -FY2008 Appropriations and President's FY2009 Request (rounded)	Agency with Jurisdiction	Target At-Risk Youth Population
Comprehensive Community Mental Health Services for Children with Serious Emotional Disturbances	Public Health Service Act of 1974, as amended 42 USC §290ff	To provide community-based systems of care for children and adolescents with a serious emotional disturbance and their family.	FY2006: $104 million FY2007: $104 million FY2008: $102 million FY2009: $114 million	U.S. Department of Health and Human Services	Youth under age 22 with a serious emotional disorders.
National Child Traumatic Stress Initiative	Children's Health Act of 2000 (Section 582(d)) 42 USC §290aa	To create a national network that develops, promotes, and disseminates information related to a wide variety of traumatic events.	FY2006: $29 million FY2007: $29 million FY2008: $33 million FY2009: $16 million	U.S. Department of Health and Human Services	Children and youth who have experienced traumatic events.
Strategic Prevention Framework State Infrastructure Grant	Public Health Service Act of 1974, as amended 42 U.S.C. 290bb	To provide funding to states for infrastructure and services that implement a five-step strategy for preventing substance and alcohol abuse among youth.	FY2006: $106 million FY2007: $106 million FY2008: $105 million FY2009: $95 million	U.S. Department of Health and Human Services	Youth at risk of using and abusing drugs.
Assertive Adolescent and Family Treatment Program (Family Centered Substance Abuse Treatment Grants for Adolescents and their Families)	Public Health Service Act of 1974, as amended 42 U.S.C. 290bb-2	To provide substance abuse treatment practices to adolescents and their families using previously proven effective family-centered methods.	FY2006: $5 million FY2007: $10 million FY2008: $10 million FY2009: $0	U.S. Department of Health and Human ervices	Youth using drugs.
Juvenile Treatment Drug Court	Public Health Service Act of 1974, as amended 42 U.S.C. 290bb-2	To provide effective substance treatment and reduce delinquent activity.	FY2006: $10 million FY2007: $10 million FY2008: $3 million FY2009: $38 (for adult, juvenile, and family treatment drug court programs)	U.S. Depart-ment of Health and Human Services	Youth using drugs who are found delinquent.

Table A-1. (Continued)

Program	Authorizing Legislation and U.S. Code Citation	Objective(s) of Program	FY2006 -FY2008 Appropriations and President's FY2009 Request (rounded)	Agency with Jurisdiction	Target At-Risk Youth Population
Community-Based Abstinence Education	Social Security Act of 1935 (Section 1110 using the definitions contained in Section 510(b)(2), as amended 42 U.S.C. §710	To provide project grants to public and private institutions for community-based abstinence education project grants.	FY2006: $109 million FY2007: $109 million FY2008: $109 million FY2009: $137 million	U.S. Department of Health and Human Services	Youth ages 12 to 18.
Abstinence Education Program	Social Security Act of 1935 (Section 510), as amended 42 U.S.C. §710	To provide formula grant funding for states to provide abstinence education and, at the option of the state, where appropriate, mentoring, counseling, and adult supervision to promote abstinence from sexual activity.	FY2006: $50 million FY2007: $50 million FY2008: $50 million FY2009: $50 million	U.S. Department of Health and Human Services	Youth likely to bear children outside of marriage.
Adolescent Family Life Demonstration Projects	Public Health Services Act of 1974, as amended 42 U.S.C. §3002	To provide project grants to establish innovative, comprehensive, and integrated approaches to the delivery of care services for pregnant and parenting adolescents with primary emphasis on adolescents who are under age 17.	FY2006: $30 million FY2007: $30 million FY2008: $30 million FY2009: $30 million (Funding for the Adolescent Family Life Demonstration Projects and Research Grants is combined.)	U.S. Department of Health and Human Services	Pregnant and parenting youth, non-pregnant youth and their families.
Adolescent Family Life Research Grants	Public Health Services Act of 1974, as amended 42 U.S.C. §3002	To provide project grants to encourage and support research projects and dissemination activities concerning the societal causes and consequence of adolescent sexual activity, contraceptive use, pregnancy, and child rearing.	FY2006: $30 million FY2007: $30 million FY2008: $30 million FY2009: $30 million (Funding for the Adolescent Family Life Demonstration Projects and Research Grants is combined.)	U.S. Department of Health and Human Services	Pregnant and parenting youth, non-pregnant youth and their families.
National and Community Service					
AmeriCorps State and National	National Community Service Act, as amended	To address the educational, public safety, human, or environmental needs through	FY2006: $265 million FY2007: $265 million	Corporation for National and	Youth up to age 25 with excep-tional or special needs, or who are economically disadvantaged and for whom one or more

Table A-1. (Continued)

Program	Authorizing Legislation and U.S. Code Citation	Objective(s) of Program	FY2006 -FY2008 Appropriations and President's FY2009 Request (rounded)	Agency with Jurisdiction	Target At-Risk Youth Population
	42 U.S.C. §12571 et seq, 42 U.S.C. §12061 et seq	services that provide a direct benefit to the community.	FY2008: $257 million FY2009: $274 million	Community Service	of the following apply: 1) out-of-school, including out-of-school youth who are unemployed; 2) in or aging out of foster care; 3) limited English proficiency; 4) homeless or have run away from home; 5) at-risk of leaving school without a diploma; and 6) former juvenile offenders or at risk of delinquency.
AmeriCorps VISTA	Domestic Volu-nteer Service Act, as amended 42 U.S.C.§ 4951, 42 U.S.C. §12061 et seq.	To bring low-income individuals and communities out of poverty through programs in com-munity organizati-ons and public agencies.	FY2006: $95 million FY2007: $95 million FY2008: $94 million FY2009: $92 million	Corporation for National and Community Service	Youth up to age 25 with exceptional or special needs, or who are economically disadvantaged and for whom one or more of the following apply: 1) out-of-school, including out-of-school youth who are unemp-loyed; 2) in or aging out of foster care; 3) limited English proficiency; 4) homeless or have run away from home; 5) at-risk to leave school without a diploma; and 6) former juvenile offenders or at risk of delinquency.
AmeriCorps National Civilian Community Corps	National Community Service Act, as amended 42 U.S.C.§12611 et seq., 42 U.S.C. §12061 et seq.	To address the educational, public safety, environmental, human needs, and disaster relief through services that provide a direct benefit to the community.	FY2006: $37 million FY2007: $27 million FY2008: $24 million FY2009: $9 million	Corporation for National and Community Service	Youth up to age 25 with exceptional or special needs, or who are economically disadvantaged and for whom one or more of the following apply: 1) out-of-school, including out-of-school youth who are unemployed; 2) in or aging out of foster care; 3) limited English proficiency; 4) homeless or have run away from home; 5) at-risk of leaving school without a diploma; and 6) former juvenile offenders or at risk of delinquency.
Learn and Serve America	National Community Service Act, as amended	To involve students in community service projects that address the educational, public	FY2006: $37 million FY2007: $37 million	Corporation for National and	Youth up to age 25 with exceptional or special needs, or who are economically disadvantaged and for whom one or more

Table A-1. (Continued)

Program	Authorizing Legislation and U.S. Code Citation	Objective(s) of Program	FY2006 -FY2008 Appropriations and President's FY2009 Request (rounded)	Agency with Jurisdiction	Target At-Risk Youth Population
	42 U.S.C. §12521-12547, 42 §U.S.C. 121561 et seq.	safety, human, or environmental needs in ways that benefit both the student and community.	FY2008: $37 million FY2009: $32 million	Community Service	of the following apply: 1) out-of-school, including out-of-school youth who are unempl-oyed; 2) in or aging out of foster care; 3) limited English proficiency; 4) homeless or have run away from home; 5) at risk of leaving school without a diploma; and 6) former juvenile offenders or at risk of delinquency.
Senior Corps Foster Grandparents	Domestic Volunteer Service Act, as amended 42 U.S.C. §5011 et seq.	To provide service to children with special or exceptional needs.	FY2006: $111 million FY2007: $111 million FY2008: $109 million FY2009: $68 million	Corporation for National and Community Service	Youth up to age 25 with excepti-ional or special needs, or who are economically disadvantaged and for whom one or more of the foll-owing apply: 1) out-of-school, including out-of-school youth who are unempl-oyed; 2) in or aging out of foster care; 3) limited English proficiency; 4) homeless or have run away from home; 5) at risk of leaving school without a diploma; and 6) former juvenile offenders or at risk of delinquency.
Senior Corps RSVP	Domestic Volunteer Service Act, as amended 42 U.S.C. 5001	To involve seniors in community service projects that address the educational, public safety, human, or environmental needs in ways that benefit both the senior and community.	FY2006: $60 million FY2007: $60 million FY2008: $58 million FY2009: $60 million	Corporation for National and Community Service	Youth up to age 25 with excepti-onal or special needs, or who are economically disadvantaged and for whom one or more of the foll-owing apply: 1) out-of-school, including out-of-school youth who are unempl-oyed; 2) in or aging out of foster care; 3) limited English proficiency; 4) homeless or have run away from home; 5) at risk of leaving school without a dipl-oma; and 6) former juvenile offenders or at risk of delinquency.

Source: Table created by the Congressional Research Service.

Table A-2. Relevant CRS Reports and Analyst Contact Information

Issue Area(s)	Corresponding CRS Report(s)	Analyst	Contact Information
• Individuals with Disabilities Education Act, Part B Grants to States • National and Community Service Programs	• CRS Report RL32913, *The Individuals with Disabilities Education Act (IDEA):Interactions with Selected Provisions of the No Child Left Behind Act (NCLB)*, by Richard N. Apling and Nancy Lee Jones • CRS Report RL33931, *The Corporation for National and Community Service:Overview of Programs and FY2009 Funding*, by Ann Lordeman and Abigail B. Rudman	Ann Lordeman	alordeman@crs.loc.gov x7-2323
• Title IV: Safe and Drug Free Schools	• CRS Report RL33980, *School and Campus Safety Programs and Requirements in the Elementary and Secondary Education Act and Higher Education Act*, by Rebecca R. Skinner and Gail McCallion	Gail McCallion	gmccallion@crs.loc.gov x7-7758
• Vulnerable Youth and Youth Programs (generally) • Chafee Foster Care Independence Program and Education and Training Voucher Program • Runaway and Homeless Youth Program (Basic Center, Transitional Living, and Street Outreach Programs) • Missing and Exploited Children's Program • Mentoring Children of Prisoners	• CRS Report RL34499, *Youth Transi-tioning From Foster Care: Background, Federal Programs, and Issues for Congress*, by Adrienne Fernandes • CRS Report RL33785, *Runaway and Homeless Youth: Demographics and Programs*, by Adrienne L. Fernandes • CRS Report RL34050, *Missing and Exploited Children: Background, Policies, and Issues*, by Adrienne L. Fernandes • CRS Report RL34306, *Vulnerable Youth: Federal Mentoring Programs and Issues*, by Adrienne L. Fernandes	Adrienne L. Fernandes	afernandes@crs.loc.gov x7-9005
• Title VII: Education of Homeless Children	• CRS Report RL30442, *Homelessness: Targeted Federal Programs and Recent Legislation*, coordinated by Libby Perl	Gail McCallion	gmccallion@crs.loc.gov x7-7758
• Upward Bound • Education Opportunity Centers	• CRS Report RL31622, *Trio and GEAR UP Programs: Status and Issues*, by Jeffrey J. Kuenzi	Jeffrey J. Kuenzi	jkuenzi@crs.loc.gov x7-8645

Table A-2. (Continued)

Issue Area(s)	Corresponding CRS Report(s)	Analyst	Contact Information
• Student Support Services • Talent Search • Gaining Early Awareness and Readiness for Undergraduate Programs • School Dropout Prevention Program	• CRS Report RL33963, *High School Graduation, Completion, and Dropouts: Federal Policy, Programs, and Issues*, by Jeffrey J. Kuenzi		
• Workforce Development (generally) • YouthBuild • — Job Corps	• CRS Report RL33687, *The Workforce Investment Act (WIA): Program-by-Program Overview and FY2007 Funding of Title I Training Programs*, by Blake Alan Naughton and Ann Lordeman	Blake Alan Naughton	bnaughton@crs.loc.gov x7-0376
• Juvenile Justice (generally)	• CRS Report RS22070, *Juvenile Justice: Overview of Legislative History and Funding Trends*, by Blas Nuñez-Neto • CRS Report RL33947, *Juvenile Justice: Legislative History and Current Legislative Issues*, by Blas Nuñez-Neto	Blas Nuñez-Neto	bnunezneto@crs.loc.gov x7-0622
• Title I: Education for the Disadvantaged • Title I-D: Prevention and Intervention Programs for Children and Youths Who Are Neglected, Delinquent, or At Risk	• CRS Report RL31487, *Education for the Disadvantaged: Overview of ESEA Title I-A Amendments Under the No Child Left Behind Act*, by Wayne C. Riddle	Wayne C. Riddle	wriddle@crs.loc.gov x7-7382
• Migrant Education • Migrant High School Equivalency Program • Title III: English Language Acquisition	• CRS Report RL31325, *The Federal Migrant Education Program as Amended by the No Child Left Behind Act of 2001*, by Jeffrey J. Kuenzi • CRS Report RL31315, *Education of Limited English Proficient and RecentImmigrant Students: Provisions of the No Child Left Behind Act of 2001*, by Jeffrey J. Kuenzi	Rebecca R. Skinner	rskinner@crs.loc.gov x7-6600
• Community-Based Abstinence Education • Abstinence Education Program • Adolescent Family Life Demonstration Projects	• CRS Report RS20873, *Reducing Teen Pregnancy: Family Life and Abstinence Education Programs*, by Carmen Solomon-Fears	Carmen Solomon-Fears	csolomonfears@crs.loc.gov x7-7306

Table A-2. (Continued)

Issue Area(s)	Corresponding CRS Report(s)	Analyst	Contact Information
• Adolescent Family Life Research Grants	• CRS Report RS20301, *Teenage Pregnancy Prevention: Statistics and Programs*, by Carmen Solomon-Fears		
• Foster Care • Court Appointed Special Advocates Program • Children's Advocacy Centers	• CRS Report RL32976, *Child Welfare: Programs Authorized by the Victims of Child Abuse Act of 1990*, by Emilie Stoltzfus • CRS Report RL31242 *Child Welfare: Federal Program Requirements for States*, by Emilie Stoltzfus	Emilie Stoltzfus	estoltzfus@crs.loc. gov x7-2324

Source: Table created by the Congressional Research Service.

End Notes

[1] U.S. Census Bureau, American Fact Finder, *Age Groups and Sex: 2000*, available at [http://factfinder.census.gov/servlet/QTTable?_bm=y&-geo_id   000US&-qr_name=D   EC   _2000   _SF   1_U_QTP 1 &-ds _name=DEC _2000 _SF 1_U].

[2] Carnegie Corporation of New York, Carnegie Council on Adolescent Development, *Great Transitions: Preparing Adolescents for a New Century* (October 1995), pp. 20-21.

[3] Wayne G. Osgood et al., eds., *On Your Own Without a Net: The Transition to Adulthood for Vulnerable Populations*. Chicago: The University of Chicago Press, 2005, pp. 4-6. (Hereinafter Wayne G. Osgood et al., eds., *On Your Own Without a Net*.)

[4] Claudia Goldin, Lawrence F. Katz, and Ilyana Kuziemko, "The Homecoming of American College Women: The Reversal of the College Gender Gap," *Journal of Economic Perspectives*, vol. 20, no. 4, Fall 2006.

[5] U.S. Census Bureau, American Fact Finder, *Median Age for First Marriage for Men* and *Median Age of First Marriage for Women: 2000-2003*, available at [http://www.census.gov/ population/socdemo/hh-fam/ms2.pdf].

[6] Bob Schoeni and Karen Ross, "Material Assistance Received from Families During the Transition to Adulthood." In Richard A. Settersten, Jr., Frank F. Furstenburg, Jr., and Rubén Rumbaut, eds., *On the Frontier of Adulthood: Theory, Research, and Public Policy*, pp. 404- 405. Chicago: University of Chicago Press, 2005.

[7] Brett Brown, Kristin Moore, and Sharon Bzostek, *A Portrait of Well-Being in Early Adulthood: A Report to the William and Flora Hewlett Foundation*, Child Trends, October 2007, available at [http://www.hewlett.org/NR/rdonlyres/B0DB0AF1-02A4-455A-849A-AD582B767AF3/0/ FINALCOMPLETEPDF.pdf]. The data are based on the authors' analysis of data from the Current Population Survey, U.S. Census Bureau.

[8] See CRS Report RS22501, *Child Welfare: The Chafee Foster Care Independence Program (CFCIP)*, by Adrienne Fernandes.

[9] See Richard A. Settersten, Jr., Frank F. Furstenburg, Jr., and Rubén Rumbaut, eds., *On the Frontier of Adulthood: Theory, Research, and Public Policy*. Chicago: University of Chicago Press, 2005. See also Osgood et al., eds., *On Your Own Without a Net*.

[10] Based on calculation of the percentage of adults ages 25 to 34 who have received a bachelor's degree. Current Population Survey, *Educational Attainment of Employed Civilians 18 to 64, by Industry, Age, Sex, Race, and Hispanic Origin, 2007*, available at [http://www.census.gov/population

[11] Kristin Anderson Moore, "Defining the Term 'At Risk,'" Child Trends Research-toResults Brief, Publication #2006-12, October 2006. (Hereinafter Kristin Moore, "Defining the Term 'At-Risk.'")

[12] J. Jeffries McWhirter et al., *At-Risk Youth: A Comprehensive Response*. California: Thomson Brooks/Cole, 2004, p. 6. (Hereinafter J. Jeffries McWhirter, *At-Risk Youth*.)

[13] Kristin Moore, "Defining the Term 'At-Risk.'"

[14] Martha R. Burt, Gary Resnick, and Nancy Matheson, *Comprehensive Service Integration Programs for At-Risk Youth*, The Urban Institute, 1992, pp. 13-22.

[15] J. Jeffries McWhirter, *At-Risk Youth*, pp. 7-9.

[16] See, for example, Osgood et al., eds., *On Your Own Without a Net*, and Michael Wald and Tia Martinez, *Connected by 25: Improving the Life Chances of the Country's Most Vulnerable 14-24 Year Olds*, William and

Flora Hewlett Foundation Working Paper, November 2003. *On Your Own Without a Net* focuses on the seven groups, in addition to youth reentering the community from the juvenile justice system. "Connected by 25" focuses on four groups: high school dropouts, young unmarried mothers, juvenile justice- involved youth, and foster youth.

[17] Wayne G. Osgood et al., eds., *On Your Own Without a Net*, p. 10.

[18] Ibid., pp. 10-12.

[19] J. Jeffries McWhirter, *At-Risk Youth*, pp. 9, 13, and 14.

[20] Mark E. Courtney and Darcy Hughes Heuring. "The Transition to Adulthood for Youth "Aging Out" of the Foster Care System" in Osgood et al., eds., *On Your Own Without a Net*, pp. 27-32.

[21] Ibid.

[22] Section 497(b)(3)(B) of the Social Security Act requires that no more than 30% of federal independent living funds administered through the Chafee Foster Care Independence Program may be spent on housing for youth between the ages of 18 to 21. The act authorizes $140 million each year for the program. The estimate of less than $800 for each youth is based on the author's calculations that as many as 60,000 youth ages 18, 19, and 20 are eligible to receive housing assistance totaling $47 million (or 30% of $140 million).

[23] Peter J. Pecora et al., *Improving Foster Family Care: Findings from the Northwest Foster Care Alumni Study*, Casey Family Programs, 2005, pp. 1-2, available at [http://www.casey. org/Resources/Publications/Northwest AlumniStudy.htm]. (Hereinafter Peter J. Pecora et al., *Improving Foster Family Care*.)

[24] This discussion is based on Martha R. Burt, Gary Resnick, and Nancy Matheson, *Comprehensive Service Integration Programs for At-Risk Youth*, The Urban Institute, 1992, pp. 13-22.

[25] Steven R. Holloway and Stephen Mullherin, "The Effects of Adolescent Neighborhood Poverty on Adult Employment," *Journal of Urban Affairs,* vol. 26, no. 4, 2004.

[26] Peter Edelman, Harry J. Holzer, and Paul Offner, *Reconnecting Disadvantaged Young Men*. Washington, DC: Urban Institute Press, 2006, pp. 19-21. (Hereafter Peter Edelman, Harry J. Holzer, and Paul Offner, *Reconnecting Disadvantaged Young Men*.)

[27] See for example, Weinberg, Reagan, and Yankow, *Do Neigborhoods Matter?*; Katherine M. O'Regan and John M. Quiley, "Where Youth Live: Economic Effects of Urban Space on Employment Propsects," *Urban Studies*, vol. 35, no.7, 1998 and Stephen Raphael, "Inter- and Intra-Ethnic Comparisons of the Central City-Suburban Youth Employment Differential," *Industrial & Labor Relationship Review*, vol. 51, no. 3, April 1998.

[28] William Julius Wilson, *When Work Disappears: The World of the New Urban Poor*. New York: Vintage Books, 1996, pp. 25-29.

[29] Peter Edelman, Harry J. Holzer, and Paul Offner, *Reconnecting Disadvantaged Young Men,* p. 21.

[30] U.S. Department of Health and Human Services, Administration for Children and Families *AFCARS Report #13: Preliminary Estimates for FY2005,* September 2006, at [http://www.acf.hhs.gov/programs/cb/ stats_research/afcars/tar 3 .htm].

[31] Peter J. Pecora et al., *Improving Foster Family Care.*

[32] See, for example, Campaign for Youth, "Memo on Reconnecting our Youth From a Coalition of Voices," January 2005, available at [http://www.clasp.org/CampaignFor Youth/].

[33] This analysis was conducted with the assistance of Thomas Gabe, CRS Specialist in Social Legislation.

[34] These rates do not appear to be comparable to the Edelman, Holzer, and Offner analysis of March 2000 CPS data. Edelman, Holzer, and Offman examined rates of disconnection in the previous year only — 1999.

[35] This discussion based in part on CRS Report RL32871, *Youth: From Classroom to Workplace?*, by Linda Levine.

[36] U.S. Department of Justice, Bureau of Justice Statistics, *Prison and Jail Inmates at Midyear 2006*, p. 1, available at [http://www.ojp.usdoj.gov/bjs/pub/pdf/pjim06.pdf].

[37] *Disadvantaged Young Men*, p. 13.

[38] U.S. Congressional Budget Office, *What Is Happening to Youth Employment Rates*, *Table 6*, November 2004, at [http://www.cbo.gov/showdoc.cfm?index=60 1 7&sequence=0].

[39] Michael Wald and Tia Martinez, *Connected by 25: Improving the Life Chances of the Country's Most Vulnerable 14-24 Year Olds*, William and Flora Hewlett Foundation Working Paper, November 2003, pp. 14-17, available at [http://www.hewlett.org/ NR/rdonlyres/60C 1 7B69-8A76-4F99-BB3B-8425 1 E4E5A 1 9/0/Final VersionofDisconne ctedYouthPaper.pdf].

[40] National Youth Development Information Center, *What is Youth Development?*, available at [http://www.nydic.org/nydic/programming

[41] National Research Council, *Community Programs to Promote Youth Development*. Washington, DC: National Academy Press, 2002, pp. 6-7.

[42] Discussion based on U.S. Department of Health and Human Services, Family and Youth Services Bureau, *Understanding Youth Development: Promoting Positive Pathways of Growth*, 1997.

[43] Karen Pittman, Merita Irby, and Thaddeus Ferber, *Unfinished Business: Further Reflections on a Decade of Promoting Youth Development,* The Forum for Youth Investment, 2000, p. 9, available at [http://www.ppv.org/ppv/publications/assets ydv_1 .pdf]. (Hereafter Karen Pittman, Merita Irby, and Thaddeus Ferber, *Unfinished Business.*)

44 Carnegie Corporation of New York, Carnegie Council on Adolescent Development, *A Matter of Time: Risk and Opportunity in the Nonschool Hours* (December 1992), p. 11.
45 4-H, The National Conversation on Youth Development in the 21st Century: Final Report. 2002, p. 4.
46 See for example, Karen Pittman, "Some Things Do Make a Difference and We Can Prove It: Key Take-Aways" from *Finding Out What Matters for Youth: Testing Key Links in a Community Action Framework for Youth Development*, The Forum for Youth Investment, April 2003, available at [http://www.ydsi.org/ydsi/pdf/WhatMatters.pdf]; 4-H, *The National Conversation on Youth Development in the 21st Century: Final Report,* 2002; National Research Council, *Community Programs to Promote Youth Development*, 2002; U.S. Department of Health and Human Services, Administration for Children and Families, Publications on Positive Youth Devlopment, available at [http://www.acf.hhs.gov/programs/fysb/content/positiveyouth/publications.htm].
47 Karen Pittman, Merita Irby, and Thaddeus Ferber, *Unfinished Business*, pp. 20-22.
48 Ibid., pp. 30-31.
49 Ibid., pp. 14-27.
50 G. Stanley Hall, "Adolescence: Its Psychology and Its Relations to Physiology, Anthropology, Sociology, Sex, Crime, Religion, and Education," (1904) in John H. Bremner, Tamara K. Hareven, and Robert M. Mennel, eds., *Children & Youth in America, Vol. II: 1866-1932, Parts 1-6*. Cambridge, MA: Harvard University Press, 1971, pp. 81-85.
51 John H. Bremner, Tamara K. Hareven, and Robert M. Mennel, eds., *Children & Youth in America, Vol. II: 1866-1932, Parts 1-6*. Cambridge, MA: Harvard University Press, 1971, p. 440.
52 Kriste Lindenmeyer, *"A Right to Childhood:" The U.S. Children's Bureau and Child Welfare, 1912-46*. Urbana: University of Illinois Press), pp. 10-11. (Hereafter Kriste Lindenmeyer, *A Right to Childhood.*)
53 Ibid., pp. 127, 137-138.
54 Ibid., pp. 148-153.
55 In 1962 (P.L. 87-543), child welfare services were formally defined under Title IV-B as "public social services which supplement, or substitute for parental care and supervision for the purpose of (1) remedying or assisting in the solution of problems which may result in, the neglect, abuse, exploitation, or delinquency of children, (2) protecting and caring for homeless, dependent, or neglected children, (3) protecting and promoting the welfare of children, including the strengthening of their own homes where possible or, where needed, the provision of adequate care of children away from their homes in foster family homes or day-care or other child-care facilities."
56 Kriste Lindenmeyer, *A Right to Childhood*, p. 193.
57 John H. Bremner, Tamara K. Hareven, and Robert M. Mennel, eds., *Children & Youth in America, Vol. III: 1933-1973, Parts 1-4*. Cambridge, MA: Harvard University Press, 1971, pp. 91-96.
58 Ibid., pp. 99-104.
59 For additional information about the creation of HEW, see CRS Report RL3 1497, *Creation of Executive Departments: Highlights from the History of Modern Precedents*, by Thomas P. Carr.
60 Executive Office of the President, Conference Proceedings from the Golden Anniversary White House Conference on Children and Youth, March 27-April 2, 1960 (Washington: GPO, 1960), p. 212.
61 Executive Office of the President, *Conference Proceedings from the White House Conference on Youth, 1971*. Washington: GPO, 1971.
62 This discussion is based on correspondence with U.S. Department of Health and Human Services, Administration for Children and Families, April 2007.
63 American Youth Policy Forum, *A Youth Development Approach to Services for Young People: The Work of the Family and Youth Services Bureau*, Forum Brief, June 11, 1999.
64 The FY2009 funding levels will be updated when the final figures become available.
65 A state-by-state expenditure data report for these and other categories of services is available at [http://www.acf.hhs.gov/programs/ocs/ssbg/annrpt/2005/index.html].
66 For additional information on Job Corps and WIA Youth Activities, see CRS Report RL33 687, *The Workforce Investment Act (WIA): Program-by-Program Overview and FY2007 Funding of Title I Training Programs*, by Blake Alan Naughton and Ann Lordeman.
67 Peter Z. Schochet, John Burghardt, and Steven Glazerman, *Does Job Corps Work?: Summary of the National Job Corps Study*, Mathematica, June 2001, available at [http://wdr.doleta.gov/opr/fulltext/0 1 -jcsummary.pdf].
68 The 109th Congress considered legislation (H.R. 27) to make the Youth Councils optional. For additional information, see CRS Report RL32778, *The Workforce Investment Act of 1998 (WIA): Reauthorization of Job Training Programs in the 109th Congress*, by Blake Alan Naughton and Ann Lordeman.
69 For additional information, see CRS Report RL3 1284, *K-12 Education: Highlights of the No Child Left Behind Act of 2001 (P.L. 10 7-110)*, coordinated by Wayne C. Riddle and CRS Report RL33960, *The Elementary and Secondary Education Act, as Amended: A Primer*, by Wayne C. Riddle and Rebecca R. Skinner.
70 For additional information, see CRS Report RL31622, *Trio and GEAR-UP Programs: Status and Issues*, by Jeffrey J. Kuenzi.

[71] The precise definition of disadvantaged varies between the programs. It generally refers to individuals who are low-income, first-generation college students, or disabled.

[72] These two programs are the Staff Development program and Dissemination Partnership Grants program. The Staff Development program supports training of current and prospective Trio staff. The Dissemination Partnership Grants funds partnerships with institutions of higher education or community organizations not receiving Trio funds but that serve first-generation and low-income college students.

[73] For additional information, see CRS Report RS22 138, *Individuals with Disabilities Education Act (IDEA): Overview of P.L. 108-446*, by Nancy Lee Jones and Richard N. Apling.

[74] This section was prepared by CRS Analyst Blas Nuñez-Neto. For an expanded discussion of juvenile justice legislation and issues, please see CRS Report RL33947, *Juvenile Justice: Legislative History and Current Legislative Issues*, by Blas Nuñez-Neto.

[75] For additional information, see CRS Report RL34306 V*ulnerable Youth: Federal Mentoring Programs and Issues*, by Adrienne L. Fernandes.

[76] Two additional child welfare programs, Court Appointed Special Advocates and Children's Advocacy Centers, are discussed in the chart below. The programs are administered by the U.S. Department of Justice.

[77] For additional information, see CRS Report RL3 1242, *Child Welfare: Federal Program Requirements for States*, by Emilie Stoltzfus.

[78] With an exception, discussed below, the income and asset tests, as well as family structure/living arrangement rules are identical to the federal /state rules that applied to the now-defunct cash aid program, Aid to Families with Dependent Children (AFDC), as they existed on July 16, 1996. Under the prior law AFDC program, states established specific AFDC income rules (within some federal parameters). The federal AFDC asset limit was $1,000, however, P.L. 106-169 raised the allowable counted asset limit to $10,000 for purposes of determining Title IV-E eligibility. In addition to meeting the income/asset criteria in the home from which he/she was removed, a child must meet the AFDC family structure/living arrangement rules. Those rules granted eligibility primarily to children in single-parent families (parents are divorced, separated, or never-married and one spouse is not living with the child; or the parent is dead). In some cases a child in a two-parent family may be eligible (if one parent meets certain unemployment criteria).

[79] For additional information, see CRS Report RS22501, *Child Welfare: Chafee Foster Care Independence Program (CFCIP)*, by Adrienne Fernandes.

[80] See Sections 102 and 472 of the Higher Education Act of 1965.

[81] For additional information, see CRS Report RL34306 *Vulnerable Youth: Federal Mentoring Programs and Issues*, by Adrienne L. Fernandes.

[82] For additional information, see CRS Report RL33785*, Runaway and Homeless Youth: Demographics, Programs, and Emerging Issues*, by Adrienne L. Fernandes.

[83] Other program activities include a national communications system for runaway youth and their families, logistical support for grantee organizations, HHS's National Clearinghouse on Families and Youth, demonstrations, and the administration of the management information system that tracks data on runaway and homeless youth, known as NEO-RHYMIS.

[84] For additional information, see CRS Report RL33997 *Substance Abuse and Mental Health Services Administration (SAMHSA): Reauthorization Issues*, by Ramya Sundararaman.

[85] Other SAMSHA funds are made available for the National Suicide Prevention Lifeline and training to organizations and individuals developing suicide prevention programs.

[86] For additional information, see CRS Report RS20873, *Reducing Teen Pregnancy: Adolescent Family Life and Abstinence Education Programs* and CRS Report RS2030 1, *Teenage Pregnancy Prevention: Statistics and Programs,* by Carmen Solomon-Fears.

[87] This information was provided by the Corporation for National and Community Service in correspondence in March and April 2008.

[88] For additional information, see CRS Report RL3393 1, *The Corporation for National and Community Service: Overview of Programs and FY2009 Funding*, by Ann Lordeman and Abigail B. Rudman.

[89] For further information, see [http://www.cns.gov/about/focus_areas/index.asp].

[90] The programs are also called AmeriCorps*State and National Direct by CNCS, and is titled National Service Trust Programs in Title I-C of the NCSA.

[91] This program is called AmeriCorps*VISTA by CNCS, and VISTA in Title I-A of DVSA.

[92] This program is called AmeriCorps*NCCC by CNCS, and the Civilian Community Corps in Title I-E of NCSA.

[93] This number includes campuses that are scheduled to open in 2008 and 2009.

[94] In its definition of disadvantaged, the program also include students who are enrolled in schools where 50% or more of students receive free or reduced-priced meals.

[95] For additional information about rationales for coordination, see CRS Report RL3 1357, *Federal Interagency Coordinative Mechanisms: Varied Types and Numerous Devices*, by Frederick M. Kaiser. For a discussion of

federal efforts to coordinate and integrate various social service programs, see CRS Report RL32859, *The "Superwaiver" Proposal and Service Integration: A History of Federal Initiatives*, by Cheryl Vincent.

[96] U.S. General Accounting Office, *At-Risk and Delinquent Youth: Multiple Federal Programs Raise Efficiency Questions*, GAO/HEHS-96-34, March 1996, at [http://www.gao. gov/archive/1996/he96034.pdf]. (GAO is now known as the U.S. Government Accountability Office.)

[97] The programs provide services such as: academic support; support for adults who work with youth; after-school programs; AIDS prevention activities; counseling; mental health services; mentoring; self-sufficiency skills; tutoring; and violence and crime prevention. See Executive Office of the President, *White House Task Force for Disadvantaged Youth Final Report*, October 2003, pp. 165-179, at [http://www.acf.hhs.gov/programs/fysb/content/ docs/white_house_task_force.pdf]. (Hereafter *White House Task Force for Disadvantaged Youth Final Report*.)

[98] U.S. Congress, House Committee on Government Reform, *Redundancy and Duplication in Federal Child Welfare Programs: A Case Study on the Need for Executive Reorganization Authority*, hearing, 108th Cong., 2nd sess., May 20, 2004 (Washington: GPO, 2004), available at [http://www.gpoaccess.gov/chearings/1 08hcat1 .html].

[99] U.S. Congress, House Commitee on Education and the Workforce, Subcommittee on Select Education, *Coordination Among Federal Youth Development Programs*, hearing 109th Cong., 1st sess., July 12, 2005, statements of Rep. Tom Osborne and Marguerite W. Sallee, Alliance for Youth (Washington: GPO, 2005), available at [http://www.gpoaccess.gov/ chearings/1 09hcat1 .html].

[100] Executive Order 13459. "Improving the Coordination and Effectiveness of Youth Programs." *Federal Register*, vol. 73 (February 7, 2008), pp. 8003-8005.

[101] For further discussion of concerns with coordination at the state and local levels and local initiatives to improve coordination in the early 1990s, see CRS Report 96-369, *Linking Human Services: An Overview of Coordination and Integration Efforts*, by Ruth Ellen Wasem (out of print). The report is available upon request at x7-5700.

[102] U.S. Congress, Senate Committee on Labor and Human Resources, *Human Services Reauthorization Act*, report to accompany P.L. 101-501, 101st Cong., 2nd sess., S.Rept. 101- 421 (Washington, DC: GPO, 1990), p. 1963.

[103] *White House Task Force for Disadvantaged Youth Final Report*, pp. 33-34.

[104] U.S. Department of Justice, Coordinating Council on Juvenile Justice and Delinquency Prevention, Minutes from the Quarterly Meeting on November 30, 2006, p. 10, available at [http://www.juvenilecouncil.gov/meetings.html].

[105] Ibid., pp. 8-9.

[106] Based on correspondence with staff from the National Corporation for National and Community Service, December 2007.

[107] For additional information about the programs in each state, see [http://www.doleta.gov/ ryf/Resources/TechnicalAssistanceForum.cfm].

[108] U.S. Department of Health and Human Services, SAMHSA, *Transition to Adulthood: SAMHSA Helps Vulnerable Youth*, SAMHSA News, vol. XI, no. 1 (2003).

[109] For additional information, see [http://samhsa.gov/grants

[110] U.S. Congress, House Committee on Education and the Workforce, Subcommittee on Select Education, *Coordination Among Federal Youth Development Programs*, hearing, 109th Cong., 1st sess., July 12, 2005, statement of Dr. Michael O'Grady, U.S. Department of Health and Human Services, (Washington, DC: GPO), available at [http://www.gpoaccess. gov/chearings/1 09hcat1 .html].

[111] U.S. Congress, House Committee on Economic and Educational Opportunities, Subcommittee on Early Childhood, Youth, and Families, *Youth Development*, hearing, 1 04th Cong., 1st sess., September 19, 1996.

[112] The Older Americans Act is the major vehicle for the delivery of social and nutritional services for older persons.

[113] For additional information, see [http://www.helpingamericasyouth.gov/].

[114] See [http://guide.helpingamericasyouth.gov/].

[115] For additional information, see CRS Report RS2 1844, *The Compassion Capital Fund: Brief Facts and Current Development*, by Joe Richardson.

[116] The five surviving presidents (at that time) convened the summit to mobilize Americans in all sectors to ensure that all youth have adequate resources that will assist them in leading healthy, productive lives.

[117] The organization's website provides additional information about the Five Promises: [http://www.americaspromise.org/].

[118] For funding in FY2008, the appropriations committees expect that America's Promise will be eligible to compete for merit-based grants under the AmeriCorps program. See U.S. House, *Congressional Record*, H1 6282, December 17, 2007.

[119] America's Promise: The Alliance for Youth, *Every Child, Every Promise: Turning Failure to Action*, p. 4, 2006, available at [http://www.americaspromise.org/uploaded Files/AmericasPromise/Our _Work/Strategic _Initiatives/Every _Child _Every_ Promise/EC-EP_Documents/MAIN%20REPORT%20DRAFT%20 11.1 .pdf].

[120] For more information, see the Family and Youth Services Bureau page on grantees [http://www.acf.hhs.gov/programs/fysb/content/youthdivision/initiatives/highlights.htm].

In: Vulnerable and Disconnected Youth: Background...
Editor: Dierk Neumann

ISBN: 978-1-60741-488-9
© 2010 Nova Science Publishers, Inc.

Chapter 4

VULNERABLE YOUTH: FEDERAL MONITORING PROGRAMS AND ISSUES

Adrienne L. Fernandes

SUMMARY

Youth mentoring refers to a relationship between youth — particularly those most at risk of experiencing negative outcomes in adolescence and adulthood — and the adults who support and guide them. The origin of the modern youth mentoring concept is credited to the efforts of charity groups that formed during the Progressive era of the early 1900s to provide practical assistance to poor and juvenile justice- involved youth, including help with finding employment.

Approximately 2.5 million youth today are involved in formal mentoring relationships through Big Brothers Big Sisters (BBBS) of America and similar organizations. Contemporary mentoring programs seek to improve outcomes and reduce risks among vulnerable youth by providing positive role models who regularly meet with the youth in community or school settings. Some programs have broad youth development goals while others focus more narrowly on a particular outcome. A 1995 evaluation of the BBBS program and studies of other mentoring programs demonstrate an association between mentoring and some positive youth outcomes, but the effects of mentoring on particular outcomes and the ability for mentored youth to sustain gains over time is less certain.

The current Administration has proposed new federal structured mentoring since FY2001 (though the Administration has also proposed phasing some of these services out beginning in FY2007). Two programs — the Mentoring Children of Prisoners (MCP) program and Safe and Drug Free Schools (SDFS) Mentoring program — provide the primary sources of dedicated federal funding for mentoring services. The Mentoring Children of Prisoners program was created in response to the growing number of children under age 18 with at least one parent who is incarcerated in a federal or state correctional facility. The program is intended, in part, to reduce the chance that mentored youth will use drugs and skip school. Similarly, the Mentoring program (proposed for elimination for FY2009 by the

Administration) provides school-based mentoring to reduce school dropout and improve relationships for youth at risk of educational failure and with other risk factors. The Administration has also supported a pilot project, the Mentoring Initiative for System Involved Youth (MISIY), which seeks to identify and expand effective mentoring programs for youth in the juvenile justice or foster care systems (Congress appropriated funds for MISIY only in FY2006). Finally, other federal initiatives support mentoring efforts, including the Federal Mentoring Council and dedicated funding for mentoring organizations like BBBS.

Five bills have been introduced in the 110th Congress that primarily concern mentoring (S. 379, H.R. 2611/S. 1812, H.R. 5660, and H.R. 5810). Issues relevant to the federal role in mentoring include the limitations of research on outcomes for mentored youth, the potential need for additional mentors, grantees' challenges in sustaining funding, and the possible discontinuation of federal mentoring funding. This report will be updated as legislative activity warrants.

Since the mid-1990s, Congress has supported legislation to establish structured mentoring programs for the most vulnerable youth. The Department of Justice's Juvenile Mentoring Program (JUMP), the first structured federal mentoring program, was implemented in 1 994 to provide mentoring services for at-risk youth ages five to 20. The purpose of contemporary, structured mentoring programs is to reduce risks by supplementing (but not supplanting) a youth's relationship with his or her parents. Some of these programs have broad youth development goals while others focus more narrowly on a particular outcome such as reducing gang activity or substance abuse, or improving grades. Research has shown that mentoring programs have been associated with some positive youth outcomes, but that the long-term effects of mentoring on particular outcomes and the ability for mentored youth to sustain gains over time are less certain.

While there is no single overarching policy today on mentoring, the federal government supports multiple mentoring efforts for vulnerable youth. Since FY2001, Congress has passed legislation to provide mentoring services for three groups of these youth: children of prisoners through the Mentoring Children of Prisoners (MCP) program; children at risk of educational failure, dropping out of school, or involvement in delinquent activities through the Safe and Drug Free Schools (SDFS) Mentoring program; and youth in the foster care and juvenile justice systems through the Mentoring Initiative for System Involved Youth (MISIY). The purpose of the three programs is to improve the outcomes of vulnerable youth across a number of areas, including education, criminal activity, health and safety, and social and emotional development.

The federal government also supports other mentoring efforts. Programs under the Corporation for National and Community Service (CNCS) provide mentoring services, among other supportive activities for youth. In partnership with the U.S. Department of Health and Human Services (HHS), CNCS also leads the Federal Youth Mentoring Council, convened in 2006 to address the ways federal agencies can combine resources and training and technical assistance to federally administered mentoring programs. Further, the Office of Juvenile Justice and Delinquency Prevention in the U.S Department of Justice (DOJ) provides funding for Big Brothers and Big Sisters of America and other mentoring organizations.

This report begins with an overview of the purpose of mentoring, including a brief discussion on research of structured mentoring programs. The report then describes the evolution of federal policies on mentoring since the early 1 990s. The report provides an overview of the components and funding for each of the three major federal mentoring programs, as well as a discussion of other federal mentoring initiatives that are currently funded. Note that additional federal programs and policies authorize funding for mentoring activities, among multiple other activities and services.[1] These programs are not discussed in this report. The report concludes with an overview of issues that may be relevant to mentoring legislation in the 110th Congress and any discussions concerning the federal role in mentoring. These issues include the limitations of research on outcomes for mentored youth, the potential need for additional mentors, grantees' challenges in sustaining funding, and the possible discontinuation of federal mentoring funding.

OVERVIEW AND PURPOSE OF MENTORING

Mentoring refers to a relationship between two or more individuals in which at least one of those individuals provides guidance to the other. In the context of this report, mentoring refers to the relationship between a youth and an adult who supports, guides, and assists the youth.[2] Youth can receive mentoring through informal and formal relationships with adults. *Informal* relationships are those that develop from a young person's existing social network of teachers, coaches, and family friends. This report focuses on *formal* mentoring relationships for vulnerable youth. These relationships are cultivated through *structured* programs sponsored by youth-serving organizations, faith-based organizations, schools, and after-school programs. Volunteers in structured programs are recruited from communities, churches, and the workplace, and undergo an intensive screening process. Youth eligible for services through structured mentoring programs are often identified as at "high risk" of certain negative outcomes.[3]

The purpose of modern structured mentoring programs is to reduce risks by supplementing (but not replacing) a youth's relationship with his or her parents. Some programs have broad youth development goals, while others focus more narrowly on a particular outcome such as reducing gang activity or substance abuse, or improving grades. Structured mentoring programs are often *community based*, meaning that mentored youth and adults engage in community activities (e.g., going to the museum and the park, playing sports, playing a board game, and spending time together outside of work and school). Other programs are characterized as *school based* because they take place on school grounds or some other set location, like a community center. The co-location of mentoring programs in schools facilitates relationships with teachers, who can meet with mentors and refer youth to the programs.[4] Mentors provide academic assistance and recreational opportunities and expose youth to opportunities that promote their cognitive and emotional development.

Origins of Contemporary Mentoring Programs

The origin of today's structured mentoring programs is credited to the efforts of charity groups that formed during the Progressive Movement of the early 1900s. These groups sought adult volunteers for vulnerable youth — defined at the time as youth who were poor or had become involved in the then nascent juvenile court system.[5] These early organizations provided practical assistance to youth, including help with finding employment, and created recreational outlets. The most prominent mentoring organization at the time, Big Brothers (now known as Big Brothers Big Sisters of America), continues today as the oldest and largest mentoring organization in the country with over 275,000 youth ages five to 18 served in 5,000 communities.[6]

The contemporary youth mentoring movement began in the late 1980s with the support of foundations and corporations, including Fannie Mae, Commonwealth Fund, United Way of America, Chrysler, Procter & Gamble, and the National Urban League.[7] In addition, nongovernmental organizations such as One to One in Philadelphia and Project RAISE in Baltimore were established by entrepreneurs seeking to expand mentoring services to vulnerable youth.

The federal government has supported structured mentoring programs and initiatives since the beginning of the contemporary mentoring movement. At that time, mentoring was becoming increasingly recognized by the government as a promising strategy to enrich the lives of youth, address the isolation of youth from adult contact, and provide one-to-one support for the most vulnerable youth, particularly those living in poverty.[8] Among the first projects undertaken by the federal government was a youth mentoring initiative in the early 1 990s implemented by the newly created Points of Light Foundation, a federally funded nonprofit organization that promotes volunteering.[9] Then, Secretary of Labor Elizabeth Dole made the case for mentoring as a way to improve the lives of youth and prepare them for the workforce.[10] Other early initiatives included the Juvenile Mentoring Program (see below). The federal government also signaled the importance of mentoring during the 1997 Presidents' Summit, which was convened by the living Presidents (at the time) to pledge their support for policies that assist youth. The Presidents and other national leaders called for adults to volunteer as mentors for over two million vulnerable youth.[11]

Characteristics of Successful Mentoring Programs

Studies of structured mentoring programs, including those that have received federal funding, indicate that the programs are most successful when they include a strong infrastructure and facilitate caring relationships. Infrastructure refers to a number of activities including identifying the youth population to be served and the activities to be undertaken, screening and training mentors, supporting and supervising mentoring relationships, collecting data on youth outcomes, and creating sustainability strategies.[12] The mentor screening process provides programs with an opportunity to select those adults most likely to be successful as mentors by seeking volunteers who can keep their time commitments and value the importance of trust. Further, these studies assert that orientation and training ensure youth and mentors share a common understanding of the adult's role and help mentors develop realistic expectations of what they can accomplish. Ongoing support and supervision of the matches assist mentored pairs in negotiating challenges. Staff can help the pairs maintain a relationship over the desired period (generally a year or more). According to the studies, successful programs are known to employ strategies to retain the support of current funders and garner financial backing from new sources. Finally, the studies demonstrate that successful programs attempt to measure any effects of mentoring services on the participating youth. Programs can then disseminate these findings to potential funders and participants. **Figure 1** summarizes the elements, policies, and procedures of successful mentoring programs.

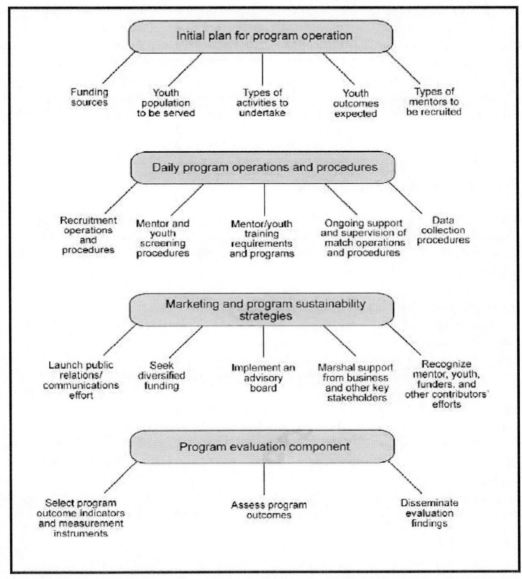

Source: Congressional Research Service, based on Figure 1 in GAO, *Student Mentoring Programs*. This information was originally presented in MENTOR/National Mentoring Partnership, "Elements of Effective Practices," 2nd ed., 2003.

Figure 1. Elements, Policies, and Procedures of Successful Mentoring Programs

Characteristics of Successful Mentoring Relationships

Research on youth mentoring demonstrates that mentoring relationships are likely to promote positive outcomes for youth and avoid harm when they are close, consistent, and enduring.[13] Closeness refers to a bond that forms between the youth and mentor, and has been found to have benefits for the youth. Mentor characteristics, such as prior experience in helping roles or occupations, an ability to appreciate salient socioeconomic and cultural influences, and a sense of efficacy for mentoring youth appear to facilitate close mentoring relationships. Consistency refers to the amount of time mentors and youth spend together. Regular contact has been linked to positive youth outcomes, and relationships become strong if they last one year or longer. Youth in relationships that lasted less than six months showed declines in functioning relative to their non-mentored peers.

Evaluation of Mentoring Programs

Some studies have found that formal mentoring programs in community-based and school-based settings are associated with improved academic and behavioral outcomes for youth, but that the effects of mentoring on particular outcomes and the ability for mentored youth to sustain gains over time is less certain.

Examples of the Positive Effects of Mentoring

A landmark study in 1995 of the Big Brothers Big Sisters of America program compared outcomes of eligible youth who were randomly selected to receive mentoring services (the treatment group) against those eligible youth who were randomly selected to remain on a waiting list for mentoring services (the control group). The study found that 18 months after the youth were assigned to their groups, the mentored youth skipped half as many days of school, were 46% less likely than their control group counterparts to use drugs, 27% less likely to initiate alcohol use, and almost one-third less likely to hit someone.[14]

A 2002 review of studies of major community-based programs (the 1995 Big Brothers Big Sisters evaluation and evaluations of Across Ages, Project BELONG, and Buddy System, among others[15]) with an experimental design — meaning that some youth were randomly assigned to get a mentor — found that the outcomes for youth with a mentor were better than outcomes for their counterparts without a mentor.[16] These outcomes included the following:

- *Improved educational outcomes:* Youth in the year-long Across Ages mentoring program showed a gain of more than a week of attended classes. Evaluations of the program also showed that mentored youth had better attitudes toward school than non-mentored youth.

- *Reduction in some negative behaviors:* All studies that examined delinquency showed evidence of reducing some, but not all, of the tracked negative behaviors. Mentored youth in the BELONG program committed fewer misdemeanors and felonies. In the Buddy System program, youth with a prior history of criminal behavior were less likely to commit a major offense compared to their nonmentored counterparts with a prior history.

- *Improved social and emotional development:* Youth in the Across Ages program had significantly more positive attitudes toward the elderly, the future, and helping behaviors than non-mentored youth. Participants in the Big Brothers Big Sisters program felt that they trusted their parents more and communicated better with them, compared to their non-mentored peers.

Similarly, a 2007 study of Big Brothers Big Sisters school-based mentoring programs demonstrated some positive results. This study — among the most rigorous scientific evaluations of a school-based mentoring program — found that mentored youth (randomly selected into the treatment group) made improvements in their first year in overall academic performance, feeling more competent about school, and skipping school, among other areas, compared to their non-mentored counterparts (randomly selected into the control group).[17]

Some Outcomes Do Not Improve or Are Short Lived

Although research has documented some benefits of mentoring, findings from studies of mentoring programs show that mentoring is limited in improving all youth outcomes. The 2002 review of mentoring program evaluations found that programs did not always make a strong improvement in grades and that some negative behaviors — stealing or damaging property within the last year — were unaffected by whether the youth was in a mentoring program.[18] In the Big Brothers Big Sisters school-based mentoring evaluation, the nonschool, related outcomes, including substance use and self worth, did not improve.[19] Other research has indicated that mentored youth make small gains or do not sustain positive gains over time.[20] The 1995 Big Brothers Big Sisters study found that mentored youth and non-mentored youth showed decreased functioning over time, although those in the mentoring group declined more slowly than those in the non-mentoring group. Further, the Big Brothers Big Sisters school- based mentoring evaluation found that, in the second year of the program, none of the academic gains were maintained (however, mentored youth were less likely to skip school, and more likely to feel that they would start and finish college).[21] The evaluation also pointed to weaknesses in the program's design, such as high attrition (due likely to the transitioning for some youth to middle school, or high school), limited contact with mentors and youth over the summer, and delays in beginning the program at the start of the school year.[22] The remainder of this report provides an overview of the federal role in mentoring and select federal programs, as well as a discussion of mentoring issues.

CURRENT FEDERAL MENTORING PROGRAMS

As discussed above, there are currently three primary federal mentoring programs, all of which were created since FY2001:

- Mentoring Children of Prisoners program administered by the U.S. Department of Health and Human Services (HHS);

- Safe and Drug Free Schools Mentoring program administered by the U.S. Department of Education (ED); and
- Mentoring Initiative for System-Involved Youth administered by the U.S. Department of Justice (DOJ).

Table 1 shows the appropriation funding levels since FY2002 for the programs, where applicable.

For FY2009, the Administration proposes to fund the Mentoring Children of Prisoners program at $50 million and to eliminate funding for the Safe and Drug Free Schools Mentoring program. No funding is proposed for the Mentoring Initiative for System Involved Youth initiative. The initiative was funded under a one-time appropriation in FY2006.

The remainder of this report describes these three programs, other current federal mentoring activities and services, and issues that may arise in any discussions of the federal role in mentoring.

Table 1. Appropriations for Current Federal Mentoring Programs, FY2002-FY2009
(dollars in millions)

Program	FY 2002 Actual	FY 2003 Actual	FY 2004 Actual	FY 2005 Actual	FY 2006 Actual	FY 2007 Actual	FY 2008 Estimate	FY 2009 Request
Mentoring Children of Prisoners (HHS)	n/a	10.0	49.7	49.6	49.5	49.5	48.6	50.0
Safe and Drug Free Schools Mentoring (ED)	17.5	17.4	49.7	49.2	48.8	19.0	48.5	0
Mentoring Initiative for System Involved Youth (DOJ)	n/a	n/a	n/a	n/a	2.6[a]	n/a	n/a	n/a

Source: FY2002 to FY2007 funding data based on information provided by the U.S. Department of Health and Human Services, Family and Youth Services Bureau; U.S. Department of Education, Office of Safe and Drug Free Schools; and U.S. Department of Justice, Office of Justice Programs, 2007. FY2008 funding data based on U.S. House, Committee on Rules, *Joint Explanatory Statement to Accompany FY2008 Consolidated Appropriations Amendment to H.R. 2764/P.L. 110-161, Division G*. FY2009 funding based on U.S. Department of Health and Human Services, Administration for Children and Families, *FY2009 Justification of Estimates*, pp. D-53 through D-55 and U.S. Department of Education, Safe Schools and Citizenship Education, *FY 2009 Justifications of Appropriation Estimates*, pp. F-8, F-16.

a. Funding for the initiative is authorized under Part G of the Juvenile Justice and Delinquency Prevention Act. Part G received $10 million for FY2006, of which $2.6 was a one-time allocation for the Mentoring Initiative for System Involved Youth. No other DOJ funding source for mentoring is included in this table.

MENTORING CHILDREN OF PRISONERS PROGRAM
(U.S. DEPARTMENT OF HEALTH AND HUMAN SERVICES)

Overview

The Mentoring Children of Prisoners (MCP) Program was proposed as part of the President's FY2003 budget and was signed into law under the Promoting Safe and Stable Families Amendments of 2001 (enacted in law in 2002 under P.L. 107-133) as Section 439 of the Social Security Act. The program is administered by the Family and Youth Services Bureau in the U.S. Department of Health and Human Services' Administration for Children and Families. The program funds public or private entities — in areas of high concentrations of children with parents in prison, including urban, rural, and tribal areas — to provide mentoring services to children of prisoners. Mentoring through the MCP is defined as a structured program that matches each eligible child (with the permission of one or both their parents) to a screened and trained adult volunteer who serves as a positive role model to the child. This one-on-one relationship, involving activities based in the community and not primarily on school grounds or the workplace, is intended to improve academic and behavioral outcomes. Mentors are to supplement existing caring relationships that the child has with his or her parents, teachers, and other adults. The Child and Family Services Improvement Act of 2006 (P.L. 109-288) expanded the scope of the program by authorizing HHS to enter into a three-year cooperative agreement with a national mentoring support organization to operate a new program that provides vouchers for mentoring services.

Purpose

The MCP program was created in response to the growing number of children under age 18 with at least one parent who is incarcerated in a federal or state correctional facility. Between 1991 and 1999, the children-of-prisoners population grew from 936,000 to 1.5 million.[23] Today, an estimated two million children between the ages of four and 18 have a parent in prison or jail.[24] Minority youth are overrepresented among the population. Less than 1% of white children have a parent in prison, compared to 7% of African American children and 3% of Hispanic children.[25]

Studies of children of prisoners show that parental confinement can lead to stress, trauma, and separation problems.[26] The living arrangements of these children often change when a parent is imprisoned. Nearly 65% of children of incarcerated mothers must live with another relative and 6% are placed under the care of a foster care agency.[27] Further, children of prisoners may need to contend with compounding issues, such loss of emotional and financial support provided by the imprisoned parent and stigmatization by peers and others.[28] The trauma of parental incarceration can trigger anti-social behavior in these children. Some children may also have difficulty maintaining contact with their parents. The majority of incarcerated parents reside over 100 miles away from their previous home, and long-distance phone calls may be prohibitively expensive.

In passing P.L. 107-133, Congress cited the success of the Amachi program[29] as a reason for supporting a national program for children of incarcerated parents.[30] The Amachi program was developed by Public/Private Ventures and Big Brothers Big Sisters in Southeastern

Pennsylvania, in partnership with secular and faith-based organizations to provide mentors to eligible youth of incarcerated parents.

Grantee Requirements

A number of entities may apply for an MCP grant: any state or local government unit, independent school districts, federally recognized American tribal governments, Native American tribal groups (other than federally recognized groups), private nonprofit organizations, and community and faith-based groups. In awarding grants, HHS must consider the qualifications and capacity of the applicants to carry out a mentoring program for children of prisoners; the need for mentoring services in local areas, taking into consideration data on the number of children (and in particular of low-income children) with an incarcerated parent (or parents) in the area; and evidence of consultation with existing youth and family services.[31] Grant funds are to be expended within one year and are to be used for mentoring services exclusively (i.e., not wraparound services or other social services).[32]

Grantees may recruit mentors from the child's family and community, church congregations, religious nonprofit groups, community-based groups, service organizations, Senior Corps, and from the business community. Grantees provide mentor training and criminal background checks, and monitor mentoring relationships. They also evaluate youth outcomes. Grantees are expected to incorporate a message of positive youth development into their programs and coordinate with other organizations to develop a plan that addresses the needs of the entire family.[33] (Positive youth development refers to a philosophy of serving youth that emphasizes youth empowerment and the development of skills and assets that prepare youth for adulthood.)

Mentored Youth and Mentors

Children ages four to 18 (as specified in the MCP grant announcement) are eligible for the program only if their parent is in state or federal prison, although they may continue to receive services if their parent is released from prison during the mentoring relationship; children whose parents are in halfway houses, under supervision, or house arrest are not eligible unless the detention follows a federal or state prison sentence.

Since the creation of the program, through March 2007, the program has served over 57,000 youth in 44 states, the District of Columbia, and Puerto Rico.[34] In FY2006, over 27,500 youth were served by the MCP.[35] Nearly 70 MCP programs are administered by the Big Brothers and Big Sisters programs (some of these same programs may receive funding through Department of Justice funds for Big Brothers Big Sisters of America; see below for further discussion).[36]

Mentors undergo screenings that include in-depth interviews and criminal background checks. They must commit to attending training and meeting with their assigned youth one hour per week for one year. Mentors are not paid for their participation, except for reimbursement for incidental expenses such as food and mileage on a case-by-case basis.

Voucher Demonstration Project: Caregiver's Choice Program

The Child and Family Services Improvement Act of 2006 (P.L. 109-2 88) extended funding and authorization for the Mentoring Children of Prisoners program and authorized a demonstration project to test the effectiveness of using vouchers to deliver MCP services more broadly to youth who have not already been matched to a mentor. The law specified that vouchers would be distributed by an organization with considerable experience in mentoring services for children, and in developing program standards for planning and evaluating mentoring programs for children.[37] In November 2007, HHS awarded a competitive three-year cooperative agreement grant (which may be renewed for an additional two years) to MENTOR, a national mentoring advocacy group and clearinghouse on mentoring issues, to administer the program. The voucher program is known as the Caregiver's Choice Program.

According to HHS, in the first year of the demonstration project, MENTOR is to begin the program, targeting efforts in geographically diverse targeted communities with high rates of incarceration, crime or poverty, rural populations, or areas with American Indian children.[38] These areas are Atlanta, Chicago, and Philadelphia, as well as the Arizona, Connecticut, Idaho, Massachusetts, North Carolina, and Washington.[39] HHS has stated that these targeted efforts are to allow systems to be implemented, reviewed, and adjusted when needed. In years two and three of the demonstration program, the demonstration is to be expanded nationally. In year one, no less than 3,000 vouchers are to be distributed to children and families; in year two, no less than 8,000 vouchers are to be distributed and in year three, no less than 10,000 vouchers are to be distributed.

As required by law, MENTOR is not providing direct mentoring services. HHS reports that the organization is to coordinate with national networks for re-entry and incarcerated families, caregiver support networks, school districts, social service agencies, and faith- and community-based organizations to identify children to participate in the program. Families and caregivers are to be directed to a national call center to enroll in the voucher program and provided with a mentoring information packet that corresponds to the family's stated preferences and provides mentoring options in their community. The voucher for mentoring services is included in the packet and contains an identification code. (This identifier becomes the primary means of data collection and system management for the voucher demonstration project.) The families redeem the vouchers at organizations deemed to be quality providers of mentoring services.

MENTOR is conducting an advertising campaign to encourage mentoring programs to become certified as "quality providers" (allowing them to receive MCP vouchers).[40] MENTOR, in consultation with FYSB, is required to identify quality standards for these providers, including, at minimum, criminal background checks of mentors. It must also monitor and oversee delivery of mentoring services. MENTOR has established several requirements for programs: they must also meet certain volunteer screening and matching requirements, have at least one year of experience matching and supporting mentoring relationships, provide training and orientation to mentors and mentored children and youth, provide ongoing support and case management to matches, and offer clear policies and procedures for ending matches, among other requirements.[41] To be eligible for voucher funding, mentoring organizations must also demonstrate that significant mentoring services can be provided for an eligible child and that after the voucher expires, they can continue providing such services through non-federal resources. For those organizations with general

234 Adrienne L. Fernandes

MCP grants, they must exhaust these funds before receiving funds through the voucher project.

Funding and Grant Awards

The MCP program, including the voucher component, is authorized to receive "such sums as may be necessary" for every year through FY2011. Funding for the general grant program is distributed on a competitive basis to eligible applicants for up to three years. The size of the average grant is $186,245 for each year of the three-year period, with grants ranging from $26,000 to $2 million per year.[42] (Some of these organizations make sub-awards to other organizations for mentoring services.) Grantees are required to provide a nonfederal share or match of at least 25% of the total project budget in the first and second years of the project, rising to 50% in the third year.

Funding may not be awarded to the national mentoring support organization (i.e., MENTOR for FY2008 to FY2010) to distribute the vouchers unless $25 million in program appropriations is first available for site-based grants. If funding is available, the organization is to receive up to $5 million in the first year of the cooperative agreement, $10 million in the second year, and $15 million in the third year. The organization's administrative expenditures for the demonstration project may not exceed 10% of the amount awarded. Individual vouchers of up to $1,000 can be awarded on behalf of an individual child to redeem for mentoring services.[43]

The MCP program received initial funding of $10 million in FY2003 and has been funded at approximately $50 million in each year since then. For FY2009, the Administration proposes to fund the program at $50 million. **Table 2** shows the level of funding for the program and the number of general grants and vouchers awarded from FY2003 to FY2008, where applicable.

Table 2. Mentoring Children of Prisoners: Funding and Grant and Voucher Awards, FY2003-FY2009 (dollars in millions)

	FY 2003 Actual	FY 2004 Actual	FY 2005 Actual	FY 2006 Actual	FY 2007 Actual	FY 2008 Estimate	FY 2009 Request
Funding Appropriated	10.0	49.7	49.6	49.5	49.5	48.6	$50.0
New Grants Awarded	52	169	0	76	144	0	188
Grants In Progress	n/a	52	221	169	220	220	144
Vouchers Awarded	n/a	n/a	n/a	n/a	n/a	8,000	13,000

Source: FY2002 to FY2007 funding data based on information provided by the U.S. Health and Human Services, Family and Youth Services Bureau, 2007. FY2008 funding data based on U.S. House, Committee on Appropriations, *Joint Explanatory Statement to Accompany FY2008 Consolidated Appropriations Amendment to H.R. 2764/P.L. 110-161, Division G.* FY2009 funding based on U.S. Department of Health and Human Services, Administration for Children and Families, *FY2009 Justification of Estimates*, pp. D-53 through D-55.

Program Performance and Oversight

Of all MCP funds, 4% must be set aside for research, evaluation, and technical assistance related to site-based and voucher-related mentoring services.[44]

Research

HHS collects caseload demographics and characteristics from grantee progress reports and from an online data collection instrument, administered by HHS, and used by grantees to input caseload data. This information allows HHS to assess the average number of days that a child is on the waitlist for a mentor, the number of hours that the child met with their mentor over the course of a reporting period, the average number of hours in pre-training/orientation and post-training that mentors received, and the number of staff contacts with mentors to address mentor skills or critical issues. **Table A-1**, in the appendix, displays demographics and characteristics for youth enrolled in the program in FY2006.

In 2006, HHS introduced the Relationship Quality Survey Instrument (RQI) to assess the dynamics of the mentor/mentored youth relationship. The RQI seeks information from youth ages nine and above engaged in long-term (i.e., minimum of nine months by the time the survey is administered in July of each year) mentoring relationships. The survey asks the youth about their satisfaction with the relationship, the extent to which mentors have helped them cope with their problems, how happy the youth feel when they are with their mentors, and whether there is evidence of trust in the mentoring relationship.[45] According to HHS, research has demonstrated that answers to the questions are predictive of the psychological and academic benefits of mentoring.

Evaluations

Pursuant to the original legislation (P.L. 107-133) authorizing the MCP, HHS was required to evaluate the program and submit its findings to Congress no later than April 15, 2005 (see below). The reauthorizing legislation (P.L. 109-288) requires the Secretary to evaluate the voucher demonstration project. The evaluation of the project is to be submitted to the House Ways and Means Committee and the Senate Finance Committee no later than 90 days after the end of the second fiscal year the project is conducted. The report is to include the number of children who received vouchers for mentoring services and any conclusions regarding the use of vouchers to deliver mentoring services to children of prisoners. In addition to the evaluations, HHS is required to submit to Congress, within 12 months after the reauthorizing legislation was passed (i.e., September 28, 2007), a report that includes the following: 1) the characteristics of the funded general MCP programs; 2) the plan for implementing the voucher demonstration project; 3) a description of the outcome-based evaluation of the programs, and how the evaluation has been expanded to include an evaluation of the demonstration project; and 4) the date HHS will submit the final report on the evaluation to Congress.

In response to some of these legislative requirements, HHS subcontracted with Abt Associates to conduct process and outcome evaluations of the general mentoring program. A report about the features of the program was submitted to Congress on September 12, 2007. The report discusses the general program's design, strategy, implementation, current operation status, and characteristics. The outcome evaluation has not yet been completed, as required by P.L. 107-133, but survey instruments have been approved by the Office of Management and Budget (OMB), grantee sites have been selected, and participating grantee staff have received training on administering the surveys. This evaluation is to measure child baseline characteristics and status in a sample of the program's caseload when a mentoring match is first formed. Outcomes are to be measured in a follow-up survey of participating youth 12 to 15 months following the baseline survey. The results are to be matched, through a data sharing agreement, against similar at-risk youth who served as controls in the recent evaluation of the Big Brothers Big Sisters school-based mentoring program (discussed above). (Abt plans to use consistent definitions and other methods to make valid comparisons between the groups.) The evaluation is to assess the operational design of the program as well as child outcomes, including attitude towards and performance in school; relationships with parents, peers, and teachers; self-esteem; and engagement in risky behaviors, including alcohol and drug use. Findings from the evaluation of the general program are likely be available during FY2010.

As required by P.L. 109-288, an evaluation of the voucher component is in the planning stages and according to HHS, will attempt to use the same methodology and definitions as the general mentoring program, to the extent practicable, given the program design. HHS is to produce an interim report, sometime in calendar year 2008, on the status of the voucher component of the program.

PART Evaluation

As part of the FY2005 budget process, the MCP program was evaluated by the Performance Assessment Rating Tool (PART), an instrument developed by the current Administration to examine the performance of certain programs across federal agencies. The PART evaluation assessed the MCP's purpose and design, strategic planning, management, and results/accountability. While the program received maximum scores for these first three measurements, it was rated as "Results Not Demonstrated" because the program performance data to assess results had only recently begun to be collected from grantees. In addition, the program also did not meet its mentor match goal. (By FY2007, the program was targeted to make 75,000 matches to date, but instead, 70,425 matches had been made.[46]) According to HHS, mentor match targets were not met because many MCP grantees had never previously received a federal grant and/or were new and formed specifically to operate the grant.[47] In its 2007 Report to Congress, HHS stated that it has taken steps to improve the number of matches, such as conducting site visits to grantees.[48] The program missed the goal of increasing the percentage of mentoring matches that endure at least 12 months in FY2007 (the goal was 60% but the actual share was 34%) and reducing the percentage of matches that terminate at three months or less to 20% (the actual share was 26%). However, the program increased the share of mentored youth in active relationships that have already been sustained more than 12 months, surpassing the goal of 20% by 13 percentage points in FY2007.

Training and Technical Assistance

HHS has contracted with Dare Mighty Things (DMT) to serve as the training and technical assistance provider for the program. DMT conducts a needs assessment for MCP grantees, and organizes an annual national conference for all MCP grantees and multiregional workshops throughout the year. DMT also conducts up to 100 days of site visits and provides on-site assistance as needed by phone and email.[49] Through its newsletters, DMT conveys important federal information, a mentor/mentored youth of the month highlight, funding opportunities, and general mentoring information.[50]

In addition to the assistance provided by DMT, the National Child Welfare Resource Center for Youth Development at the University of Oklahoma (the contractor for FYSB on select child welfare issues and the Runaway and Homeless Youth program) is developing a peer-to-peer monitoring tool that is to allow for grantees to join federal staff on visits to other grantees to monitor compliance with the legislative intent of the program and to encourage cross-fertilization of ideas between peer mentoring professionals.[51] If the peer reviewers determine that technical assistance is needed (or is requested by an organization), DMT is to be notified and develop a plan for delivering services.

Finally, HHS staff provide direct assistance to grantees.[52] Program specialists assist grantees in grant management, service delivery planning, program start-up and implementation, reporting, and building partnerships. HHS staff monitor grantee activities and oversee detailed quarterly narrative and financial information. The staff also facilitates transfers of promising practices from experienced to less experienced grantees.

SAFE AND DRUG FREE SCHOOLS MENTORING PROGRAM (U.S. DEPARTMENT OF EDUCATION)

Overview

The Safe and Drug Free Schools (SDFS) program was enacted as Title IV-A of the Elementary and Secondary Education Act (ESEA) of 1994 (P.L. 103-382) in response to concerns about increased school violence and drug use among school-aged youth. The program awards funding to states to support activities that promote school safety. In 2001 (P.L. 107-110), the No Child Left Behind Act reauthorized and amended ESEA, and enacted a school-based mentoring program under the SDFS program.[53]

The SDFS Mentoring program is administered by the Office of Safe and Drug Free Schools in the U.S. Department of Education, and provides grants to establish and support mentoring programs that are school based. School-based mentoring refers to mentoring activities that are closely coordinated with school (i.e., involve teachers, counselors, and other school staff who identify and refer students for mentoring services) and assist youth with improving their academic achievement, reducing disciplinary referrals, and increasing their bonding to school.[54] Generally, mentored youth are paired with one adult[55] who serves as a positive role model and provides the child with academic assistance (e.g., tutoring, helping with homework, learning a game like chess, developing computer skills), exposure to new experiences that promote positive youth development (e.g., attending concerts and plays, visiting colleges, shadowing mentor at his/her job), and recreational opportunities (e.g., playing sports, creating arts and crafts projects, attending professional sports games).[56] According to a June 2004 GAO report of the program, many of these mentoring activities are carried out on school grounds, but some activities take place in the community and in the workplace.[57]

Purpose

The mentoring program targets children with the greatest need, defined as those children at risk of educational failure or dropping out of school, involved with criminal or delinquent activities, or who lack strong positive role models. The purpose of the program is to provide school-based mentoring programs that improve academic outcomes, improve interpersonal relationships, and reduce involvement in delinquency and gang involvement.

Grantee Requirements

The Secretary of the Department of Education is authorized to award competitive grants to three entities to carry out the SDFS Mentoring program: (1) local education agencies (LEAs); (2) nonprofit community- based organizations (CBOs), including faith-based groups; and (3) partnerships between LEAs and CBOs. The Secretary prioritizes grant applications that propose a school-based mentoring program, provide high quality background checks and technical assistance, and serve children with greatest need living in particular areas.

In applying for grants, an eligible entity must provide information on the children for which the grant is sought; a description of the method to match children with mentors based on the needs of the children; information on how the entity will recruit, screen, and provide training to mentors; information on the system for managing and monitoring information related to the program's background checks of mentors and procedures for matching children to mentors. Grantees must also make assurances that no mentor will be matched with so many children that the assignment will undermine the mentor's ability to be an effective mentor or the mentor's ability to establish a close relationship (i.e., a one-to-one relationship, where practicable), with each mentored child. Further, grantees must assure that the mentoring program will provide children with certain supports (i.e., emotional, academic, and exposure to new experiences) and assign a new mentor if the relationship between the original mentor and the child is not beneficial to the child.

Mentored Youth and Mentors

As noted above, the SDFS Mentoring program targets children with the greatest need. In awarding grants, the Secretary is to prioritize entities that serve children in grades four to eight with greatest need living in rural areas, high-crime areas, or troubled home environments *or* who attend schools with violence problems.[58] The Department of Education does not aggregate demographic and other data on youth participants, and therefore, the number and characteristics of youth that have been served by the program is unknown.[59]

Mentors may be a responsible adult, a postsecondary school student, or a secondary school student. While the Department of Education does not mandate a set amount of hours that mentors and students must meet, it advises that programs require at least one hour each week.[60] Mentors are screened using appropriate reference checks, child and domestic abuse record checks, and criminal background checks; and receive training and support in mentoring. Mentors are uncompensated.

Table 3. Safe and Drug Free Schools Mentoring Program: Funding and Grant Awards, FY2002-FY2009 (dollars in millions)

Program	FY 2002 Actual	FY 2003 Actual	FY 2004 Actual	FY 2005 Actual	FY 2006 Actual	FY 2007 Actual	FY 2008 Estimate	FY 2009 Request
Funding Appropriated	17.5	17.4	49.7	49.2	48.8	19.0	48.5	0
New Grants Awarded	122	0	163	90	0	170	110	0
Grants In Progress	n/a	122	122	163	253	86	170	170

Source: FY2002 to FY2007 funding data based on information provided by the U.S. Department of Education, Office of Safe and Drug Free Schools, 2007. FY2008 funding data based on U.S. House, Committee on Appropriations, *Joint Explanatory Statement to Accompany FY2008 Consolidated Appropriations Amendment to H.R. 2764/P.L. 110-161, Division G.* FY2009 data based on U.S. Department of Education, Safe Schools and Citizenship Education, *FY2009 Justifications of Appropriation Estimates*, pp. F-8, F-16.

Funding and Grant Awards

The mentoring program is one component of the Safe and Drug Free Schools program. The SDFS program has two funding streams: one for state grants awarded by formula and another for discretionary national grants. The SDFS mentoring program is funded through the national grants component.[61] The program has received about $17 million to $49 million each year since grants were first awarded in FY2002. The average amount awarded for FY2008 to each grantee was $167,000.[62] There is no match requirement and grantees are ineligible to apply for subsequent SDFS mentoring grants if they are currently receiving funds through the program (though they may apply for other Department of Education grants for which they are eligible).[63] **Table 3** shows the amount of funding appropriated for the program and the number of grants awarded.

In the FY2007, FY2008, and FY2009 budget justifications, the President proposed no funding for the program, on the basis that it has met its objectives. The FY2009 budget also proposes to consolidate the SDFS national grants component, which currently has several sub-programs, into a single-flexible discretionary program.[64]

Program Performance and Oversight

The No Child Left Behind Act does not specify whether or how the SDFS mentoring program is to be monitored and evaluated, or how grantees are to receive technical assistance and support. However, regulations promulgated in March 2004 specify that grant applicants must include in their application an assurance that they will (1) establish clear, measurable performance goals; and (2) collect and report to the agency data related to the established Government Performance and Results Act (GPRA) performance indicators for the mentoring program's grant competition.[65] The Department of Education requires grantees to provide an evaluation of their program at the end of the three-year grant period. Further, the agency established three performance measures for assessing the effectiveness of the mentoring program:

(1) The percentage of mentor-youth matches that are sustained for a period of nine months. The goal for 2007 was 44.9% and the actual figure was 38.6%.
(2) The percentage of mentored students who demonstrate improvement in core academic subjects as measured by grade point average after 12 months. The goal for 2007 was 49.6% and the actual figure was 22%.
(3) The percentage of mentored students who have unexcused absences from school. The goal for 2007 was 3 9.6% and the actual figure was 28.9%.[66]

Evaluation

In 2004, GAO conducted a study of the program and made three recommendations to the Department of Education to facilitate monitoring and evaluation of the program: (1) explore ways to facilitate the sharing of successful practices and lessons learned among grantees, (2) ensure that the agency uses grantees' single audit reports, and (3) undertake a national study of the program's outcomes.[67] (This second recommendation refers to audit reports of grantees that provide information on weaknesses related to grantee financial management, internal control, and compliance issues; these reports are available through the Office of Management and Budget's Federal Auditing Clearinghouse.) In response to GAO's first recommendation, the Department of Education has developed an electronic listserve to promote communication among grantees. To ensure that the agency monitors single audit reports, the agency began to provide a comprehensive training to grant monitors (of the audit reports) to assist them access the information. In addition, the agency added a requirement to the grant monitoring procedures that directs staff to review audit findings at least annually.

Finally, in response to GAO's third recommendation, the Department of Education has subcontracted with Abt Associates to conduct process and outcome evaluations. To conduct the process evaluation, data on the nature of mentoring program services are to be collected through a survey of the program grantees and mentors to provide context for the outcome evaluation and to provide information to the agency about how the program can improve. According to the department, the outcome evaluation will use a randomized control trial with a sample size of approximately 2,600 students in grades four through eight that are or were mentored at 32 grant sites from the 2004 and 2005 cohorts of mentoring projects.[68] Data are being collected for the student sample on school engagement, academic performance, dropping out of school, the quality of interpersonal relationships, and involvement with high-risk and delinquent behaviors. To measure program impact, student surveys and student school records are to be collected both at baseline and at the end of the school year. The agency expects the findings to be available in October 2008.[69]

Training and Technical Assistance

In 2004, the Department of Education awarded a performance-based contract to EMT Associates, Inc., to operate the Mentoring Program Resource Training and Technical Assistance Center until 2009.[70] The purpose of this center is to ensure that programs funded under the mentoring program receive assistance, as appropriate, in the management and implementation of their projects. Grantees receive assistance with (1) training to ensure that they are using high-quality, evidence-based programs; (2) identifying gaps and weaknesses in their program design; and (3) collaborating with other organizations; and (4) planning for program sustainability.[71] In FY2007, EMT held three regional meetings for more than 500 participants that focused on sustaining projects; and with Department of Education staff, EMT conducted three webinars (web-based seminars).[72] For FY2008, the agency reports that EMT will develop and deliver four webinars; produce four manuals that capture best practices; develop six fact sheets for distribution to grantees via the program's resource center website; develop four new case studies around promising prevention practices among mentoring programs; and conduct two regional training sessions.[73]

Department of Education staff also provide needed assistance to grantees. Mechanisms to assist grantees include a post-award call to ensure that grantees understand established outcomes and to offer technical assistance, semiannual calls to grantees to determine the implementation process and issues and to provide technical assistance, reviews of annual grantee performance reports to determine successes and needed corrective action, monitoring of expenditure rates to determine if grants were expended at an appropriate rate, and visits to a limited number of grantees.[74]

MENTORING INITIATIVE FOR SYSTEM-INVOLVED YOUTH (U.S. DEPARTMENT OF JUSTICE)

Overview

As noted above, the Department of Justice is the first federal agency to have funded a structured mentoring program. The 1992 amendments (P.L. 102-586) to the Juvenile Justice and Delinquency Prevention Act (JJDPA) added Part G to the act, authorizing the Office of Juvenile Justice and Delinquency Prevention (OJJDP) to establish a mentoring program, which came to be known as the Juvenile Mentoring Program (JUMP). The program was created in response to the perception that youth in high-crime areas would benefit from one-on-one adult relationships.[75] The objectives of JUMP were to reduce juvenile delinquent behavior and improve scholastic performance, with an emphasis on reducing school dropout. From FY1 994 through FY2003, Congress appropriated a total of $104 million ($4 million to $15.8 million each year) to the program.

JUMP was repealed by the 21st Century Department of Justice Appropriations Authorization Act of 2001 (P.L. 107-273). This law incorporated the Juvenile Justice and Delinquency Prevention Act of 2001 (H.R. 1900), which eliminated several juvenile justice programs, including Part G (Mentoring), and replaced it with a block grant program under new Part C (Juvenile Delinquency Prevention Block Grant Program, to be used for activities designed to prevent juvenile delinquency). The act also created a new Part D (Research, Evaluation, Technical Assistance and Training) and a new Part E (Developing, Testing, and Demonstrating Promising New Initiatives and Programs). According to the accompanying report for H.R. 1900, the small amount of funding for JUMP may have been a factor in its elimination. The report states: "In creating this block grant, the [Senate Judiciary] Committee has eliminated separate categorical programs under current law.... Funding for the Part E — State Challenge Activities and Part G — Mentoring Program received minimal funding."[76] [77]

The report goes on to say that the Committee does not discourage mentoring activities under the new block grant program.[78]

Since the JUMP program was discontinued, the Administration has requested funding for mentoring under Part C (Juvenile Delinquency Prevention Block Grant Program) and Part E (Developing, Testing, and Demonstrating Promising New Initiatives and Programs), which can fund mentoring demonstration projects.[79] However, Congress has appropriated mentoring funds under a separate mentoring line item titled "Mentoring Part G" or "Mentoring" for FY2005 through F72008 (no mentoring funds were appropriated for FY2004); the line item does not specify under which part of the JJDPA, as amended, the funding is authorized.[80] The Department of Justice has interpreted the appropriations language as requiring the agency to allocate funds pursuant to old Part G.[81]

Most DOJ mentoring activities are coordinated through the Office of Juvenile Justice and Delinquency Prevention.[82] Pursuant to the mentoring line item, OJJDP has allocated funding for mentoring initiatives. For FY2006, OJJDP proposed a new juvenile mentoring project, the Mentoring Initiative for System Involved Youth (MISIY), to provide mentoring to youth involved in the juvenile justice system or foster care, or juvenile offenders re-entering the community.[83] Congress appropriated $10 million for mentoring (under the mentoring line item) that fiscal year, with approximately $2.6 million for the MISIY program and the balance for specific set asides for jurisdictions and other organizations that support youth mentoring, including Big Brothers Big Sisters of America (see page 31 for further discussion of DOJ's other mentoring efforts).

Grantees

Entities eligible to apply for MISIY funds include public agencies (state agencies, units of local government, public universities and colleges, and tribal governments) and private organizations (including secular and nonprofit, faith-based groups).[84] The initiative awarded a total of $1.6 million to four sites ($400,000 per site) for a four-year period (FY2006 to FY2009).[85] (See below for a discussion on the $1 million in funding for the training and technical assistance provider and the organization conducting the evaluation.) Grantees are not required to provide a match.

The four grantees are nonprofit, youth-serving organizations, and the City of Chicago. (As part of its grant requirements, the City of Chicago was to develop a pilot mentoring program that sub-contracts with community-based organizations.) Each of the organizations is required to meet performance standards that focus on building protective factors (e.g., youth are to gain at least two responsible nonparent adults in their life that support them, experience improved self esteem, and develop better relationships with their families and peers) and improving school outcomes (e.g., greater attendance, higher reading and math scores, and fewer behavior referrals). The four MISIY grantees are described below.

- *The Boys and Girls Aid Society's Mentor Portland* program in Portland, Oregon provides mentoring to youth ages 10 to 14 who are in the foster care system or have an incarcerated parent. With its MISIY grant, the organization is implementing a mentoring program for 136 youth in foster care that focuses on one-on-one and team-based mentoring in the community. The youth are to be referred primarily by the Oregon Department of Human Services. Each mentoring pair is to be placed on a team with six other pairs. In addition to meeting with their mentors, youth are expected to attend monthly team activities and community events, and attend a weekend camp with their mentor.[86]

- *Lutheran Family Services of Virginia's Mentor Match* in Roanoke, Virginia, provides one-on-one, community-based mentoring to youth ages 8 to 18 in foster care and the juvenile justice system. With the MISIY grant, the organization anticipates serving 140 additional youth by 2010. Youth are to be recruited through established relationships with the local juvenile court system, the local social services agency, and Lutheran Family Services. The program is to include the following: (1) therapeutic mentoring for children in treatment foster care provided by mentors employed by Lutheran Family Services, involving structured recreation and goal setting, and open dialogue about emotions and problems or other topics; (2) therapeutic mentoring for court-involved youth provided by mentors who work with the juvenile justice system; (3) non-therapeutic mentoring for foster care children provided by volunteers; and (4) a volunteer mentor pilot project for system-involved youth provided by volunteers trained in therapeutic mentoring.[87]

- *The City of Chicago, Department of Children and Youth Services,* is using its MISIY funds to support four community-based organizations that provide mentoring to adolescent males who are involved in the juvenile justice system or are at risk for entering the system. These organizations include Agape, Southwest Youth Collaborative, Uchlich Children's Advocacy network, and Building with Books. Youth are to enter the program in 8th to 10th grade and are eligible to remain in the program through the 12th grade. Participants are to be walk-ins or be referred by the Chicago Juvenile Intervention Support Center (JICS), Cook County State's Attorneys Office, and the Cook County Juvenile Probation Department. Each youth is to receive a case manager and service referrals, and is to be assigned a mentor (known as a youth advocate) to help them overcome obstacles to successful enrollment and completion of JICS programs and to achieve regular attendance in the appropriate school program. The MISIY program anticipates assisting youth develop an individual plan to ensure that they are connected to work and/or school.[88]

- *The Mentoring Center* in Oakland, California, serves youth reentering the community from the Alameda County juvenile residential rehabilitation facility. The organization is using its MISIY funds to develop the Camp Sweeney Transformative Mentoring Program with the long-term goal of reducing re-arrest and re-commitment rates among 240 youth ages 15 to 18. Youth in the program are to participate in: (1) group mentoring and a group counseling program that focuses on behavior change through weekly curriculum-based cognitive behavior sessions; (2) pre-release individual mentoring and case management provided by a case manager that focuses on identifying the needs and services for the youth; and (3) post-release mentoring. The individual mentoring is to be provided through the program's case manager.[89]

Evaluations

OJJDP awarded a four-year grant of approximately $500,000 to the Pacific Institute for Research and Evaluation in FY2006 to conduct process and outcome evaluations of the program.[90] The process evaluation is to document how the selected mentoring sites adapt mentoring approaches (e.g., individual, group mentoring, counseling); how the programs and/or strategies are being implemented for the target populations; and how these types of mentoring approaches and strategies could impact outcomes for mentoring.[91] The evaluator is also to gather data from the grantees, through annual site visits and telephone interviews, to inform best practices in the mentoring field. These data are to be shared with the training and technical assistance provider.

The outcome evaluation is underway and the first wave of data collection was reported to OJJDP by the end of calendar year 2007. The evaluation measures youth behaviors and their school performance at intake into their respective programs, three months after youth are matched with mentors, and nine months after they are matched. Measured outcomes include short-term outcomes (i.e., quality of match), intermediate outcomes (i.e., academic self-esteem, aggression and violence, delinquency, and substance use), and long-term outcomes (i.e., improved academic performance, involvement with the juvenile justice system, and stability in the foster care system). These data are to be aggregated and compared across the four grant recipients. The data are also to be analyzed in sub-groups, based on race and ethnicity, gender, age, type of participant (foster care youth, juvenile justice youth, or both), and the individual grantee.[92]

The outcome evaluation includes a treatment group — those youth who are in the mentoring programs — and a control group made up of youth who either agree to be on a waiting list for at least six months or are in a local geographic area not served by the grant recipient. The same demographic and survey data is collected from youth in the control group (except they are not be asked for information about the quality of their match) and are to be compared to the data from the treatment group.

According to OJJDP, the Administration will await results from the evaluation prior to determining whether the program should be expanded.[93]

Training and Technical Assistance

The Education Development Center (EDC) was awarded a two-year grant of approximately $500,000 in FY2006 to provide training and technical support to the grantees.[94] To date, EDC had conducted telephone pre-assessments and in-depth assessments of all grantees to determine what type of assistance is needed, as well as on-site and off-site training. EDC has also researched and created a literature review containing resources related to mentoring system-involved youth; created two technical assistance briefs on mentor recruitment and retention; and identified a series of teleconferences targeted to the specific needs of grantees, including one that focuses on recruiting African American male mentors to their programs, among other types of assistance.[95] EDC is working with the grant recipients to develop their plans for becoming financially sustainable.

OTHER FEDERAL MENTORING SUPPORT

In addition to the three primary mentoring programs, the federal government supports other mentoring initiatives, administered both independently and jointly by the Corporation for National and Community Service, Department of Health and Human Services, Department of Justice, and Department of Defense.[96]

FUNDING PROVIDED BY THE CORPORATION FOR NATIONAL AND COMMUNITY SERVICE

The Corporation for National and Community Service is an independent federal agency that administers programs to support volunteer services, including volunteering. CNCS is authorized by two statutes: the National and Community Service Act (P.L. 101-610) of 1990, as amended, and the Domestic Volunteer Service Act (P.L. 93-113) of 1973, as amended. The agency has provided mentoring through two of its volunteer organizations, AmeriCorps and SeniorCorps. In FY2005, CNCS devoted more than $250 million to support approximately 400,000 youth, including 16,000 children of prisoners, through mentoring, tutoring, and related services.[97] (The amount of funding for mentoring alone cannot be disaggregated.[98]) CNCS has also partnered with MENTOR, the mentoring advocacy group, in an effort to match three million youth with mentors by 2010.[99] The campaign has also secured commitments from corporate and foundation partners for funding to support mentoring programs.

America's Promise

America's Promise, a national nonprofit children's advocacy organization, was formed after the Presidents' Summit for America's Future was convened in Philadelphia in 1997.[100] The organization promotes five "commitments" (or factors) that attendees at the summit determined to be essential for the success of young people. One of the factors was caring adults who are actively involved in a child's life, such as mentors, parents, teachers, and coaches.[101] America's Promise has promoted mentoring, and the organization is funded through a combination of federal and private funds. The Corporation for National and Community Service has provided some funding. In FY2006, Congress appropriated $5 million for the organization from the CNCS budget.[102] (Congress did not appropriate funds in FY2007 and FY2008.)

Funding Provided by the Department of Justice

Mentoring Funding Generally

Since JUMP was discontinued in FY2003, through FY2007, the Office of Juvenile Justice and Delinquency Prevention has awarded more than $31 million total in funding to support mentoring programs across the country (no funds were appropriated for mentoring programs through the DOJ budget in FY2004).[103] These funds were appropriated under a mentoring line item. Some of this funding has gone to the MISIY program ($2.6 million in FY2006 only). The balance of this funding has been allocated to community- and faith-based mentoring organizations through competitive awards and specific set asides in appropriation bills. Most of the funding for these organizations has gone to Big Brothers Big Sisters of America (see below). OJJDP has also funded youth-serving organizations such as the National Network of Youth Ministries, Youth Friends, Virginia Mentoring Partnership, People for People, the Pittsburgh Leadership Foundation, and the Messiah College, among others, to provide mentoring to at-risk youth.

Big Brothers Big Sisters of America

In most years from FY1 998 to FY2007, the Department of Justice allocated more than $40 million to Big Brothers Big Sisters of America and its affiliates in specific set asides in appropriation bills.[104] Funding for the national organization ($12.4 million in FY1998, $5.0 million in FY2003, $6.0 million in FY2004, and $7.0 million in FY2005 and in FY2006) has been used to build a national infrastructure that supports 450 local affiliates in serving one million children (this initiative is known as "Building Capacity for High-Volume Quality Growth").[105] Congress has also appropriated funds directly to state and regional affiliates, including Kansas Big Brothers Big Sisters ($497,750 in 2003 and $246,807 in FY2006) and Big Brothers Big Sisters of South Georgia ($98,948 in FY2004).

Also in FY2007, the Department of Justice awarded Part E (Developing, Testing, and Demonstrating Promising New Initiatives and Programs) funds to Big Brothers Big Sisters under a competitive solicitation (Prevention and Intervention Programs) designed to advance juvenile justice, child protection, or delinquency prevention by expanding knowledge in these areas.[106] The funding is used to support mentoring services for Alaskan Native youth.

Funding for Targeted Mentoring Activities Beginning in FY2008

The FY2008 appropriations law (P.L. 110-161) provides a line item of $70 million for mentoring grants and directs the Office of Justice Programs (which oversees the Office of Juvenile Justice and Delinquency Prevention) to provide a report and spending plan to congressional appropriations committees that detail the scope of the grant program and the criteria and methodology DOJ will employ to award these grants. In its joint explanatory statement to accompany H.R. 2764 (which was signed into law as P.L. 110-161), Congress stated that it expects national programs that have received funding under the Byrne discretionary program[107] or the JJDPA Part E program to be eligible for funding under the mentoring grant program.[108]

Pursuant to P.L. 110-161, the Department of Justice is funding three new mentoring programs beginning in FY2009: National Mentoring Programs, Strengthening Youth Mentoring Through Community Partnerships Program, and Latino Youth Mentoring Program.[109] Although the programs have different purposes, they seek to support mentoring programs in communities and schools and to provide vulnerable youth with one-on-one mentors for at least one year. They also intend to achieve specific goals for the youth, such as improved academic performance or social or job schools and to deter youth from engaging in truancy and gang activity. The programs require applicants to meet three broad objectives, including (1) improve youth outcomes, (2) establish or improve the administration of mentoring programs and strategies, and (3) enhance and improve the organizational capacity and cost effectiveness through training and technical assistance and other strategies. Entities funded by the three programs must report performance data to DOJ that focuses on the number of mentoring program partnerships in place, the number of youth served, the number of youth who offend or reoffend, the number of mentors, and average length of time mentors remain in the program, among other data.

The National Mentoring Programs funding is available for national organizations, including community- and faith-based non-profit entities, that engage in mentoring activities or provide training and technical assistance on mentoring in multiple states. In particular, the program targets organizations that work to increase participation of mentors by underrepresented groups, involve single-parent families, and focus on truancy prevention. The initiative also seeks to promote collaboration among both national youth service organizations and community organizations that support mentoring activities. The program is to fund multiple awards (funding levels not specified) for up to three years.

Entities eligible to apply for the Strengthening Youth Mentoring Through Community Partnerships Program include state governments, units or subunits of local government, and federally recognized tribal governments. These entities must demonstrate they have formed a community partnership with one or more community-based organizations to provide mentoring services. The program is intended to encourage collaboration among nontraditional partners (including those that may not have mentoring as their primary mission), but have areas of common or overlapping interest in serving at-risk youth. The program is to fund multiple awards of $250,000 to $500,000 for up to three years.

Finally, the Latino Youth Mentoring Program seeks applications from school districts with a demonstrable Latino gang problem. The school district is to establish a mentoring program that reaches Latino youth before they are recruited to gangs as well as to develop their protective factors against gang involvement and other problem behaviors. Mentoring is to take place at high schools; is to be directed by a teacher, social worker, or school psychologist; and is to involve incoming students as mentored youth and older peers as mentors. The program is to award four awards up to $500,000 each for three years.

Funds have been set aside to evaluate the programs; however, DOJ has not determined how the funds will be used.[110] All program grantees will have access to training and technical services through the National Training and Technical Assistance Center, which contracts with DOJ to assist OJJDP grantees generally.

FY2009 Budget Request

As with the FY2008 budget, the Administration's FY2009 budget request does not provide a specific sum of funding for mentoring.[111] The budget proposes to consolidate grants now authorized under the Missing Children's Assistance Act, Juvenile Justice and Delinquency Prevention Act, Victims of Child Abuse Act, and other acts into a "single flexible grant program," and OJP would use the funds to make competitive discretionary grants to assist state and local governments "in addressing multiple child safety and juvenile justice needs to reduce incidents of child exploitation and abuse, including those facilitated by the use of computers and the Internet, improve juvenile justice outcomes, and address school safety needs."

Funding Provided by the Department of Defense

Youth ChalleNGe Program[112]

The Youth ChalleNGe Program is a quasi-military training program administered by the Army National Guard to improve outcomes for youth who have dropped out of school or have been expelled. The program was established as a pilot program under the National Defense Authorization Act for FY2003 (P.L. 102-484), and Congress permanently authorized the program under the National Defense Authorization Act for FY1998 (P.L. 105-85). Congress has since provided an annual appropriation for the program as part of the Department of Defense authorization acts. For FY2008, Congress appropriated $83.1 million to the program. Currently, 35 programs operate in 28 states, the District of Columbia, and Puerto Rico.

Youth are eligible for the program if they are ages 16 to 18 and enroll prior to their 19th birthday; have dropped out of school or been expelled; are unemployed; are not currently on parole or probation for anything other than juvenile status offenses and not serving time or awaiting sentencing; and are drug free.[113] From 1993 through 2007, nearly 94,000 youth enrolled and approximately 74,000 youth have graduated from the program.[114] The program consists of three phases: a two-week pre-program residential phase where applicants are assessed to determine their potential for completing the program; a 20-week residential phase; and a 12-month post-residential phase.[115] During the residential phase, youth — known as cadets — work toward their high school diploma or GED and develop life-coping, job, and leadership skills. They also participate in activities to improve their physical well-being, and they engage in community service. Youth develop a "Post-Residential Action Plan (P-RAP)" that sets forth their goals, as well as the tasks and objectives to meet those goals. The post-residential phase begins when graduates return to their communities, continue in higher education, or enter the military. The goal of this phase is for graduates to build on the gains made during the residential phase and to continue to develop and implement their P-RAP.

A core component of the post-residential phase is mentoring in which a cadet works with a mentor to meet his or her goals set forth in the P-RAP. This component is referred to as the "Friendly Mentor Match" process. Parents and youth are asked to nominate at least one prospective mentor prior to acceptance into the program. They are advised to identify an individual who is respected by the youth and would be a good role model. Cadets tend to know their mentors before enrolling in the program; however, members of an applicant's immediate family or household and ChalleNGe staff members and their spouses are not eligible to become mentors. By week 13 of the residential phase, and prior to the formal matching of a cadet and a mentor, programs are required to use a National Guard-approved curriculum to train the mentors and the cadets for their roles and responsibilities during the formal mentoring relationship.

Mentors be at least 21 years old, of the same gender as the youth (unless otherwise approved by the director of the program), and within reasonable geographic proximity. Mentors must also undergo a background check that includes two reference checks, an interview, and a criminal background investigation that includes a sex offender registry check. In some programs, the mentors are required to initiate the background investigation and have the results provided to the program prior to their acceptance as a mentor. Mentors and cadets begin weekly contact during the last two months of the residential phase and maintain monthly contacts during the post-residential phase. Cadets and mentors are encouraged to participate in community service activities or job placement activities. Although the program prefers that the pair meet in person, contact may be made by telephone calls, emails, or letters, particularly for those cadets who enlist in the military or attend school in a different community.

Mentors report each month during the post-residential phase about the cadets' placement activities, progress toward achieving their goals, and the activities associated with the mentoring relationship. Some programs also require the cadets to report monthly about their progress. At the end of the post-residential phase, an exit interview is conducted between program staff and the mentor, and the match is formally concluded.

Federal Mentoring Council

The chief executive officer of CNCS and the Commissioner of HHS's Family and Youth Services Bureau chair the Federal Mentoring Council ("Council"), which is comprised of the leadership teams of eight federal agencies with multiple youth-focused programs.[116] The Council was created in 2006 to address the ways these agencies can combine resources and training and technical assistance to federally administered mentoring programs, and to serve as a clearinghouse on federal mentoring.[117] The Council was funded in FY2007 through CNCS, the Department of Education, and the Department of Health and Human Services; CNCS has pledged to continue funding the initiative in FY2008.[118] (The current director of the initiative is funded in FY2008 through the CNCS budget.) A national working group comprised of leading mentoring experts and practitioners (including the chief executive officers of MENTOR, Big Brothers Big Sisters of America, the Boys and Girls Club, and America's Promise, among others) advises and shares effective mentoring practices with the Council.[119]

Since the Council was convened, it has met quarterly to identify federal programs with mentoring components, and training and technical assistance resources for mentoring organizations, which is to be posted on a CNCS-sponsored website; to develop a common set of criteria and broad description of mentoring that can be used across agencies; and to explore how agencies can collaborate in research on youth mentoring.[120] The Council has held a public forum on mentoring and is now developing a mentoring initiative for young people aging out of foster care tentatively known as the Foster Youth Mentoring Campaign.[121] The campaign is working to recruit federal employees to serve as mentors. The initiative is to incorporate the recommendations of the White House Task Force for Disadvantaged Youth, including strategies to assist foster youth as they transition to adulthood. Finally, the Council is drafting an Executive Order on mentoring, which would promote mentoring across agencies, including engaging federal employees as mentors.

FEDERAL ISSUES IN MENTORING

Six bills have been introduced in the 110th Congress that primarily concern mentoring.[122] The Mentoring America's Children Act (H.R. 2611/S. 1812) would make changes to the

SDFS Mentoring program. The Foster Care Mentoring Act (S. 379) seeks to provide additional mentoring services for youth in the foster care system.[123] Another pending bill (H.R. 5660), introduced by Representative Kendrick Meek, provides tax incentives for adults who provide or facilitate mentoring for adults ages 18 through 21. Finally, the Mentor-Mentee Teen Pregnancy Reduction Act of 2008 (H.R. 5810) would authorize grants for school-based mentoring programs for at risk teenage girls to prevent and reduce teen pregnancy, and to provide student loan forgiveness for mentors participating in the programs.

Issues that may be relevant to any discussions around the federal role in mentoring include (1) the limitations of research on outcomes for mentored youth; (2) the potential need for additional mentors, particularly for vulnerable populations; (3) grantees' challenges in sustaining funding; and (4) the possible discontinuation of federal mentoring funding.

Limited Research on Mentored Youth Outcomes

A few positive evaluations of mentoring programs may have provided some justification for federal support of these programs.[124] The 1995 landmark study of community-based mentoring programs at select Big Brothers and Big Sisters chapters demonstrated that mentored youth were less likely than their non-mentored counterparts to use drugs and alcohol, hit someone, and skip school, among other outcomes. A recent evaluation of the Big Brothers Big Sisters school-based mentoring program found similar promising results for mentored youth. Nonetheless, findings from these and other studies are limited and/or show that mentoring is limited in improving all youth outcomes. The long-term influence of mentoring for youth is unknown. The 1995 study tracked youth for 18 months, which is among the longest periods of time mentored youth have been studied. No study appears to address issues around how well youth transition to adulthood, such as whether they attend college or secure employment. Further, studies of mentoring programs have shown that some gains made by mentored youth, compared to their non-mentored counterparts, are short-lived and that mentored youth do not improve in certain areas.

A related issue is the use of mentoring techniques, such as group mentoring, that have not been rigorously evaluated. The Mentoring Initiative for System-Involved Youth grant solicitation encouraged applicants to "consider a variety of mentoring approaches, such as one-to-one, group, student/peer, team education, and sports mentoring; professional development coaching; and other approaches best suited to meet the needs of the target population."[125] Two of the MISIY grantees appear to use group mentoring or team-based mentoring as a primary technique, and one of the programs uses therapeutic mentoring provided by paid case managers.[126] The 2004 GAO report on the Safe and Drug Free Schools Mentoring program found that 3% of grantees used group mentoring exclusively and that 20% used group mentoring in combination with one-to-one mentoring.[127] Compared to mentoring pairs, these other mentoring techniques have not been thoroughly evaluated.

Finally, researchers have noted that evaluations of certain mentoring techniques are often not in place prior to implementation. In response to GAO's finding that the SDFS Mentoring program lacked an evaluative component, the Department of Education has contracted with a research organization to evaluate outcomes of students in programs funded by the program.

Gap in Mentoring Services

A 2002 poll by MENTOR, a mentor advocacy group, estimated that 15 million at-risk[128] youth need a mentor.[129] Recruiting and retaining volunteers appears to be a major challenge for mentoring organizations, including those funded through federal mentoring programs.[130] In its 2004 report of the Safe and Drug Free Schools Mentoring program, GAO found that new grantees had more difficulty than established grantees in recruiting and supporting mentors.[131] Similarly, HHS reports that some mentors in organizations that receive Mentoring Children of Prisoners' funding have dropped out before being matched with a youth because of the time and energy commitment mentoring entails.[132] While research on mentor recruitment and retention is nascent, it reveals that mentoring organizations tend to attract individuals who are middle aged, educated, and have children in their household, and that word of mouth is among the top strategies for recruiting new volunteers.[133] Further, individuals are likely to remain in formal mentoring programs if they feel adequately prepared to serve as mentors. According to the research on mentoring, retention may be high when programs continually monitor mentoring relationships for effectiveness and respond to the needs of mentors.

To address the perceived mentoring gap, the Corporation for National and Community Service has partnered with MENTOR to match three million youth with mentors by 2010. The campaign has also secured commitments from corporate and foundation partners for funding to support research on mentoring programs and engage their networks of employees in mentoring. The Federal Mentoring Council is also undertaking efforts to recruit federal employees to serve as mentors.

A related issue is that the mentoring gap may be wider for special populations. Mentoring programs primarily serve youth ages 9 through 11 who come to the attention of a parent or teacher, rather than the most at-risk populations, which include, but are not limited to, older youth, runaway and homeless youth, and youth in foster care or the juvenile justice system.[134] According to a 2005 study by MENTOR, less than one-fifth of mentors reported mentoring a youth involved in the juvenile justice or foster care systems or with a parent in prison.[135] However, most of these mentors said they would be willing to work with vulnerable youth populations. Recent efforts to recruit volunteers for vulnerable populations are also underway, as evidenced by two of the three current federal mentoring programs that target youth involved in the foster care or juvenile justice systems and children with imprisoned parents. The three recent DOJ mentoring grants target vulnerable youth, including Latino high school students that attend schools in areas with a significant gang presence. In addition, provisions in the proposed Foster Care Mentoring Act (S. 379) are intended to help recruit mentors for children in the foster care system. These provisions would forgive the federal student loan debt of mentors who serve 200 hours each year, at $2,000 each year, not to exceed $20,000 total. Nonetheless, potential mentors may still be discouraged from working with youth facing serious personal difficulties. In addition, creating financial incentives for mentors may raise the concern that this type of mentoring would not be strictly voluntary.

Sustaining Resources

Some organizations that receive federal mentoring grants report challenges with securing diverse sources of funding and expanding their programs because of limited funding.[136] While the Safe and Drug Free Schools Mentoring program does not require grantees to provide a match, they are ineligible to apply for subsequent grants, even in the last year of the grant cycle. (They may, however, apply for other Department of Education grants for which they are eligible and/or apply for subsequent SDFS Mentoring grants after the grant cycle ends.) For example, grantees awarded funds in FY2007 are only eligible to apply for a subsequent grant after FY2009, the final year of their grant. This may lead to gaps in funding for organizations that rely on federal dollars to sustain their services. According to the Department of Education, grantees must wait to reapply for continuation grants because the agency would like to provide funding opportunities for new grantees and to encourage current grantees to secure other sources of funding.[137]

To improve the prospects that organizations continue providing mentoring services beyond the life of their grants, the three federal mentoring programs provide training and technical assistance to help grantees in becoming financially sustainable.[138] For example, the Education Development Center is working with MISIY grantees to develop strategies and tools to secure additional financial resources. EDC has conducted pre-assessments of the grantees to gauge their need for this type of assistance.[139] Further, pending legislation to reauthorize the Safe and Drug Free Schools program would enable grantees to reapply for additional funding after their grant terminates. The Mentoring America's Children Act (H.R. 2611/S. 1812) would enable grantees to seek additional funding. Specifically, the act provides that in awarding grants, the Secretary must consider entities who have received prior grant funding only if they meet specific criteria: (I) performance during the initial grant cycle was satisfactory, in terms of program design and number of children served (*the bills do not specify which entity or persons are to determine if the performance was satisfactory*); (ii) the subsequent grant is to support expanded services to a new geographic area or target population; and (iii) the eligible entity demonstrates that it is able to provide a 50% match to federal funds for all three years of the new grant. The act would also require first-time grantees to provide a match of at least 10% in the first year, at least 25% in the second year, and 50% in the third year.

Possible Discontinuation of Select Federal Mentoring Funding

Funding appears uncertain for two of the three primary federal mentoring programs. The Administration has proposed eliminating the Safe and Drug Free Schools Program, claiming that the program has met its objectives.[140] Funding for the program will continue in FY2008, pursuant to the FY2008 appropriations law (P.L. 110-161) signed by the President on December 26, 2007. MISIY is funded as a pilot project that may not continue beyond FY2009, the last year of grant funding. The Administration plans to await results from the evaluation prior to determining the feasibility of expanding the program.[141] However, a pending omnibus crime control bill (S. 2237) proposes to expand the MISIY program to additional sites and authorize an annual appropriation of $4.8 million for FY2008 to FY2012.[142]

APPENDIX

Table A-1. Mentoring Children of Prisoners: Demographics and Characteristics of Children, Mentors, and Relationships (FY2006)

Demographic or Characteristic	
Total Number of Matches	27,525
Average age of youth	11 years
Percent of children who were male	44%
Percent of mentors who were male	38%
Total number of matches that began in FY2006 and were across gender (e.g., female mentor and male youth)	2,461 (8.9%)
Total number of matches that began in FY2006 and were across race or ethnicity (e.g., Asian mentor and white youth)	6,380 (23.2%)
Average number of days youth was waiting for a mentor	53 days
Share of children with fewer than 12 hours of regular mentor/youth contact during the past quarter (i.e., four-month period)	24%
Share of children with 12 to 24 hours of regular mentor/youth contact during the past quarter	22%
Share of children with more than 24 hours of regular mentor/youth contact during the past quarter	32%
Share of children for whom the frequency or length of their contacts with mentors is unknown	22%
Average number of initial pre-match training/orientation(s) per mentor	5
Average number of hours post-match training per mentor	4.5
Average number of staff follow-up contacts in person or by phone per mentor per fiscal quarter addressing the following: key mentor skills, commitment, or mentor's response to child crisis or other critical issue in child's life	15.7

Source: Congressional Research Service presentation of data provided by the U.S. Department of Health and Human Services, Administration for Children and Families, Family and Youth Services Bureau, June and December 2007.

End Notes

[1] The White House Task Force for Disadvantaged Youth, convened in 2003 to identify issues in coordinating federal youth policy, identified approximately 123 federally funded programs administered by 10 agencies with a mentoring component. The task force's final report is available at [http://www.acf.hhs.gov/programs/fysb/content/docs/white_house_ task_force.pdf].

[2] See U.S. General Accounting Office, *Student Mentoring Programs: Education's Monitoring and Information Sharing Could Be Improved*, GAO Report GAO-04-581 (Washington, June 2004), p. 6. (Hereafter referenced GAO, *Student Mentoring Programs*.) After this report was issued, the name of the General Accounting Office was changed to the Government Accountability Office.

[3] For further discussion of risk factors and groups of at-risk youth, see CRS Report RL33975, *Vulnerable Youth: Background and Policies*, by Adrienne L. Fernandes.

[4] U.S. Government Accountability Office, *Student Mentoring Programs*, p. 6.

[5] George L. Beiswinger, *One to One: The Story of the Big Brothers Big Sisters Movement in America.* (Philadelphia: Big Brothers Big Sisters of America, 1985), pp. 15-20.

[6] U.S. Department of Justice, Office of Juvenile Justice and Delinquency Prevention, "OJJDP Helps Big Brothers Big Sisters Celebrate 100th Anniversary," *OJJDP News @ a Glance*, vol. 3, no. 3, May/June 2004, p. 1. (Hereafter referenced as U.S. Department of Justice, *Big Brothers Big Sisters.*)

[7] Marc Freedman, *The Kindness of Strangers: Mentors, Urban Youth, and the New Volunteerism* (San Francisco: Jossey-Bass Publishers, 1993), p. 5. (Hereafter referenced as Mark Freedman, *The Kindness of Strangers.*)

[8] U.S. Department of Justice, "Juvenile Mentoring Program (JUMP) Guidelines," 59 *Federal Register* 3820, July 28, 1994.

[9] Marc Freedman, *The Kindness of Strangers*, p. 4.

[10] Ibid, p. 16.

[11] The Presidents' Summit on America's Future, Remarks at the Presidents' Summit on America's Future, available at [http://clinton3.nara.gov/WH/New/Summit/Remarks_index. html].

[12] See, Jean Baldwin Grossman, ed., *Contemporary Issues in Mentoring, Public/Private Ventures*, p. 6.; Mentor/National Mentoring Partnership, "Elements of Effective Practice," 2nd ed., 2003; and Jean E. Rhodes and David L. DuBois, "Understanding and Facilitating the Youth Mentoring Movement," Social Policy Report, vol. 20, no. 3 (2006), pp. 8-11. (Hereafter referenced as Rhodes and DuBois, "Understanding and Facilitating the Youth Mentoring Movement.")

[13] Rhodes and DuBois, "Understanding and Facilitating the Youth Mentoring Movement," p. 9.

[14] Joseph P. Tierney and Jean Baldwin Grossman, with Nancy L. Resch, *Making A Difference: An Impact Study of Big Brothers Big Sisters*, Public/Private Ventures, reissued September 2000, available online at [http://www.ppv.org/ppv/publications/assets 1_ publication.pdf].

[15] These programs are a sampling of some of the programs profiled.

[16] Susan Jekielek et al., *Mentoring Programs and Youth Development: A Synthesis*, Child Trends, January 2002, available at [http://www.childtrends.org/what_works/clarkwww/mentor/mentorrpt.pdf]. (Hereafter reference Jekielek et al., *Mentoring Programs and Youth Development.*)

[17] Carla Herrera et al., *Making a Difference in Schools: The Big Brothers Big Sisters School- Based Mentoring Impact Study*, Public/Private Ventures, August 2007, pp. 34-35, available at [http://www.ppv.org/ppv/publications/assets _publication.pdf]. (Hereafter referenced as Herrera et al., *Making a Difference in Schools.*)

[18] Jekielek et al., *Mentoring Programs and Youth Development*, p. 15.

[19] Herrera et al., *Making a Difference in Schools*, pp. 37-38.

[20] Jean E. Rhodes and David L. DuBois, "Understanding and Facilitating the Youth Mentoring Movement," pp. 3-5.

[21] Herrera et al., *Making a Difference in Schools*, pp. 47-78.

[22] Ibid., pp. iv-v.

[23] Christopher J. Mumola, *Incarcerated Parents and Their Children*, U.S. Department of Justice, Bureau of Justice Statistics, August 2000, p. 2, available at [http://www.ojp.usdoj. gov/bj s/pub/pdf/iptc.pdf].

[24] U.S. Department of Health and Human Services, Administration for Children and Families, *The Mentoring Children of Prisoners Program*, Report to Congress, September 12, 2007, p. 3. (Hereafter referenced as *The Mentoring Children of Prisoners Program*, Report to Congress.)

[25] Ibid.

[26] Executive Office of the President, Office of Management and Budget, *Mentoring Children of Prisoners Assessment*, 2005, available at [http://www.whitehouse.gov/omb/expectmore/ summary/10003505.2005.html]. (Hereafter referenced as Office of Management and Budget, *Mentoring Children of Prisoners Assessment.*)

[27] Elizabeth Inez Johnson and Jane Waldfogel, *Children of Incarcerated Parents: Cumulative Risk and Children's Living Arrangements*, July 2002, p. 2, available at [http://www.jcpr.org/wpfiles/johnson_waldfogel.pdf].

[28] Nancy G. La Vigne, Elizabeth Davies, and Diana Brazzell, *Broken Bonds: Understanding and Addressing the Needs of Children with Incarcerated Parents*, Urban Institute, Research Report, February 2008, available at [http://www.urban.org/publications/411616.html].

[29] For further information about the Amachi program, see [http://www.amachimentoring.org/ index.html].

[30] U.S. Congress, House Committee on Ways and Means, *Promoting Safe and Stable Families Amendments*, report to accompany H.R. 2873, 107th Cong., 1st sess., H.Rept. 107- 281 (Washington: GPO, 2001), p. 19.

[31] HHS has given preference to grantees that have demonstrated a need for mentoring services in their areas based on the concentration of children of prisoners who are currently not mentored. Grantee applicants have determined the number of eligible participants by contacting local school systems for student/parent information and/or the Bureau of Prisons. Others have collaborated with child social service programs such as the foster care system and/or their state prisons. Organizations with well-established ministry programs recruited participants as part of their ministry work.

[32] Office of Management and Budget, *Mentoring Children of Prisoners Assessment.*

[33] U.S. Department of Health and Human Services, Administration for Children and Families, *Mentoring Children of Prisoners Competitive Grant Announcement*, 2007, pp. 5-6, available at [http://www.acf.hhs.gov/grants (Hereafter referenced as U.S. Department of Health and Human Services, *Mentoring Children of Prisoners Competitive Grant Announcement*, 2007).

[34] Six states (Indiana, Nebraska, New Mexico, Oklahoma, Utah, and Vermont) do not appear to have programs funded by the MCP grant.

[35] Based on correspondence with the U.S. Department of Health and Human Services, Administration for Children and Families, Family and Youth Services Bureau, December 2007.

[36] Ibid., June 2007.

[37] HHS is required to provide a description of how the organization should ensure collaboration and cooperation with other interested parties, including courts and prisons, with respect to the delivery of mentoring services under the demonstration project.

[38] Based on correspondence with the U.S. Department of Health and Human Services, Administration for Children and Families, Family and Youth Services Bureau, December 2007. Receipt of a voucher is not counted for purposes of determining eligibility of federal or federally supported assistance for the child's family.

[39] See [http://www.mentoring

[40] For information about the publicity campaign, see [http://www.mentoring choice].

[41] For additional information about the program's eligibility requirements, see [http://www.mentoring

[42] *The Mentoring Children of Prisoners Program*, Report to Congress, p. 1.

[43] U.S. Department of Health and Human Services, *Mentoring Children of Prisoners Competitive Grant Announcement*, 2007.

[44] The percentage of funds set aside for this purpose was increased from 2.5% to 4% under P.L. 109-288.

[45] Department of Health and Human Services, *Mentoring Children of Prisoners Competitive Grant Announcement*, 2007, p. 7.

[46] Based on correspondence with the U.S. Department of Health and Human Services, Administration for Children and Families, Family and Youth Services Bureau, December 2007.

[47] *The Mentoring Children of Prisoners Program*, Report to Congress, p. 11.

[48] Ibid.

[49] Based on correspondence with the U.S. Department of Health and Human Services, Administration for Children and Families, Family and Youth Services Bureau, June 2007.

[50] Based on correspondence with U.S. Department of Health and Human Services, Administration for Children and Families, Family and Youth Services Bureau, July 2007. See also *Case Study: Supporting a Government Agency, Mentoring Children of Prisoners Program* on the DMT website, [http://www.daremightythings.com/company/casestudy/MCP %20052507_v2.pdf].

[51] This on-site monitoring tool is to be similar to one that has been used by FYSB's Runaway and Homeless Youth program for the past twenty years. Based on correspondence with U.S. Department of Health and Human Services, Administration for Children and Families, Family and Youth Services Bureau, October 2007.

[52] *The Mentoring Children of Prisoners Program*, Report to Congress, p. 8.

[53] The SDFS program supports two major grant programs — one for states and one for national programs. The mentoring program is authorized under the national programs grant. For further information, see CRS Report RL33980, *School and Campus Safety Programs and Requirements in the Elementary and Secondary Education Act and Higher Education Act*, by Rebecca R. Skinner and Gail McCallion.

[54] U.S. Department of Education, "Notice of Final Priorities, Requirements, and Selection Criteria Under the Mentoring Program," 69 *Federal Register* 30794, May 28, 2004. (Hereafter referenced as U.S. Department of Education, "Notice of Final Priorities.")

[55] In a 2004 GAO analysis of the 121 SDFS Mentoring Program grantees who received awards in FY2002, 75% provided one-to-one mentoring only; 22% provided both one-to-one mentoring and group mentoring; and 3% provided group mentoring only.

[56] GAO, *Student Mentoring Programs*, p. 17.

[57] Ibid.

[58] U.S. Department of Education, "Notice of Final Priorities."

[59] Based on correspondence with the U.S. Department of Education, Office of Safe and Drug Free Schools, October 2007.

[60] Based on correspondence with the U.S. Department of Education, Office of Safe and Drug Free Schools, July 2007.

[61] State grants are awarded to states based on a formula that incorporates poverty and population factors. States must use 93% of their allocation to make formula grants to local educational agencies (LEAs) based on poverty factors and each LEA's share of student enrollment in public and private nonprofit elementary and secondary schools. National grants are used primarily for a variety of discretionary programs designed to prevent drug abuse and violence in elementary and secondary schools. For further information, see CRS

Report RL33980, *School and Campus Safety Programs and Requirements in the Elementary and Secondary Education Act and Higher Education Act*, by Rebecca R. Skinner and Gail McCallion.

[62] U.S. Department of Education, Safe Schools and Citizenship Education, *FY 2009 Justifications of Appropriation Estimates*, pp. F-37. (Hereafter referenced U.S. Department of Education, *FY 2009 Justifications of Appropriation Estimates*.)

[63] Based on correspondence with U.S. Department of Education, Office of Safe and Drug Free Schools, December 2007. Also, see U.S. Department of Education, "Office of Safe and Drug-Free Schools: Notice of Final Eligibility Requirement," 71 *Federal Register* 70369, December 4, 2006.

[64] U.S. Department of Education, *FY 2009 Justifications of Appropriation Estimates*, p. F-30.

[65] U.S. Department of Education, "Notice of Final Priorities."

[66] U.S. Department of Education, *FY 2009 Justifications of Appropriation Estimates*, pp. F-39, F-40.

[67] GAO, *Student Mentoring Programs*.

[68] Approximately half of this sample is to be randomly assigned to be matched with a mentor. The study uses a nonrandom sample of 33 mentoring grantees, meaning that Abt is to select certain grantee organizations for the study. According to ED, many programs could not support a study that randomly assigns students to mentoring. According to ED, the agency will spend $5.6 million for the national evaluation. Funding began in FY2005 and extends through FY2008. Based on correspondence with U.S. Department of Education, Office of Safe and Drug Free Schools, July 2007.

[69] U.S. Department of Education, *FY 2009 Justifications of Appropriation Estimates*, p. F-47.

[70] Funding for training and technical assistance is approximately $5.5 million from FY2004 through FY2008. Based on correspondence with the U.S. Department of Education, Office of Safe and Drug Free Schools, July 2007.

[71] Based on correspondence with the U.S. Department of Education, Office of Safe and Drug Free Schools, October 2007.

[72] U.S. Department of Education, *FY 2009 Justifications of Appropriation Estimates*, p. 46.

[73] Ibid.

[74] This process is described in greater detail in GAO, *Student Mentoring Programs*, pp. 24-26.

[75] Sen. Frank R. Lautenberg, "Juvenile Justice and Delinquency Prevention Authorization Act," remarks in the Senate, *Congressional Record*, daily edition, vol. 138 (October 7, 1992).

[76] U.S. Congress, House Committee on Education and the Workforce, *Juvenile Justice and Delinquency Prevention Act of 2001*, report to accompany H.R. 1900, 107th Cong., 1st sess. H.Rept. 107-203 (Washington; GPO, 2001), p. 31.

[77] An evaluation of JUMP found that the program did not recruit the desired number of mentors, that many of the relationships appeared to have ended prematurely, and that some youth outcomes did not improve. Nonetheless, the results of the evaluation do not appear to have been a factor in eliminating the program.

[78] The Department of Justice did not request that these funds be discontinued. According to the agency, no letters or budget justifications advocating for these funds to be discontinued were submitted to Congress. Based on correspondence with the U.S. Department of Justice, Office of Justice Programs, Office of Juvenile Justice and Delinquency Prevention, November 2007.

[79] Based on correspondence with the U.S. Department of Justice, Office of Justice Programs, Office of Juvenile Justice and Delinquency Prevention, March 2006 and U.S. Department of Justice, *2007 Congressional Authorization and Budget Submission*, p. 141.

[80] See, for example, House Committee on Appropriations, *Making Appropriations for Science, the Departments of State, Justice, and Commerce, and Related Agencies for the Fiscal Year Ending September 30, 2006, and for Other Purposes*, report to accompany H.R. 2862, 109th Cong., 2nd sess., CP-3 (Washington: GPO, 2006).

[81] Based on correspondence with the U.S. Department of Justice, Office of Justice Programs, Office of Juvenile Justice and Delinquency Prevention, November 2007.

[82] The Bureau of Justice Assistance has provided some funding for mentoring.

[83] U.S. Department of Justice, Office of Justice Programs, *FY2005 Budget Justifications*.

[84] U.S. Department of Justice, Office of Justice Programs, Office of Juvenile Justice and Delinquency Prevention, "Application for Funding: Mentoring Initiative for System Involved Youth," available at [http://www.ojj dp.ncjrs.gov/grants initiative.pdf]. (Hereafter referenced as U.S. Department of Justice, "Application for Funding: Mentoring Initiative for System Involved Youth.")

[85] U.S. Department of Justice, Office of Justice Programs, Office of Juvenile Justice and Delinquency Prevention, "OJJDP Awards Foster Mentoring for System Involved Youth," available at [http://www.ojj dp.ncjrs.gov/enews/07juvjust/070 123 .html].

[86] The Boys and Girls Aid Society's Mentor Portland, Grant Application for Mentoring Initiative for System Involved Youth, provided to the Congressional Research Service by the U.S. Department of Justice, Office of Justice Programs, September 2007.

[87] Lutheran Family Services of Virginia, Grant Application for Mentoring Initiative for System Involved Youth, provided to the Congressional Research Service by the U.S. Department of Justice, Office of Justice Programs, September 2007.

[88] City of Chicago, Grant Application for Mentoring Initiative for System Involved Youth, provided to the Congressional Research Service by the U.S. Department of Justice, Office of Justice Programs, September 2007.

[89] The Mentoring Center, Grant Application for Mentoring Initiative for System Involved Youth, provided to the Congressional Research Service by the U.S. Department of Justice, Office of Justice Programs, September 2007.

[90] U.S. Department of Justice, Office of Justice Programs, Office of Juvenile Justice and Delinquency Prevention, "Application for Evaluation of Mentoring Initiative for System Involved Youth," available at [http://www.ojj dp.ncjrs.gov/grants eval.pdf].

[91] The process evaluation involves the monthly collection of data on the date of each mentoring and related activity, duration of each activity, the type of activity (e.g., recreational, academic), location of activity (e.g., at mentoring agency, school), structure of activity (e.g., face to face, by phone), and whether the activity was conducted one-on-one or in a group. These data are to be submitted by each of the four grant recipients electronically.

[92] Based on correspondence with the U.S. Department of Justice, Office of Justice Programs, Office of Juvenile Justice and Delinquency Prevention, November 2007.

[93] Ibid, September 2007.

[94] U.S. Department of Justice, Office of Justice Programs, Office of Juvenile Justice and Delinquency Prevention, "Application for Training and Technical Assistance for Mentoring Initiative for System Involved Youth," available at [http://www.ojj dp.ncjrs.gov/grants solicitations/ttamentoring06.pdf]. In FY2007, EDC received a supplement of $197,446.

[95] Based on correspondence with the U.S. Department of Justice, Office of Justice Programs, Office of Juvenile Justice and Delinquency Prevention, September 2007.

[96] This section is not exhaustive of the mentoring services that may be available through other federal programs and initiatives. See, for example, Executive Office of the President, *White House Task Force for Disadvantaged Youth Final Report*, October 2003, pp. 165-179, available online at [http://www.acf.hhs.gov/programs/fysb/content/docs/white_house_task_ force.pdf].

[97] Corporation for National & Community Service, I*ssue Brief: National Service and Mentoring*, available at [http://www.nationalservice.gov/pdf/06_0503_mentoring brief.pdf].

[98] Based on correspondence with the Corporation for National and Community Service, December 2007.

[99] Corporation for National and Community Service, "Cross-Sector Leaders Unveil Major New Plan to Close Mentoring Gap," press release, May 3, 2006, available at [http://www.usafreedomcorps.gov/about_usafc/newsroom/announcements_dynamic.asp? ID= 1299]. (Hereafter referenced as Corporation for National and Community Service, "Close Mentoring Gap.")

[100] The five surviving Presidents (at that time) convened the summit to mobilize Americans in all sectors to ensure that all youth have adequate resources to assist them in leading healthy, productive lives.

[101] The organization's 2006 report, *Every Child, Every Promise: A Report on America's Young People*, correlated the presence of the five commitments in young people's lives with success in adolescence and adulthood. The report concluded that children who have at least four of the five commitments are more likely to be academically successful, civically engaged, and socially competent, regardless of their race or family income. The report is available online at [http://www.americaspromise.org/uploadedFiles/AmericasPromise/Our_ Work/Strategic _Initiatives/Every _Child _Every _Promise/EC-EP _Documents/MAIN%20 REPORT%20DRAFT%20 11.1 .pdf].

[102] U.S. Congress, House of Representatives, *Making Appropriations for the Departments of Labor, Health and Human Services, and Education, and Related Agencies for the Fiscal Year Ending September 30, 2006, and for Other Purposes*, report to accompany H.R. 3010, 109th Cong., 2nd sess., H.Rept. 109-337 (Washington: GPO, 2006), p. 41.

[103] Based on correspondence with the U.S. Department of Justice, Office of Justice Programs, Office of Juvenile Justice and Delinquency Prevention, December 2007.

[104] Ibid, November 2007.

[105] Ibid.

[106] U.S. Department of Justice, Office of Justice Programs, Office of Juvenile Justice and Delinquency Prevention, *OJJDP FY2007 Prevention and Intervention Programs* grant solicitation, available online at [http://www.ojj dp.ncjrs.gov/grants intervention.pdf].

[107] Byrne Discretionary Grant program funds activities that are to improve the functioning of the criminal justice system. For additional information, see CRS Report RS224 16, *Edward Byrne Memorial Justice Assistance Grant Program: Legislative and Funding History*, by Nathan James.

[108] U.S. House, Committee on the Appropriations, *Joint Explanatory Statement to Accompany FY2008 Consolidated Appropriations Amendment to H.R. 2 764/P.L. 110-1 61, Division G*, available at [http://www.gpoaccess.gov/congress 08conappro.html].

[109] The solicitations are available online at [http://ojjdp.ncjrs.gov/grants FY2008/CommMentoring.pdf], [http://ojjdp.ncjrs.gov/grants/solicitations/FY2008/Natl Mentoring.pdf], and [http : //ojj dp .ncj rs . gov/grants/solicitations/FY2008/Latino Mentoring.pdf].

[110] Based on correspondence with the Department of Justice, Office of Justice Programs June 9, 2008.

[111] U.S. Department of Justice, Office of Justice Programs, *FY2009 Performance Budget*, pp. 23 through 26.

[112] Unless otherwise noted, this information is based on correspondence with the U.S. Department of Defense, National Guard, June 12, 2008.

[113] U.S. Department of Defense, National Guard, *Youth ChalleNGe Program 2007 Performance and Accountability Highlights*, 2008.

[114] Ibid.

[115] U.S. Department of Defense, National Guard, "Youth *ChalleNGe* Program, About Us," at [http://www.ngycp.org/aboutus_dependant_T2_R29.php].

[116] These leadership teams also serve on the Coordinating Council on Juvenile Justice and Delinquency Prevention ("Coordinating Council"), established by the Juvenile Justice and Delinquency Prevention Act of 1974 (P.L. 93-415) and administered by the Department of Justice's Office of Juvenile Justice and Delinquency Prevention. The Council's primary functions are to coordinate federal programs and policies concerning juvenile delinquency prevention, unaccompanied juveniles, and missing and exploited children. The Council is led by the Administrator of OJJDP. The Federal Mentoring Council consults with the Coordinating Council.

[117] U.S. Department of Justice, Coordinating Council on Juvenile Justice and Delinquency Prevention, Minutes from the Quarterly Meeting on November 30, 2006, p. 10, available at [http://www.juvenilecouncil.gov/meetings.html].

[118] Based on correspondence with the Corporation for National and Community Service, December 2007.

[119] Ibid.

[120] U.S. Department of Justice, Office of Justice Programs, Office of Juvenile Justice and Delinquency Prevention, Coordinating Council on Juvenile Justice and Delinquency Prevention, September 14, 2007, meeting, available at [http://www.juvenilecouncil.gov/ materials/2007_09/MeetingSummary%209- 14-07-ed.doc].

[121] Based on correspondence with the U.S. Department of Health and Human Services, Administration for Children and Families, April 2007.

[122] Other legislation (most notably, H.R. 3168 and S. 990/H.R. 1692) would authorize programs and funding for mentoring, among additional activities. Three resolutions (H.Res. 29, H.Res. 908, and S.Res. 61) establish January as national mentoring month or support the goals of national mentoring month.

[123] An amendment to the College Opportunity and Affordability Act (H.R. 4137) would allow community college students to have $10 forgiven from their student loans for every hour they dedicate to mentoring an at-risk child. Another bill, the Families Beyond Bars Act of 2008 (H.R. 5654), would authorize a grant program through the Department of Justice for youth-serving organizations that carry out visitation programs for incarcerated parents and their children.

[124] Gary Walker, "Youth Mentoring and Public Policy," in David L. Dubois and Michael J. Karcher, eds., *Handbook of Youth Mentoring* (Thousand Oaks, California: Sage Publications, 2005), pp. 510-512. (Hereafter referenced as Walker, "Youth Mentoring and Public Policy.")

[125] U.S. Department of Justice, "Application for Funding: Mentoring Initiative for System Involved Youth."

[126] Mentoring programs for juvenile justice-involved youth that employ paraprofessionals may be the most appropriate and cost effective. See Elaine A. Blechman and Jedediah M. Bopp, "Special Populations: Youth Offenders," in David L. Dubois and Michael J. Karcher, eds., *Handbook of Youth Mentoring* (Thousand Oaks, California: Sage Publications, 2005).

[127] GAO, *Student Mentoring Programs*, p. 15.

[128] This definition encompasses youth with poor academic performance or substance abuse issues, or are sexually active, and may overstate the number of youth who need mentoring.

[129] MENTOR, "The National Agenda For Action: How to Close America's Mentoring Gap," 2006, available at [http://www.mentoring p. 10.

[130] Arthur Astukas and Chris Tanti, "Recruiting and Sustaining Volunteer Mentors," in David L. Dubois and Michael J. Karcher, eds., *Handbook of Youth Mentoring*, (Thousand Oaks, California: Sage Publications, 2005), p. 245. (Hereafter referenced as Astukas and Tanti, "Recruiting and Sustaining Volunteer Mentors.")

[131] GAO, *Student Mentoring Programs*, pp. 20-21.

[132] U.S. Department of Health and Human Services, *Report to Congress: The Mentoring Children of Prisoners Program*, September 2007.

[133] Astukas and Tanti, "Recruiting and Sustaining Volunteer Mentors," pp. 235-249.

[134] Walker, "Youth Mentoring and Public Policy," pp. 509-510.

[135] MENTOR, "Mentoring in America 2005: A Snapshot of the Current State of Mentoring," 2006, available at [http://www.mentoring

[136] Erika Fitzpatrick, "Surviving Without Uncle Sam's Money: Mentoring Grant Cutoff Sparks Talk About How to Diversify Funding," *Youth Today*, June 2007, p. 10.

[137] Based on correspondence with U.S. Department of Education, Office of Safe and Drug Free Schools, December 2007. Also, see U.S. Department of Education, "Office of Safe and Drug-Free Schools: Notice of Final Eligibility Requirement," 71 *Federal Register* 70369, December 4, 2006.

[138] Based on correspondence with the U.S. Department of Health and Human Services, Family and Youth Services Bureau, November 2007; U.S. Department of Education, Office of Safe and Drug Free Schools, September 2007; and U.S. Department of Justice, Office of Justice Programs, September 2007.

[139] Ibid.

[140] U.S. Department of Education, *FY 2009 Justifications of Appropriation Estimates*, p. F16.

[141] Based on correspondence with the U.S. Department of Justice, Office of Justice Programs, September 2007.

[142] The bill proposes to amend Section 261(a) of the Juvenile Justice and Delinquency Prevention Act of 1974 (42 U.S.C. 5665(a)) by adding, "The Administrator shall expand the number of sites receiving [MISIY] grants from 4 to 12." *This proposed change appears to be a drafting error.* Section 261(a) does not currently authorize funding *specifically* for MISIY or any other pilot project; rather, it authorizes funds *generally* for demonstration grants and projects.

CHAPTER SOURCES

The following chapters have been previously published:

Chapter 1 – This chapter is edited and excerpted testimonies before the SubCommittee on Income and Security and Family Support of the Committee on Ways and Means, U.S. House of Representatives on June 19, 2007.

Chapter 2 – This is an edited, excerpted and augmented edition of a United States Government Accountability Office (GAO), Report to the Chairman, Committee on Education and Labor, House of Representatives. Publication GAO-08-313, dated February 2008.

Chapter 3 – This is an edited, excerpted and augmented edition of a United States Congressional Research Service publication, Report Order Code RL33975, dated September 3, 2008.

Chapter 4 - This is an edited, excerpted and augmented edition of a United States Congressional Research Service publication, Report Order Code RL34306, dated June 20, 2008.

INDEX

#

21st Century Community Learning Center, 179

A

abstinence, 184, 211

academic performance, 168, 203, 229, 240, 244, 246, 258

academic progress, 51

academic settings, 148

academic success, 55

academics, 14, 87

accountability, 37, 84, 85, 121, 158, 188, 236

ACF, 183, 207

achievement, 25, 82, 159, 171, 179, 202, 237

activism, 85

addiction, 43, 101

adjudication, 149

adjustment, 80, 164

administration, x, 162, 219, 246

administrators, 37

adolescence, ix, x, 33, 161, 162, 163, 164, 166, 168, 169, 170, 171, 172, 173, 177, 197, 223, 257

adolescent behavior, 101

adolescent problem behavior, 24

adolescents, ix, 17, 19, 23, 36, 163, 164, 167, 173, 174, 176, 183, 184, 210, 211

adult education, 23, 154

adult learning, 148

adult population, 27, 37, 91

adulthood, ix, x, 6, 7, 8, 35, 41, 55, 80, 91, 101, 115, 119, 145, 161, 162, 163, 164, 165, 171, 172, 173, 197, 198, 223, 232, 250, 257

advocacy, 53, 79, 84, 99, 126, 172, 209, 233, 245, 251

African American, 2, 24, 26, 27, 107, 118, 159, 163, 231, 244

African Americans, 107, 163

after-school, 22, 25, 179, 185, 193, 220, 225

aid, 55, 176, 179, 180, 186, 203, 204, 219

AIDS, 22, 220

Air Force, 89

alcohol, 16, 19, 43, 52, 109, 168, 179, 183, 184, 193, 196, 202, 210, 228, 236, 250

alcohol abuse, 184, 210

alcohol problems, 43

alcohol use, 228

ALL, 89

alternative, 3, 21, 22, 23, 26, 37, 38, 39, 56, 83, 84, 85, 92, 104, 116, 125, 133, 146, 152, 184, 194

alternatives, 27, 28, 86, 171

American Indian, 233

antecedents, 166, 167

antisocial behavior, 118

anxiety, 16, 19

application, 92, 104, 185, 239

appropriations, 102, 119, 151, 160, 177, 181, 188, 197, 220, 234, 242, 246, 252

Arizona, 54, 55, 56, 60, 193, 233

Armed Forces, 169

armed robbery, 30, 31

Army, 99, 248

arrest, 81, 232, 243

assault, 16, 18

assessment, 7, 8, 98, 141, 172, 184, 188, 236

assets, 109, 140, 171, 182, 194, 198, 217, 232, 254

assignment, 11, 238

attachment, 82, 132

attitudes, 26, 106, 108, 172, 228

Attorney General, 143, 190, 192

availability, 3, 24, 171, 180

awareness, 17, 19, 102, 184, 194, 196

B

babies, 9, 22, 88
back, 10, 14, 21, 30, 31, 32, 40, 42, 44, 45, 46, 56, 57, 60, 61, 62, 65, 88, 130
background information, 151
barrier, 23, 82, 134, 153
barrier-free, 23
barriers, 25, 37, 45, 87, 88, 91, 92, 100, 101, 104, 136, 162, 163, 165
basic competencies, 87
Basic Life Support, 91
basketball, 109
behavior, 25, 95, 101, 130, 142, 163, 173, 229, 231, 241, 242, 243
beliefs, 26, 85, 171
benchmarks, 121, 159
benefits, 36, 51, 54, 98, 127, 228, 229, 235
biological parents, 10
Blacks, 34
Boston, 111, 123, 124, 150, 152
boys, 15, 17, 18, 19, 22
Bureau of the Census, 111
bureaucracy, 28
Bush Administration, 106

C

caregiver, 233
caregivers, 98, 104, 233, 255
cash aid, 219
CCC, 174
Census, 81, 82, 83, 111, 135, 168, 170, 216
Census Bureau, 135, 168, 170, 216
central city, 82
CEO, 99
child abuse, 205, 206, 207, 209
child development, 87, 184
child labor, 172, 173
child maltreatment, 44
child poverty, 59
child protection, 246
child protective services, 104
child rearing, 211
child welfare, 20, 23, 26, 27, 33, 44, 46, 79, 84, 92, 94, 95, 96, 101, 102, 103, 104, 118, 159, 168, 172, 173, 183, 188, 208, 218, 219, 237
childbearing, 25
childcare, 88
childhood, ix, 93, 163, 173, 191, 193
citizens, 2, 53, 62, 108, 149, 153, 200
citizenship, 107, 144

civil rights, 64, 81
civil society, 144
civilian, x, 159, 161, 169
class size, 10, 37
classes, 10, 11, 12, 14, 16, 30, 31, 32, 56, 64, 65, 87, 107, 125, 228
classroom, 22, 51, 52, 53, 87, 117, 125, 129, 186
classroom settings, 53
classrooms, 13
clients, 3, 25, 26, 27, 138, 159
close relationships, 134
coaches, 4, 197, 225, 245
coalitions, 194
cohort, 62, 180
collaboration, 37, 97, 99, 117, 124, 128, 138, 139, 144, 145, 147, 152, 159, 189, 190, 191, 193, 198, 247, 255
collaborative approaches, 131
college campuses, 186, 209
College Cost Reduction Act, 6, 8
college students, 58, 175, 179, 203, 204, 219, 258
colleges, 82, 109, 123, 163, 179, 203, 237, 242
Columbia, 24, 33, 34, 56, 86, 88, 116, 152, 196, 232, 248
Columbia University, 33, 34
Committee on Appropriations, 234, 239, 256
communication, 10, 87, 98, 99, 139, 149, 186, 189, 193, 198, 240
Community Development Block Grant, x, 145, 148, 162, 163
community service, x, 85, 86, 87, 106, 108, 117, 126, 130, 144, 145, 149, 162, 172, 176, 186, 195, 196, 197, 198, 199, 212, 248, 249
community support, 117, 128
community-based services, 205
complexity, ix, 163, 186
compliance, 2, 3, 92, 104, 237, 240
components, xii, 38, 114, 117, 119, 126, 129, 131, 181, 182, 188, 225, 249
confidence, 37, 109, 131
confinement, 231
conflict, 27, 44, 132, 173, 177
conflict resolution, 132, 177
congenital heart disease, 165
Congressional Budget Office, 217
Congressional Record, 220, 256
constraints, 114, 117, 118, 132, 134, 135, 136, 143, 159, 198
construction, 27, 31, 32, 37, 87, 106, 110, 124, 126, 129, 135, 146, 149, 153, 192
contracts, 27, 101, 113, 114, 117, 118, 121, 132, 136, 137, 138, 142, 143, 242, 247

control, 15, 18, 51, 54, 155, 169, 171, 181, 205, 206, 228, 229, 240, 244, 252
control group, 228, 229, 244
costs, 4, 27, 45, 134, 135, 142, 164, 178, 180, 181
counseling, 16, 19, 21, 22, 23, 25, 27, 54, 56, 100, 106, 108, 109, 117, 126, 129, 133, 145, 149, 175, 177, 179, 180, 182, 183, 200, 204, 205, 211, 220, 243, 244
courts, 6, 21, 23, 173, 255
CPR, 91
CPS, 168, 169, 170, 217
crime, ix, 4, 24, 28, 36, 80, 81, 91, 106, 113, 165, 169, 177, 220, 233, 238, 241, 252
crimes, 51, 52, 142, 205
criminal activity, xii, 177, 224
criminal behavior, 229
criminal justice, 2, 33, 34, 38, 45, 62, 80, 119, 134, 257
criminal justice system, 2, 38, 45, 62, 80, 119, 134, 257
crisis intervention, 100
critical thinking, 87
cross-fertilization, 237
CRS, 166, 167, 170, 176, 189, 200, 214, 215, 216, 217, 218, 219, 220, 254, 255, 257
cultural influence, 228
cultural norms, 171
culture, 59, 171
Current Population Survey (CPS), 168, 170, 216
curriculum, 11, 130, 180, 243, 248

D

data collection, 138, 139, 192, 233, 235, 244
data set, 100
database, 42, 121
dating, 25, 28
death, 5, 24, 110, 174
death rate, 5
deaths, 24, 26
debt, 179, 251
decision-making process, 146
decisions, 30, 32, 37, 61, 64, 171
Defense Authorization Act, 248
deficit, 133, 194
deficits, 95, 131
definition, 5, 35, 40, 119, 151, 158, 159, 163, 164, 168, 187, 219, 258
delinquency, ix, x, 161, 162, 172, 173, 174, 175, 176, 181, 185, 199, 207, 212, 213, 218, 228, 238, 244, 246
delinquent behavior, 95, 184, 193, 240, 241
delinquents, 173, 207

delivery, x, 83, 85, 86, 115, 138, 142, 162, 163, 176, 184, 191, 208, 211, 220, 233, 237, 255
demographic transition, 35
demographics, 235
Demonstration Project, 184, 198, 215, 233
Department of Agriculture, 150, 201
Department of Defense, 245, 248, 258
Department of Education, 37, 120, 154, 175, 178, 180, 201, 203, 204, 230, 237, 238, 239, 240, 241, 249, 250, 252, 255, 256, 259
Department of Health and Human Services, xii, 42, 55, 111, 115, 154, 157, 171, 181, 183, 184, 188, 193, 207, 208, 217, 218, 220, 224, 229, 230, 231, 234, 245, 249, 253, 254, 255, 258, 259
Department of Housing and Urban Development, 37, 46, 106, 111, 138, 145, 146, 147, 148, 149, 151, 159, 178, 192
Department of Justice (DOJ), xi, xii, 46, 81, 95, 111, 120, 155, 169, 171, 180, 181, 192, 204, 205, 206, 209, 217, 219, 220, 224, 230, 232, 241, 242, 245, 246, 254, 256, 257, 258, 259
Department of the Interior, 200
depression, 16, 19, 132
detention, 22, 28, 44, 110, 184, 232
development policy, 172
developmental disabilities, 101
diplomas, 5, 87, 106, 148
disabilities, 3, 46, 101, 118, 133, 151, 165, 175, 178, 180, 186, 187, 198, 204
disability, 66, 101, 200
disabled, 153, 175, 203, 219
disadvantaged students, 179, 180
discipline, 24, 171
discretionary, 104, 177, 181, 188, 197, 205, 206, 207, 209, 239, 246, 247, 255
discretionary programs, 255
discrimination, 2, 101, 171
disseminate, 179, 194, 227
distress, 81, 84
distribution, 43, 143, 241
District of Columbia, 24, 52, 56, 86, 88, 116, 152, 196, 232, 248
diversity, 37, 151, 152
domestic policy, 110
domestic violence, 101
donors, 57, 58
doors, 105, 110
drinking, 43, 109
dropout rates, 51, 52, 114, 116, 118, 122, 126, 135, 178, 202
dropouts, 5, 22, 34, 36, 37, 82, 83, 84, 86, 92, 104, 106, 107, 111, 118, 119, 126, 146, 148, 153, 165, 177, 179, 202, 204, 217

drug abuse, ix, x, 16, 19, 140, 161, 193, 255
drug addict, 183
drug treatment, 184
drug use, 171, 236, 237
drugs, xi, 21, 22, 26, 30, 32, 43, 52, 64, 109, 134, 168, 179, 183, 195, 202, 210, 223, 228, 250
duplication, 98, 141, 142, 188, 189, 191
duration, 36, 257
duties, 141, 188, 191
dyslexia, 66

E

earnings, 82, 137, 167
economic assistance, 7
economic development, 4, 159
economic growth, 33
economic indicator, 24
economic resources, 15, 18
economically disadvantaged, 185, 200
Education for All, 175, 204
education reform, 84
education/training, 93, 104
educational attainment, 35, 52, 54, 133, 168, 178
educational background, 11
educational institutions, 171, 196
educational programs, 201, 203
educational services, 155, 180, 192, 193
Elementary and Secondary Education Act, 144, 146, 150, 175, 178, 201, 202, 218, 237, 255, 256
elementary school, 18
eligibility criteria, 119, 126
email, 2, 7, 8, 88, 89, 237
emerging issues, 26
emotional abuse, 101
emotional disabilities, 133
emotional disorder, 140, 193, 210
employability, 153
employees, 249, 251
employers, 37, 109, 128, 134, 136, 167
empowerment, 232
encouragement, 53, 66
engagement, 25, 85, 129, 130, 151, 170, 197, 236, 240
English Language, 179, 215
enrollment, 61, 92, 93, 104, 105, 119, 180, 203, 243
environment, 12, 30, 32, 53, 55, 57, 82, 84, 87, 93, 101, 109, 117, 124, 127, 145, 148, 164, 170, 193
Environmental Protection Agency, 187
ethnicity, 36, 43, 244, 253
evidence-based program, 140, 241
Executive Office of the President, 218, 220, 254, 257
Executive Order, 190, 220, 249

F

F-16, 230, 239
failure, xi, 24, 53, 85, 158, 224, 238
faith, 37, 64, 100, 182, 190, 197, 225, 232, 233, 238, 242, 246, 247
family conflict, ix, x, 24, 44, 101, 161, 162
family income, 198, 257
family life, 173
family literacy, 123, 154
family members, 62, 101
family structure, 167, 171, 182, 219
family support, 23, 93, 96, 103, 159
federal funds, 114, 165, 175, 178, 181, 252
federal government, x, xi, xii, 12, 24, 27, 38, 55, 56, 99, 108, 138, 142, 151, 161, 162, 172, 173, 174, 176, 177, 181, 182, 187, 199, 224, 226, 245
federal grants, 114, 117, 121, 138, 152
Federal Register, 220, 254, 255, 256, 259
financial aid, 179, 180, 203, 204
financial resources, 252
financial support, 4, 174, 231
financing, 63, 96
first generation, 203
focus groups, 65
focusing, ix, 62, 79, 134, 163, 171, 189, 190, 195
food, 24, 63, 109, 123, 126, 232
food stamps, 24
foster mothers, 13
FSA, 174

G

gangs, 134, 205, 247
GEAR, 179, 204, 214, 218
gender, 35, 244, 248, 253
gender differences, 35
General Accounting Office, 53, 220, 253
general education, 89, 90
generation, 203, 204, 219
Georgia, 64, 246
gifted, 66
global economy, 4, 33, 34, 35
goal setting, 243
goals, ix, x, xi, 12, 89, 90, 92, 94, 98, 109, 113, 114, 115, 117, 118, 121, 124, 126, 127, 132, 133, 136, 137, 138, 141, 142, 143, 147, 151, 169, 177, 180, 187, 188, 189, 193, 195, 196, 198, 223, 224, 225, 239, 246, 248, 249, 258
going to school, 63
Government Accountability Office (GAO), 104, 187, 220, 253, 254, 261

Government Performance and Results Act (GPRA), 239

Government Reform Committee, 188

GPO, 218, 220, 254, 256, 257

grades, xi, 178, 185, 224, 225, 229, 238, 240

grants, ix, 55, 113, 114, 117, 119, 120, 128, 135, 138, 139, 141, 152, 174, 178, 179, 181, 182, 183, 185, 186, 193, 194, 198, 203, 208, 209, 211, 220, 232, 234, 237, 238, 239, 241, 246, 247, 250, 251, 252, 255, 256, 257, 258, 259

groups, x, xi, 2, 4, 41, 53, 54, 65, 66, 85, 98, 139, 165, 166, 169, 170, 172, 176, 182, 185, 187, 188, 192, 193, 194, 198, 217, 223, 224, 225, 228, 232, 236, 238, 242, 244, 247, 254

guidance, 8, 30, 31, 32, 83, 87, 113, 114, 118, 121, 123, 137, 142, 143, 147, 172, 176, 182, 194, 196, 225

guidelines, 3, 131

H

H1, 220

handicapped, 173

hardships, 6, 8

harm, 162, 228

Head Start, 175

health, ix, x, xii, 6, 7, 8, 20, 22, 24, 25, 29, 38, 44, 45, 58, 87, 100, 101, 117, 124, 129, 132, 145, 146, 159, 161, 162, 165, 168, 170, 173, 174, 180, 182, 183, 184, 185, 187, 193, 199, 207, 224

health care, 6, 7, 8, 20, 22, 29, 38, 45, 58, 87, 92, 124, 145, 146, 165, 193

health insurance, ix, x, 159, 161, 162, 165, 168

health policy issues, 174

health problems, 44

health services, 24, 129, 132, 159, 184, 185, 207, 220

hearing, 1, 2, 3, 4, 5, 6, 7, 9, 12, 20, 23, 58, 59, 63, 65, 66, 78, 79, 91, 93, 97, 105, 107, 165, 188, 220

hearing impairment, 165

high risk, 21, 40, 41, 111, 195, 225

high school degree, 169

higher education, 61, 92, 107, 164, 179, 180, 182, 203, 204, 219, 248

Higher Education Act (HEA), 164, 175, 178, 179, 180, 182, 203, 204, 214, 219, 255, 256

high-level, 141

high-risk, 40, 94, 100, 165, 240

high-tech, 167

Hispanic, 35, 81, 82, 168, 169, 170, 216, 231

Hispanics, 34, 35, 107, 169, 170

HIV infection, 25

HIV/AIDS, 16, 18

holistic approach, 26, 114, 117, 128

homelessness, ix, x, 2, 3, 4, 6, 8, 14, 15, 16, 17, 18, 19, 24, 29, 40, 41, 43, 44, 45, 46, 58, 90, 91, 92, 93, 94, 100, 101, 102, 103, 104, 111, 114, 115, 116, 122, 126, 138, 159, 161

House, ix, 1, 2, 16, 19, 20, 22, 86, 98, 145, 146, 149, 174, 175, 195, 196, 220, 230, 234, 235, 239, 254, 256, 257, 261

House Committee on Government Reform, 220

House Ways and Means Subcommittee, 86

household, 59, 82, 248, 251

housing, 3, 4, 7, 17, 19, 20, 22, 23, 24, 27, 28, 37, 38, 45, 46, 88, 89, 92, 100, 101, 102, 103, 104, 106, 108, 110, 116, 117, 119, 123, 126, 130, 132, 134, 145, 147, 148, 149, 150, 153, 154, 159, 164, 165, 168, 178, 185, 196, 200, 217

Housing and Urban Development (HUD), 37, 45, 46, 106, 107, 111, 138, 139, 145, 146, 147, 148, 149, 151, 159, 178, 187, 190, 192, 196, 199

human, 6, 8, 45, 63, 64, 97, 129, 211, 212, 213

human immunodeficiency virus (HIV), 16, 18, 25, 129

I

identification, 93, 147, 170, 233

immigrants, 82, 163

immigration, 80, 101, 102

Immigration and Customs Enforcement, 192

implementation, 37, 118, 142, 143, 159, 190, 199, 235, 237, 240, 241, 250

incarceration, 27, 28, 34, 35, 36, 46, 58, 84, 94, 115, 118, 169, 231, 233

incentive, 54, 95, 108, 137

incentives, 84, 121, 129, 130, 137, 142, 143, 178, 200, 251

incidence, 36, 169, 195

inclusion, 1, 169, 184, 191

income, 12, 24, 27, 38, 52, 56, 57, 79, 89, 92, 93, 95, 101, 103, 104, 106, 107, 108, 118, 130, 134, 146, 147, 153, 165, 174, 175, 176, 177, 178, 179, 182, 192, 195, 198, 199, 200, 201, 203, 204, 207, 212, 219, 232, 257

incomes, 24

independence, 7, 21, 55, 86, 101, 125, 171, 177

indicators, 93, 105, 168, 172, 189

individual character, 170

individual characteristics, 170

individual development, 109

Individuals with Disabilities Education Act (IDEA), 175, 180, 204, 214, 219

industry, 37, 87, 88, 130, 144, 146, 149

information sharing, 141, 189

infrastructure, 6, 8, 79, 80, 85, 107, 108, 184, 226, 246
instability, 2, 4, 23, 51, 53, 100
institutions, 20, 23, 41, 45, 46, 58, 80, 100, 111, 155, 169, 171, 178, 180, 181, 196, 201, 203, 211, 219
institutions of higher education, 180, 203, 219
instruction, 25, 54, 123, 136, 149, 179, 180, 186
integration, 98
intelligence, 109
interaction, 2, 165, 170, 171
interactions, 127
Interagency Forum on Child and Family Statistics, 188, 189
internship, 89, 91
interpersonal relations, 238, 240
interpersonal relationships, 238, 240
intervention, 17, 19, 21, 28, 29, 36, 40, 41, 42, 45, 64, 79, 80, 100, 104, 107, 139, 177, 183, 193, 257
intervention strategies, 183
interview, 45, 248, 249
interviews, 116, 133, 134, 140, 144, 151, 152, 232, 244
investment, 22, 28, 29, 41, 45, 63, 79, 80, 83, 102, 108, 113, 114, 117, 118, 121, 132, 136, 138, 142, 143, 159, 178

J

jails, 41, 169
job skills, 21, 38, 52, 106, 154, 178, 185, 207
job training, 7, 16, 19, 51, 92, 108, 144, 150, 172, 174, 176, 177, 192
jobless, 4
jobs, 4, 11, 15, 38, 59, 62, 63, 80, 82, 85, 87, 88, 93, 101, 104, 107, 108, 110, 118, 128, 134, 136, 159, 163, 167, 170, 171
junior high, 14
jurisdiction, 27, 103, 106, 174, 176
jurisdictions, 27, 38, 85, 101, 138, 198, 242
Justice Assistance Grant, 257
juvenile crime, 195
juvenile delinquency, 120, 139, 155, 173, 180, 181, 192, 204, 205, 206, 241, 258
juvenile delinquents, 173, 207
juvenile detention facilities, 110
juvenile justice, x, xi, 20, 21, 22, 23, 26, 28, 34, 35, 36, 46, 79, 92, 101, 102, 115, 118, 119, 120, 139, 149, 151, 155, 161, 162, 165, 172, 175, 176, 181, 183, 193, 198, 199, 204, 205, 206, 207, 209, 217, 219, 223, 224, 241, 242, 243, 244, 246, 247, 251, 258

Juvenile Justice and Delinquency Prevention Act (JJDPA), 139, 175, 176, 180, 181, 182, 192, 230, 241, 242, 246, 247, 256, 258, 259
juveniles, 27, 110, 155, 181, 192, 205, 258

K

K-12, 178, 218

L

labor, ix, x, 33, 34, 35, 79, 80, 82, 83, 84, 85, 86, 121, 159, 161, 167, 168, 172, 198
labor force, 33, 34, 35
language, 87, 101, 123, 189, 242
language barrier, 101
Latino, 33, 107, 246, 247, 251, 258
law, 11, 14, 23, 60, 61, 85, 102, 103, 104, 105, 134, 137, 173, 177, 180, 183, 188, 192, 193, 197, 204, 208, 219, 231, 233, 241, 246, 252
law enforcement, 134, 183, 193, 208
laws, 61, 101, 116, 151, 173
LEA, 255
leadership, 12, 20, 21, 23, 38, 85, 87, 90, 91, 93, 105, 106, 108, 109, 114, 117, 126, 128, 131, 142, 145, 150, 153, 176, 197, 199, 207, 248, 249, 258
learning, 11, 13, 23, 31, 33, 38, 53, 54, 61, 66, 80, 84, 85, 87, 94, 100, 106, 114, 117, 118, 123, 125, 129, 133, 144, 147, 148, 178, 186, 202, 237
learning disabilities, 118, 133
learning environment, 84, 85, 147
learning process, 53, 54
legislation, x, xi, xii, 5, 7, 41, 54, 55, 85, 92, 93, 95, 98, 102, 141, 162, 163, 172, 173, 174, 175, 176, 178, 179, 188, 191, 194, 195, 196, 199, 218, 219, 224, 225, 235, 252, 258
lifetime, 12, 43, 44, 93, 104
likelihood, 40, 44, 167, 184
limitations, xi, xii, 42, 101, 224, 225, 250
listening, 17, 19, 59, 60
literacy, 7, 8, 38, 87, 89, 109, 118, 123, 137, 148, 154, 177, 194, 200, 202
living arrangements, 92, 104, 231
living environment, 147
local community, 128, 195
local educational agencies, 181, 255
local government, 51, 55, 115, 121, 139, 175, 181, 182, 189, 232, 242, 247
long-distance, 231
longevity, 128, 141
love, 4, 9, 13, 63, 108, 109

low-income, 12, 24, 27, 38, 52, 56, 79, 104, 106, 108, 118, 130, 134, 146, 153, 174, 175, 177, 178, 179, 192, 195, 199, 200, 201, 203, 204, 207, 212, 219, 232

M

mainstream, 65, 85, 146
maintenance, 87, 92, 95, 96, 103, 200, 207
major cities, 24, 27, 28
males, 25, 36, 43, 95, 118, 163, 169, 243
management, 24, 42, 114, 128, 131, 138, 149, 170, 184, 207, 219, 233, 236, 237, 240, 243
manufacturing, 4, 146, 167
market, ix, x, 20, 79, 80, 82, 83, 84, 85, 86, 145, 161, 167, 168, 198
marriage, 163, 176, 184, 211
matching funds, 108
Maya, 124, 147
MCP, xi, 223, 224, 231, 232, 233, 234, 235, 236, 255
meals, 219
measures, 6, 8, 54, 136, 137, 142, 159, 168, 176, 240, 244
median, 163
Medicaid, 7, 8, 24, 52
medical care, 193
medical services, 129
medicine, 57
membership, 26, 99, 100, 102, 173
mental disorder, 165, 198
mental health, 44, 46, 52, 62, 84, 94, 100, 101, 102, 117, 121, 129, 132, 139, 159, 170, 183, 193, 196, 207, 208, 220
mental illness, 40, 101, 140, 165, 193
mentor, 226, 228, 232, 233, 235, 236, 237, 238, 240, 243, 244, 248, 249, 251, 253, 254, 256
mentoring program, x, xi, xii, 139, 181, 182, 192, 223, 224, 225, 226, 228, 229, 232, 233, 235, 236, 237, 238, 239, 240, 241, 242, 244, 245, 246, 247, 249, 250, 251, 252, 255
metropolitan area, 20, 22
middle class, 14, 21, 27, 59
middle schools, 178
migrant, 151, 175, 178, 180, 189, 194, 200, 201, 203
migrant workers, 175
migrants, 194
military, 35, 83, 87, 163, 176, 248, 249
minorities, 43
minority, 35, 40, 43, 79, 80, 81, 82, 83, 85, 86, 169, 187
minors, 40, 42
missions, 6, 7, 119, 187
mobility, 33, 34, 35, 162, 176

models, x, 64, 65, 94, 108, 115, 121, 144, 151, 193, 194, 223, 238
money, 14, 15, 16, 17, 18, 26, 30, 31, 32, 41, 43, 62, 63, 64, 87, 109, 121, 134, 135, 149
mothers, 13, 22, 25, 33, 35, 36, 37, 41, 165, 169, 186, 217, 231
movement, 17, 19, 28, 46, 84, 110, 171, 172, 226
music, 15, 60, 63

N

nation, 4, 6, 7, 8, 22, 27, 29, 33, 54, 79, 80, 91, 92, 93, 94, 97, 99, 100, 101, 103, 104, 105, 107, 115, 139, 162, 191, 195, 196
National Defense Authorization Act, 248
National Guard, 248, 258
National Park Service, 201
National Research Council, 171, 217, 218
national security, 79
Native American, 107, 232
Native Americans, 107
natural resources, 178, 200
Navy, 88
NCLB, 214
NCS, 249
negative consequences, ix, x, 161
negative influences, 24
negative outcomes, x, 115, 164, 166, 168, 169, 223, 225
neglect, 5, 6, 8, 24, 25, 29, 44, 85, 94, 100, 101, 104, 133, 168, 173, 209, 218
negotiating, 226
network, 45, 107, 108, 144, 151, 164, 172, 183, 195, 210, 225, 243
networking, 100
New York, 37, 39, 44, 53, 54, 80, 81, 106, 110, 145, 171, 196, 198, 216, 217, 218
No Child Left Behind, 178, 180, 194, 214, 215, 218, 237, 239
no voice, 14, 17
nongovernmental organization, 226
non-institutionalized, 159
non-profit, 38, 86, 97, 106, 185, 186, 247
non-violent, 36

O

offenders, 27, 37, 85, 101, 107, 148, 153, 180, 184, 185, 194, 201, 204, 205, 206, 207, 212, 213, 242
Office of Justice Programs (OJP), 230, 246, 247, 256, 257, 258, 259

Office of Juvenile Justice and Delinquency
    Prevention (OJJDP), xii, 46, 120, 155, 171, 180,
    181, 192, 194, 224, 241, 242, 244, 245, 246, 247,
    254, 256, 257, 258
Office of Management and Budget (OMB), 137, 187,
    236, 240, 254
Office of National Drug Control Policy, 184, 190,
    192, 194, 197
Office of Vocational and Adult Education, 120, 154
online, 2, 111, 121, 194, 196, 235, 254, 257, 258
on-the-job training, 124, 126, 129, 175
organizational capacity, 246
organizational development, 197
orientation, 30, 32, 226, 233, 235, 253
outreach programs, 17, 19
oversight, 52, 56, 142, 188

P

parental care, 218
parental involvement, 189
parental support, 174
parent-child, 171
parenthood, ix, x, 2, 4, 161, 163
parenting, 22, 100, 101, 102, 118, 123, 130, 146,
    168, 177, 183, 184, 208, 211
parole, 119, 154, 248
PART, 187, 236
partnership, xii, 22, 38, 46, 108, 129, 180, 181, 193,
    196, 198, 224, 232, 247
partnerships, 139, 140, 180, 196, 219, 237, 238, 247
pathways, 3, 37, 79, 82, 85, 107, 110, 119, 171
peer, 53, 54, 109, 134, 193, 237, 250
peer group, 53, 54
peer review, 237
peer support, 109
peers, 5, 11, 13, 52, 54, 59, 61, 64, 95, 102, 168, 170,
    201, 228, 229, 231, 236, 242, 247
penalties, 121, 184
percentile, 168
perception, 135, 170, 241
performance indicator, 239
personal autonomy, 170
personal responsibility, 80, 106
persons with disabilities, 3
philosophy, 29, 107, 173, 174, 194, 199, 232
physical abuse, 173
physical health, 44, 102
physical well-being, 248
planning, 10, 91, 123, 147, 155, 170, 177, 181, 207,
    233, 236, 237, 241
play, 84, 85, 93, 98, 107, 109, 110, 119, 142, 159,
    171, 190

police, 17, 19, 25, 126, 198
policy makers, 36
policymakers, 54, 55, 133, 134, 162, 164, 172, 196,
    199
political parties, 93
poor, ix, x, 24, 29, 52, 53, 54, 79, 80, 86, 93, 101,
    107, 163, 165, 167, 168, 171, 173, 174, 176, 195,
    223, 225, 258
poor health, 29, 101
population, ix, 10, 15, 16, 18, 19, 20, 21, 27, 28, 33,
    34, 35, 37, 42, 44, 45, 51, 52, 86, 91, 108, 113,
    115, 116, 118, 121, 134, 137, 142, 151, 159, 163,
    164, 165, 166, 168, 169, 170, 173, 176, 177, 181,
    185, 193, 198, 199, 216, 226, 231, 250, 252, 255
population group, 137, 169
positive attitudes, 229
positive behaviors, 169, 170
Post Traumatic Stress Disorder, 19
postsecondary education, 137, 154, 167, 175, 178,
    179, 180, 204
poverty, 2, 4, 14, 15, 18, 21, 23, 24, 29, 59, 79, 80,
    81, 82, 83, 84, 85, 86, 88, 94, 104, 107, 153, 165,
    167, 174, 185, 202, 204, 212, 226, 233, 255
poverty line, 81
poverty rate, 80
pregnancy, 22, 25, 29, 40, 43, 52, 168, 171, 177,
    183, 184, 211, 250
pregnant, 21, 43, 95, 109, 146, 183, 184, 195, 200,
    208, 211
premature infant, 186
preschool, 202
preschoolers, 154
president, 110, 191, 199
President Bush, 190, 197, 199
prevention, x, 22, 23, 25, 26, 28, 29, 85, 104, 106,
    121, 140, 151, 161, 162, 172, 173, 174, 176, 177,
    180, 181, 183, 184, 186, 192, 193, 199, 205, 207,
    209, 219, 220, 241, 246, 247, 258
primary care, 183
primary caregivers, 183
prisoners, xi, 185, 208, 224, 231, 232, 235, 245, 254
prisons, 169, 254, 255
private, 10, 12, 13, 20, 22, 34, 35, 42, 54, 56, 58, 59,
    60, 61, 108, 114, 115, 116, 119, 121, 122, 135,
    141, 152, 171, 172, 176, 180, 181, 182, 190, 197,
    211, 231, 232, 242, 245, 255
private schools, 13
private sector, 20, 22, 34, 35
probation, 31, 33, 140, 248
problem behavior, 162, 164, 166, 247
problem behaviors, 162, 164, 166, 247
problem solving, 24, 170
professional development, 102, 250

professions, 32
profit, 38, 86, 97, 106, 185, 186, 247
profits, 97
programming, 22, 38, 79, 83, 84, 99, 135, 139, 171, 198, 217
progress reports, 235
Progressive era, x, 223
prosocial behavior, 171
prostitution, 14, 17, 43, 208
protection, 26, 101, 103, 172, 173, 207, 246
protective factors, ix, 163, 198, 242, 247
protocol, 139, 192
psychological assessments, 129
psychologist, 173, 247
puberty, 163
public awareness, 102
public education, 100, 154, 180
public health, x, 101, 102, 129, 162, 172, 176
Public Health Service, 174, 209, 210, 211
public policy, 24, 27, 56, 102
public safety, 159, 211, 212, 213
public schools, 10, 11, 13, 85, 110, 123, 125, 175
public service, 99, 159, 184
public welfare, 80
pupil, 178
pupils, 178, 201

R

race, 36, 43, 170, 198, 244, 253, 257
racial groups, 170
racism, 165
range, x, 20, 22, 35, 42, 61, 79, 87, 105, 115, 116, 118, 119, 122, 124, 125, 126, 127, 128, 144, 147, 151, 159, 162, 163, 171, 177, 184, 186
reading, 27, 37, 60, 87, 117, 125, 133, 136, 186, 242
reading skills, 37
recidivism, 107, 108, 149
recidivism rate, 107, 108
recognition, 127
recreation, 100, 243
recruiting, 244, 251
recurrence, 36
redundancy, 188
regulations, 116, 151, 185, 191, 239
rehabilitation, 28, 150, 153, 243
reimbursement, 181, 232
relationship, x, xi, 64, 101, 223, 224, 225, 226, 231, 232, 235, 238, 248, 249
relationships, x, xi, 25, 28, 29, 51, 53, 54, 61, 86, 117, 126, 127, 128, 134, 141, 163, 170, 171, 195, 223, 224, 225, 226, 228, 231, 232, 233, 235, 236, 238, 240, 241, 242, 243, 251, 256

remediation, 87
rent, 15, 95, 130
rent subsidies, 130
replication, 115, 151, 197
resilience, 63
resolution, 132, 177
responsibilities, 37, 79, 118, 139, 188, 248
retention, 38, 86, 137, 175, 179, 203, 244, 251
retrenchment, 83
reunification, 96
risk behaviors, 165, 195
risk factors, xi, 21, 24, 26, 44, 139, 192, 224, 254
risk management, 170
robbery, 30, 31
runaway, 8, 20, 22, 23, 24, 29, 41, 43, 45, 99, 100, 102, 109, 116, 118, 119, 123, 125, 129, 149, 151, 154, 162, 165, 175, 176, 177, 183, 200, 208, 219, 251
rural areas, 238
rural communities, 83, 119, 134
rural population, 233

S

safety, xii, 23, 83, 87, 92, 93, 101, 103, 134, 170, 180, 213, 224, 237, 247
Salvation Army, 99
sanctions, 93, 105, 121, 171
satisfaction, 55, 65, 235
savings, 96, 130
savings account, 130
scholarship, 15, 18, 51, 54, 55, 56, 59, 61, 180
Scholarship Program, 65
scholarships, 51, 52, 54, 55, 56, 60, 90, 109, 130, 175
school performance, 168, 244
school support, 28
school work, 130
schooling, 23
scores, 51, 52, 168, 236, 242
secondary education, 80, 82, 84, 87, 92, 106, 178
secondary schools, 255
security, 29, 79, 93, 103
selecting, 45, 179
self esteem, 242
self worth, 229
self-confidence, 147, 170
self-esteem, 236, 244
self-regard, 170
self-report, 122
Senate, 87, 174, 191, 195, 196, 220, 235, 241, 256
Senate Finance Committee, 235
separation, 3, 42, 100, 171, 231

service provider, 6, 97, 98, 104, 117, 118, 128, 137, 143, 144, 189
sex, 15, 25, 28, 43, 57, 248
sexual abuse, ix, x, 161, 208
sexual activity, 25, 211
sexual assault, 16, 18
sexual orientation, 101
sexually transmitted disease, 22
sharing, 62, 66, 138, 141, 189, 236, 240
shelter, 7, 16, 18, 20, 21, 22, 23, 24, 27, 43, 44, 45, 63, 90, 100, 101, 147, 149, 154, 175, 183
short-term, 132, 135, 136, 244
sites, 123, 190, 236, 240, 242, 244, 253, 259
skills training, 53, 54, 87, 108, 116, 126, 128, 144, 146, 149, 152
social acceptance, 25
social behavior, 231
social benefits, 54
social cohesion, 79
social environment, 167, 168, 170
social isolation, 24, 84
social justice, 58
social network, 51, 53, 151, 168, 225
social policy, 33, 176
social relations, 28
social relationships, 28
Social Security, 93, 95, 139, 173, 181, 193, 207, 208, 211, 217, 231
social services, x, 11, 20, 23, 38, 47, 51, 55, 162, 172, 174, 176, 177, 181, 184, 191, 193, 197, 199, 207, 218, 232, 243
Social Services Block Grant, 177
social support, 38, 118, 126, 136, 168
social work, 10, 33, 247
social workers, 10
special education, 11, 12, 13, 53, 65, 165, 178, 186, 198, 201
spectrum, 24
spina bifida, 165
spirituality, 170
sponsor, 121, 195
sports, 225, 237, 250
SSBG, 177
stability, 6, 8, 9, 10, 12, 14, 24, 25, 51, 54, 55, 60, 61, 101, 128, 132, 244
stabilization, 24
stabilize, 46
statistics, 21, 40, 42, 45, 62, 80, 82, 94, 106, 111, 135, 169
statutes, 184, 245
stereotype, 26
stigma, 18, 57, 83, 133
stigmatization, 231
strategic planning, 236
strategies, 37, 41, 93, 105, 127, 173, 183, 184, 190, 206, 226, 244, 246, 249, 251, 252
streams, 58, 83, 183, 185, 188, 239
stress, 171, 173, 231
stressors, 100, 165
structuring, 143
student enrollment, 255
Student Support Services, 175, 179, 215
students, 5, 10, 11, 12, 26, 30, 31, 33, 37, 51, 52, 53, 54, 55, 56, 58, 65, 80, 82, 84, 88, 106, 107, 130, 133, 145, 146, 148, 174, 175, 178, 179, 180, 183, 186, 193, 202, 203, 204, 205, 212, 219, 237, 238, 240, 247, 250, 251, 256, 258
substance abuse, xi, 2, 22, 44, 45, 46, 62, 101, 129, 134, 139, 159, 168, 183, 186, 194, 210, 224, 225, 258
substance use, 26, 229, 244
substances, 26
suburban, 9, 82, 135
suicide, 16, 18, 19, 183, 209, 219
summer, 63, 85, 111, 179, 186, 193, 194, 196, 229
supervision, 29, 31, 33, 40, 41, 42, 103, 211, 218, 226, 232
supervisors, 87, 129
supply, 2, 172, 200
support services, 25, 86, 87, 96, 117, 126, 128, 129, 148, 150, 177, 180, 182, 200, 203
surviving, 63, 220, 257

T

talent, 86
target population, 98, 189, 244, 250, 252
target populations, 98, 189, 244
targets, 55, 178, 184, 200, 236, 238, 247
task force, 105, 187, 188, 192, 253
tax incentive, 250
tax incentives, 250
taxes, 88
taxpayers, 87, 162
teachers, 4, 5, 11, 12, 30, 31, 32, 33, 53, 106, 189, 197, 225, 231, 236, 237, 245
teaching, 16, 65, 108, 124, 184
technical assistance, xii, 79, 97, 98, 114, 118, 121, 136, 142, 143, 188, 189, 192, 224, 235, 236, 237, 238, 239, 241, 242, 244, 247, 249, 252, 256
technicians, 146
teenage girls, 250
teenagers, 9, 11, 20, 22, 23, 56, 169, 186
teens, 24, 26, 82, 147, 183
telephone, 3, 40, 244, 249

Temporary Assistance for Needy Families (TANF), 9, 24, 92, 93, 104, 105, 174, 177

testimony, 1, 5, 12, 16, 20, 21, 24, 29, 33, 34, 39, 40, 41, 50, 52, 59, 60, 62, 63, 65, 79, 86, 98, 105, 111, 194

time allocation, 230

time commitment, 226

time frame, 114, 117, 132, 134, 136, 142

time periods, ix, 118, 163

Title I-A, 178, 201, 215, 219

Title III, 175, 179, 182, 202, 215

tobacco, 168, 179, 196, 202

tolerance, 34, 35

training programs, 93, 104, 137, 159, 192, 199

transformation, 83, 106

transformations, 83, 85

transition, ix, x, 2, 35, 45, 46, 58, 80, 84, 86, 113, 118, 119, 125, 126, 133, 134, 139, 142, 144, 145, 148, 154, 161, 162, 163, 164, 166, 168, 170, 171, 172, 177, 193, 198, 207, 249

transition period, 45

transition to adulthood, ix, x, 58, 80, 113, 118, 126, 142, 161, 162, 164, 166, 168, 170, 171, 172, 177, 249

transitions, 13

trauma, 25, 91, 132, 231

traumatic events, 183, 210

treatment programs, 205

trial, 240

tribes, 185, 186, 198

truancy, 52, 168, 176, 246, 247

tuition, x, 51, 54, 55, 59, 159, 161, 164, 168

tutoring, 54, 56, 88, 179, 180, 185, 186, 193, 220, 237, 245

U

U.S. Department of Agriculture (USDA), 150, 194, 196

unemployment, 24, 29, 33, 34, 35, 36, 80, 101, 169, 219

unemployment rate, 36

Uniform Crime Reports, 81

United States, ix, 10, 15, 18, 24, 32, 33, 34, 47, 56, 81, 90, 96, 100, 111, 158, 161, 163, 164, 181, 261

United Way, 226

universities, 163, 175, 242

unpredictability, 135

upward mobility, 162

urban areas, 80, 167

urban centers, 134

urban population, 191

V

values, 13, 59, 60, 85, 101, 106, 108, 171

victims, 7, 8, 18, 169

violence, 2, 22, 26, 28, 29, 88, 134, 140, 177, 179, 193, 197, 202, 220, 237, 238, 244, 255

violent, 36, 82, 95

violent behavior, 95

violent crime, 82

violent offenders, 36

vision, 86, 109, 128

vocational education, 23, 125, 126, 144

vocational schools, 21, 165

vocational training, ix, 25, 124, 161, 163, 166, 182, 200

volunteerism, 87

volunteers, 175, 185, 225

vouchers, 12, 51, 54, 55, 56, 60, 92, 103, 130, 164, 182, 208, 231, 233, 234, 235

W

wages, ix, x, 82, 88, 108, 134, 136, 161, 162, 164, 166

welfare, 5, 7, 9, 20, 22, 23, 25, 26, 27, 33, 34, 38, 44, 46, 52, 79, 92, 94, 95, 96, 101, 102, 103, 104, 118, 159, 168, 169, 172, 173, 183, 188, 208, 218, 219, 237

welfare system, 22, 23, 26, 27, 92, 94, 103, 104, 168

wellness, 100, 102

White House, 116, 119, 139, 151, 158, 175, 184, 187, 188, 194, 196, 218, 220, 249, 253, 257

White House Office, 184, 194

white women, 169

whites, 35, 36, 169

work environment, 85, 87, 129

work ethic, 85

workers, 33, 34, 35, 58, 62, 82, 100, 132, 146, 149, 162, 175

workforce, x, 21, 23, 25, 27, 35, 37, 79, 84, 86, 100, 101, 102, 113, 114, 117, 118, 119, 121, 132, 136, 138, 142, 143, 145, 153, 159, 161, 162, 164, 168, 172, 174, 176, 177, 178, 192, 193, 199, 200, 226

Workforce Investment Act, 84, 85, 88, 114, 115, 117, 153, 159, 177, 200, 215, 218

workplace, 8, 58, 82, 84, 100, 123, 124, 135, 148, 154, 162, 225, 231, 237

Y

young adults, ix, 5, 20, 22, 27, 37, 38, 42, 43, 44, 62, 87, 93, 100, 106, 108, 109, 119, 145, 146, 149, 161, 163, 165, 169, 176

young men, 2, 86, 95, 107, 110, 126, 146, 148
young women, 36, 95, 118
younger children, 51, 55
youth projects, 104, 188
youth transition, 119, 171, 193, 250